KASZTNER'S CRIME

Jewish Studies Series
William B. Helmreich, editor

Jewish Studies is an interdisciplinary series devoted to the study of Jewish history, religion, and culture.

KASZTNER'S CRIME

PAUL BOGDANOR

Transaction Publishers
New Brunswick (U.S.A.) and London (U.K.)

Library of Congress Catalog Number: 2016026729
ISBN: 978-1-4128-6340-7 (hardcover); 978-1-4128-6443-5 (paperback)
eBook: 978-1-4128-6363-6
Printed in the United States of America

Library of Congress Cataloging-in-Publication Data

Names: Bogdanor, Paul, author.
Title: Kasztner's crime / Paul Bogdanor.
Description: New Brunswick : Transaction Publishers, [2016] | Includes
   bibliographical references and index.
Identifiers: LCCN 2016026729| ISBN 9781412863407 (hardcover) |
   ISBN 9781412864435 (pbk.)
Subjects: LCSH: Kasztner, Rezsno Rudolf, 1906-1957. | World War,
   1939-1945--Jews--Rescue--Hungary. | Holocaust, Jewish
   (1939-1945)--Hungary. | Journalists--Hungary--Biography. |
   Lawyers--Hungary--Biography.
Classification: LCC D804.6 .B64 2016 | DDC 940.53/18092 [B] --dc23
LC record available at https://lccn.loc.gov/2016026729

Contents

Acknowledgments

I would like to thank the staff at the following archives for their assistance: Central Zionist Archives (Jerusalem), Haganah Archives (Tel Aviv), Jabotinsky Institute (Tel Aviv), Joint Distribution Committee Archives (New York), Labor Party Archive (Beit Berl College, Kfar Saba), National Archive and Records Administration (College Park, MD), Strochlitz Institute for Holocaust Research (Haifa), The National Archives (London), Wiener Library (London), and Yad Vashem (Jerusalem).

I would also like to thank the following individuals: Edward Alexander, Dan Anbar, Zvi Atir, Adam Bogdanor, Judy Bogdanor, Nigel Bowles, Randolph Braham, Noga and Ehud Duchovni, Stefan Fischer, Mark Gardner, Moshe Golan, Michael Hay and Amanda Mackenzie Stuart, Suzanna Harsanyi, Nadav Kaplan, Zsuzsi Kasztner, Ruth Landau, Ruth Linn, Ladislaus Löb, Jacob Lyons, Karla Müller-Tupath, Ayala Nedivi, Ofra Offer, Akiva Orr, Ann Pasternak-Slater, Michael Pinto-Duschinsky, Susan Pollack, Joseph Ragaz, Dave Rich, Alvin Rosenfeld, Ruth Tamir, Zoltán Tibori Szabó, Bill Treharne Jones, Rafael Vago, Margaret Vermès, Robin Vrba, Gerta Vrbova, Zuza Vrbova, Menahem Weber, and Lily Zamir.

Special thanks to Michael N. Ezra, whose interest in Kasztner spurred me on as I was writing. Michael generously read and commented on every chapter; his invaluable feedback substantially improved the book. Dr. Eli Reichenthal of Ben-Gurion University gave me access to the documents from the Kasztner and Dinur Archives cited in this book, and he made some of the translations from Hebrew and all of the translations from Hungarian.

My final debt is to the highly professional people at Transaction for their hard work in guiding this book to publication: Mary E. Curtis, Lauren Bridges, Aileen Bryant-Allen, Andrew McIntosh, Eileen Ramos, Jeffrey Stetz, and Mindy Waizer.

None of the arguments in this book should be attributed to any of those just named; a few of them totally reject my conclusions. Responsibility for any errors is mine.

Introduction

This book is about one of the most intense controversies of the Holocaust. It explains how an attempt to save the innocent became an instrument of their murder. It shows how the illusion of rescue was used to camouflage the reality of genocide and then turned into an alibi for war criminals—and how the protests of the survivors have been consigned to oblivion.

By 1944 the majority of Jews in the Nazi sphere of influence were dead. Yet Hungary's Jewish community, though far from unscathed, was largely intact. Moreover, many Hungarian Jews were still oblivious to the fate that had befallen millions of their coreligionists under Hitler's rule. On March 19, 1944, their innocence was suddenly and cruelly shattered when the Nazis occupied Hungary. Accompanying the German armed forces were Adolf Eichmann and his SS staff. Their mission was to organize the deportation of all the Jews in Hungary—over three-quarters of a million men, women, and children[1]—to Auschwitz.

Eichmann had only 150–200 SS personnel at his disposal. He also had very little time: the Nazis were losing the war, and it would not be long before the Germans were beaten back by the Red Army. It was no simple matter to murder so many people in such a brief interval. Nevertheless, Eichmann performed his grisly task with extraordinary speed and efficiency: for eight weeks, beginning in mid-May 1944, he was able to load Jews onto the death trains at the rate of up to twelve thousand souls per day.

As they were making the arrangements for this tremendous slaughter, officers of the SS conducted "rescue negotiations" with representatives of Hungary's Jewish population. One of the aims of these negotiations, from the Nazi standpoint, was to lull the Jewish side into a false sense of security and to abort any effective steps to save Jewish lives. The key Jewish figure in the talks with the SS was Rezső Kasztner, acting head of a small Zionist rescue committee in Budapest. Kasztner had already compiled a record of courageous activism in saving Jews from extermination in Poland and Slovakia. Recognizing his importance, the SS officers granted him special exemptions from their antisemitic measures and treated him as the major spokesman for Hungary's Jews.

In the fateful weeks of the mass deportations to Auschwitz, Kasztner and Eichmann were locked in heated discussions about the possibility of sparing Jewish lives. Ultimately Eichmann agreed to gather a special group of 1,684 Jews, who were first taken hostage and later sent to Switzerland by train. By that point, Eichmann and his local henchmen had rounded up well over four hundred thousand other Jews and sent them to a terrible destination. At the end of the war, the Jewish death toll from the Nazi occupation of Hungary stood at half a million.

During the negotiations, Eichmann presented a "rescue plan" that was as far-reaching as it was far-fetched. He announced to Kasztner's colleague Joel Brand that he was prepared to free a million Jews from Nazi-occupied Europe in exchange for ten thousand trucks and other goods from the West. Brand traveled to Turkey to explain the offer—the so-called Goods for Blood deal—to the Zionist movement. The latter duly informed the British and lobbied for their support. But Eichmann, who had promised to postpone the destruction of Hungary's Jews until the end of Brand's mission, was already delivering hundreds of thousands to the gas chambers.[2]

Given the obstacles facing Eichmann's tiny SS unit at the time of the Nazi occupation in the penultimate year of the war, it is remarkable that the Hungarian Jews were sent to their deaths so quickly. Only outside pressure forced the Hungarians to call a halt to the deportations in July 1944, at the eleventh hour. Otherwise, Eichmann would have achieved the total destruction of the country's Jewish population during the few short months of his "rescue negotiations" with Kasztner and his "rescue offer" to Brand.

Kasztner survived the war under Nazi protection. After the Holocaust he was hailed as a savior by many of the passengers of his special train—which came to be known as the Kasztner Train—but condemned as a collaborator by many of the death camp survivors from Hungary. It was alleged that, as a condition of his deal with the killers, he had knowingly misled the victims about their fate. In his home city of Kolozsvár (now Cluj-Napoca) in North Transylvania, there was a campaign to try him *in absentia*: the suspicion was that he had encouraged the local Jewish leaders to save their own lives by deceiving many thousands of ordinary Jews into boarding the trains to Auschwitz.

In December 1947, Kasztner moved from Switzerland to Palestine. Although there was ongoing controversy surrounding his dealings with the Nazis, he succeeded in becoming an Israeli government official. But his wartime record finally caught up with him in 1954, when the government prosecuted an elderly Jew, Malkiel Grünwald, for branding him a Nazi collaborator. The case, now known as the Kasztner Trial, became a *cause célèbre*. In his verdict, the trial judge agreed with Grünwald that Kasztner had collaborated with the SS, remarking that in doing so he had "sold his soul to the Devil." This finding provoked public uproar and led to the collapse of the government. The verdict was appealed to the Supreme Court, but it was too late for Kasztner: in March 1957, he was assassinated by right-wing extremists in Tel Aviv.

Delivering their decision, the majority of the Supreme Court judges voted to overturn the trial verdict. But they were very far from exonerating Kasztner: all of the judges agreed that he had wrongfully saved SS officer Kurt Becher from punishment at the Nuremberg Trials. Subsequently, it was discovered that Kasztner had intervened on behalf of several other SS war criminals at Nuremberg.

That was not the only evidence unknown to the Supreme Court judges. They did not have access to most of Kasztner's communications with his foreign contacts during the destruction of the Hungarian Jews. The analysis of those messages in the following pages will help us to understand, for the first time, how the Nazis were able to mislead world opinion for several crucial weeks as they did their inhuman work.

This book also exposes, for the first time, the conveyor belt of deception from Budapest that enabled the Nazis to manipulate Jewish leaders in ghettos throughout Hungary. Readers will learn why hundreds of thousands of Hungarian Jews boarded the death trains either in total ignorance of where the trains were taking them or in the belief that they were being resettled for labor. Understanding the Kasztner affair allows us to unlock one of the central mysteries of the Holocaust in Hungary: the secret of how Eichmann was able to prevent panic among the Jewish population of the ghettos and secure their obedience to the SS machinery of mass murder.

Despite decades of anguished debate among Jewish communities, Holocaust survivors, and historians in Israel and abroad, there is still no consensus on whether Kasztner was a savior or a collaborator—a Jewish version of Oskar Schindler or a Jewish equivalent of Vidkun Quisling. This investigation aims to resolve the controversy once and for all. It reproduces extensive testimony from the Kasztner Trial, most of it never before seen in English. It uncovers in Kasztner's statements shocking new information that previous research has missed. It is also the first book to give an accurate account of his messages to the outside world during the deportations to Auschwitz. And it contains new evidence from his private papers.[3] It asks the following questions:

- Were Hungary's Jews aware that the Nazis intended to murder them?
- What preparations did the Zionists make before the Nazi occupation? Did they succeed in building a viable underground rescue network?
- Was there any connection between Eichmann's success in deporting the Hungarian Jews to Auschwitz and his negotiations with Kasztner?
- What did Kasztner tell the outside world as the mass murder of Hungary's Jews was taking place?
- Did Kasztner really help to rescue tens or even hundreds of thousands of Jews, as he asserted after the war?
- Why did Kasztner intervene on behalf of several of his wartime Nazi contacts at Nuremberg?

The answers to these questions will bring us to the most disturbing issue of all: was the head of the Jewish rescue operation in Budapest working as an accomplice of the Nazis during the genocide of his country's Jews?

Notes

1. At the time of the occupation, there were 762,000 Jews in Hungary: Randolph L. Braham, *The Politics of Genocide: The Holocaust in Hungary*, Vol. 2 (Boulder, CO: Social Science Monographs in association with Columbia University Press, 1994), 1298, Table 32.1.
2. On May 15, 1944, Eichmann gave Brand two weeks to return from his mission. Within that space of time, Eichmann deported the first two hundred thousand Hungarian Jews: Braham, *The Politics of Genocide*, Vol. 1, 673.
3. Kasztner's personal papers were made available to my fellow researcher Eli Reichenthal by the Kasztner family and have since been donated by them to Yad Vashem.

1

The Underground

When the Nazis occupied Hungary on March 19, 1944, the Jewish public was caught by surprise. Many ordinary Jews did not know what to expect. The Jewish community leaders were also in shock.

Major disasters had already struck the country's Jewish population. From 1941, many Jewish men were drafted to the Hungarian army's labor units on the Soviet front. Some of the army officers were made to understand that the draftees were not to return alive. As a result, tens of thousands of Jews died from starvation, typhus, shooting, and other brutalities.

Then in July–August 1941, Hungary resolved to expel all Jews from the East who could not prove their Hungarian citizenship. Some fourteen thousand to sixteen thousand Jews were deported to Nazi-controlled Galicia, where they were massacred by the local SS at the site of Kamenets-Podolsk.

Finally, a third atrocity was carried out: when Hungarian gendarmes were killed in January 1942 by insurgents in the Bácska area (recently annexed from Yugoslavia), Hungarian forces rounded up and massacred three thousand to four thousand Serbs and Jews in and around Újvidék (now Novi Sad).

These horrors were, of course, dwarfed by the genocide taking place in the rest of Nazi-occupied Europe. Between the beginning of the Holocaust and the Nazi occupation of Hungary, most of Europe's Jews had been put to death. Helpless men, women, and children had been rounded up and shot at mass execution sites, starved to death in ghettos, or deported to the death camps and gassed.

In early 1942, Holocaust survivors from Poland and Slovakia began to cross the border into Hungary. The challenge of helping these refugees provoked a group of Zionists in Budapest to establish a Relief and Rescue Committee at the end of the year. This rescue committee came into contact with Zionist outposts in Istanbul and Geneva and was soon granted official recognition by the Jewish Agency. The committee also

1

received funds from the non-Zionist American Jewish Joint Distribution Committee (JDC), via its Swiss delegate Saly Mayer.

The Zionist rescue committee quickly compiled an impressive record of humanitarian achievements. It saved Jews from the Holocaust in most of the countries around Hungary. Having made contact with foreign Jewish bodies, the Zionists in Budapest became vital sources of intelligence on the Final Solution and provided some of the first information about Auschwitz. To rescue Jews from the surrounding Nazi-occupied lands, they enlisted the aid of German military agents, high-ranking Hungarians, and citizens on both sides of the border. Thanks to their achievements, when the Nazis decided to destroy the Jews in Hungary, an underground Zionist rescue apparatus with an experienced leadership and hundreds of Jewish personnel was ready for action. Nothing of the kind existed in any other country before its subjugation by the Germans.

The Jewish rescue committee's achievements before 1944 were the work of a small group of activists. The most important of them was Rezső Kasztner.

Who Was Kasztner?

Rezső Kasztner was born in 1906 in the Transylvanian city then known as Kolozsvár (now Cluj-Napoca). He grew up in a Zionist home, and one of his brothers soon immigrated to Palestine. Kasztner gained a legal doctorate and worked as the political editor of the Jewish newspaper *Új Kelet*. His journalism was highly regarded—so highly regarded that he was granted an interview by Romania's prime minister.[1] In 1937, he married the daughter of József Fischer, the head of the city's Jewish community. The marriage was advantageous: Fischer was a preeminent Jewish figure in Transylvania and a representative of the Jewish Party in Romania's Chamber of Deputies. Before long, Kasztner became the chairman of the Jewish Party's parliamentary group.[2]

Kasztner's good fortune did not last. Hungary's annexation of North Transylvania ended his parliamentary role, while its antisemitic laws forced the closure of *Új Kelet*. All of a sudden, his public career had vanished. In late 1940, the newly unemployed Kasztner moved to Budapest. There he became deputy head of Ihud—one of the smallest of the Zionist factions—and was reduced to earning his living as a Zionist fundraiser.[3]

In July 1942, Kasztner was drafted into a Jewish forced labor unit. His friends in Budapest tried but failed to secure his release. His unit was ordered to the front to assist the Hungarian troops against the Red Army—a virtual death sentence. However, Kasztner was never sent: in December 1942 his entire unit was suddenly discharged and the Jewish conscripts returned home.[4] According to Joel Brand, his friend and rescue committee colleague, he was widely suspected of draft evasion: "Another claim, which hung in the air long afterwards, was that the circumstances of his release were ethically suspect and that Kasztner had played a role in it. The exemption of his entire unit from the battlefield at the time is shrouded in fog to this day."[5]

The true explanation for these events has since come to light. After Kasztner's release, Jewish leaders in Budapest began to receive complaints. It was alleged that Kasztner had freed his unit through bribery—using funds embezzled from his Jewish community. A commission was appointed to investigate; but its chairman was none other than József Fischer, the father-in-law of the accused. Kasztner's exoneration, predictable as it was, did not impress his Zionist colleagues in Budapest: he was promptly fired from his fundraising position.[6]

These allegations shed some light on the character of Rezső Kasztner, or at least the general perception of his character. The descriptions by friends and acquaintances are remarkably consistent.

- Sámuel Springmann, an early member of the rescue committee, regarded him as "a very capable and experienced Zionist worker of the cold intellectual variety. Rather bohemian in his way of life, and at the same time an opportunist, he was not very well-liked by many of his fellow Zionists, as he was tight with his money and often did not repay his debts."[7]
- Joel Brand described him as "a courageous man who put his whole heart and soul into the rescue of the Jewish people and who achieved a great deal." All the same, Brand viewed him as "a typical Jewish intellectual, with all the good and bad qualities of his kind . . . to many people he seemed to be the prototype of the snobbish intellectual who lacked the common touch."[8]
- Fülöp Freudiger, the Orthodox leader in Budapest, praised his political idealism and fearless approach to danger, but drew attention to several faults. He was unreliable in keeping appointments and commitments. He was "dictatorial" and "jealous of the success of others." Worse yet, "It is probable that he had the ambition to become the sole master and leader of the Hungarian Jews, i.e., almost one million souls."[9]
- Moshe Krausz, director of the Jewish Agency's Palestine Office in Budapest—a man who repeatedly clashed with Kasztner—acknowledged his ability and personal charm. On the other hand, "I considered him a megalomaniac. He had delusions of grandeur. . . . He tried hard to

be the focus of attention in every group. And when it came to his own interests, he was without conscience or consideration."[10]

- Moshe Alpan, a Zionist youth activist, remembered him as "a very, very bright, intelligent man, capable of analyzing political things brilliantly," who was also "an egomaniac" with "boundless and unrestrained ambition and drive."[11]

In the various profiles of Rezső Kasztner by friends and foes, a number of character traits loom large: exceptional intelligence, resourcefulness, vision, and boldness, combined with vanity, amorality, and relentless ambition for power and status. In the words of one of his academic champions, Yechiam Weitz, he had "courage and nerves of steel," but he also "assumed titles and honors he was not entitled to, obsessively tried to take center stage," and displayed "cunning and the ability to lie without batting an eyelid."[12]

In the context of wartime underground operations that required self-confidence and unconventional thinking, such traits were sometimes an asset. As the rescue operations expanded, Kasztner became the committee's dominant figure. The committee's chairman was Ottó Komoly, a Zionist leader and decorated World War I army officer. But according to Brand, its "political director and operational manager" was Kasztner.[13]

Gathering Intelligence

In the Hungarian Jewish community before 1944, the Zionist rescue committee quickly became the main repository of information on the Final Solution. From mid-1942, wrote Kasztner, there were "countless reports, eye-witness testimonies and accounts from escapees about what was happening in Poland."[14] Brand described how the committee set up an intelligence center in Budapest to interview the survivors and send reports to world Jewry. Upon arrival, "the refugees would be closely questioned so that we could ascertain and record the situation in the ghettos from which they had come." The rescue committee sent "hundreds of these records" to the Zionists abroad.[15]

The rescue activists in Hungary received vital information from their counterparts in Slovakia (the Jewish "Working Group"), who had approached the SS offering ransom payments to stop the killing. From their correspondence, which he forwarded to the Jewish Agency after mid-1942, Kasztner learned that Adolf Eichmann was the SS officer coordinating the deportation and murder of Europe's Jews.[16]

One of the most authoritative sources on the destruction of Polish Jews was Oskar Schindler, the German industrialist and Holocaust rescuer. Schindler visited Budapest in November 1943 to meet Spring-mann and Kasztner, who reported his observations to the Jewish Agency.

"It is not part of the art of war to trample the heads of infants under your jackboots," began Schindler. The SS was led by "coarse people with the instincts of brutes" who "find it hard to drop the habit of shooting a few dozen or a few hundred Jews a day."

Schindler was asked how many Jews had perished at the hands of the Nazis: "I can only speak of the figures given by the SS leaders. They speak of 4–4.5 million. But I reckon that this number is exaggerated. They pride themselves on such numbers."

The discussion turned to the fate of Jewish children: "They have been virtually exterminated. I believe that 90% of the children up to the age of 14 were shot or gassed. . . . The old folk have suffered the same fate. Not a single person over the age of 50 has remained alive."

When Schindler referred to the Jewish workers in "Oswiencim," Kasztner interjected: "We have heard that Oswiencim [Oświęcim, i.e., Auschwitz] is a death camp." Came the reply: "That may be the case as far as children and old people are concerned. I have also heard that Jews were burnt and gassed there. A scientific method of extermination has been developed there."[17]

From this source alone it was possible to learn every important fact about the Holocaust: the death toll ran into several millions; children and the elderly had been wiped out; the SS was in charge of the slaughter; mass killing had been industrialized in death camps; and the process consisted of gassing and burning.

"I gave Dr. Kasztner a precise description of what was happening to the Jews, the increasingly ruthless actions of the SS, the primary threats, the most effective forms of aid and possible escape routes," wrote Schindler. As he soon realized, "Dr. Kasztner's sources of information and intelligence were always exceptionally good, positively first-rate."[18]

In postwar testimony at Nuremberg, Kasztner revealed how much the Hungarian Zionist rescue activists knew:

> In Budapest we had a unique opportunity to follow the fate of European Jewry. We had seen how they had been disappearing one after the other from the map of Europe. At the moment of the occupation of Hungary, the number of dead Jews amounted to over 5 million. . . . We had, as early as 1942, a complete picture of what had been happening in the East with the Jews deported to Auschwitz and the other extermination camps.[19]

Kasztner and his Zionist colleagues were not the only Jews in Budapest who had amassed accurate and detailed information about the Holocaust. Anti-Zionist establishment figures such as Samu Stern, leader of the reformist Neolog community, were also well aware of the Nazi genocide of the Jews.[20] These anti-Zionist leaders made no attempt to inform their community members about the Holocaust because they thought that the Nazis would not turn their attention to Hungarian Jewry. The Zionists on Kasztner's rescue committee were less optimistic, but they too failed to spread the alarm in the Jewish community before 1944. This mistake would return to haunt them after the Nazi occupation.

Recruiting Couriers

From the beginning of its operations, the rescue committee had to make a fateful decision: since the committee members could not themselves travel abroad to send and collect messages and funds, they had to identify reliable couriers. The problem was solved, but at the price of choosing messengers whose loyalty ranged from uncertain to nonexistent.

The first of the couriers was Bandi Grosz, a converted Hungarian Jew and professional smuggler. As early as 1941, Grosz had offered his services to the Wehrmacht's intelligence arm, the Abwehr. Later, to protect himself from arrest for smuggling, he worked for Hungarian military intelligence. At various times of the war, Grosz served other intelligence agencies, both Axis and Allied.[21] Following a meeting in a cafe, he was also recruited as a courier for the Jewish rescue committee by Springmann.

Opinions of Grosz's character and role vary. Teddy Kollek, who was responsible for the Jewish Agency's clandestine rescue effort, considered him "a double-crossing rat," whereas Joel Brand found him "strictly honest in money matters" and commented that "without his help, we could not have achieved much of our work."[22]

It was Grosz who coordinated many of the couriers used by the rescue committee. Indeed, Springmann went so far as to say that the committee's messenger network was really Grosz's organization: often the couriers were introduced to Springmann only after they had made several trips, and some of them he never met at all.[23] The key figures were Erich Wehner/Popescu, Joseph Winninger, Rudi Scholz, and Rudolf Sedlacek, all of whom turned out to be agents of the Abwehr; and Ferenc Bagyoni, who was an agent of Hungarian counter-espionage.[24]

Doubts about the integrity of such messengers set in early; Grosz was plainly using them for smuggling purposes. But when Springmann wrote to the Jewish Agency in Istanbul questioning the reliability of the Grosz network, he was assured that there was no cause for concern.[25]

In truth, the Jewish rescue committee in Budapest had ample warning that its clandestine communications were not secure. In summer 1943, for example, Moshe Krausz cautioned Springmann that Wehner was a known Gestapo agent. When Springmann confronted Wehner in panic, the courier replied that he was merely "zur Wehrmacht." Kasztner, however, saw no reason for alarm: he argued that Wehner's allegiances were probably already known to the Jewish Agency.[26]

On another occasion, Winninger—who was also known to be "zur Wehrmacht"[27]—promised to keep the rescue committee's "more important" letters secret, but added that there was little need to conceal "unimportant" messages. The implication was that these messages were being shown to the German censors. But the committee members decided to trust him anyway. Their rationale was somewhat naive: "as [Winninger] had said he was hiding the important letters, they could not be compromised by the unimportant ones."[28] Springmann did not explain why he believed Winninger's assurance that the important messages were being hidden from the German authorities. Such incidents give some indication of the rescue committee's surprisingly lax attitude to the security of its illegal communications.

Perhaps the most dangerous person to become involved in the Jewish rescue committee's courier network was Fritz Laufer.[29] Initially an agent of the Abwehr, Laufer subsequently served the combined Gestapo and SD (the SS security service) in Hungary. Laufer had allegedly infiltrated the Czech underground, had certainly penetrated a significant American spy operation (the "Dogwood" network), and surely performed the same task in the Zionist courier network along the Budapest–Istanbul route.

According to Springmann, it was Laufer who in 1943 first made the proposal to exchange some Jews in Nazi captivity for goods from the Allies, such as trucks.[30] This initiative may have had more than one purpose at the time: testing the readiness of the Zionists to discuss a ransom deal with Germany or testing their usefulness as intermediaries between the Abwehr and the West. Laufer's gambit, revived by Eichmann on behalf of the SS, would become known as the "Goods for Blood" offer, and subsequently formed an integral part of the deception tactics surrounding the destruction of Hungary's Jews under Nazi rule.

The Rescue Underground

Setting aside the security risks, the benefits of using these couriers were not slight. As a result of their activities, the Jewish rescue committee in Budapest was able to maintain contact with ghettos in Poland, rescue activists in Slovakia, and the Jewish Agency outpost in Turkey. With the aid of other messengers, the committee communicated with two vital rescue contacts in Switzerland: Saly Mayer of the JDC and Nathan Schwalb of the international Zionist youth.

The central activity of the Jewish rescue committee in Hungary was extracting Jews from Nazi-occupied territory. This mission, involving cross-border smuggling, was organized by Brand from a small office in a Budapest side street. Among the targets of the smuggling campaign were surviving Jews in Poland. Brand was able to build up a list of some two hundred to three hundred contacts there. About half of them were non-Jews; others were Jews held in labor camps or living illegally in Polish society.[31]

There were two routes for smuggling Polish Jews. One was across Slovakian territory via Kassa (now Košice). In this case the refugees would typically cross the Polish border by themselves and travel to Kassa's synagogue; there they would be met by one of Brand's representatives, who would escort them into Hungary. The other, more dangerous route was across the Polish–Hungarian border. Here the security measures were such that it was often necessary to bandage the refugees and pass them off as sick, so that they would not be expected to reply to questions in Hungarian.[32] There is no doubt that the rescue committee managed to save thousands of Polish Jews from certain death through such smuggling efforts. Later in the war, Brand stated, with an element of hyperbole, "I have saved many Polish Jews from the very doors of the gas chamber."[33]

Once they were in Hungary, the troubles of the Polish Jewish refugees were not over; they had to be given false identity papers to disguise them as Christians in order to be allowed to work in the capital or in certain provincial towns. According to Kasztner, there were about one thousand two hundred such Polish refugees in Budapest and eight hundred to one thousand two hundred in the provinces. There were also three children's camps housing dozens of mostly orphaned children; Jewish soldiers in the Polish army who were interned in military camps; and some individual Polish Jews who managed to obtain their own Christian identity papers or who remained in hiding.[34]

In addition to smuggling, the rescue committee used its messengers to deliver letters and money to ghettos in Poland. The Abwehr courier Sedlacek also traveled three times to Krakow to bring money to the seven thousand to eight thousand Jews employed in Oskar Schindler's factories.[35]

Slovakia was another focus of the rescue committee's underground activities. The border was near enough to the Hungarian capital for messages to be sent back and forth twice a day. Some of the mail was taken by Grosz's couriers, and some by smugglers. Smuggling operations were greatly aided by the Slovak police, who had been bribed by the Slovak Jewish community: refugees were arrested, brought by the local police to the Hungarian border, and released.[36]

The smuggled refugees were not supposed to remain in Hungary; the objective was to send them to Palestine via Romania. To that end, the rescue committee sent several of its Hungarian members to Bucharest, where they were to establish an apparatus for sending refugees by ship to Turkey and then to the Jewish homeland.[37]

The rescue committee also helped Jews who were hiding underground in Austria, known as "U-Boats." These efforts were largely coordinated with a single rescue worker, codenamed Austern ("Oysters"), who operated from Vienna. Out of the two thousand Jewish U-Boats in Vienna, between five and twenty were smuggled to Hungary each week.[38] Contact was established using the driver of the vehicle that made the daily delivery of the Nazi newspaper *Völkischer Beobachter* from Vienna to Budapest; Kasztner took advantage of the same means to travel secretly on this route.[39]

Repeated attempts were made to establish links with the Yugoslav Partisans; these were the responsibility of two Polish Zionists working with the Budapest rescue committee. Both succeeded in infiltrating men across the border, but failed to establish a permanent line of communication. The aim was to send men for training in guerrilla tactics that might be used to resist the Nazis in the event of a German military occupation of Hungary; but these ambitions remained unfulfilled.[40]

There are several estimates of the numbers of Jews helped in various ways by the rescue committee before the Nazi occupation of Hungary. In November 1943, the committee reported a figure of fifteen thousand refugees, broken down as follows:

- Slovakia: six thousand to eight thousand
- Poland: one thousand six hundred to two thousand
- Germany: three thousand to four thousand
- Yugoslavia: three hundred to four hundred
- Czech Protectorate: five hundred to one thousand[41]

A document obtained by the Office of Strategic Services in Washington at the end of February 1944 estimated the numbers as

- Slovakia: eight thousand to ten thousand
- Poland: two thousand five hundred
- Croatia, Serbia, Germany: a few hundred[42]

These figures excluded Jews who traversed Hungary to other countries. A final and all-inclusive estimate of the numbers saved or assisted by the Zionist rescue committee in Budapest was given by Brand at the Eichmann Trial: twenty-two thousand to twenty-five thousand Jews.[43]

Self-Defense or Negotiations?

From mid-1943, according to Springmann, the Zionists—especially the Polish and Slovak refugees—had been concerned about a possible Nazi occupation of the country. The refugees, "filled with pessimism and a desire to avenge themselves," repeatedly encouraged the Hungarian Zionists to set up an armed underground movement in preparation for the arrival of the Nazis. But "nothing concrete" was done for some time.[44]

In October or November 1943, Brand decided to force his colleagues to act. He called a meeting to which he invited the leaders of the Zionist underground. It was resolved to set up an armed defense committee—the Hungarian Haganah—and to procure weapons by theft and by raiding small police stations and military posts.[45] It was also thought that arms could be obtained from Tito's Partisans in Yugoslavia. The Hungarian Haganah was to forge links with other armed movements in Poland and Slovakia. All Zionist parties except the right-wing Revisionists were to be involved, and there were plans to recruit non-Zionists as well.[46]

The defense activity soon moved into high gear. Bunkers were set up throughout the country; strategic points for resistance were identified; Polish and Slovak refugees carried out training in guerrilla warfare tactics; and food and medicines were stockpiled.[47] The task of actually obtaining weapons posed a far greater challenge. It was Brand's hope to arm as many as two thousand people, but the results of the project were disappointing: by May 1944, the Zionists had succeeded in obtaining only one hundred and fifty pistols, forty grenades, three small carbines, and two machine guns, one of them unserviceable.[48]

On instructions from the Jewish Agency in Istanbul, in February 1944 the defense committee was placed under the command of Moshe

Schweiger. Because of the latter's ill health, he was soon replaced by Moshe Rosenberg. From the Jewish Agency, the committee received what was then considered the princely sum of $15,000 for making preparations. This money was used to set up a workshop for the production of false identity papers.[49]

In 1943 the Jewish rescue committee in Budapest became aware of an apparent alternative to underground activity: the option of negotiating with the Nazis in the hope of ransoming Jews. The model for this alternative was the strategy of the rescue committee's counterpart in Slovakia, the so-called Working Group, led by the Orthodox Rabbi Michael Weissmandel and the Zionist Gisi Fleischmann.

The negotiations in Slovakia unfolded in two stages. In the first stage, the Working Group tried to bribe Dieter Wisliceny, the SS officer supervising the liquidation of Slovakia's Jews, to stop the deportations from that country. This was known as the Slovakia Plan. In the second stage, mistakenly believing that its bribe to Wisliceny had caused the ending of the deportations from Slovakia, the Working Group pursued a more ambitious scheme to pay the Nazis $2 million to stop the Final Solution throughout Europe. This attempt was named the Europa Plan.

In June 1942, Rabbi Weissmandel, who had heard that Wisliceny was susceptible to bribes, conceived of the idea of paying him $50,000 to halt the deportations from Slovakia entirely. Wisliceny was approached and the first instalment of $25,000 duly handed over. When deportations were postponed for several weeks, Weissmandel concluded that the payment had worked, and so he decided to hand over the remaining instalment.[50] This was delayed because of difficulties in raising the money.

In August 1942, the decision to stop deportations from Slovakia was taken by the Slovak Council of Ministers. The deportations actually ended in October, by which point fifty-nine thousand of the country's ninety-five thousand Jews had been sent to their deaths. Wisliceny had no power to overrule the suspension by the Slovak regime. Making the best of the situation, he agreed that some Jews could remain in the country for the time being. According to a report by the SD in Slovakia, he continued to press for renewed deportations.[51]

The members of the Working Group, delighted with the ending of the deportations, were unaware of the real reasons for this turn of events. Instead they inferred that their payments to Wisliceny were the decisive factor. They soon hatched a more far-reaching plan to end the Final Solution throughout Europe by means of a single ransom deal for

$2 million. They hoped to raise this amount from the JDC and from the Zionists in Switzerland and from Hungarian Jews.

On receiving the second instalment of the original bribe in October 1942, Wisliceny informed his superior Eichmann and prepared a report for Himmler. He continued to tempt the Working Group with the prospect of a deal, even after February 1943, when he was sent to Greece to organize mass deportations there. At last, not having received any of the $2 million ransom, he broke off negotiations at the beginning of September 1943. Afterwards, he taunted his Jewish interlocutors with the possibility that the Final Solution might have been stopped if the money had been paid.[52]

Was there a genuine possibility of rescue in the Europa Plan talks? The consensus among historians is that the idea of ending the Holocaust by means of a ransom payment was a delusion. At most the Nazis were willing to contemplate the release of small groups of "preferred" Jews in return for large quantities of foreign currency.[53]

Crucial here is not only the fact that the Nazis were unwilling to conduct mass rescue negotiations in good faith, but also the fact that the rescue committee in Budapest, which closely followed the Europa Plan talks, did not realize that the Nazi readiness to negotiate was a sham.[54] The successful deception of the Slovak Working Group—and through it, the Jewish rescue committee in Hungary—was to have a fateful impact on the rescue committee's reaction when the Germans marched into Budapest.

A Fork in the Road

By the first months of 1944, there was an established Zionist rescue operation in Hungary. This rescue apparatus had clandestine contacts with Zionist agents (in Istanbul and Geneva) and substantial funding (from the Jewish Agency in Palestine and the JDC in Switzerland). The apparatus had succeeded in penetrating the surrounding Nazi-occupied countries, spiriting thousands of refugees across international borders and sending humanitarian aid to the remotest ghettos in Poland. The rescue committee had bribed police officials and border guards in several countries and had recruited German intelligence agents as couriers. The committee's leadership had funded a major rescue operation by a German industrialist, Oskar Schindler, in the heart of Nazi-ruled Poland. They had prepared a network of hundreds of young Zionist activists who could be mobilized to take information and false identity papers to ordinary Jews, to smuggle escapees across borders, and to undertake clandestine sabotage. The existence and effectiveness of this Zionist rescue apparatus was due in no small measure to the talent, industry, and initiative of Rezső Kasztner.

It is clear that in the event of Nazi occupation, the Zionist activists would have been well placed to start a new rescue campaign. Like previous rescue missions, these activities would be illegal. To execute such a rescue campaign, Kasztner and his colleagues would have to go underground. The alternative was to negotiate: to halt illegal activity, to cooperate with established Jewish leaders in a Nazi-appointed Jewish Council (*Judenrat*), to identify "reasonable" SS commanders, and to approach them with an offer to ransom the Jewish masses.

This alternative path—rescue via negotiations—would involve far less immediate personal danger. Subconsciously, it might be perceived as the safer option. In practice, it would mean gambling the outcome of the rescue effort on the permission of the murderers. The odds of such a gamble were—as Kasztner would later point out—"very slim." The consequences of losing would be horrific.

Notes

1. Andre Biss, *A Million Jews to Save* (London: New English Library, 1975), 44–45.
2. Kasztner, London Affidavit, 1.
3. Springmann-SIME1, para. 75, Springmann-SIME2, para. 101.
4. For the dates, see Kasztner's London Affidavit, 1.
5. Joel Brand and Hansi Brand, *Ha'Satan veha'nefesh* [*The Devil and the Soul*] (Tel Aviv: Ladori, 1960), 26–27. Brand describes his own methods of draft evasion in Brand-SIME1, paras. 13–15.
6. Eli Reichenthal, *Ha'omnam nirzach paamayim? Parashat Kastner breija mechudeshet* [*A Man Who Was Murdered Twice? A Re-examination of the Kasztner Affair*] (Jerusalem: Bialik Publishing, 2010), 63–64.
7. Springmann-SIME2, para. 100.
8. Alex Weissberg, *Desperate Mission: Joel Brand's Story* (New York: Criterion Books, 1958), 18.
9. *Freudiger Report*, 27; Fülöp Freudiger, "Five Months," in *The Tragedy of Hungarian Jewry*, ed. Randolph L. Braham (Boulder, CO: Social Science Monographs in association with Columbia University Press, 1986), 258.
10. Kasztner Trial testimony, July 1, 1954.
11. Annie Szamosi, *Rudolf Kasztner in History, in Testimony and in Memory* (MA Thesis, Toronto: York University, 2006), 61–62; Yechiam Weitz, *The Man Who Was Murdered Twice: The Life, Trial and Death of Israel Kasztner* (Jerusalem: Yad Vashem, 2011), 61.
12. Weitz, *The Man Who Was Murdered Twice*, 323.
13. Joel Brand and Hansi Brand, *Ha'Satan veha'nefesh*, 28.
14. Rezső Kasztner, *Der Bericht des jüdischen Rettungskomitees aus Budapest 1942–1945* (Basel: Vaadat ezrah ve'hatsalah be'Budapest, 1946), vii.

15. Weissberg, *Desperate Mission*, 22–23.

16. Kasztner, Interrogation 1581a, 2.

17. TNA FO 371/42807, *Bulletin of the Jewish Agency Committee For the Jews of Occupied Europe*, February 1944, 11–13; also Yad Vashem, P 32/11, *Die Bekenntnisse den Herrn X*, November 1943. The report was drawn up by Kasztner: Springmann-SIME2, para. 43.

18. Szabolcs Szita, *Trading in Lives? Operations of the Jewish Relief and Rescue Committee in Budapest, 1944–1945* (Budapest: Central European University Press, 2005), 10.

19. Kasztner's Veesenmayer Trial testimony, March 19, 1948, Kasztner Trial prosecution exhibit 4, 3620, 3622.

20. Samu Stern, "'A Race with Time': A Statement," in *Hungarian Jewish Studies*, ed. Randolph L. Braham (New York: World Federation of Hungarian Jews, 1973), 5–6.

21. Béla Vágó, "The Intelligence Aspects of the Joel Brand Mission," *Yad Vashem Studies* 10 (1974): 113ff.

22. Richard Breitman, "Other Responses to the Holocaust," in *US Intelligence and the Nazis*, eds. Richard Breitman, Norman J. W. Goda, Timothy Naftali and Robert Wolfe (Cambridge: Cambridge University Press, 2005), 53; Brand-SIME1, para. 116; Brand's Eichmann Trial testimony, May 29, 1961.

23. Springmann-SIME1, para. 39. For Grosz's account, much of it no doubt unreliable, see Grosz-SIME3, paras. 49–51, 58, 66–67, 78, 82, 87–89, 95, 126, 174, 176, 186, 204.

24. For profiles of these individuals, see Springmann-SIME2; Tuvia Friling, *Arrows in the Dark: David Ben-Gurion, the Yishuv Leadership and Rescue Attempts During the Holocaust* (Madison: University of Wisconsin Press, 2005), Vol. 1, 301–4. Under British interrogation, Brand claimed that he only met the Abwehr couriers and Grosz a week or two before Springmann's final departure from Hungary: Brand-SIME1, para. 49; Brand-SIME2, para. 3.

25. Springmann-SIME1, para. 41.

26. Springmann-SIME2, paras. 19–20.

27. Springmann-SIME2, para. 26. Brand claimed under interrogation that the couriers only admitted to being Abwehr agents about "two weeks" before the German occupation in 1944: Brand-SIME1, para. 48.

28. Springmann-SIME3, para. 47; cf. ibid., para. 56, Springmann-SIME2, para. 27.

29. For background on Fritz Laufer ("perhaps one of the most important double-agents of World War II"), see Shlomo Aronson, *Hitler, the Allies and the Jews* (Cambridge: Cambridge University Press, 2004), 203–6, 211, 322; idem, "OSS X-2 and Rescue Efforts During the Holocaust," in *Secret Intelligence and the Holocaust*, ed. David Bankier (New York: Enigma Books, 2006), 71–74; Friling, *Arrows in the Dark*, Vol. 1, 308.

30. Aronson, *Hitler, the Allies and the Jews*, 205, citing his interview with Springmann.

31. Brand-SIME1, para. 61.

32. Weissberg, *Desperate Mission*, 22.

33. Quoted in the report of the US vice-consul in Istanbul, Leslie Albion Squires, "Activities of André Antal Gyorgy and Joel Brand," June 4, 1944, in John Mendelsohn, *The Holocaust: Selected Documents, Vol. 15, Relief in Hungary*

and the Failure of the Joel Brand Mission (New York: Garland Publishing, 1982), 102.

34. Kasztner, *Bericht*, 9–10.
35. Ibid., 13–14.
36. Brand-SIME1, para. 62.
37. Brand-SIME1, para. 66.
38. Brand-SIME1, para. 63.
39. Kasztner, *Bericht*, 8; Szita, *Trading in Lives?*, 11.
40. Brand-SIME1, para. 65.
41. The Jewish rescue committee's report to Saly Mayer, November 22, 1943, Kasztner Archive, cited in Reichenthal, *Ha'omnam nirzach paamayim?*, 77. Slightly different figures are given by Kasztner in the *Bericht*, 9.
42. NARA RG 226, Entry 191A: OSS, Dissemination A-24178, Report 18087, cited in Reichenthal, *Ha'omnam nirzach paamayim?*, 78.
43. Eichmann Trial testimony, May 29, 1961.
44. Springmann-SIME3, paras. 3–4.
45. Brand-SIME1, paras. 41–42.
46. Springmann-SIME3, para. 5.
47. Springmann-SIME3, para. 7.
48. Brand-SIME1, para. 43; cf. Brand-JAE2, para. 67.
49. Rafi Benshalom's filmed interview on Ynet, January 30, 2010: http://www.ynet.co.il/articles/0,7340,L-3840571,00.html (accessed May 18, 2010).
50. Livia Rothkirchen, "The 'Europa Plan': A Reassessment," in *American Jewry During the Holocaust*, ed. Seymour Maxwell Finger (New York: American Jewish Commission on the Holocaust, 1984), Appendix 4:7, 8.
51. Aronson, *Hitler, the Allies and the Jews*, 175–7.
52. Rothkirchen, "The 'Europa Plan': A Reassessment," 10.
53. This is clear from a note by Himmler in December 1942, when the Europa Plan talks had just begun: "I have asked the Führer about the releasing of Jews against hard currency. He had authorized me to approve such cases, provided they bring in genuinely substantial sums from abroad." Ibid., 3.
54. Kasztner, *Bericht*, iv.

2

Negotiating with Nazis

On March 10, 1944, Adolf Eichmann addressed his fellow Holocaust perpetrators in a conference at the Mauthausen concentration camp. The audience included Hermann Krumey, his assistant in the annihilation of Polish Jewry; Dieter Wisliceny, who had destroyed the Jews of Slovakia and Greece; and Otto Hunsche, a specialist in the legal arrangements for the Final Solution. Eichmann announced that he was preparing his SS unit, the *Sondereinsatzkommando-Eichmann* (or *Eichmann-Kommando*), for his mission in Hungary: organizing the fastest possible deportation of the entire Jewish population to Auschwitz.[1]

In the same week (perhaps on the same day), the Jewish rescue committee's couriers in the Abwehr arranged an interview for Kasztner and Brand with their commanding officer, Dr. Johann Schmidt. This individual (described by Brand as "an unpleasant, sexual, sadistic, disgusting character") asked them to inform the Jewish Agency that there had been a power struggle among the German elite, which had now concluded with the victory of his military superiors over the SS. The outcome would be a revolutionary improvement in Nazi conduct toward the Jews: there would be "no further mass executions" and the survivors would be used as slave labor, just like "other peoples" in occupied Europe. Not only would the German army maintain tolerable living conditions in the concentration camps, but the rescue committee in Budapest would also be allowed to take foreign humanitarian aid directly to camp inmates in Poland and Italy. To bring about this miracle, Kasztner's committee had to raise a large sum of money abroad. The Zionists also had to send the Americans and the British a report praising the Abwehr cell's vital contribution to their rescue work; here was a transparent bid for a postwar alibi.[2]

Soon afterwards, Schmidt's subordinate Winninger (also among the "creatures of the lowest order," according to Brand)[3] privately informed the rescue committee of the impending occupation of Hungary. Kasztner and Brand agreed to convey the Abwehr's reassuring falsehoods to the Jewish Agency (which they did) and to send the alibi report to the Allies (which they did not). In return, they asked the Abwehr group to contact the *Eichmann-Kommando* officer Wisliceny, with a view to reopening the rescue talks cut off the previous year in Slovakia.[4]

Schmidt's baseless offer to the rescue committee set the pattern for the following months: at each stage of the planning and execution of the Final Solution in Hungary, someone on the German side proposed another rescue deal to the Jews.

Meanwhile, the Hungarian head of state Miklós Horthy was summoned to meet Adolf Hitler, who accused his government of disloyalty to the Axis. Horthy was informed of the imminent German occupation of his country and instructed to surrender hundreds of thousands of Jews for labor in the Third Reich. This was, of course, the official pretext for their transfer to the gas chambers.[5]

On March 19, the Nazis occupied Hungary. Horthy returned as a mere figurehead. On the same train was Hitler's representative, Edmund Veesenmayer, who now installed a pro-German regime led by Döme Sztójay. Key posts in the Interior Ministry were given to the virulent antisemites László Baky and László Endre, while a special security force of twenty thousand gendarmes was placed under the command of László Ferenczy. These men would become the chief Hungarian tormentors and destroyers of the Jews.

With the eager support of the new regime, the *Eichmann-Kommando* set to work on the Final Solution in Hungary. As elsewhere in Nazi-occupied Europe, the plan unfolded in stages: *isolation* of the victims from the general population; *concentration* of the victims in ghettos; *deportation* of the victims to the place of extermination.

The process began at once. The new regime issued a barrage of antisemitic decrees. These included measures to remove the Jews from social and economic life (dismissal of public servants, disbarment of lawyers, expulsion from professional and cultural bodies, closure of businesses, freezing of bank accounts); measures to cut off all communication and information (confiscation of telephones and radios); and measures to immobilize and identify the victims (exclusion from public and private transport, obligation to wear the Yellow Star).[6] Within a month, Hungary's Jews were stripped of their civil rights.

The Nazi Initiative

As the German forces arrived in Budapest, Eichmann's henchmen Krumey and Wisliceny entered the Jewish headquarters and ordered the Jewish leadership to assemble within twenty-four hours. The next day's meeting consisted of the standard Nazi deception tactics. The Jewish leaders were told that only economic restrictions would be imposed, while cultural and religious life would continue. The community had to "ensure that people remained quiet and maintained order," which necessitated the immediate formation of a Jewish Council (*Judenrat*).[7]

The Hungarian Jewish leaders had neither foreseen nor planned for the occupation, but the same anti-Zionist personalities who had spent their lives preaching the virtue of blind loyalty to the Magyar nation—men like Samu Stern and Ernő Pető—now organized the central *Judenrat* in Budapest and demanded blind obedience to the Nazis from the Jewish community.

The Zionist activists, in contrast, knew just what to expect. On the morning of the occupation, the Abwehr agents took Brand into protective custody. Contrary to the assurances they had given just a few days earlier, the Abwehr men were pessimistic about their future and regretted their loss of power to the SS.[8] That afternoon, Winninger visited Kasztner's home. According to Kasztner, he warned that the Nazis would wipe out the Hungarian Jews with even greater cruelty than they had used against Polish Jews.[9] As Kasztner testified at Nuremberg, "with the German occupation we could not have any illusion. We knew that it is the beginning of the end. It was something like a death sentence for about 800,000 Jews existing at that time in Hungary."[10]

As soon as Brand was released on March 22, the rescue activists debated their options. On the one hand, there were orders from the Jewish Agency to prepare the Jewish masses for self-defense and self-preservation if the Nazis came. On the other hand, it was tempting to resume the previous year's negotiations in Slovakia, in the hope of somehow moderating the Nazi killers. The prerequisite for such negotiations was, of course, official recognition of the Jewish rescue activists by the Nazis.

Here it is intriguing that the Abwehr agents now offered Kasztner's rescue committee control over the official *Judenrat*. Brand writes that the committee "brusquely refused" to nominate the *Judenrat* members, "for we knew what had happened in Poland." In spite of this rebuff, the committee was immediately placed under Abwehr protection.[11] This was important because the Nazis were combing the country for the purpose of rounding up their opponents, seizing hostages, and creating a climate of terror: more than three thousand Jews were arrested in the first week of the occupation.[12]

A decision had to be made now. Should the rescue activists go underground, or should they try to start negotiations? Kasztner favored negotiations. Insisting that it had been "a fatal mistake" not to deliver the ransom promised in Slovakia, he proposed to pay the Nazis $200,000 per month for ten months in the expectation that Germany would lose the war in the meantime.[13] "Our main aim," he later explained, "was to buy time. We told ourselves that we had to make this attempt and open negotiations and promise and so postpone the date of destruction for as long as possible. Postponement by negotiation. To this end we decided to offer $2 million."[14]

The Nazis were eager to negotiate. On March 24, Wisliceny arrived in Bratislava. There he retrieved the codex of antisemitic decrees that had been used to send most of the Slovak Jews to Auschwitz—decrees that would be re-enacted in Hungary.[15] He also obtained a letter of recommendation from the local Jewish rescue leader, Rabbi Weissmandel. The letter confirmed Wisliceny's good faith and advised Hungarian Jews to save themselves by paying him a ransom of $2 million. It gave exact instructions for the direction of the negotiations, stating that everything had already been agreed and that the entire Jewish population would be spared.[16]

Just as Kasztner was urging his colleagues to approach Wisliceny on the rationale of "buying time" for the rescue effort, the very same Nazi was preparing to trick the Jews into making the very same offer, with the aim of buying time for the extermination effort.

Rabbi Weissmandel instantly suspected Wisliceny's true purpose. In his memoirs he describes both the "open letter" he had to write for Wisliceny and a "secret letter" he sent at the same time, without Wisliceny's knowledge. The secret letter essentially revoked his open letter and outlined the dangers of negotiating with Nazis. Weissmandel formulated a simple test of German willingness to bargain in good faith: if negotiations took place, there should be no ghettoization; but if ghettoization took place, then the negotiations were a trick. "I explained," wrote Weissmandel, "that the killings began with the gathering of everyone into a ghetto, and after that there was no escape."[17] In such a scenario, he recommended alerting the Jews of Hungary to the meaning of Auschwitz, as the resulting disobedience would make it harder for the killers to round up their victims.

Wisliceny returned to Budapest on March 27 bearing Weissmandel's open letter, which he showed to the Orthodox leader Fülöp Freudiger.[18] The resulting exchange sheds light on the immediate goal of the exercise. As Freudiger relates:

> He tore [Weissmandel's letter] into small pieces and threw them into the stove. Then he asked me: "What do you have to say about the letter?" I said to him: "I am at your disposal." He said to me: "From today onwards, we need the funds that are reaching you from abroad."[19]

Wisliceny's demand for the funds from abroad referred to the money sent by Jewish institutions for the refugees in Hungary. Funds previously used for illegal rescue activities would now be given to the SS instead.

On March 31, Eichmann received a delegation from the *Judenrat*. He announced that his priority in Hungary was the deployment of Jewish labor for the war effort. The burdens imposed on the Jewish population were only temporary:

> After the war, the Jews would be free to do whatever they wanted. Everything taking place on the Jewish question was in fact only for the wartime period, and with the end of the war the Germans would again become good-natured and permit everything, as in the past.

If Jews tried to join the anti-fascist resistance, they would be crushed. But as long as the Jews were passive and obedient, "not only would they not come to any harm, they would be protected from it." Eichmann "emphatically wanted this idea of his to be propagated among the widest strata of Jewry." He vowed to punish even street-level antisemitic harassment: any such incident "should be reported to him and he would deal with the attackers."[20]

The Jewish leaders exposed to this charade were familiar with the precedents in Nazi-occupied Europe. Yet not only were they deceived by Eichmann, they were also enlisted in his effort to deceive "the widest strata of Jewry."

Having won the collaboration of the anti-Zionists (through duress), Eichmann's SS unit now dangled the lure of "rescue negotiations" before the Zionists.

"Money for Blood"[21]

On April 4, a new message for the rescue committee arrived from Bratislava: the Slovak Zionist leadership had received Wisliceny's personal promise not to deport the Hungarian Jews. If a ransom deal was made, even the Jewish survivors in Poland would be allowed to leave Europe.[22]

Kasztner and Brand took the bait: they bribed their Abwehr contacts to ask Wisliceny to negotiate "on a financial basis" about "moderating the anti-Jewish measures" in Hungary.[23]

Meeting No. 1

The first meeting was held on April 5.[24] Brand and Kasztner spoke for the Jewish rescue committee, and Wisliceny represented the *Eichmann-Kommando*. Also present (as silent spectators) were Schmidt and Winninger of the Abwehr and an officer Erich Klausnitzer of the Gestapo/SD.

Brand and Kasztner offered Wisliceny $2 million in return for four points:

1. No executions.
2. No ghettos.
3. No deportations.
4. Emigration. They specifically requested exit permission for six hundred Jews holding British entry certificates to Palestine.[25]

Wisliceny's replies seemed too good to be true. He appeared to accept points 1–3. As for point 4, he not only agreed to Jewish emigration but also encouraged the rescue activists to aim higher: he asked them to draw up a plan for the mass exodus of tens or hundreds of thousands. Wisliceny also dismissed the $2 million offer as too low, but he suggested no alternative price—and demanded the first $200,000 within a week.[26]

Wisliceny was quick to add an important caveat. There would be no deportations, and emigration would be allowed—but the emigrants would have to be deported from Hungary "in order to make the bodies into German goods" before they could leave Europe.[27]

Wisliceny's qualification showed that the rescue negotiations were a sham. What would happen if the talks succeeded and emigration took place on his terms? First, the Jewish masses would be moved into camps. "The main idea of the plan," according to Freudiger, "was to concentrate Jews in labor camps where they would have to carry out various kinds of work," and it was understood that "the construction of the camps in question would be imposed on the Jews."[28] Second, the Jewish masses would be deported from Hungary; only then would the Nazis let them emigrate from Europe. Wisliceny injected an element of blackmail: he could prevent deportation to Poland by telling his superiors that "it was an unnecessary waste, when these Jews were due to go in another direction."[29]

In short, if the negotiations failed, the Jews would be concentrated and deported; and if the negotiations succeeded, the Jews would be concentrated and deported. If the talks with the SS continued on this basis, how could the Jewish rescue committee oppose the concentration and deportation of Jews? When Brand asked "that the concentrations with a view to these deportations should not be as brutal as they had been in other parts of German Europe," Wisliceny would not even concede this much. It was, he replied, a matter for the Hungarians.[30]

Kasztner and Brand fell right into the Nazi trap. Deciding that their four points had been accepted, they started work on a mass emigration plan and began to raise money from the Jewish community in Budapest.

April 5—the date of the first meeting with the *Eichmann-Kommando*—was the day when the Yellow Star became compulsory for Hungarian Jews. Only one group was exempt: Kasztner's rescue committee.[31] Two days later, Baky and Endre circulated a secret order approved by the *Eichmann-Kommando*: the entire country would be "purged of Jews." The victims would be confined to concentration camps before their deportation. Not even small children or hospital patients would be spared.[32]

Meeting No. 2

The second meeting between the rescue committee and the *Eichmann-Kommando* was held around April 12.[33] Again Kasztner and Brand spoke for the Jews, but Krumey and Hunsche replaced Wisliceny on the German side. Kasztner and Brand delivered most of the $200,000 advance payment, but not all of it; the Nazis agreed to accept the rest later on.

By now there were signs that the concentration process was beginning in Subcarpathia, but the Jewish rescue committee's protests were ignored.[34] Krumey insisted that he would need to verify Wisliceny's statements, which would take time as Wisliceny was in Berlin. This was both false (Wisliceny was in the provinces preparing the ghetto drive) and absurd (Wisliceny was Krumey's subordinate). When the rescue committee presented its plan for the immediate emigration of one hundred and fifty thousand Jews, Krumey was evasive, claiming that he needed further instructions.[35]

Having dismissed their protests and ignored their proposals, Krumey distracted Kasztner and Brand: he agreed to forgo the detention of a few of their colleagues and granted the rescue committee several immunity passes guaranteeing freedom of movement and freedom from arrest. Brand had requested these passes in the hope of making contact with the provincial communities, but it soon emerged that further permission was required to leave the capital. Kasztner received such permission; Brand did not.[36] In mid-April—and again at the beginning of May—Kasztner was allowed to visit Kolozsvár in North Transylvania. On top of this benefit, Kasztner and Brand were allowed to use their own cars and telephones and not to wear the Yellow Star. Not even the leaders of the *Judenrat* received all these privileges.[37]

As activists in the leftist Mapai party, Brand and Kasztner represented a small fraction of the Hungarian Zionist movement, which represented a small fraction of the country's Jewish population. Yet "in the few days that followed the German invasion *we became the leaders of Hungarian Jewry.*" Even Samu Stern, the head of the *Judenrat*, who had always treated them with contempt, now deferred to their decisions.[38]

On April 12, the regions of Subcarpathia and North Transylvania were designated "military operational zones"—a pretext for driving their Jewish residents into ghettos. On April 14, Veesenmayer confirmed the Hungarian regime's promise to send one hundred thousand Jewish workers to the Third Reich—a camouflage for the deportations to Auschwitz.[39] On that date, the Zionist movement was officially banned. There was only one exception: Kasztner's rescue committee, which had traded the protection of the Abwehr for the protection of the SS.[40]

SS protection was not a free gift. Kasztner had to avoid or prevent any action that might provoke his new patrons to break off contact. Clearly he could expect nothing from Eichmann's officers if he antagonized them by spreading panic in the Jewish community, promoting large-scale flight, helping rescue activists to evade arrest, setting up underground bunkers, or—most dangerous of all—preparing for resistance.

This became clear on April 15, when a member of the Zionist youth, Avri Lissauer, was caught trying to arrange an escape route to the Partisans in Yugoslavia. The next morning, Kasztner's aide Ernő Szilágyi was taken by the SS for interrogation, disregarding his immunity pass.[41] Kasztner was furious. As noted by one of the Zionist youth leaders, Rafi Benshalom, Kasztner was "opposed in principle" to the cross-border escape effort: "Here and there the Germans were turning a blind eye, but on this issue they were not joking."[42] Kasztner ordered the Zionist youth to stop all of their illegal operations, as these were endangering his talks with the SS. When the youth movements refused, Kasztner yielded "quite unwillingly." He had no choice, writes Benshalom, "because most of the Zionist leaders supported us."[43]

Thanks to Kasztner's relations with the SS, the Zionists now had to fight the head of their own rescue committee in order to continue their own rescue missions.

Meeting No. 3

The third meeting was held on April 21. Kasztner and Brand still did not bring the whole of their advance payment. Krumey and Hunsche rebuked them and threatened to stop the talks. By now one hundred thousand Jews in Subcarpathia had been driven into ghettos.[44] The issue was plainly nonnegotiable and it vanished from the agenda. As for preventing deportation, the Nazis would not even discuss the subject.[45]

Krumey was amenable to the emigration of a limited number of Jews, if America or a neutral country would take them. But to avoid provoking the Hungarian regime, even this small-scale departure would need to be disguised as a Nazi deportation. The rescue activists pointed out that the "disguise" was unnecessary: not only was the government in favor of emigration, but the Hungarian Foreign Ministry had also sent the German Embassy an official request to allow the exit of six hundred Jews to Palestine.[46] The Nazis were unmoved. They warned the Jewish side not to contact the Hungarian regime and classified the talks as a "Reich secret."

The outcome of this third meeting on April 21 proved that the initial "Money for Blood" plan was null and void. Any remaining doubts vanished as soon as Krumey and Hunsche left the room. The Abwehr commander Schmidt stayed behind to tell Kasztner and Brand that concentration and deportation were now a foregone conclusion; according to Brand, he warned explicitly that the Jews would be sent to Auschwitz.[47] Schmidt held out a slight hope that more payments would achieve something. But by now it was clear that the four points raised by Kasztner and Brand had been rejected. As their colleague Andre Biss recognized, "there was no longer any question of delaying the deportations." While the Jews had to pay for the privilege of negotiating, "the Germans just made promises and took engagements which all, without exception, were never kept."[48]

The only issue still on the table was exit permission for a few hundred people. And the conditions attached were sinister in the extreme.

The Nazis insisted on turning the emigration into a deportation—and their rationale (official Hungarian opposition) was transparently false.

Nazi "Concessions"

The Nazis expertly manipulated the negotiations to entrap the Jewish side. In this way they could proceed with their genocidal plans without fear of an underground rescue campaign or mass panic resulting in cross-border flight, passive disobedience, and active resistance.

The Nazis were shrewd enough to understand that they could not sustain the charade without appearing to make concessions.[49] While driving provincial Jews into ghettos and preparing the deportations, the *Eichmann-Kommando* not only bestowed various privileges (such as immunity passes) on the national Jewish leaders but also pretended to spare individuals. The tactic of arresting and then releasing the friends and relatives of prominent figures (such as Kasztner's aide Szilágyi) was a strong incentive to continue the talks, no matter what was happening to the provincial communities.

It soon became clear that these "concessions" were unrelated to any rescue deals and were not really concessions. In the second half of April, Fülöp Freudiger visited the SS headquarters with a *Judenrat* official, Imre Reiner, to request the release of the latter's elderly parents from their ghetto. They encountered Eichmann, who not only agreed, but also gave instructions to move the immediate relatives of *all* central *Judenrat* members to Budapest. And this was just the start of the *Eichmann-Kommando*'s "generosity." When Freudiger requested the transfer of provincial *Judenrat* members as well, Wisliceny promptly agreed.[50] So Eichmann's unit accepted the "rescue" of certain Jewish VIPs and their families without negotiating with Kasztner or anyone else.

As Freudiger slowly realized, Eichmann's "concessions" to Jewish leaders were nothing of the kind: "With hindsight I see that he just did it to coerce them . . . . A person cares about his nearest and dearest and it's more horrible to kill his family."[51] The targets of these SS-sponsored "rescue actions" had been given a temporary reprieve because they were still useful to the Nazis as hostages.

Within hours of the Nazi occupation of Hungary, Kasztner had been informed by German intelligence that the Jewish population was doomed. He immediately understood that the occupation was a "death sentence" for all Hungarian Jews. Within days of the disaster, Kasztner persuaded his colleagues to disobey the Jewish Agency's instructions to foment a Zionist uprising—and to approach the Nazis instead. Meanwhile, he tried unsuccessfully to induce them to abandon all illegal rescue operations, including efforts to hide Jews and smuggle them across the border.

During the first meeting with the *Eichmann-Kommando*, Kasztner agreed to negotiate a "rescue plan" based on emigration of Jews through deportation by the Nazis. During the second meeting, his committee was granted official SS protection. Kasztner and his minions became the only Jews in Hungary who were exempt from the Yellow Star and allowed to retain their cars and telephones. A month after the occupation, Kasztner became the only Jew in Hungary with official permission to travel from the capital to the provinces. At the third meeting, Kasztner accepted the brutal concentration process as a *fait accompli*, when most of the Jews were still outside ghettos; immediately afterwards, he was told by a German agent that mass deportations were inevitable.

Throughout this period, Kasztner's negotiations succeeded only in enhancing his own status. So rapid was Kasztner's ascent that his committee managed to usurp the political contacts with the Nazis from the official *Judenrat*, which increasingly deferred to his wishes.

Eichmann's officers had not, of course, bestowed this extraordinary promotion on the head of the rescue committee for free. The price for the rise of Kasztner would be paid by the Jewish population of Hungary.

Notes

1. Braham, *The Politics of Genocide*, Vol. 1, 417. For Eichmann's mission, see his Statement to the Israeli Police, Eichmann Trial exhibit T/37, 1879. See also the interview published in *Life Magazine*, November 28, 1960: "In Hungary my basic orders were to ship all Jews out of the country in as short a time as possible. Now, after years of working behind a desk, I had come out into the raw reality of the field."
2. Brand-SIME1, paras. 68–71 (specifying the date of March 10 and the sum of $250,000); Kasztner, *Bericht*, 14–15 (March 13 and $200,000). According to Brand, Schmidt also promised to free Gisi Fleischmann from captivity in Slovakia. According to Kasztner, he promised to place the camps under Red Cross supervision.
3. Brand-JAE2, para. 19.
4. Brand-SIME1, paras. 72, 74; Kasztner, *Bericht*, 15-15a.
5. Braham, *The Politics of Genocide*, Vol. 1, 388–401, 663.
6. For a chronological list, see Braham, *The Politics of Genocide*, Vol. 2, Appendix 3, 1371–84.
7. Freudiger, Eichmann Trial testimony, May 24, 1961. NB Komoly's immediate reaction to this news: "we [the Zionists] will not join the *Judenrat*." *Komoly Diary*, March 20, 1944.
8. Brand-JAE2, para. 10; Brand-SIME1, paras. 75–77; Brand-SIME4, para. 9(b); Weissberg, *Desperate Mission*, 66–68. Brand requested the same protection

for his friends (i.e., Kasztner and other committee members) but was told that they were "not so important": Brand-SIME1, para. 76.

9. Kasztner, *Bericht*, 16.

10. Kasztner Trial prosecution exhibit 4: Kasztner's Veesenmayer Trial testimony, March 19, 1948, 3622–3.

11. Weissberg, *Desperate Mission*, 71–72. According to Grosz, the Abwehr now used "terroristic methods" against Brand and Kasztner "to blackmail them out of their Zionist funds." Brand described the payments as voluntary: Grosz-SIME3, para. 234, Brand-SIME4, para. 9(c).

12. Szita, *Trading in Lives?*, 24.

13. Weissberg, *Desperate Mission*, 72.

14. Kasztner Trial testimony, February 18, 1954.

15. Kasztner, *Bericht*, 24.

16. Ibid.; Michael Dov Weissmandel, *Min ha'meitzar* [*From the Abyss*] (New York: Emunah, 1960), 112–14; *Freudiger Report*, 17; Freudiger's Kasztner Trial testimony, August 12, 1954.

17. Weissmandel, *Min ha'meitzar*, 117; for a translation of Weissmandel's chapter on Hungary, see *Jewish Guardian*, Neturei Karta USA (Summer 1987): http://www.truetorahjews.org/images/guardian3-2.pdf (accessed June 18, 2012). Weissmandel's story includes a verifiable detail: when Freudiger asked him to explain the acronym "PKR" in his secret letter, he answered that it meant Subcarpathia and repeated his statements about ghettos. Weissmandel's advance warning of the ghetto drive in "PKR" is mentioned by Freudiger in "Five Months," 253.

18. *Freudiger Report*, 17; Freudiger's Kasztner Trial testimony, August 12, 1954 (giving a premature date of Thursday, March 23); Eichmann Trial testimony, May 25, 1961 (equivocating between Friday, March 24 and Monday, March 27); "Five Months," 245–6 (referring to "the next Wednesday," i.e., March 29). The "open letter" was also addressed to Baroness Edith Weiss (as Neolog representative) and Nison Kahan (as head of the Zionists). The former was in hiding and the latter was excluded from the meeting; Freudiger alone saw the open letter. Yehuda Bauer falsely states that the "open letter" was addressed to Freudiger, Weiss and Kasztner, and that since the first two evaded their duties, Kasztner became the official Jewish negotiator by default: *Jews for Sale? Nazi-Jewish Negotiations, 1933–1945* (New Haven, CT: Yale University Press, 1994), 154–5.

19. Freudiger's Eichmann Trial testimony, May 25, 1961.

20. From the *Judenrat*'s minutes of the meeting in Braham, *The Politics of Genocide*, Vol. 1, 465–8. The German participants were Eichmann, Krumey and Wisliceny; the Jewish delegates were Samu Stern, Ernő Boda, Ernő Pető and Janos Gabor.

21. The phrase is Brand's: see his Krumey-Hunsche Trial testimony as quoted in the *New York Times*, May 21, 1964.

22. Oskar Neumann to Eliahu Dobkin, April 4, 1944, TNA WO 208/685A (item 91B, para. 8); Budapest to Geneva, May 9, 1944, Haganah Archive, 14/798.

23. Kasztner, *Bericht*, 24.

24. Ibid.; implicitly, Brand-JAE2, para. 10 (under British interrogation, Brand became confused and described a pair of meetings with Wisliceny on March 29 and April 2: Brand-SIME1, paras. 81, 84–87).

25. Kasztner, *Bericht*, 24; Brand-JAE1, 2; Brand-JAE2, para. 11; Brand-SIME1, paras. 81–82; *Brand Report*, 20; *Shertok Report*, 4; Weissberg, *Desperate Mission*, 73.

26. Brand-JAE1, 2–3; Brand-JAE2, paras. 11–12; Brand-SIME1, paras. 82–83; *Brand Report*, 20–22; Weissberg, *Desperate Mission*, 73–75; Brand, Eichmann Trial testimony, May 29, 1961; Kasztner, *Bericht*, 24–25. Only Kasztner mentions that the first payment was to be made in a week.

27. Brand-JAE2, paras. 11, 14. In the Jewish Agency's protocol, Wisliceny proposes to deport the first transport of seven hundred and fifty Jews, and Eichmann later insists on deporting all Jewish emigrants: Brand-JAE1, 3, 5. Cf. Brand, Eichmann Trial testimony, May 29, 1961 ("Wisliceny . . . said that he could not sell Hungarian Jews directly from Hungary. They would have to be brought to German-occupied territory first, become German merchandise, and then they could be delivered. However, this sounded very ominous to us.") Kasztner does not mention Wisliceny's insistence on turning the emigrants into German "merchandise": *Bericht*, 25.

28. *Freudiger Report*, 18. See also *Brand Report*, 20. Kasztner refers to the labor camps in Slovakia in the *Bericht*, 24.

29. Brand-SIME1, para. 83.

30. Brand-JAE2, para. 14.

31. Brand-JAE2, para. 58; Kasztner, Kasztner Trial testimony, March 9, 1954; Freudiger, "Five Months," 248.

32. Braham, *The Politics of Genocide*, Vol. 1, 573–6.

33. On April 5, Wisliceny set a one-week deadline for the $200,000. On April 12, "Brand informed me that Krumey demanded the money for the next day" (Freudiger, "Five Months," 247–8). Brand, who often confused the dates, specified April 9 (Brand-SIME1, para. 88).

34. Weissberg, *Desperate Mission*, 79, 81.

35. On the mass emigration plan, see Brand-SIME1, para. 85 (confusing Krumey with Wisliceny); *Brand Report*, 22; Weissberg, *Desperate Mission*, 80; Brand, Eichmann Trial testimony, May 29, 1961. For Krumey's evasions, see Kasztner, *Bericht*, 25.

36. Weissberg, *Desperate Mission*, 82–83.

37. The *Judenrat* members had immunity passes but they had no freedom of travel, no private vehicles and no exemption from the Yellow Star: Freudiger's Kasztner Trial testimony, August 13, 1954; Kasztner Trial verdict, s. 36.

38. Weissberg, *Desperate Mission*, 76–77, emphasis added.

39. Braham, *The Politics of Genocide*, Vol. 1, 581, 663.

40. Kasztner, *Bericht*, 26, 47.

41. *Komoly Diary*, April 16, 1944.

42. Rafi Benshalom, *We Struggled For Life: The Hungarian Zionist Youth Resistance During the Nazi Era* (Jerusalem: Gefen, 2001), 35.

43. Benshalom's filmed interview posted on Ynet, January 30, 2010: http://www.ynet.co.il/articles/0,7340,L-3840571,00.html (accessed May 18, 2010; translation adjusted slightly for grammar and syntax). See also Asher Arányi, *One Eye Cries While the Other Laughs* (Kibbutz Dalia: Maarechet, 2004), 149.

44. Szita, *Trading in Lives?*, 32.

45. Kasztner, *Bericht*, 27.

46. Miklós (Moshe) Krausz, *Memorandum über die Tätigkeit des Palästina-Amtes in Budapest in den kritischen Kriegsjahren 1941–45* (Budapest: March 4, 1946), Kasztner Trial prosecution exhibit 124, 3; Krausz, Kasztner Trial testimony, June 25, 1954.
47. Kasztner, *Bericht*, 27; Weissberg, *Desperate Mission*, 84–85.
48. Biss, *A Million Jews to Save*, 29, 30. As Freudiger testified in the Kasztner Trial on August 12, 1954, "after 3–4 weeks . . . there was no more talk of the Europa Plan."
49. Szita, *Trading in Lives*, 87–88; Braham, "Rescue Operations in Hungary," 42–44, 47–48.
50. Kasztner Trial testimony, August 12, 1954.
51. Kasztner Trial testimony, August 12, 1954. See also *Freudiger Report*, 37.

3

Salvation or Extermination?

On April 24, 1944, Adolf Eichmann and Dieter Wisliceny embarked on a tour of the major ghettos in the provinces. Joining them were László Endre of the Interior Ministry, gendarme commander László Ferenczy, and other Hungarian antisemites. In his official report of the tour, Endre stated that the ghettos had "a veritably sanatorium-like character." The Jews, he added, "are finally getting fresh air and have changed their old lifestyle for a healthier one."[1] Meanwhile, victims in the ghettos were committing suicide after torture at the hands of Ferenczy's men.

The *Eichmann-Kommando* had arrived in Hungary with a staff of 150–200 people.[2] Using these personnel (which included secretaries, drivers, and the like), Eichmann was expected to deport over three-quarters of a million people to their deaths. Such an operation could only be completed with the full support of Hungary's Interior Ministry, which supplied a force of twenty thousand gendarmes to carry out the segregation, expropriation, concentration, and expulsion of the victims. But Hungarian collaboration hinged on the pretense that the Jews would be sent for "work," with their families joining them only for the sake of "morale."[3] Any breach of secrecy about the mass murder of the deportees would shatter this official cover story.

Eichmann's tactics were also carefully regulated by his masters in the SS. Himmler, in particular, was obsessed with the prospect of a repeat of the Warsaw Ghetto uprising—the fear that the rage and the despair of those condemned to death would drive them to acts of last-ditch resistance. This notion, however paranoid—Jews in Hungary were isolated both physically and socially, their combat-worthy young men had been drafted into forced labor units, and they had no access to weapons—dictated the conduct of the murderers. Eichmann testified at his trial about the camouflage orders he received from Himmler: "as the front came closer and contacts were made with the Jewish masses . . . there were fears that there would be uprisings, and the [German] defences would be weakened. This found its expression in strategic reasoning. . . ."[4]

The outcome of these constraints was the extraordinary effort made by the Nazis to distract and mislead the central Jewish leadership by means of negotiations. Since the *Eichmann-Kommando*'s operations in Hungary were undertaken at lightning speed, the Jewish leaders had to be discouraged at each stage of the campaign from spreading panic among the victim population or provoking an international outcry that might end in Allied reprisals.

The collaboration of the anti-Zionist establishment in the capital was secured without much difficulty: by April 24, the *Judenrat* in Budapest was summoning selected Jews for "internment"—which in reality meant death—at the hands of the Nazis.[5]

The Zionists were another matter. The most dynamic element in the Jewish community, they had built an underground network capable of organizing illegal rescue efforts and spreading the alarm both at home and abroad—which the Nazis wanted to avoid at any cost. To distract the Zionists from these options, the Nazis began "rescue negotiations" with the committee led by Kasztner, who urged his colleagues to open official contacts at the very moment when they should have been preparing to go underground.

Only the head of this committee could have sabotaged the illegal Zionist rescue plans and crippled the Zionist rescue network in the hour of crisis.[6] That is why the Nazis bestowed unique privileges on Kasztner during the first few weeks of the occupation. They enabled a marginal activist from the provinces to pole-vault his way over the established community officials in Budapest so that he became *de facto* leader of Hungarian Jewry. And he was pleased with his new status. As one sympathetic researcher notes, "from Kasztner's point of view, his relations with senior Nazi officers were not only an unavoidable necessity but part of his self-image and sense of belonging to 'high society' and to the circle of decision makers."[7]

"Goods for Blood"

On April 25, Kasztner wrote to Saly Mayer, the JDC's delegate in Switzerland. Kasztner listed the committee's four points and repeated the specifics of the ransom plan; he wrote that Wisliceny had accepted it in principle; that the meetings with Krumey and Hunsche showed that the German negotiators were official representatives and not a private party seeking bribes; that the $200,000 advance payment had been raised and delivered; that the JDC's assistance in paying the full $2 million would save Hungarian Jewry; and that there were now prospects for the immigration of six hundred Jews by ship to Palestine.[8]

None of this was true. The rescue committee's four points had not been satisfied; the ransom deal was not on the agenda; Wisliceny had not made any real promises; Krumey and Hunsche had not officially endorsed his supposed promises; the rescue committee had not collected and delivered the whole $200,000; the Nazis were not even pretending that $2 million would save Hungary's Jews; and six hundred Jewish immigrants were not about to travel by ship to Palestine, since the *Eichmann-Kommando* was proposing to deport them to the Reich before sending them to a neutral country.

Kasztner's letter also cushioned the news of the ghetto drive, stating that the rescue committee's major demands—no deportation and no killing—had been met "so far." Kasztner knew all too well that under Nazi rule, ghettos were the prelude to deportation and mass slaughter.

Kasztner's letter of April 25 was calculated to create a false sense of optimism. It encouraged Jewish institutions to channel their rescue efforts into ransom negotiations that had already failed. This did not serve the interests of Hungary's Jews, but it did serve the interest of the Nazis, who were anxious to deceive the outside world about their plans. And the Zionist rescue activists in the free world were in fact deceived: their conclusion from this letter was that Kasztner's rescue committee had "succeeded in postponing the deportation."[9]

Either that day or a few days afterwards, Eichmann summoned Brand to the SS headquarters at Schwabenberg.[10] At this meeting, the obsolete ransom plan, or "Money for Blood," was replaced with an even more far-fetched barter plan: the so-called Goods for Blood deal.

Brand's later account of Eichmann's proposal differs fundamentally from the explanation he gave at the time. We begin with his postwar version, which has entered the popular imagination. At the Kasztner Trial, Brand testified that Eichmann greeted him with these words:

> You know who I am? I ran the [anti-Jewish] actions in Germany, Austria, Poland, Slovakia and so on. I was assigned to run the actions in Hungary. . . . I want to do business with you: goods for blood, blood for goods. I'm willing to sell you a million Jews. What do you want to save? Women who can give birth, men who can reproduce, children, the elderly? Talk!

Stunned by the tone and content of this diatribe, Brand replied that he would not choose Eichmann's victims for him. In any case, he would need to consult his comrades abroad.

> [Eichmann] answered: "Then go abroad. Go to Switzerland, Turkey, Spain or wherever you want: bring me the goods." I asked him which goods. "Bring me all sorts of goods," he said. "Trucks, for example! For 10,000 trucks I'm ready to sell you a million Jews: add 1,000 tons of tea, coffee and soap as well, I need it all."

Brand pointed out that no one would believe in the sincerity of the offer. Who would trust the Nazis to exchange a million Jews for ten thousand trucks? Eichmann responded: "We won't use the trucks on the Western front, only on the Eastern front." To Brand—testifying a decade later—this was "a clear attempt to drive a wedge between the Allies."

According to Brand's postwar version, Eichmann offered another guarantee of his good faith:

> So he suggested that he was willing to give 100,000 Jews as a "down payment" and only then require payment of 10% of the goods. Then he would give another 100,000 down payment: I could select my Jews from Hungary, Auschwitz, Theresienstadt, Slovakia or wherever I liked.... Instead [of Palestine] he wanted to send the Jews to Spain; we would have to take them to Africa, South or North America and so on.

Brand was now convinced. "I had nothing to lose," he explained. "If I gained a down payment of 100,000 Jews, and if the deportations were suspended in the meantime—I didn't consider his motives and objectives, and I wasn't interested in them."[11]

Such is Brand's postwar version. He gave similar accounts in his memoirs and at the Eichmann Trial. There his story caused some embarrassment when Eichmann began to use it in his defense, insisting that he had tried in good faith to save Hungarian Jewry and feigning outrage that the Allies had frustrated his efforts. The judges hastened to correct Brand's "mistaken" testimony in their verdict.[12]

In his original wartime interrogations, Brand said nothing about the immediate liberation of one hundred thousand Jews. He told the Jewish Agency that "a certain number would be allowed to cross the frontier before any payment had been made, as a token of goodwill, but no specific number was mentioned."[13] Brand did not even hint that Eichmann had offered to stop the deportation. In fact he said the opposite: the offer *depended* on mass deportations, because the

Nazis "would first have to convert the Jews into Reichs-chattels" or "German goods" (meaning that the Nazis had to deport Hungarian Jews into German territory in order to be able to treat them as German "merchandise").[14] For this reason, the Hungarian Jews would be sent to camps in Nazi Germany; only then would they be allowed to leave Europe.[15] Plainly, this condition was calculated to disguise the true purpose of the deportations.

Brand's first meeting with Eichmann was supervised by a Nazi officer who did not identify himself. This was Kurt Becher, the economic agent of the Waffen-SS, who had been sent to Budapest by Heinrich Himmler.[16] At the time of the Goods for Blood offer, Becher was also trying to buy trucks through Ferenc Chorin, the nation's preeminent Jewish industrialist. In the course of extracting "economic intelligence" from the frail elderly captive, Becher urged him to visit Switzerland and surrender his financial assets there, which would be used to buy the vehicles.[17] When this proved impractical, Becher terrorized Chorin and his family into handing over the Weiss-Manfréd factories, a pillar of the regional arms industry. He considered the acquisition a "perfect way to make procurements for the German army."[18]

Becher's postwar statements on the Goods for Blood deal were self-serving and contradictory, but under interrogation at Nuremberg, the truth slipped out. Becher's mandate from Himmler was straightforward: "Take what you can get from the Jews. Promise them what you like. What we keep is another matter."[19] In testimony submitted to the Eichmann Trial, Becher conceded that the Goods for Blood deal "was not meant as a serious proposal."[20]

Interviewed fifty years after the destruction of Hungary's Jews, Becher took credit for Eichmann's offer while admitting that it had nothing to do with rescue:

> Q: Did you ever believe that this grand "Jews For Goods" deal—a million Jews for 10,000 trucks—could succeed?
> A: No.
> . . .
> Q: You didn't believe Hitler would release a million Jews?
> A: No.[21]

Thus Becher flatly denied that the Goods for Blood deal could have saved Hungary's Jews. Becher's mission was not to sell the living but to force the victims to pay for their own murder—to achieve a self-financing genocide.[22]

Brand, it seems, was the only true believer in Eichmann's proposal; his colleagues were "shattered" when they heard the news.[23] Even his wife Hansi was skeptical:

> At first we just could not grasp it, we were just totally unable to imagine it, since we were aware that [Eichmann] had already exterminated 5 million Jews. . . . And then, suddenly he comes to him with an offer like this, and we had also heard that there had been various offers made in various countries, and the Jews had been robbed and they had all been killed, despite promises that they would be sent abroad. They had negotiated, and at the end of the negotiations they finished up in the gas chambers.[24]

These apprehensions were fully justified, as the rescue committee would now find out.

The Auschwitz News

Events during the negotiations exposed the Nazi plans for Hungarian Jewry and the dangers of trusting the promises of the SS. These included the ghetto drive in Subcarpathia; the railway negotiations with Slovakia; the first actual deportations from Hungary; and eye-witness evidence of preparations for a new extermination campaign in Auschwitz.

In the first few days of the occupation, Eichmann and his henchmen had assured the Jewish establishment that they had no wish to harm the Jews of Hungary. Wisliceny repeated this to Brand and Kasztner. By the second half of April it was clear that these assurances were false. The news of the ghetto drive in Subcarpathia soon reached the capital, followed by reports of the inhuman cruelty of the Hungarian gendarmes who were putting it into effect. There was little doubt that the ghetto drive would end in deportations. The central *Judenrat* submitted a formal protest to the Interior Ministry, where it was ignored.[25] Kasztner's committee was now in close contact with the *Judenrat* and maintained an office at its headquarters.[26]

After preparing the ghettos, the next challenge facing the Nazis was to transport the Hungarian Jews out of the country. As early as April 23, Veesenmayer updated the German Foreign Office:

> Negotiations about transportation have been started. They call for a daily shipment of 3,000 Jews, mainly from the Carpathian area, beginning on May 15. If transportation facilities permit, there will be later on also simultaneous shipments from other ghettos. Auschwitz is designated as receiving station.[27]

From his counterparts in Bratislava, Kasztner learned that negotiations on the transfer of 150 trains were under way between the Hungarian and Slovak railway officials. This was in the direction of Auschwitz.[28] On May 4, a conference to establish the train timetables opened in Vienna. The *Eichmann-Kommando* was represented by its transport specialist Franz Novak—"the stationmaster of death."[29]

Even more terrifying was the joint testimony of two Auschwitz escapees, Rudolf Vrba and Alfred Wetzler, who had witnessed preparations for further mass murders in the camp. Thanks to their long imprisonment and their contacts with other inmates, the pair had extensive knowledge of the numbers and origins of those killed and the methods of killing. The reorganization of the camp for the imminent arrival of large numbers of new victims provoked Vrba and Wetzler to escape in the hope of issuing a warning. Arriving in Slovakia on April 21, they gave the Zionist leadership a comprehensive account of the history of the mass murders at Auschwitz. Based on their information, the Slovak Zionists compiled a detailed report (the Vrba–Wetzler report or Auschwitz Protocols) and sent it on to Hungary. But the report never reached its intended recipients, the Hungarian Jewish public; nor was it published abroad for several vital weeks.[30]

Oskar Krasniansky, the Slovak Zionist official who compiled the Vrba–Wetzler report, wrote that at the end of April 1944 he personally handed a copy to a Hungarian visitor: Rezső Kasztner.[31] This was confirmed by Vrba: according to him, Krasniansky assured the escapees at the end of April that their report was already in Kasztner's hands.[32] The point remains uncertain, as Kasztner never admitted to receiving a copy of the report, let alone visiting Slovakia at this time. He did, however, refer to an important message from Bratislava warning about the preparations in the death camp for the imminent arrival of the Hungarian Jews. According to the warning message received by Kasztner, the SS were about to renovate the gas chambers and crematoria at Auschwitz, SS personnel at the camp had been reinforced, and one of the noncommissioned officers had been overheard commenting: "Soon we'll eat fine Hungarian salami"—a reference to the provisions that the unsuspecting Jews would be bringing with them. Reacting to this information, on April 28 Kasztner demanded an emergency meeting with Krumey.[33] Whether he had been given the Vrba–Wetzler report in person in Bratislava or he had merely received the warning message in Budapest, the timing of Kasztner's demand to meet Krumey indicates that he learned of the preparations to gas Hungarian Jews in Auschwitz no later than April 28.[34]

Over the next forty-eight hours came the trial deportation of three thousand eight hundred Hungarian Jews. From the Kistarcsa prison camp there were one thousand eight hundred victims and from Topolya there were two thousand. To sustain the fiction that the able-bodied were being sent for work, on this occasion the SS deported only those aged fourteen to sixty; but Kasztner was not fooled by this ruse. By April 29, he had received confirmation that the first train had been seen traveling past Bratislava *en route* to the death camp.[35] Out of three thousand eight hundred deportees, two thousand seven hundred were sent straight to the gas chambers.

Kasztner now had concrete evidence of the imminent massacre of huge numbers of innocent people: accounts of full-scale ghetto concentration in Subcarpathia; news of negotiations to send scores of deportation trains to Poland; a warning message describing the arrangements for gassing and incinerating the deportees; and the initial deportation of several thousand Hungarian Jews to Auschwitz.

It was obvious that the rescue negotiations were a trap and that the promises of the *Eichmann-Kommando* were worthless. Kasztner understood what was happening: "All signs showed that deportation could be postponed no longer—except by a miracle," he explained. To verify the status of the talks with the SS, he opted to call an immediate meeting.[36] But what did the Jews of Hungary have to gain from further negotiations if there was no chance of postponing the deportation? Did Kasztner's decision to arrange another meeting with the SS indicate that his priority was the fate of the Jews or the future of his relationship with the SS?

Kasztner's Reaction to the Auschwitz News

What did Kasztner do in response to the Auschwitz news, apart from renewing contact with the Nazis? Did he tell the Jews of Hungary? Did he tell the outside world?

Kasztner claimed after the war that at this point he "sent messengers to Jewish communities to warn them of the danger of deportation."[37] He referred to messages sent to "many provincial ghettos" encouraging people to flee and to resist boarding the trains. Such warnings, he complained, were rejected by a complacent Jewish public.[38]

These apologetic claims contradict his own words at the time. In mid-July, only a week after the end of the deportations from the provinces, Kasztner discussed his actions with Becher. Among his statements: "I've wondered many times whether, instead of the negotiations, it wouldn't have been better to call on the Zionist youth and rally the people to active resistance to entering the brickyards and the wagons."[39]

Kasztner not only failed to spread the Auschwitz news through the Zionist activists but also sabotaged their warning missions by pretending that he had no such information. In late April and early May, Hannah Ganz made several dangerous journeys from Budapest to Kolozsvár and back. On arriving in Kolozsvár, she approached people she knew and tried to warn them about the Nazis. But her information came from Jewish refugees who had escaped the slaughter in Poland; she had been given no specific information by Kasztner; and so she knew nothing of the Nazi plans to deport Hungary's Jews to Auschwitz.[40]

During the Kasztner Trial, one of the Zionist leaders from Kolozsvár, Hillel Danzig, was asked about his encounters with Hannah Ganz:

> Q: What did she tell you on Kasztner's behalf?
> A: She told us one thing: the situation was severe . . .
> Q: She didn't tell you about anticipated dangers on his behalf?
> A: She didn't tell us and she didn't know what would happen.
> Q: Did you speak to her about what would happen?
> A: I asked her.
> Q: What did she reply?
> A: She didn't know. They didn't know the intentions of the Germans or the Hungarians.[41]

Kasztner *did* know the genocidal plans of the Germans and the Hungarians—but he told his messenger that he knew nothing. Far from seeking to raise the alarm, he deceived his own messenger and, through her, the Jews she wanted to help.

Kasztner also made no effort to communicate the truth to the outside world.[42] In fact, as the portents of evil multiplied, more disinformation was sent to the foreign rescue activists. On May 1, a coded message was cabled to the Jewish Agency outpost in Istanbul:

> Payments were made to Wisliceny. Negotiations with Wisliceny aim at avoidance of death and deportation. A chance of success exists only if you intervene quickly and positively for the sake of large financial means. Let Saly [Mayer] and all his associates know that delay can work out catastrophically here . . . . Large organized *aliya* from here to Palestine is difficult, so permission for emigration to America is necessary so that a ship can leave Constanza [in Romania] for an American port. Make efforts for emigration to America via Lisbon for non-visa-holders as well . . . [43]

In truth, the payments had achieved nothing except for depleting the Zionist rescue funds and buying time for the ghetto drive; Wisliceny had long since vanished from the talks; "all signs showed" that negotiations would *not* prevent deportation and death; and under the policy of "emigration disguised as deportation," Jews seeking permission to leave the country had to be named by Kasztner's committee and handed over to the SS.

The rescue negotiations had rescued no one. The Nazis were planning to massacre over three-quarters of a million Hungarian Jews. But instead of alerting the intended victims and the outside world, Kasztner deceived the Zionist youth and his Zionist contacts abroad so that he could continue to deal with the murderers.[44]

Notes

1. Braham, *The Politics of Genocide*, Vol. 1, 606.
2. Ibid., Vol. 1, 415.
3. Ibid., Vol. 1, 391, 393–4, 397–401; Zoltán Vági, László Csősz, and Gábor Kádár, *The Holocaust in Hungary: Evolution of a Genocide* (Lanham, MD: AltaMira Press in association with the United States Holocaust Memorial Museum, 2013), 117.
4. Eichmann Trial testimony, July 21, 1961.
5. The leaders were told that "the Jews would have nothing to fear if they collaborated without friction" and those present "were enjoined to reassure their co-religionists," according to the *Freudiger Report*, 7. On the "internments" through the *Judenrat*, see Braham, *The Politics of Genocide*, Vol. 1, 610–13. For a detailed analysis of the *Judenrat*, see Braham, "The Role of the Jewish Council in Hungary: A Tentative Assessment," *Yad Vashem Studies* 10 (1974): 69–109. As Braham notes, the *Judenrat* leaders "lulled the masses into a false sense of security, issued the internment summonses, requisitioned apartments, distributed the yellow star badges, moved Jews into specially marked buildings, and surrendered large sums of money. Against their will and against their intention, they had become one of the major instruments through which the Nazis carried out their evil designs." Ibid., 86.
6. See Kasztner Trial verdict, s. 65.
7. Weitz, *The Man Who Was Murdered Twice*, 61.
8. Kasztner and Brand to Mayer, April 25, 1944, JDC Archive, New York, Saly Mayer Collection, file 20(2); for a Hebrew translation, see Kasztner Trial prosecution exhibit 25. This was supposedly a joint letter, but Kasztner is mentioned in the first person and Brand in the third. Kasztner apologizes for his brevity: he had only been given an hour to write before the courier's departure. If true, Brand had no time to read the letter with any care, if he even saw it; if false, Brand surely did not see it.
9. Schwalb to Istanbul, May 1, 1944, TNA WO 208/685A (item 91B, para. 5).
10. Brand gave several dates: April 16 (Brand-SIME1, para. 90), April 25 (*Desperate Mission*, Eichmann Trial), May 8 (Krumey-Hunsche Trial). Kasztner

indicated May 8 (*Bericht*, 34). Komoly mentioned a "new offer" on April 27 and he discussed it with Brand the next day (*Komoly Diary*, April 27, 28, 1944). Grosz heard of the offer on May 1–2 (Grosz-SIME3, paras. 259–62, 264). The meeting with Eichmann certainly preceded Brand's request for a Turkish visa on May 2 (Budapest to Istanbul, May 2, 1944, Haganah Archive, 14/798).

11. Kasztner Trial testimony, April 1, 1954. Cf. Brand-JAE1, 4; Brand-JAE2, para. 15; Brand-SIME1, paras. 92–93; Weissberg, *Desperate Mission*, 91–95; Eichmann Trial testimony, May 29, 1961.

12. Eichmann Trial verdict, s. 116.

13. Brand-JAE2, para. 31; cf. Brand-SIME1, para. 100. According to another source, Brand mentioned a figure of five thousand Jews: *Shertok Report*, 6. If Eichmann had really offered to free one hundred thousand Jews, it is certain that Brand would have told the Jewish Agency officials he met on May 19 (Istanbul) and June 11 (Aleppo). Not until his meeting with Ira Hirschmann of the War Refugee Board on June 22 (in Cairo) did he mention figures of ten thousand to fifty thousand Jews (probably pulled out of thin air in the hope of saving his mission): see Brand-WRB. By January 1945, the numbers had inflated to fifty thousand to one hundred thousand: *Brand Report*, 23. By the time of Brand's Kasztner Trial testimony, the figure had peaked at one hundred thousand.

14. Brand-JAE1, 5; Brand-JAE2, para. 22.

15. Brand-JAE1, 5; *Shertok Report*, 6. Not until January 1945 did Brand mention a Nazi promise to halt the deportations if his mission succeeded: *Brand Report*, 23.

16. Brand's Eichmann Trial testimony, May 29, 1961.

17. Gábor Kádár and Zoltán Vági, *Self-Financing Genocide: The Gold Train, the Becher Case and the Wealth of Hungarian Jews* (Budapest: Central European University Press, 2004), 199–200; Szita, *Trading in Lives*, 128.

18. Kádár and Vági, *Self-Financing Genocide*, 201, 204. See also Karla Müller-Tupath, *Reichsführers gehorsamster Becher* (Berlin: Aufbau-Verlag, 1999), 126–9; Sofia Leite and Antonio Louça, "Bechers Ziel: Der Fall Manfred Weiss und die Parallel-Diplomatie der SS (1944)," *Theresienstädter Studien und Dokumente* 15 (2008): 148–79.

19. Becher's Nuremberg interrogation, March 2, 1948, in Mendelsohn, *Relief in Hungary*, 52.

20. Becher's Eichmann Trial testimony, submitted to the Court of First Instance, Bremen, June 20, 1961, para. 59.

21. Interview with Ilana Dayan on Israel's Channel 2, December 22, 1994, in Müller-Tupath, *Reichsführers gehorsamster Becher*, 218.

22. Kádár and Vági, *Self-Financing Genocide*, 175–278.

23. Brand-SIME1, para. 94.

24. Hansi Brand, Eichmann Trial testimony, May 31, 1961.

25. Braham, *The Politics of Genocide*, Vol. 1, 607–9.

26. Asher Cohen, *The Halutz Resistance in Hungary 1942–1944* (Boulder, CO: Social Science Monographs in association with Columbia University Press, 1986), 132.

27. Veesenmayer to Foreign Office, April 23, 1944, NMT Vol. XIII, NG-2233, 348–9.

28. Kasztner, *Bericht*, 30; cf. his London Affidavit, 6 (mentioning 120 trains) and his Kasztner Trial testimony, February 18, 1954. At the Kasztner Trial, it was wrongly assumed that he was aware of the train *agreement* when he met Krumey on May 2; it is now known that the conference was held on May 4–6. His London Affidavit and trial testimony do mention the agreement, but the *Bericht* refers to *negotiations*—and these were already under way when Veesenmayer cabled Berlin on April 23. Kasztner's diverse claims on this point can be reconciled on the hypothesis that he learned of the negotiations before the conference and received confirmation after the conference (via Freudiger) that an agreement had been reached.

29. Szita, *Trading in Lives*, 66. Kasztner's London Affidavit states that Novak left for Vienna on April 14.

30. On the escapees, their report, its publication and its impact, see Braham, *The Politics of Genocide*, Vol. 2, 824–40; Henryk Świebocki, ed., *London Has Been Informed: Reports by Auschwitz Escapees* (Oświęcim: Auschwitz-Birkenau State Museum, 1997); Rudolf Vrba, *I Escaped From Auschwitz* (London: Robson Books, 2006); and Ruth Linn, *Escaping Auschwitz: A Culture of Forgetting* (Ithaca, NY: Cornell University Press, 2004).

31. Braham, *The Politics of Genocide*, Vol. 2, 826, 835–6.

32. Vrba, *I Escaped From Auschwitz*, 403–4.

33. Kasztner, *Bericht*, 30; see also London Affidavit, 6.

34. Unlike the message from Bratislava to Kasztner, the Vrba-Wetzler report did not mention the planned massacre of Hungarian Jews. This has persuaded some historians that at the time of their escape Vrba and Wetzler were unaware of the impending deportations from Hungary: see Miroslav Karny, "The Vrba and Wetzler Report," in *Anatomy of the Auschwitz Death Camp*, eds. Yisrael Gutman and Michael Berenbaum (Bloomington: Indiana University Press, 1998), 559–60; and Vrba's response in *I Escaped From Auschwitz*, 411–15. In his memoirs (written in 1946 but published a decade later), the Slovak Zionist leader Oscar Neumann acknowledged that the "Hungarian salami" comment had been reported by the two escapees: *Im Schatten des Todes* (Tel Aviv: Olamenu, 1956), 178–81.

35. Kasztner, *Bericht*, 30.

36. Ibid.

37. Kasztner Trial testimony, February 18, 1954.

38. Kasztner, *Bericht*, 35.

39. Kasztner-Becher minutes, July 15, 1944, Dinur Archive.

40. Ganz later explained that she had gone from house to house speaking to people. In her own words, "I said what I had to say; I did not say, '[Going to] Budapest will be better than [going to] Auschwitz.'" See discussion with Hannah Ganz and other members of the Zionist youth movements, Strochlitz Institute For Holocaust Research, Haifa, H3 C5 4/4, 16; cf. 7–8, 13–15.

41. Kasztner Trial testimony, August 19, 1954.

42. More than one researcher has advanced baseless claims about attempts by Kasztner to publicize the Vrba–Wetzler news. For example, Anna Porter writes (without citing a source) that he took the report to the Swiss diplomat-rescuer Carl Lutz: *Kasztner's Train: The True Story of an Unknown Hero of the Holocaust* (New York: Walker Publishing Company, 2007), 136.

43.   Budapest to Istanbul, May 1, 1944, Haganah Archive, 14/798. Just as his April 25 letter to the JDC was also sent in Brand's name, so the May 1 message to the Jewish Agency was also sent in the names of his colleagues Komoly, Brand and Goldfarb.

44.   Springmann-SIME1, para. 67: "Very little news was in fact received from Hungary after the occupation. . . . [Springmann] and Pomerany [sic] both received one from Kastner which did not give cause for alarm."

4

Two Days in May

Having learned the imminent fate of Hungary's Jews, Kasztner had requested a crisis meeting with Eichmann's aide Krumey on April 28, 1944. The fateful meeting took place four days later, on May 2.

Krumey announced with a smile that the emigration of six hundred Jews had been approved in Berlin and could take place in one to two weeks. He accepted Kasztner's request to bring three hundred from the provinces—mostly from Kolozsvár—to the capital. There they would stay under SS guard in a "preferred camp" until the entire group was ready to leave. He even offered to enlarge the quota by one hundred Jews in return for a large ransom.[1]

When Kasztner asked about the deportees from the Kistarcsa camp, who had been gassed in Auschwitz only a few hours earlier, Krumey feigned innocence: "Haven't these people written yet?" he asked. Kasztner wondered where such letters could have been written. "From Waldsee," said Krumey. Unimpressed by the Nazi's subterfuge, Kasztner answered, "there's no point in playing hide-and-seek."

Forcing new arrivals in Auschwitz to write postcards reassuring their relatives at home that they were alive and well in Waldsee (in Germany) was one of the many deception tactics of the SS. Kasztner, by his own account, was not fooled. He demanded to meet both Krumey and Wisliceny within twenty-four hours to clarify the plans of the *Eichmann-Kommando*.[2]

What did Kasztner tell his Zionist colleagues about this meeting? His defenders insist that he regarded the transport of six hundred emigrants as the first of many: it was a test of German willingness to barter the lives of all Hungarian Jews. His accusers allege that he accepted the promise to release the six hundred in the knowledge that it was a decoy from the impending slaughter of everyone else. Each theory yields a testable prediction. On the pro-Kasztner hypothesis, the news of the emigration transport and the likely salvation of the wider public should have been greeted with relief by his colleagues. On the anti-Kasztner hypothesis, news of the imminent fate of the masses and the promised survival of a select few would have provoked a frenzied contest to join the emigration transport—a contest among the leaders alone, who would have kept their knowledge to themselves lest the Nazis revoke even this minor concession.

On this point we have the evidence of Ottó Komoly, the chairman of Kasztner's committee, who wrote in his diary immediately after the news of the deal with Krumey:

> Dr. Kasztner tells me that the Germans have given permission for a transport of 600, they are demanding a list [of names], etc. Maybe it can leave at the end of next week. . . . The job of drawing up the list goes to myself and Szilágyi (an appalling siege). . . . The endless exhaustion and agitation are draining me badly. I can't take people's constant pressures and the inevitable injustice that accompanies the selection.[3]

Kasztner himself purports to quote a still more dramatic statement allegedly made by Komoly: "A list of 600 is impossible to draw up. 600 names—out of 800,000."[4] This remark—which is not in Komoly's diary—suggests that choosing six hundred names was not a means to negotiating the rescue of the remainder. It implies that the promise to free several hundred Jews was not part of a plan for general rescue but the "compensation" offered by the Nazis for the general *non*-rescue of the Jewish population of Hungary.

Kasztner's Final Visit to Kolozsvár

In spite of Kasztner's demand to see Wisliceny within twenty-four hours, Krumey arrived at the May 3 meeting alone. He explained that Wisliceny was in Kolozsvár and gave Kasztner permission to travel there—after paying the rest of the $200,000 negotiating fee. Kasztner handed over the money and promptly set out for Kolozsvár.[5]

This, at least, is Kasztner's explanation for his journey to Kolozsvár. It was accepted at face value by all the judges involved in the Kasztner Trial and has been given credence by historians and commentators interested in the subject ever since. It is, nevertheless, a transparent falsehood.

According to Kasztner's version, Krumey refused to provide a straight answer about the intentions of the Germans or the status of Wisliceny's "promises" to the Jewish rescue committee; Kasztner therefore requested and received Krumey's permission to ask Wisliceny in person—and Wisliceny just happened to be in Kolozsvár.

This would mean that on May 2 Kasztner more or less openly accused Krumey of lying to him about the fate of the deportees in "Waldsee"; that Krumey did not deny the accusation; that Kasztner decided to circumvent Krumey by approaching his *subordinate* Wisliceny; that on May 3 Krumey gave permission to make this "appeal" to Wisliceny; and that at this very moment, the latter just happened to be in Kolozsvár, Kasztner's home city, which Kasztner already planned to visit. Here is a chain of absurdities that defies belief. Kasztner's version—taken at face value by almost everyone—is an invention. His real reason for traveling to meet Wisliceny in Kolozsvár on May 3 was quite different.

The true explanation is not hard to find. On the evening of May 2, the Jews of Kolozsvár had been placed under house arrest, and in the morning of May 3 the local newspaper announced the formation of a ghetto.[6] Wisliceny was in the city for the purpose of directing the transfer of the Jews into that ghetto. Kolozsvár was the provincial capital of North Transylvania, and May 3 was the launch date for the ghetto drive throughout the region. Kasztner's cover story in his postwar account ("the *Bericht*") was designed to forestall the natural questions: Why did the Nazis send the head of the Jewish rescue committee to meet the officer directing the ghetto drive in Kolozsvár within hours of the ghetto's creation? And why was Kasztner the only Jewish leader in Budapest to receive Nazi permission to travel to a provincial ghetto— and on that specific day?

Arriving on the afternoon of May 3, Kasztner found Wisliceny in the Kolozsvár police station. There the SS officer told him that Eichmann had pulled him out of the talks with the rescue committee and sent him to oversee the ghetto concentration of the Jews. "I eased up wherever I could," protested Wisliceny, "but Endre wants to eat all Hungarian Jews alive, and Eichmann definitely isn't the one to tame him."[7] In Kasztner's eyes, this meant that Wisliceny's mission was "not saving Jews but exterminating them, as one of the top murderers."[8] Kasztner nonetheless demanded explicit confirmation that full-scale deportation was imminent. Feigning ignorance, Wisliceny promised to ask Eichmann and enlighten Kasztner back in Budapest.

But the conversation did not end there. This point was clarified during Kasztner's testimony in Israel:

> [Wisliceny] asked me to tell my friends in Kolozsvár that they had increased the guard at the Romanian border just 4 km away (a place of escape we used constantly): I had to tell those who wanted to escape to Romania to be more careful and to use other ways.[9]

The significance of these Nazi instructions becomes clearer if we consider the apologetic remarks of Holocaust historian Yehuda Bauer:

> In May 1944 what could a person like Kastner, the most active of the group around Komoly, do? He was a "foreigner," a Transylvanian journalist, unknown outside his own town, [Kolozsvár], and a fairly small circle in Budapest. Jews were forbidden to go by railway, and Kastner could not have traveled to dozens of ghettos. . . . How else could he have warned the Jews of Hungary? By radio? Through the press? By giving lectures? These questions are so ridiculous that they do not deserve an answer.[10]

Contrary to Bauer's argument, Kasztner did have the opportunity to contact the Jews in his home city—the regional capital—on the day when the ghetto drive began in North Transylvania. *He was in fact sent to do so by the Nazis.*

In assessing Kasztner's visit to Kolozsvár on May 3, 1944, the key question is not why the head of the Jewish rescue committee wanted to visit a Jewish ghetto. The single most important question is why *the Nazis* wanted the head of the Jewish rescue committee to visit a major Jewish ghetto.

The head of the Jewish rescue committee had received evidence that the Jews in the provincial ghettos were about to be deported to their deaths in Auschwitz. The victims had been systematically isolated from the general population, from each other, and from all sources of information. The victims in North Transylvania were also next to the Romanian border and had the best opportunity to flee. On the first day of the ghetto drive, all but a fraction of them were still at home awaiting transfer to the local brickyard. By placing the head of the Jewish rescue committee in contact with a major Jewish community within hours of the ghetto announcement, the Nazis took the risk that he would spread panic among those doomed to die and incite mass flight to the Romanian border, just 4 km away. It is as certain as anything can be that Krumey would not have sent Kasztner to see Wisliceny, and Wisliceny would not have sent him to see the city's Jewish community, unless they were sure that Kasztner would do the opposite. The head of the Jewish rescue committee was sent to contact this community on the eve of its destruction because the Nazis knew that he would help them to sabotage the rescue of the victims.[11]

What did Kasztner make of Wisliceny's instructions to discourage the exodus to Romania? There were just two possibilities: either

Eichmann's henchman wanted Kasztner's help in saving Jews; or he wanted Kasztner's help in preventing the escape of Jews. During the Israeli libel trial, Kasztner was asked which of these interpretations was correct:

> Q: Was Wisliceny doing the Jews a favor, otherwise how do you explain this?
>
> A: For this one has to explain Wisliceny's personality. On one hand, he was careful to appear loyal to Eichmann; on another, he made gestures to us when he could. It was a gesture: if he couldn't keep his promises to us, then at least make gestures. He said that he knew about the flight, that orders had been given to increase the number of guards and that I must warn my friends to look for safer ways. He also told me that not a few had been caught and sent back [to Kolozsvár].[12]

According to Kasztner's testimony, Eichmann's assistant Wisliceny, who had broken all of his "promises" to the Jews of Hungary, was determined to help the victims. He did so by offering Kasztner a friendly warning that cross-border escape was no longer a viable rescue option. It is not easy to believe Kasztner's psychological profile of Wisliceny, murderer of the Jews of Slovakia and Greece, who was now preparing the Final Solution in Hungary. Kasztner certainly did not believe it at the time. He realized that Wisliceny's mission was "not saving Jews but exterminating them, as one of the top murderers."

Kasztner understood very well on May 3, 1944, that Eichmann's henchman wanted him to prevent the escape of the city's Jews before their deportation to Auschwitz. And that is exactly what he did. This is clear from the evidence about his statements to the Jewish leaders and to the Jewish public in Kolozsvár.

What Did Kasztner Tell the Jewish Leaders in Kolozsvár?

The Jewish leaders in Kolozsvár during the Nazi occupation were Kasztner's relatives and friends. The Nazi-appointed leader of the Kolozsvár *Judenrat* was Kasztner's father-in-law, József Fischer. Other members of the local *Judenrat* included his brother, Ernő Kasztner, and his close friends Zsigmond Léb, József Gottlieb, and Dezső Hermann. The Jewish administration of the Kolozsvár Ghetto was in the hands of Fischer's cousin, Endre Balázs. The local Jewish rescue committee was the responsibility of Kasztner's friends Ernő Marton and Hillel Danzig.[13]

Kasztner met several of these Jewish leaders during his final visit to Kolozsvár on May 3, 1944. According to his testimony:

> I spoke to my father-in-law [Fischer], my brother, Dr. Marton, Zsig-mond Léb . . . [and] József Gottlieb. I don't remember if I spoke to Danzig on the first or the second occasion [i.e., during Kasztner's first visit on April 16 or his second visit on May 3] . . . . I remember that the meeting with him wasn't so important because he was ill then. I don't remember if I saw Hermann but I may have met a few people. I was in the community and met several Jews. I remember speaking to them.

Kasztner was asked:

> Q: In Kolozsvár, whom did you tell about the outcome of your meeting with Wisliceny?
> A: Marton and my late father-in-law.
> Q: Who else?
> A: I'm sure about those two.
> Q: What did you tell them about the situation?
> A: I told them that the situation was severe, there was a danger of deportation and they had to use all means to save as many as possible. I recommended escalating the escape and hiding people.[14]

This is not, of course, what Wisliceny had told Kasztner to say. Is it possible that Kasztner played a trick on the Nazis—that he won their trust, convinced them that he would betray his fellow Jews, persuaded them to send him into Kolozsvár, and then took the opportunity to deliver an accurate warning? But in that case, why did the escape effort come to a standstill in the aftermath of his visit? After lengthy questioning, Kasztner finally gave an explanation:

> I think my friends in Kolozsvár, including my father-in-law, didn't do everything they could and should have done. Perhaps they should have escalated not just the escape activities but also the warning activities. I don't say that they didn't do so; but apparently they did less than they could have done.[15]

Kasztner implied that he double-crossed the SS; that he urged local Jewish leaders to *increase* Jewish flight to Romania—and that the leaders ignored his advice and spontaneously decided to *stop* Jewish flight to Romania, thus inadvertently complying with the wishes of the SS. This version is incredible. And it is refuted by the evidence.

The first discussion mentioned by Kasztner was held with Fischer, his father-in-law. There were no eavesdroppers during this conversation (so far as is known) but its contents can be inferred from the reported account of a Jewish resident of Kolozsvár, Avram Feuerman. After the founding of the ghetto, Feuerman's father consulted Fischer—the chairman of the local *Judenrat*—about his plan to escape to Romania. Fischer allegedly advised him to abandon the idea and enter the ghetto, as the inmates would be resettled in "Kenyérmező" in Hungary. Fischer warned that Jews attempting to cross the border were shot by guards.[16] This "information" about border guards resembles what Kasztner was instructed to say by Wisliceny. Judging from this account, Kasztner was also told to spread the hoax that the ghetto inmates would be taken to the nonexistent site of "Kenyérmező" rather than deported to Auschwitz.

Another of Kasztner's discussions was held with Zsigmond Léb, the former head of the Orthodox community in Kolozsvár. Again, there were no eavesdroppers, but the contents of the conversation can be inferred from Léb's subsequent conduct. According to an inmate of the Kolozsvár Ghetto, Anna Nussbächer, he stood on a tree-stump and "reassured the crowd that we would be taken to work to Kenyérmező, where the families will stay together." His speech was authorized by the guards of the ghetto.[17] Léb was then allowed to leave the ghetto before the beginning of the deportations and travel to Budapest, where he helped to draw up the list of Kasztner Train candidates from Kolozsvár.[18] This is a further hint that Wisliceny had told Kasztner to have the Kenyérmező hoax disseminated in the ghetto.

Kasztner also mentioned that he spoke to Ernő Marton, the head of the city's Jewish rescue committee. Marton was in charge of organized escape from Kolozsvár. But after meeting Kasztner, he promptly fled across the border in the Romanian consul's car. He resumed the struggle to save North Transylvania's Jews from Bucharest, where he started a new rescue organization.[19] Marton's reported assessment of the events in Kolozsvár is intriguing. As Fischer wrote to Kasztner immediately after the war, Marton had acknowledged "an element of truth" in charges that individuals meant to join the Kasztner Train had worked to expedite the deportation of their community members.[20] Kasztner wrote to his father-in-law that he did not know if the reports of Marton's views were true: all he knew was that Marton was trying to defame him.[21]

If Marton did make the statements reported in this correspondence, his only factual basis for them was his encounter with Kasztner on May 3; he left the country the next day and could not have witnessed any subsequent developments in Kolozsvár. From Marton's alleged criticisms we can draw a plausible inference about what Kasztner told him on May 3: the escape route had been blocked; the SS-sponsored Kasztner Train was the only rescue option; and this option required an orderly ghettoization in Kolozsvár. Marton reacted by finding another means of escape and setting up a new base of operations in Romania.

Marton's replacement on Kolozsvár's Jewish rescue committee was Kasztner's friend Hillel Danzig. There is no doubt that they also spoke on May 3. Kasztner "didn't know then what was expected," testified Danzig. "It was a crisis point in the negotiations and Kasztner could not say anything concrete about German intentions."[22] If this testimony is to be believed, then Kasztner—who had just received first-hand confirmation that the Nazi objective was "not saving the Jews but exterminating them"—feigned ignorance of the imminent fate of the Jews who were being moved into the ghetto. Worse still, he passed on the disinformation from Wisliceny about the impossibility of fleeing across the border. Danzig also testified about the impact of this disinformation:

Q: Did you organize other people's escape by smuggling?
A: Until the ghetto, meaning until the route we were using was blocked.
   . . .
Q: In what sense?
A: The authorities reinforced the guard.[23]

This was the very "information" that Wisliceny had ordered Kasztner to pass on to the Jewish leaders. Danzig—who was testifying on Kasztner's side and trying to help him on the witness stand—inadvertently revealed Kasztner's decisive role in ruining the Jewish escape effort in Kolozsvár.

What Did Kasztner Tell the Jewish Public in Kolozsvár?

Concerning his contact with the ordinary Jews who were scheduled to be murdered, Kasztner testified: "In Kolozsvár I didn't address the Jewish masses. Not even in a small party of 30 people. I didn't advise Jews in Kolozsvár not to panic."[24] Thus he admitted his failure to warn the Jews (an omission) but not his role in deceiving them (an action). But there is eye-witness evidence that he did deceive them.

Yosef Reiss, a Holocaust survivor from a nearby town, remembered the impact of Kasztner's visit to Kolozsvár:

> I lived in Huedin (Bánffyhunyad) in Transylvania, which was under Hungarian sovereignty between the years 1940–45 . . .
>
> I had a large family and unfortunately none of them returned. I was in contact with them by letters until they were sent to Auschwitz. Every day my brother and sister went to various work in the city with other young people. From the letters I learned that they wanted to go to Romania and that it could be done easily.
>
> Kasztner was well aware that the young people wanted to escape and he spread it among the people that they should not escape and cause trouble for their families, that they would all be sent to southern Hungary (Kenyérmező) and families would remain together and work in agriculture.[25]

In some cases, Kasztner may have lied to the victims directly. Ruth Landau, the daughter of a Holocaust survivor from Kolozsvár, described the fate of her family:

> I am writing on behalf of over 50 of my relatives I was never able to meet . . . who paid the price for Kasztner's silence as to what awaited them in the final destination where the trains were taking them in May 1944.
>
> Like many others, my mother personally heard Kasztner in his home town, in the Kolozsvár Ghetto, assuring the town's Jews who were collected there before being sent to Auschwitz that they were going "to work in the bread fields."[26]

Kenyérmező—the "work" site invented by the Nazis as a camouflage for deportation to Auschwitz—is a Hungarian name meaning "bread fields."

So Kasztner not only failed to warn the victims, but also actively misled them about their imminent fate in the gas chambers. Here is the real reason why Eichmann's right-hand man in Budapest sent him to the capital of North Transylvania on the first day of the ghetto drive in that province and why Eichmann's officer in Kolozsvár sent him to contact the Jewish leaders and the Jewish public in the city.

Results of Kasztner's Visit

Yehuda Bauer has defended Kasztner against the charge of sabotaging rescue attempts in Kolozsvár. Commenting on the escape effort, he alleges that the local rescue committee in Kolozsvár did indeed try to persuade Jews to flee to Romania in order to save their lives, but "only a very few were to be found who were willing to cross the border." He also cites the existence of a cross-border smuggling network, run by the Orthodox and the Zionists, in the Romanian town of Turda.[27]

With regard to the rescue committee in Kolozsvár, not only did this organization fail to warn Jews that escape was a question of life and death, as Bauer claims, but under Kasztner's influence it also halted the escape effort entirely. As for the smuggling network in Turda, this was examined at the Kasztner Trial. Its coordinator, Arnold Dávid Finkelstein, was community secretary in Turda. In partnership with a Zionist activist, Arie Hirsch, he managed to smuggle up to one thousand two hundred Jews via North Transylvania to Romania. In spite of the close proximity of Kolozsvár, only two hundred Jews fled from that city, almost all of them before the ghetto's establishment on May 3.

At the Kasztner Trial, Finkelstein testified not *for* Kasztner but against him. Finkelstein had been appalled when the Kolozsvár *Judenrat* stopped the escapes to Romania. He suspected the worst:

> I checked my records and, unfortunately, I found that the accusation was not weakened but reinforced. The proof is that they had a beaten path, as I explained, and they knew that across the border was a group managing their absorption and welfare, but they sent only a limited number of people.... Now I did a mental exercise. I thought to myself that private individuals, who had no connections across the border, who were not public figures and who had no public funds, were still able to save themselves and other people. Unlike those who called themselves leaders and are still doing so today, who had public funds and a beaten path and made sure to save themselves and their property. As for the rest: farewell, friend! I'm reluctant to think so, but there's the impression of an irresponsible business, I would say a criminal business.

Finkelstein was asked about the border policing, which had been Kasztner's argument on May 3 for halting the escape operation. If more Jews had tried to escape from Kolozsvár, would the Hungarian and Romanian authorities have reinforced the guard and closed the exit routes? Finkelstein replied: "The question is quite logical, but reality disproved this objection as they weren't caught.... Just as 1,200 crossed the border, I assume that another 2,000 could have followed. Our system wasn't just viable for 2,000 but for 4,000 as well."[28]

Kasztner knew that the escape route to Romania was viable. Among his contacts was Zvi Zimmerman, a Polish refugee who had approached him with a plan to smuggle Jews across the border to Romania. Zimmerman had promised that any Jewish escapees to Romania would receive false identity papers and other assistance from the Polish consulate in Bucharest.[29] So Kasztner knew that Jews who crossed the border would find refuge. When Zimmerman himself decided to flee Hungary, he went by way of Kolozsvár and through Turda, using the very route that Kasztner had told the Kolozsvár *Judenrat* to abandon.

From mid-April, the Zionist youth activist Hannah Ganz had traveled back and forth from Budapest to smuggle Jews via Kolozsvár to Romania. On May 2, she transferred a local group that included the town's Neolog Chief Rabbi, Moshe Carmilly-Weinberger. How then could Kasztner have believed Wisliceny's claim the very next day that this escape route was now closed? Indeed, Hannah Ganz continued to smuggle Jews over the border—without assistance from the Kolozsvár *Judenrat*—until the end of the month, when she was arrested.[30]

On June 11, Joel Brand met Jewish Agency officials in Aleppo, Syria. Asked what could be done to save Jews in Hungary, he suggested bribing local police to allow cross-border flight. In particular, "One of the centres through which large numbers of escapees pass is Turda in Rumania. It would be useful to arrange the buying up of the police there."[31] This was, of course, the latest news available to Brand before he left Hungary in mid-May 1944, well after Kasztner's encounter with Wisliceny.

So the escape route to Romania was open as the Jews of North Transylvania were being driven into ghettos. And it remained open during and after the deportations from these ghettos to Auschwitz. On June 17, Hitler's representative in Hungary, Edmund Veesenmayer, cabled the Nazi Foreign Office with a serious complaint: "Hungarian Jews who have fled to Rumania are treated there like political refugees . . . the Rumanian Government intends to make it possible for them to emigrate to Palestine."[32] On July 11, with the deportations from Hungary's provinces complete, Veesenmayer reported that "numerous Hungarian Jews" had illegally crossed the Romanian border in the preceding weeks and that in Romania these Jews were "tolerated by the national authorities more or less openly."[33]

The evidence shows that fleeing across the Romanian border was a viable escape option for Jews in North Transylvania. Wisliceny's assertion to the contrary was designed to sever this lifeline. By repeating Wisliceny's false message in Kolozsvár, Kasztner prevented the escape of a substantial number of Holocaust victims. He must have known what he was doing when he agreed to spread this Nazi disinformation on Nazi instructions.

Kasztner returned to Budapest in a day or two.[34] The concentration of Jews in the Kolozsvár Ghetto proceeded until May 10. The Zionist escape effort collapsed as eighteen thousand victims were moved to the city's brick factory, which was surrounded by just twenty guards. And the head of the Jewish rescue committee drew ever closer to the most bloodstained officers of the SS.

Notes

1. According to Kasztner, Krumey's price for the extra one hundred emigrants was 10 million *pengős* (c\$300,000), that is, 50 percent more than the 6.5 million *pengős* (\$200,000) advance payment for the lives of many hundreds of thousands of Jews! If Krumey requested no payment for the original six hundred emigrants, Kasztner could not have believed at the time that exit permission had been given in return for money (Kasztner Trial verdict, s. 29). However, according to Brand, 10 million *pengős* was the price for the whole transport (Brand-JAE1, 4; Brand-JAE2, para. 16; Brand-SIME1, para. 89; Brand-SIME4, para. 26).

2. Kasztner, *Bericht*, 30–31. See also his London Affidavit, 6: the Kistarcsa Jews arriving in Auschwitz "were compelled to write encouraging notes to their relatives with datelines from 'Waldsee'. The notes were brought by an SS Courier to Budapest and were distributed by the Jewish Council." Also *Freudiger Report*, 27: "Later on signs of life were received from some of the deported persons from Waldsee, so that it may be assumed that the transport did after all go to Ausschwitz [sic]. The locality 'Waldsee' does not exist in reality: it is a postal pseudonym used for designating Ausschwitz-Birkenau [sic]."

3. *Komoly Diary*, May 2, 1944. The rescue committee cabled the Jewish Agency requesting a ship for 750 people: Budapest to Istanbul, May 2, 1944, Haganah Archive, 14/798.

4. Kasztner, *Bericht*, 32. Kasztner attributes this statement to Komoly's May 3, 1944 diary entry, which contains no such remark. The statement may reflect something that Kasztner heard from Komoly in person. Of course, if Kasztner actually invented the statement, it is even more revealing, for in that case it betrays his *own* understanding of the deal with Krumey.

5. Ibid., 31.

6. *Ellenzék* (Kolozsvár), May 3, 1944.

7. Kasztner, *Bericht*, 32.

8. Kasztner Trial testimony, February 18, 1954.

9. Ibid.

10. Yehuda Bauer, *Rethinking the Holocaust* (New Haven, CT: Yale University Press, 2001), 237–8. Bauer does not disclose to his readers that Kasztner's visit to Kolozsvár on the day of the ghetto's formation was one of the central issues in the Kasztner Trial. Otherwise, how could he maintain that Kasztner had no opportunity to warn Jews?

11. For recognition of this point, see Ben Hecht, *Perfidy* (Jerusalem: Gefen, 1999), 102.
12. Kasztner Trial testimony, September 16, 1954.
13. Kasztner Trial verdict, s. 50.
14. Kasztner Trial testimony, September 16, 1954.
15. Ibid.
16. Personal letter from George (György) Breiner to Zoltán Tibori Szabó, May 25, 2001, cited in Tibori Szabó, *Frontiera dintre viață și moarte: refugiul și salvarea evreilor la granița româno-maghiară (1940–1944) [Frontier Between Life and Death: Shelter and Rescue of Jews At the Romanian-Hungarian Border (1940–1944)]* (Bucharest: Compania, 2005), 134–5.
17. Anna Nussbächer, *Sentenced to Live: Memoir* (Köln-Kolozsvár: privately printed, 2010), 27. I am grateful to Michael N. Ezra for this source.
18. Kasztner Trial verdict, s. 50.
19. Ibid., s. 53; Randolph L. Braham, "What Did They Know and When?," in *Studies on the Holocaust: Selected Writings, Vol. 1*, ed. Randolph L. Braham (Boulder, CO: Social Science Monographs in association with Columbia University Press, 2000), 32. On Marton's rescue efforts in Romania, see Béla Vágó, "Political and Diplomatic Activities for the Rescue of the Jews of Northern Transylvania (June 1944–February 1945)," *Yad Vashem Studies* 6 (1967): 155–73.
20. Fischer to Kasztner, November 9, 1945, Kasztner Archive. The context of this passage is a discussion of allegations made by the Holocaust survivors from Kolozsvár.
21. Kasztner to Fischer, November 9, 1945, Kasztner Archive (this was not a reply to the letter above; the letters crossed).
22. Kasztner Trial testimony, August 19, 1954.
23. Kasztner Trial testimony, August 15, 1954. Danzig (who tended to confuse dates) initially testified that the "blocking" of the escape route occurred in late May but he subsequently corrected himself, confirming that it coincided with the ghetto's formation at "the end of April and the beginning of May."
24. Kasztner Trial testimony, March 3, 1954.
25. Letters, *Makor Rishon*, August 9, 2002.
26. Letters, *Ha'aretz*, May 13, 2008: http://www.haaretz.co.il/opinions/letters/1.1323933 (last accessed May 15, 2015). Ruth Landau is Associate Professor of Social Work at the Paul Baerwald School of Social Work and Social Welfare, Hebrew University of Jerusalem.
27. Yehuda Bauer, *Jewish Reactions to the Holocaust* (Tel Aviv: MOD Books, 1989), 185.
28. Kasztner Trial testimony, June 25, 1954.
29. Zvi Zimmerman's Eichmann Trial testimony, June 1, 1961.
30. Cohen, *The Halutz Resistance in Hungary*, 91–92.
31. Brand-JAE2, para. 64.
32. Veesenmayer to Foreign Office, June 17, 1944, NMT Vol. XIII, NG-5567, 358.
33. Veesenmayer to Foreign Office, July 11, 1944, NMT Vol. XIII, NG-5586, 361.
34. *Komoly Diary*, May 5, 1944, noting Kasztner's return from Kolozsvár by late afternoon.

5

Co-opting the Rescuers

As Kasztner was returning from Kolozsvár, Himmler was addressing the commanders of the Wehrmacht. In a speech delivered in Sonthofen in Germany on May 5, 1944, the *Reichsführer-SS* boasted that the "Jewish question" had been resolved in "an uncompromising fashion" throughout Germany and Nazi-occupied Europe. He stated his determination to murder all the Jews in his grasp, irrespective of the laws of war. Even Jewish infants had to die.[1]

The rescue committee's foreign communications told a very different story about Nazi policies. With Kasztner back in Budapest, more misleading messages were sent to the Zionists abroad. An unsigned cable to the Jewish Agency in Geneva mentioned the $2 million ransom plan and the $200,000 advance payment to Wisliceny; Brand's request for additional funds from Saly Mayer; the possibility of saving Polish and Slovak Jews; exit permission granted "in principle" for six hundred Hungarian Jews; and Wisliceny's preference for immigration to America.[2]

But by now the ransom plan was obsolete; the $2 million fee was irrelevant; the $200,000 had achieved nothing; and Wisliceny, having been removed from the talks, was busy driving hundreds of thousands of Jews into ghettos. The message to Geneva implied that six hundred emigrants were about to leave Hungary, but it gave no hint of Kasztner's intention to hand over a list of names so that these Jews could be deported by the SS.

If the Jewish Agency was being deceived by Kasztner, Brand was deceiving himself. He thought that the Nazis "must have been serious about the negotiations, because for weeks they spent hours daily listening to his complaints and propositions." Their behavior toward him betrays their opinion of his mental acumen. As he would later explain to the British, the Nazis were "continually complimenting him, saying he was a decent fellow and honest. . . . Brand felt that such people had respect for a man who was fighting for his ideals, and who had the courage to stand up for them." At one point Eichmann even told him: "You are a Jewish idealist. You fight for your Jews and I fight for my Germans." Krumey, who was now meeting Brand almost every day, constantly sought to ingratiate himself, "pretending to do his best for the Jews and trying to show what a good fellow he really was."[3]

Brand was also introduced to the Gestapo/SD agent Fritz Laufer, who was seen by Western intelligence services as a dangerous enemy spy—and who (unknown to Brand) had previously worked as one of the Jewish rescue committee's couriers.[4] Brand's summary of the encounter speaks for itself:

> I was treated to a lengthy lecture, during which I got coffee and cake. I was told that only through Eichmann's offer could the Jews be rescued, that Himmler wanted this to happen, that Himmler was really a decent human being; Himmler no longer wants the Jews to be executed, and it was our chance now to rescue the residue of Jewry that still remained.[5]

Both Jewish rescue activists enjoyed ever more cordial relations with the Nazis. Brand was driven home by Laufer's boss Klausnitzer; they proceeded to get drunk together.[6] Grosz saw Kasztner playing cards with Gestapo agents and losing large amounts of money.[7] Meanwhile Freudiger heard Kasztner's new excuse for unpunctuality: late-night gambling with German officers.[8]

From Rescue Committee to Puppet Committee

At this stage—the first week of May 1944—the Nazis took control of the Jewish rescue committee's foreign funds and communications. The occasion for this development was the second Brand–Eichmann meeting on May 5.[9] Present was the commander of the Laufer/Klausnitzer unit, Gerhard Clages. Allegedly, Clages had been assigned to monitor Eichmann in order to ensure the secrecy of the Final Solution in Hungary—and for this purpose he reported directly to Himmler.[10]

"I have sent for you because I want to give you something," began Eichmann, throwing down some packages of mail from Switzerland.[11] Inside were large amounts of cash, as well as letters to the Zionists and to various Hungarian Jews. The delivery, which had been destined for the rescue committee, had been intercepted by Grosz on orders from Clages and handed over to the Nazis.[12]

"This is for your children's relief work," Eichmann continued. "I have nothing against your children's relief activities. Here you have the money, and there you have the letters. . . . I have no time now to censor them. If they contain anything besides children's relief, report to me about it."[13] Henceforth, all deliveries of foreign mail would have to be handled via Clages, and Brand would be expected to report "anything political" in the rescue committee's letters. Furthermore, if he was found to be "mixing in politics," the Nazis "would take the ground away from all his work."[14]

Brand's perception of the incident emerges from a warning he sent at the end of the month to rescue activist Nathan Schwalb in Switzerland:

> Be careful! Do not write any letters containing political matter. . . . Do not trust anybody. Do not believe that you can find a messenger able to bring over the mail safely without its being opened. The last two despatches—the first containing $32,750 and the other one SF250,000 and $50,000—were handed to me by—no less a person than—Mr. Eichmann himself. I received the second despatch unopened, but had to give my word that in case it contained political matter I would communicate it. Thank God it did not . . .[15]

So for Brand the main issue was the security of the Zionist communications: it was no longer safe to write to the rescue committee in Budapest about political issues. The more basic point that the committee was now expected to account to the Nazis for all its actions—and that its very existence depended on avoiding "politics," meaning activities displeasing to the Nazis—had escaped his attention.[16]

Brand's third meeting with Eichmann probably took place on May 8.[17] Both Becher and Clages were present at the session.[18] By now Brand was becoming ever more confused about the proposition he was supposed to convey to the West. Indeed, after his departure from Hungary he was to give contradictory accounts of Eichmann's demands. To the Jewish Agency he explained that the Nazis needed ten thousand *railway wagons* in order to "ship the Jews across Europe."[19] To the British he announced that the Nazis wanted *trucks* for the benefit of the Waffen-SS.[20] On various occasions, according to Brand, the Nazis also requested consumer goods, money, and the repatriation of German civilians interned in the West. Throughout the discussions, Brand "had a feeling that the Germans would not say exactly what they wanted." One Nazi officer told him that "of course they needed many things, but [he] did not explain what."[21] As Brand would later admit, "I did not have a clear offer—[Eichmann] only told me some kinds of goods and money which I should bring. . . . He said I would find out for myself—he did not want to commit himself."[22] But how could Brand "find out" what the Germans wanted if the Germans themselves refused to tell him?

This vagueness about the terms of the Goods for Blood offer was, of course, another sign that the Nazis were not serious about their proposal.[23] They were, on the other hand, all too serious about the objectives they had accomplished while pretending to negotiate: efficiently concentrating hundreds of thousands of Jews in ghettos as a prelude to their deportation to Auschwitz; distracting the Jewish rescue committee from any thought of spreading the alarm, organizing mass flight, or causing disruption; co-opting the rescue committee by taking control of its communications and funds, and by making its operations conditional on Nazi permission. So dependent was the committee on the Nazis that by the time of Brand's departure from Budapest, he was receiving the committee's mail as a matter of routine from Clages—the Gestapo/SD officer.[24]

On May 8—the same day as Brand's third meeting with Eichmann—Kasztner was invited to Wisliceny's home. After confirming the Nazi decision to deport the whole of Hungarian Jewry, Wisliceny described the coming Brand Mission as the last hope; satisfying the German demands was the only way to "gain time."[25] Kasztner, who had established in their previous encounter that Wisliceny's task was not to help Jews but to kill them, was now being ordered by the same Nazi to "gain time" by promoting a Nazi "rescue plan" while the Jews were killed.

It is in this context that we should interpret the next day's coded message from the Jewish rescue committee in Budapest to Nathan Schwalb in Geneva:

> According to [the Slovak Zionist leader] Oskar Neumann's message to us on April 4, [Jewish] emigration from Poland is fine. They asked Wisliceny to help the Hungarian family [i.e., Jewish community] and received the intermediary's special promise regarding deportation and mass murder [i.e., that deportation and mass murder would not take place].[26]

Kasztner, of course, knew that Neumann's information was wrong and that Wisliceny's promise had been a lie. Kasztner had just received Wisliceny's confirmation of the imminent deportation of Hungarian Jewry. The message to Schwalb was disinformation.

Countdown to the Brand Mission

Before the Nazi occupation, Kasztner's rescue committee had been dependent on the support of the Abwehr. Its international couriers had been agents of the Abwehr. But during the occupation, Kasztner and Brand traded their relationship with the Abwehr for the protection of the SS and the Gestapo. By soliciting immunity passes from Krumey and by receiving their money and mail via Clages, they transformed their rescue committee from an underground operation into a client body of the most dangerous Nazis. Accordingly, Kasztner and Brand had no further use for their old Abwehr associates, whose financial demands were as irksome as their personal conduct was repulsive.

The SS and the Gestapo were also determined to remove the Abwehr agents in Budapest from the negotiations with the Jews. These agents were bleeding the Zionists of funds that the SS demanded for itself, and they were interfering with the plans for Brand's departure on his mission.[27] For these reasons, the SS and the Gestapo prepared for the elimination of the Schmidt group—with the aid of Kasztner and Brand.

The Gestapo/SD agent Laufer had repeatedly spoken of the imminent arrest of Schmidt's people and the need to "collect evidence" against them from the Jewish rescue committee.[28] Meanwhile, relations between the committee and the Schmidt group had become increasingly tense. Finally, Winninger threatened to have Kasztner and Brand arrested unless the committee's remaining payments were made.[29]

At this point, Laufer sprang to Kasztner's defense; on May 10, Kasztner was taken into protective custody at the SS headquarters at Schwabenberg, where he typed out a list of allegations against the Schmidt group.[30] Subsequently the entire Abwehr group—Schmidt, Winninger, Scholz, and Sedlacek—was rounded up; only Sedlacek was released.[31] Both Kasztner and Brand were called as witnesses to incriminate Schmidt and Winninger.[32] The two rescue activists were so embroiled in the internecine rivalries of the German intelligence outfits that the SS and the Gestapo could now use them against the Abwehr.[33]

While Kasztner and Brand assisted in the persecution of their own couriers, the campaign against Hungary's Jews proceeded apace. To well-connected figures who wanted to know, the impending slaughter was no secret. The Red Cross delegate, Jean de Bavier, quickly learned the truth from Jewish representatives:

> On 13 May . . . I was informed by the Jewish community that a rail-way meeting was due to take place on 15 and 16 May concerning the conveyance of 300,000 Jews to Kassa and possibly to Poland . . .
>
> It has been stated to me, not only by the Jewish community but also by a highly placed Hungarian official, that the destination of these trains is in Poland, the up-to-date installations for putting people to death by gas.[34]

Unfortunately, nothing was done by the Red Cross to publicize these facts abroad. This failure considerably simplified the next stage of the Nazi effort to deceive world opinion.

The day after the Red Cross received this horrible news from key Jewish and Hungarian sources, the Jewish rescue committee sent its longest communication yet to the JDC in Switzerland. The letter was sent in the names of Kasztner and Brand, but its style and content leave no doubt that its author was Kasztner. It provided a comprehensive review of the tragedy of Hungarian Jewry and a warning that deporta-tions were imminent. But in the middle of this factual account, Kasztner inserted some important "information":

> Two weeks ago some of the internees, aged 15–50 and several as old as 60, were taken away [from Kistarcsa and Topolya] to an unknown destination outside the country's borders. According to uncontrolla-ble rumors, the destination should be the Birkenau industrial center [*das Industriezentrum Birkenau*].

This statement amounted to a single sentence in a detailed letter of several pages, all of it phrased in a solemn and matter-of-fact tone that disguised the Nazi propaganda. Kasztner was, of course, already aware that these Jews had been sent to Auschwitz-Birkenau—not according to "uncontrollable rumors," but according to an eye-wit-ness report from the Jewish activists in Bratislava. He also knew that Auschwitz-Birkenau was no mere "industrial center" but a major Nazi death camp.

The remark about the "Birkenau industrial center" was not the only deception in the May 14 letter. "In recent days," wrote Kasztner, "the situation has been clarified. We have been introduced to new people in the negotiations, whose appearance before us can be treated to some extent as a *deus ex machina*." So Eichmann's involvement bordered on a miracle! Kasztner continued:

> These new masters seem to have in their hands the comprehensive settlement of the Jewish question; they are not friendly to us in attitude, however they seem to appreciate upright negotiating partners . . .
>
> The negotiations originally started with Wisliceny have thus reached a stage that opens up a glimmer of light in the darkness and an angle for us.

Having discerned "a glimmer of light" as the Nazis were about to massacre hundreds of thousands, Kasztner offered the most egregious distortion of all: "Our efforts so far," he wrote, "are concentrated on preventing the deportation and in this connection preparing an even bigger emigration."[35] But the rescue committee was *not* concentrating its efforts on the goal of "preventing the deportation." On the contrary: the subject matter of the "rescue negotiations" from the very first meeting with Wisliceny had been *emigration through deportation*.

In summary: on May 13, the Red Cross learned of the impending Nazi deportation of the first three hundred thousand Hungarian Jews for gassing in Poland. The next day, Kasztner sent a long letter to the Jewish relief headquarters in Switzerland in which he misdescribed Auschwitz-Birkenau as an industrial site, while hiding the fact that his "rescue negotiations" were premised on carrying out the deportations.

At the same time, Kasztner continued to misrepresent the prospects of the Goods for Blood deal to Jewish leaders in Budapest. Calling a meeting in Freudiger's office, he finally divulged the full details of Brand's forthcoming mission to Turkey. Both the terms of the mission and the identity of the emissary caused consternation.[36] Freudiger instantly saw through Eichmann's offer:

> I said it would do no good. You can't give the enemy trucks. . . . "Money can be raised and paid without a trace—but trucks?!? How do you mean to get them? From whom?"
>
> [Kasztner] said: "In Istanbul there's a rescue committee and there are Jewish Agency representatives: we can fix it."
>
> I told him I didn't think it would work.
>
> He said: "You're not a Zionist, that's why you think it won't work."
>
> I said: "True, I'm not a Zionist, but I think it's impossible in any case."
>
> So Kasztner said: "That's the point, it wasn't our offer. Eichmann made the offer."

When it was pointed out to him that Brand was unsuitable for such a sensitive diplomatic task, Kasztner responded: "It isn't up to us. Eichmann only knows me and Brand. His choice was between just the pair of us and he decided to send Brand." Freudiger urged Kasztner himself to travel instead, but the answer was firm: "It isn't up to me. Whoever Eichmann wants to go has to go."[37]

According to Freudiger, it was discovered that Brand had been chosen to convey the SS proposal because Eichmann considered him less competent than Kasztner and he wanted to be sure that the negotiations would fail. In addition, Kasztner, having been raised to the height of power and influence by the Nazis, was not about to relinquish the leadership role.[38] Here the testimony of Moshe Krausz, director of the Palestine Office in Budapest, is illuminating: "It was basically administrative contact between the *Judenrat* and the Germans, while political contact—with the *Judenrat* also—went through Kasztner."[39] Unlike Krausz, the left-wing Zionist youth leader Rafi Benshalom was sympathetic to Kasztner, but he too noticed who was giving the orders: "Distinguished members of the [Zionist] presidency, who had just held an election and left Kastner and his party in the minority, were now standing helplessly in front of this man. From time to time they tried to register a protest, but were silenced with a wave of the hand."[40]

From the beginning of the occupation, the Germans had diligently studied the Jewish rescue operation to see if its leaders could be "turned." Wisliceny's demand for emigration through deportation; Krumey's grant of official SS protection; Wisliceny's use of Kasztner to sabotage the escape effort in Kolozsvár; Eichmann's decision to return the rescue committee's intercepted funds and letters; and the liquidation of the Abwehr cell by Clages with the complicity of Brand and Kasztner—all these steps not only furthered the various Nazi plans but also served as psychological tests for the Jewish rescue operatives. If the SS drew the conclusion that Brand could be manipulated and Kasztner could be recruited as a collaborator, it is no surprise that Brand was sent to Istanbul bearing an implausible rescue proposal, while Kasztner was kept in Budapest to play the role scripted for him by the killers.

On May 15, Brand was summoned for a final meeting with Eichmann before his departure. Eichmann announced that full-scale deportation was starting immediately at the rate of twelve thousand Jews per day. Those fit for work would be used as slave labor; the rest would be available for exchange under the Goods for Blood deal. But where were they being sent? Here, yet again, we have an unreliable postwar version from Brand:

> [Eichmann] could hold back the people for 8–14 days, and they would not be sent directly to Auschwitz, but to Austria or Slovakia. However, he could not hold them back for a longer period, I would have to be back with my answer before that.[41]

But this is not at all what was said in the May 15 encounter. Only weeks after that meeting, Brand reported the opposite to his British interrogators:

> Eichmann replied that nothing would happen to the people and that they would be well-treated. Brand countered that he had definite information from Jewish contacts in Slovakia that the Jews were being *taken in the direction of Auschwitz* [emphasis added]—a red flag to the Jews, because it had been the scene of some of the most ghastly massacres and gas-chamber episodes. Eichmann laughed—"So Auschwitz has a bad name with you. It doesn't matter. They are only distributing camps."[42]

Eichmann did not deny that the deportation trains were heading straight for Auschwitz. Brand and his wife misrepresented this crucial point after the war.[43] As for Eichmann's promise to keep the Auschwitz deportees alive pending the outcome of Brand's mission, this was, of course, a lie: the vast majority were sent to the gas chambers without delay.

Before his departure, Brand had further meetings with Eichmann's SS colleagues. He still did not have a clear offer to take to Istanbul. Finally he was given a typed list of fifteen to twenty items, with no quantities specified. As Brand's British interrogator concluded, the Nazis were obviously insincere, "otherwise they would have been more thorough in discussing the goods they required."[44]

Did Kasztner Believe in Negotiations for Large-Scale Rescue?

Eichmann's parting words to Brand reveal a central feature of the "rescue plan" that Kasztner discussed with the SS for the next month: all the Jews would be deported from Hungary, no matter what. The same point is clear in Kasztner's own account of the Goods for Blood offer:

> Eichmann and other German officers repeated it to my face more than once, more than 10 times. Brand reported to me and then the rescue committee and others that Eichmann was offering to let Hungary's

Jews emigrate in exchange for goods instead of money. He specifically mentioned trucks. He was willing to release 100 Jews per truck from German-occupied territory. But he could do nothing for the Jews in Hungary. "I can only sell from Germany," he said. So he was starting with deportation of Jews to Germany.[45]

In the Goods for Blood deal, *rescue depended on deportation*. If Kasztner intended to pursue Eichmann's offer, he could do nothing to obstruct the deportation plan.

The other central feature of the "rescue plan" was revealed by Eichmann on May 15. It is also mentioned by Kasztner in his statements about the Goods for Blood deal. For instance, in an apologetic letter written soon after the end of the mass deportations, Kasztner admitted that at the time of Brand's departure, it was said that "the selection would go ahead *in Auschwitz* [emphasis added]" and that "the suitable people for the [rescue] plan would be kept there."[46] In his main affidavit for the Nuremberg Trials, Kasztner quoted Eichmann to the same effect:

> I am prepared to sell 1,000,000 Hungarian Jews for goods, primarily vehicles. I would transport them to Oswiecim [Auschwitz] and "put them on ice." If my generous offer is accepted, I will release all of them. If not, they will all be gassed.[47]

Whether Eichmann used these exact words is beside the point. The relevant issue is Kasztner's confession that *the precondition of the Goods for Blood plan was deportation to Auschwitz*.

That the head of the rescue committee was prepared to negotiate on this basis seems incredible, but Kasztner admitted it more than once. Under interrogation at Nuremberg, he summarized the Goods for Blood offer as follows:

> Eichmann was willing to release 100 Jews per truck from the German-occupied territories. He was willing to transport Brand by plane to Istanbul to forward this "generous" proposal to the Allied and Jewish bodies. Meanwhile he would totally uproot the Hungarian Jews but would *store them in Auschwitz*. He wanted a clear answer from Istanbul in two weeks at the latest, otherwise he would proceed as usual with *the Jews taken to Auschwitz*. [Emphases added.][48]

Cross-examination during the Kasztner Trial yielded this exchange:

> Q: Brand left Budapest on May 17 and he was already telling everyone in Istanbul that 12,000 Jews per day were being sent to Auschwitz.

A: I don't know what this was based on.
Q: Based on the meeting with Eichmann.
A: But Eichmann said he would wait two weeks.[49]

As the astonished trial judge asked in his verdict, did Kasztner really believe that 168,000 Jews would still be alive in Auschwitz after two weeks of deportations?[50] Kasztner had admitted in court: "I knew then the meaning of deportation to Auschwitz."[51]

In short, Kasztner claimed during and after the war that he was in contact with the murderers of Hungary's Jews because he was negotiating a Goods for Blood deal on these terms: Hungary's Jews would be deported in order to be rescued; and they would be sent to Auschwitz in order to be released. But Kasztner could not have believed in such a deal.

No less bizarre were the rescue deal's demands on the West. The Goods for Blood plan was not likely to produce an international agreement. No one could have honestly expected the West to send military supplies to the Nazis. Indeed, Kasztner stated after the war that he had never hoped for any such thing: the Jewish leaders in Hungary, himself included, had never believed that the Allies would meet the German demands.[52] Kasztner subsequently explained his approach to the Goods for Blood offer:

> We in the rescue committee told ourselves that it was a perverse approach from the Germans to make the Allies help their war effort. *We had no illusions about the realism of these demands,* but it wasn't our place to judge this. Our job was to save Jewish lives. Our duty was to convey the offer to higher Jewish authorities and pass the decision and initiative to them. *We estimated the odds as very slim,* but not impossible. But we hoped that the Jewish institutions together with the Allies would find some way to prolong the contact we had created and *gain time* this way. [Emphases added.][53]

So Kasztner did not believe Eichmann's offer to spare Hungarian Jewry and he did not expect anyone to satisfy Eichmann's demands. His intention was to "gain time" by dragging out the negotiations. That would have been reasonable if deportations had been suspended for the duration of the talks. But when thousands of Hungarian Jews were being sent to Auschwitz each day, it was the Nazis who were gaining time, and the Jews who were losing it. Continuing to negotiate meant buying time for the killers.

Did Kasztner Believe in Negotiations for Small-Scale Rescue?

If Kasztner did not seriously expect to arrange a mass rescue deal with the SS, was he at least hopeful of achieving a smaller agreement regarding the so-called Kasztner Train? The evidence suggests otherwise.

The *Eichmann-Kommando* agreed to the exit of six hundred Jews under the "disguise" of a Nazi deportation. It was not difficult for the Jewish rescue committee to understand why. As Brand recalled, Krumey repeatedly asked for lists of names, but the committee did not supply them because "we were afraid of any such emigration via Germany."[54] When Krumey proposed bringing the six hundred to a transit camp in Budapest, Brand tried to resist "because of the obvious danger of assembling the Jews in a camp for the Germans."[55] It was feared *at the time* that the emigrants would be taken hostage.

On May 2, Kasztner was suddenly assured that the emigrants would leave within two weeks. He told Komoly, chairman of his committee, that they would go "at the end of next week."[56] So the Kasztner Train (as it is now known) should have left Hungary by the weekend of May 13–14, just before the mass deportations to Auschwitz began. But the Nazis did not honor this deadline.

There is other evidence that Kasztner did not really expect the Nazis to release the six hundred Jews. The purported motive of the SS for disguising the plan as a deportation was to avoid embarrassing the Hungarian government. On learning of this, Krausz urged Kasztner to offer the Nazis evidence of Hungary's official support for Jewish emigration. But Kasztner replied that he had been forbidden to contact the Hungarian authorities. To circumvent this further restriction, Krausz arranged for the publication of three articles sympathetic to Jewish emigration in the state-sponsored newspaper *Esti Újság*. The first of the articles appeared on the paper's front page on May 3.[57] Krausz explained:

> I took the articles to Kasztner, who promised to show them to the Germans. I asked him about it several times; he found all kinds of excuses. One day I asked him directly. He admitted that the Germans had refused to hear about it or read the articles.[58]

Krausz drew the obvious conclusion: the *Eichmann-Kommando*'s stated reason for disguising the departure of the six hundred Jews as a deportation to the Third Reich was a mere pretext. He refused to have anything to do with this emigration project or to hand over the six hundred Palestine entry certificates in his possession. Yet Kasztner then announced that the Nazis were dispensing with Palestine entry certificates; they were willing to consider the emigration project even though the six hundred Jews had nowhere to go.[59]

What Kasztner knew about the Nazi-sponsored "emigration" plan was that the promised exit date was a lie, the "emigrants" were to be deported by the Nazis on a false pretext, and they had nowhere to go as their entry papers had been withdrawn. The uncomfortable truth is that Kasztner pursued this SS-sponsored plan to deport six hundred Jews when he had no reason to expect that it would lead to the release of those Jews. Just as his negotiations for a large-scale rescue deal (Goods for Blood) were bogus, so too was his pursuit of a small-scale rescue deal (the Kasztner Train).

The Truth about the "Rescue Negotiations"

The signs are that *all* of Kasztner's rescue plans, large and small, were illusory. The reality is that the acting head of the Jewish rescue operation in Hungary had been recruited as a collaborator by the Nazis.

Krausz had similar thoughts at the time. In May 1944, he realized that the SS "rescue" plans were meant to raise false hopes during the preparation and implementation of the genocide. He warned against gambling hundreds of thousands of lives on the outcome of talks with Eichmann's SS unit.[60] Having observed the psychological warfare methods of the murderers, he was able to identify their motives for negotiating with Kasztner's committee:

> First: the German aim was to show the Jews that they wanted to help. Second: to give the Jews something to keep them preoccupied. When it became known that the Germans were willing to grant exit permits to Jews, almost the entire Jewish community in Budapest entertained hopes of joining this emigration. . . . Another point: the Germans wanted to take the [Zionist] activists out of Budapest because they feared that the activists would prepare resistance. . . . They also wanted to get the Jewish leaders into their hands as hostages. And they wanted to demoralize the Jews. All these points raised the suspicion and perhaps even the certainty that here was a German diversion.[61]

The Nazis, argued Krausz, aimed to distract the attention of the Jewish community from their plans. For this they needed a Jewish leader like Kasztner to convince his own side to negotiate "rescue" deals while the Jewish masses were sent to Auschwitz.

That the "rescue negotiations" were a deception meant to allow the Nazis to exterminate the Jews of Hungary would become all too clear during the Brand Mission.

Notes

1. Peter Longerich, *The Unwritten Order: Hitler's Role in the Final Solution* (Stroud: Tempus Publishing, 2003), 210.
2. Budapest to Posner in Geneva, re: cable of May 4, 1944, Haganah Archive, 14/798.
3. Brand-SIME1, paras. 103, 105, 97, 89. See also Brand-JAE1, 5 (Krumey "went out of his way to appear kind and understanding, and made an impression of sincerity"); Brand-JAE2, para. 20 (Krumey "was a cheerful type and appeared willing to help").
4. Brand was told that he could discuss whatever he liked during his mission, but if he disclosed Laufer's identity, the Goods for Blood offer would be revoked: Brand-JAE2, para. 26.
5. Eichmann Trial testimony, May 29, 1961. See also Brand-SIME1, para. 109: "Laufer . . . assured Brand that they wanted to carry through decent, clean business and that the highest German SS would liberate the Jews." Elsewhere we find that the refreshments were not limited to coffee and cake. See Weissberg, *Desperate Mission*, 100: "We drank a lot. Klausnitzer could be described as a professional drunkard, and I needed alcohol at that time to soothe my nerves."
6. Grosz-SIME3, para. 284; Brand-SIME4, para. 32; Weissberg, *Desperate Mission*, 100, 102. Under interrogation, Brand denied that Klausnitzer slept at his home; in his memoirs, he admits it.
7. Grosz, Kasztner Trial testimony, June 13, 1954.
8. Freudiger, Kasztner Trial testimony, August 13, 1954.
9. For the date, see Grosz-SIME3, para. 275, which is probably more reliable than Brand on this point.
10. Biss, *A Million Jews to Save*, 61. For background on Gerhard Clages (often misnamed Otto Klages), see Aronson, *Hitler, the Allies and the Jews*, 239; Szita, *Trading in Lives?*, 34. Aronson describes Clages as a member of the amalgamated Gestapo/SD while Szita considers him an SD operative alone.
11. Brand-SIME1, para. 120 (confusing the second and third meetings; see Brand-SIME2, para. 46). According to Grosz, Eichmann and Clages treated Brand "very civilly": Grosz-SIME3, para. 275.
12. Grosz-SIME3, paras. 265–8.
13. Brand's Eichmann Trial testimony, May 29, 1961.
14. Brand-SIME1, para. 121–2.
15. Brand to Schwalb, May 31, 1944, TNA WO 208/685A (item 91B, para. 10), translation adjusted for code words.
16. See also Brand's various explanations of the incident in (a) Brand-SIME1, para. 124: "they wished to lull his suspicions by saying that he had only to report with the letters and they would all be returned"; (b) Weissberg, *Desperate Mission*, 104: "I could not make out what was happening. Eichmann seemed to be appointing me as a German censor . . . I was completely at sea"; (c) Brand's Eichmann Trial testimony, May 29, 1961: "they also feared

that if the money was stolen by them, then all the negotiations which they had now launched would evaporate into thin air."

17. This is the date for the *first* meeting given in Kasztner's *Bericht*, 33–34, and in Brand's testimony at the Krumey–Hunsche Trial, *New York Times*, May 21, 1964. Under British interrogation, Brand placed the *third* meeting with Eichmann around May 10: Brand-SIME1, para. 120. It is safe to assume that a meeting did indeed take place on May 8—and since this was not the first, second or fourth of the four meetings, it must have been the third.

18. Weissberg, *Desperate Mission*, 117.

19. Brand-JAE2, paras. 27, 38.

20. Brand-SIME1, paras. 130–1.

21. Brand-JAE2, paras. 27–29.

22. Brand-WRB, 3.

23. As noted by Brand's British interrogator: Brand-SIME1, para. 196.

24. Brand-SIME1, paras. 138–40.

25. Kasztner, *Bericht*, 34.

26. Budapest to Natan in Geneva, May 9, 1944, Haganah Archive, 14/798.

27. Brand-SIME1, para. 99; Brand-SIME4, para. 31.

28. Brand-SIME1, paras. 109–10; Grosz-SIME3, para. 285; Brand-SIME4, para. 33; Weissberg, *Desperate Mission*, 100, 109–10.

29. Brand-SIME4, para. 34.

30. Brand-SIME4, para. 36.

31. Brand-SIME1, para. 134.

32. Brand-SIME4, para. 36.

33. Kasztner later disguised his role, pretending that he had opposed the move against the Abwehr while Brand had supported it: *Bericht*, 33.

34. De Bavier's confidential report to the ICRC, May 30, 1944, quoted in Arieh Ben-Tov, *Facing the Holocaust in Budapest: The International Committee of the Red Cross and the Jews in Hungary, 1943–1945* (Dordrecht: Kluwer Academic Publishers, 1988), 126.

35. Kasztner and Brand to Mayer, May 14, 1944, JDC Archive, New York, Saly Mayer Collection, file 20(2); for a Hebrew translation, see Kasztner Trial prosecution exhibit 26. This is a joint letter, but the style and content (e.g., the ostentatious use of the Latin phrase "*deus ex machina*") leave no doubt that the author was Kasztner.

36. Freudiger, "Five Months," 257–8.

37. Kasztner Trial testimony, August 12, 1954. See "Five Months," *supra*, for a similar version.

38. *Freudiger Report*, 29.

39. Kasztner Trial testimony, July 8, 1954.

40. Benshalom, *We Struggled For Life*, 66.

41. Eichmann Trial testimony, May 29, 1961.

42. Brand-SIME1, para. 142 ("Ausschwytz" spelling corrected).

43. See, for example, Weissberg, *Desperate Mission*, 119–20; Hansi Brand, Eichmann Trial testimony, May 30, 1961.

44. Brand-SIME1, paras. 148, 196. One of the Nazis made verbal suggestions: 10,000 trucks, 40,000 kg of coffee, 10,000 kg of tea, 10,000 kg of cocoa or chocolate and 2 million bars of soap. Ibid., para. 144.

45. Kasztner Trial testimony, February 18, 1954.

46. Kasztner to Schwalb, July 12, 1944, Haganah Archive, 80/p187/32.

47. Kasztner, London Affidavit, 7.

48. Kasztner, Interrogation No. 1581a, 5.

49. Kasztner Trial testimony, September 16, 1954. Eichmann admitted to Brand that the Jews were being sent to Auschwitz but denied that it was a death camp: Brand-SIME1, para. 142. But he assured Brand's wife that they were being sent "to Austria or somewhere else" pending the outcome of the negotiations: Hansi Brand, Eichmann Trial testimony, May 30, 1961. Eichmann was, of course, lying in both cases.

50. Kasztner Trial verdict, s. 53. See also Kasztner Appeal, Silberg verdict, s. 13.

51. Kasztner Trial testimony, March 1, 1954.

52. Kasztner, *Bericht*, 37.

53. Kasztner Trial testimony, February 19, 1954. In some published versions of the trial verdict, a serious misprint in s. 46 reverses the meaning of the key words "very slim, but not impossible." Misled by this, one commentator gave the mistranslation "balanced, but not impossible": Leora Bilsky, *Transformative Justice: Israeli Identity on Trial* (Ann Arbor: University of Michigan Press, 2004), 275n56. The actual words in the transcript of Kasztner's testimony (correctly printed in s. 53 of the verdict) are "very slim, but not impossible."

54. Eichmann Trial testimony, May 29, 1961.

55. Brand-SIME1, para. 137. Brand only changed his mind just before his departure in mid-May.

56. *Komoly Diary*, May 2, 1944.

57. Ayala Nedivi, *Ha-Misrad ha-Erets Yisre'eli be-Budapesht: pe'ulotav bi-tehum ha-hatsalah ba-shanim 1943–1945 ve-ofen 'itsuvan ba-zikaron ha-kolektivi* [*The Palestine Office in Budapest: Its Actions in Saving Jews From 1943–1945 and Their Formulation in the Collective Memory*] (PhD Dissertation, Haifa: Haifa University, 2009), 138.

58. Krausz, Kasztner Trial testimony, June 25, 1954.

59. Kasztner Trial verdict, s. 29; Nedivi, *Ha-Misrad ha-Erets Yisre'eli be-Budapesht*, 138.

60. Kasztner Trial verdict, s. 78; Nedivi, *Ha-Misrad ha-Erets Yisre'eli be-Budapesht*, 137–9, 144–5.

61. Kasztner Trial testimony, July 2, 1954. See also Eugene [Jenő] Lévai, *Black Book on the Martyrdom of Hungarian Jewry* (Zurich: Central European Times Publishing Co., 1948), 274. On Krausz's point that the Nazis aimed "to show the Jews that they were willing to help," see Brand-JAE1, 5 (Krumey tried "to appear kind and understanding"), Brand-JAE2, para. 20 (Krumey "appeared willing to help"), and Brand-SIME1, para. 89 (Krumey was constantly "pretending to do his best for the Jews").

6

The Brand Mission

On May 19, 1944, Brand and Grosz landed in Istanbul. At the airport they were greeted not by Chaim Weizmann—as Brand had naively expected—but by the Jewish Agency's local rescue coordinator, Chaim Barlas. Brand demanded an emergency private meeting with the Zionist agents in Istanbul. One of the agents, Menachem Bader, recalled his words:

> Brand told us about the situation of the [Hungarian] Jews, about the fact that 12,000 Jews (men, women and children) were being sent for extermination every day and that most of the provincial Jews had already been moved to deportation sites; we knew that these meant extermination sites. He told us that the crematoria in Auschwitz were insufficient to burn all the bodies, so bonfires had been established in the forest near Birkenau next to Auschwitz, and people were no longer gassed but machine-gunned and loaded for burning at these bonfires.[1]

Initially, the Zionist agents were unimpressed by Eichmann's offer. Their first reaction was to exclaim, "Lies, all lies! The proposal is an evil deceit!"[2] Bader saw it as "a horrible trick" motivated by the Nazi assumption that America and Britain would refuse to admit such large numbers of Jews.[3]

The futility of Brand's task was also understood by Grosz, who had arrived with a mission of his own. Grosz had been ordered to arrange a meeting in any neutral country between SS representatives and high-ranking American and British officers. The aim of the meeting would be to negotiate a "separate peace" between the Nazis and the West. Grosz was to use the Zionists as intermediaries in arranging the talks. His instructions came not from Eichmann—whom he had never met—but from the Gestapo/SD officer Clages, who gave the rationale that since the war was leading toward a stalemate on the Western front, it would be prudent for Nazi Germany to join the United States and

Britain in order to fight the Soviets. Clages intimated that the peace offer had the backing of Himmler and was meant to provide "security"—meaning alibis—for its architects. As for Brand's mission, Clages told Grosz that it was merely a cover story designed to keep the German Foreign Office from interfering with the SS plan.[4]

At the first opportunity, Grosz warned the Zionist activists in Istanbul that the Nazis were not serious about Goods for Blood. Certain SS officers, he explained, had a "childish dream" of creating an alibi for themselves by offering to release Jews. Their sole objective was to contact their counterparts in the West and make a good impression on them. Grosz did his best to disabuse the Zionists of the idea that negotiating with the Nazis might save the lives of Jews. "The people Brand quotes, Eichmann included, have as much power to stop the ovens—or the trains—as I have to stop the world," he insisted. "And even if they could stop them, they would never have the courage to propose it to a beast like Himmler. Don't be children! Don't believe a word!"[5]

The story of the Brand Mission is the record of how Brand's news of the mass extermination and Grosz's warning about the perils of negotiations were disregarded by the rescue activists even though they were wholly accurate. As the ghettos in Hungary were being emptied at maximum speed and with utmost cruelty, the Zionist leaders in Palestine became the naive victims of a calculated deception by the killers. In this deception, the head of the Jewish rescue committee in Budapest played a key part.

Kasztner Meets Eichmann

Brand's departure from Budapest was an opportunity for his ambitious colleague to seize exclusive control of political relations between Hungarian Jewry and the Nazis. Kasztner (as one admirer put it) "exercised all his charm" on Joel Brand's wife Hansi, who agreed to introduce him to Eichmann.[6] (By exercising his masculine charm, Kasztner ensured that Brand's wife would be his pliant tool throughout the Nazi occupation—and his devoted apologist subsequently.) The meeting took place on May 20. Kasztner was aware of his interlocutor's aims. Eichmann was the coordinator of the extermination of the Jews; with him lay the choice of life or death.[7]

Kasztner and Hansi Brand presented a series of complaints to Eichmann. They asked why they had seen no sign of the VIP emigration candidates who were supposed to have been transferred from the ghettos to Budapest under the deal with Krumey. They protested against the hideous cruelties accompanying every stage of the concentration and deportation process. And they warned that the Brand Mission was unlikely to yield results under such circumstances.

Eichmann was unmoved. After expatiating for over an hour on his experiences in persecuting Jews in other countries, he declared that the emigration candidates had not been removed from the ghettos because the rescue committee had yet to supply the list of names. He dismissed the complaint that up to a hundred people were being forced into each train wagon with the "explanation" that Jewish families in the Subcarpathians had many children, who needed less room and less air than adults. He also made it clear that nothing would induce him to stop the deportations, since otherwise no one abroad would negotiate with him.[8]

Emerging from his first encounter with Eichmann, Kasztner acted immediately. As he noted in his postwar account, the *Bericht*, he cabled Istanbul that deportations were continuing.[9] Brand received the cable, but according to him, its message was not so simple. It read in full: "750 [emigrants] not granted permit. Deportation not interrupted. *Large camps have been arranged in Germany for old people and little children* [emphasis added]."[10] On its face, this meant that all of the deportees, even the most vulnerable, were being kept alive pending a negotiated deal.

However, before his departure Brand had agreed with his wife and Kasztner to use a signature code in their communications. According to this code, a message signed with a *first name only* was true, but a message signed with a *last name only* was false and its meaning had to be reversed.[11] The cable to Brand was signed with his wife's last name only, so it had to be interpreted thus: "750 granted permit. *Deportation interrupted.* Large camps have not been arranged in Germany for old people and little children." The real message to Brand was that the deportations had stopped altogether.

Whether taken at face value or reversed, the rescue committee's cable to Istanbul conveyed the same point: Eichmann had so far kept his promise not to kill any Hungarian Jews; Brand's warning to the Zionist activists about the mass murder of the deportees in Auschwitz had been premature.

But Eichmann was in fact deporting thousands of Hungarian Jews to Auschwitz every day. The cable to Brand was disinformation. The fact that it was signed with a *last name only* indicated that the sender was privy to the signature code. The only two people in Budapest who knew this code were Kasztner and Hansi Brand. And although the cable was signed by the latter, it was surely sent by Kasztner, or at his behest. Hansi Brand had no reason to mislead her husband about the destruction of Hungarian Jewry; and Kasztner himself took responsibility for the message in his *Bericht.*

The effect of the cable was catastrophic. Brand was now confused; he repeatedly cabled Budapest for clarification, but received no reply.[12] Having correctly informed the Zionist activists that the Nazis were killing thousands of Hungarian Jews every day, he apparently changed his mind and declared that Eichmann was keeping his promise to wait for two weeks. And the rescue activists in Istanbul conveyed this disinformation to their superiors in Jerusalem—who in turn passed it to the British authorities.

The Deception of the Jewish Agency

On May 24, just days after the arrival of Brand and Grosz in Istanbul, Himmler delivered another speech to Wehrmacht commanders gathered in Sonthofen in Germany. It closely resembled his previous address on May 5. The Jewish question, he announced, was "decisive for the inner security of the Reich and of Europe." Although Himmler did not consider himself a bloodthirsty person, he would not allow moral restraints to disturb him. In particular, he once again pledged to exterminate all Jewish children without exception. Anything else would be "cowardly."[13] Here was another sign that Eichmann's promises were worthless and a chilling vindication of Grosz's cautionary words to the Zionists.

The next day, Venia Pomerantz, one of the rescue activists from Istanbul, briefed the Jewish Agency Executive (JAE) in Palestine about the Brand Mission. He explained the situation in Hungary as follows: "300,000 Jews have been concentrated in Carpathian Ruthenia and Transylvania . . . . Eight thousand Jews have been deported to Poland to date, and starting next week another 12,000 will be deported every day." In fact the full-scale deportations had been under way for ten days and the number of Hungarian Jews already sent to Auschwitz was not eight thousand but nearly 139,000.[14] Unaware of this calamity, the JAE members responded predictably to the news of Eichmann's offer to Brand: they debated how to make use of it to delay the deportation and extermination drive.

The most skeptical of the participants was the head of the Jewish Agency's rescue committee in Palestine, Yitzhak Grünbaum. He at once recognized the German offer as "a satanic provocation meant to give them an opportunity to slaughter the Jews of Hungary." But he drew a most illogical conclusion: the offer had to be kept alive as long as possible, "although there is no doubt that nothing can possibly come of it." Grünbaum insisted on three conditions: any deportations had to stop at once; the first Jews had to be released from Poland instead of Hungary; and the Zionists should pay the Nazis with money instead of goods. He recommended sending Moshe Shertok, head of the Jewish Agency's political department, to Istanbul in order to investigate the offer, "because that way we buy time." The delusion that the rescuers could "buy time" by pursuing a hopeless deal with the murderers would bedevil the entire effort to save Hungary's Jews.

Grünbaum's reservations were too much for his comrades. Their reactions were even more illogical than his. Shertok, who thought the scheme "chimerical," embraced it anyway, announcing that "there is no doubt that many Jews may be saved if we respond in the affirmative." Ben-Gurion also saw the offer as "fantastic," but rebuked Grünbaum for dismissing it as a satanic plot. The Nazis, he explained, "have one plot—to destroy Jews. If there is a hope of one in a million, we should cling to it." Eliezer Kaplan found the proposed deal "puzzling" but emphasized that "it is our duty to spare no effort to rescue the Jews of Hungary.... If there is even one straw to grasp, we must not let it slip away." None of the JAE members considered the possibility that by devoting their efforts to a Nazi "rescue" proposal the Jews were *losing* time instead of gaining it. Instead, the main point of controversy was whether to pursue the matter independently or to report the offer to the British government.

At the end of the meeting, after it was decided to inform the British authorities, Ben-Gurion set the stage for the next act in the disaster: he ordered all those present "to keep these matters in total confidence and reveal them to no one."[15] Needless to say, it was the German offer and not the fate of the Jews that Ben-Gurion wanted to handle in confidence. But as it turned out, secrecy about the proposed deal was inextricably linked to secrecy about the unfolding situation in Hungary.[16]

Reviewing the Jewish Agency's immediate reaction to the news of Eichmann's offer to Brand, it is hard not to notice the multitude of illogical statements. Grünbaum, who understood that Eichmann's offer was a trick designed to give the Nazis time to murder Hungary's Jews, nevertheless recommended investigating the scheme in order to "buy time" for the victims. At the opposite pole, Shertok considered the idea bizarre and unrealistic, but had "no doubt" that pursuing it would save "many" lives. The minutes of the meeting abound with platitudes deployed as substitutes for arguments ("If there is a hope of one in a million, we should cling to it." "If there is even one straw to grasp, we must not let it slip away.") What is disturbing is that the participants recognized the impossibility of satisfying the German conditions, but then allowed their emotions to overrule their faculty of reason. Having dimly perceived the trap that Eichmann had set for them, Ben-Gurion and his colleagues walked straight into it.

On May 26, the JAE officially disclosed the German offer to the British High Commissioner in Palestine, Sir Harold MacMichael. The JAE reported that the Nazis were prepared to show their "good faith" by releasing a transport of five thousand to ten thousand Hungarian Jews (not one hundred thousand, as later asserted by Brand) as an advance payment. On the other hand, "If the offer is rejected they will proceed with their programme of wholesale liquidation." The JAE echoed Brand's mistaken assumption that prolonging the talks, even without concluding an agreement, would gain time for the victims. The basis for that argument was Brand's account of the situation in Hungary, which the JAE now repeated to MacMichael:

> 300,000 Hungarian Jews are already herded in concentration camps prior to deportation. The rounding up of other Jews is in progress. Eight thousand Jews have already been deported to Poland. Plans had been made for the daily deportation to Poland of 12,000 Jews as from 22nd May but *presumably this has been deferred pending negotiations.* [Emphasis added.]

The JAE expressed the hope that the Allied governments would not allow themselves to be deterred by "the magnitude and the seemingly fantastic character of the proposition." Finally, MacMichael was assured that Ben-Gurion and colleagues were "keeping all this information strictly secret."[17]

While Eichmann was delivering his victims to the gas chambers at a rate that was unprecedented in the history of the Holocaust, the British were thus "informed" that the destruction of the Jews in Hungary had not yet begun. Furthermore, the Jewish Agency leaders committed themselves to handling the rescue of Hungary's Jews in total secrecy. These two factors—ignorance of the ongoing mass extermination and the commitment to secret negotiations—precluded any effort to publicize the massacre and generate outside pressure on the Hungarian regime to stop collaborating with the Nazis against the Jews. Not public pressure but clandestine diplomacy became the Jewish Agency's sole method of rescue in the decisive days and weeks for the Jews in the Hungarian ghettos.

The Impact of the Brand Mission

The information about the status of Hungary's Jews that was communicated to the Jewish Agency, hence the British, as a result of the Brand Mission can be summarized as follows:

- On May 15, Brand met Eichmann, who said that he was deporting twelve thousand Hungarian Jews per day to Auschwitz, but added, falsely, that the deportees would be kept alive for two weeks. Brand was not fooled by Eichmann's assurance.
- On May 19, Brand told the Jewish Agency rescue activists in Turkey that Eichmann was deporting twelve thousand Hungarian Jews per day to Auschwitz, where they were already being killed.
- On May 20, Kasztner met Eichmann, who refused to suspend the deportations. Kasztner (or someone acting on his behalf) dispatched a coded message to Istanbul falsely indicating that Eichmann had agreed to suspend the deportations.
- On May 25, the JAE met to discuss the Brand Mission and was mistakenly informed by Pomerantz, one of the rescue activists from Turkey, that the deportations would not begin for another week. It was decided to handle the Brand Mission in strict secrecy.
- On May 26, the Jewish Agency mistakenly informed the British that the deportations from Hungary had been deferred pending the outcome of the Brand Mission.

Instead of alerting the free world and provoking intervention to halt the slaughter, or at least gain time for the victims, the Brand Mission and the related disinformation gained time for the killers to gas most of the provincial Hungarian Jews in relative secrecy. A significant contribution to this tragedy was the cable sent by Kasztner, or at his behest, after his first meeting with Eichmann. That message convinced Brand—and through him the Jewish Agency—that the massacre of Hungary's Jews had been delayed and so there was time to investigate Eichmann's offer.

An indication of Kasztner's bad faith in this affair is the fact that he continued to misrepresent the chronology of the mass murders even after the war. Interviewed by FBI investigators in 1945, he summarized the events thus:

> [I] managed to inform the Allies of Eichmann's demand for trucks through Istanbul and the Allies promptly refused to have anything to do with it. (This was during the end of May 1944.) On hearing of the Allied attitude, Eichmann issued orders for Auschwitz "to start work."[18]

In fact, the Allies did not publicly reject the Goods for Blood deal until the second half of July. Eichmann was already sending Hungarian Jews to the gas chambers in mid-May. Was Kasztner's postwar lie about the timing of the mass murders in Auschwitz meant to camouflage a wartime lie about the very same subject?

What is certain is that the Brand Mission convinced the Jewish Agency in Jerusalem that the massacre of Hungary's Jews had been delayed, when Kasztner in Budapest knew full well that many thousands were being taken to the gas chambers every day.

The insincerity of the Nazi Goods for Blood offer transmitted by Brand in Turkey—and relentlessly championed by Kasztner in his messages from Hungary—was clear from the beginning. Krausz had made the point in Budapest; Grosz had repeated it in Istanbul; and Grünbaum immediately suspected as much in Jerusalem. The evidence now available establishes this fact conclusively.

In November 1944, the British were contacted by a German defector named Karl Marcus. He claimed to represent the inner circle of the head of SS foreign intelligence, Walter Schellenberg, one of Himmler's closest advisers. Marcus urged the West to drop the demand for unconditional surrender and pursue the Schellenberg group's offer of an anti-Soviet coalition. While dismissing this idea, the British recognized his considerable importance as an intelligence asset, and he was transferred to England. There he exposed several Nazi agents and supplied the background to Eichmann's offer to Brand. Marcus told his interrogators that "Brand's mission was approved by Schellenberg and its main aim was to split the Allies."[19]

Schellenberg wanted to avoid total military defeat. He had no power to stop the trains to Auschwitz. Splitting the Allies, however, would have prolonged the war and increased the Jewish death toll accordingly. The demand for war supplies conveyed by Brand was liable to produce the same results as the German peace initiative transmitted via Grosz. If the Western governments agreed to send the trucks or drop out of the war, then Germany would be free to concentrate its military forces on the Eastern front. If, on the other hand, these governments tried to negotiate as a ruse to "gain time" for Hungarian Jews—as they were being asked to do by the Jewish Agency—then the Nazis could disclose their disloyalty to the Soviets and break up the Allied coalition.[20] In either case, a stay of execution for the Third Reich would have been a death sentence for the remainder of Europe's Jews.

Brand himself was convinced that failing to secure a deal with the Nazis would seal the fate of Hungarian Jewry. Unable to speak to any high-ranking Jewish Agency official in Istanbul and threatened by the Turkish authorities with premature expulsion to Hungary, he proceeded to Syria, on the promise of meeting Shertok.[21] He was arrested in Aleppo by British intelligence and held for four months. After the war, he castigated the Jewish Agency and the British government for allegedly conspiring to prevent his return to Budapest and for sabotaging any hope of a rescue deal.[22] However, testifying at the trial of Krumey and Hunsche just before his death in 1964, he finally acknowledged that his mission had been futile from the outset. "I made a terrible mistake in passing this [Goods for Blood offer] on to the British," he confessed. "It is now clear to me that Himmler sought to sow suspicion among the Allies as a preparation for his much-desired Nazi–Western coalition against Moscow."[23] What was now clear to him had been obvious to others twenty years earlier. Brand, observed his British interrogator at the time, gave "the impression of being a very naive idealist."[24]

Eichmann, of course, did not object to splitting the Allies at the decisive moment of the war, so long as no actual Goods for Blood deal was made and his deportation plan unfolded without interruption. No doubt he also hoped to distract the Jewish leaders and Western governments, to camouflage the fate of the victims, and to hide the truth about Auschwitz, thus neutralizing any outside rescue efforts. His false assurance that the deportees would be "well-treated" pending Brand's return from Istanbul and his pretense that Auschwitz was only a "distributing camp" for these Jews reveal his true agenda.[25] During Brand's absence, Eichmann escalated the deportations to unprecedented levels in order to exterminate the Jews in the provincial ghettos as quickly as possible. And on May 25–26—as the Jewish Agency concluded that the deportations had been deferred for the sake of negotiations—his Foreign Office liaison, Eberhard von Thadden, heard his plan to eradicate the Jews of Budapest. The SS would mobilize not only the gendarmes and police but also the city's postmen and chimney sweeps to round up the entire community in a twenty-four-hour period. All traffic in the capital would be halted as the victims were concentrated on an island in the Danube for rapid transportation to Auschwitz.[26]

By ensnaring his adversaries in hopeless diplomatic activities linked to a bogus rescue offer, Eichmann wanted to gain time to murder the Jewish population of Hungary: as he saw it, the offer of rescue negotiations would undermine any genuine possibility of rescue.[27] His calculations turned out to be accurate. The impact of the Brand Mission on the would-be rescuers abroad is described by Holocaust historian Martin Gilbert: as a result of a "brilliantly successful" Nazi deception plan, "the faith that negotiations might succeed in saving all Hungarian Jewry coincided with the destruction of more than half of the Jews of greater Hungary."[28]

And so the Jewish Agency in Palestine, which might have turned into a source of accurate information for the free world and a rallying point for an international campaign against the Hungarian regime, devoted all its efforts to secret lobbying of the British and the American governments to investigate a Nazi "rescue offer" that had been designed to fail. Meanwhile, the trains were rolling continuously, taking the unsuspecting victims on their final journey—from the ghettos of Hungary to the gas chambers in Poland.

Notes

1. Bader, Kasztner Trial testimony, March 24, 1954. See also Bader, *Sad Missions* (Tel Aviv: Sifriat Poalim, 1979), 98; Ehud Avriel, *Open the Gates!* (New York: Atheneum, 1975), 175–6.
2. Bader, *Sad Missions*, 99.
3. Bader, Kasztner Trial testimony, March 24, 1954.
4. Grosz-SIME3, paras. 302–3, 322, 324–5. Cf. the slightly different account in Grosz-SIME1, para. 10–12.
5. Avriel, *Open the Gates!*, 178–9. "We could not visualize Grosz thinking up a practical joke like this," writes Avriel. "We believed Brand's story about his talk with Eichmann. There must be something in the whole affair that we had no right to denigrate." Cf. Grosz-SIME3, para. 342.
6. Biss, *A Million Jews to Save*, 44. Hansi Brand's version: "I decided that it was not for a woman to bear such responsibility, so I went to Kasztner, and we resolved that Kasztner should go up and see [Eichmann] the same day." Eichmann Trial testimony, May 30, 1961.
7. Kasztner, *Bericht*, 38.
8. Ibid., 38–39; his Kasztner Trial testimony, February 19, 1954; Hansi Brand's Eichmann Trial testimony, May 30, 1961.
9. Kasztner, *Bericht*, 39.
10. Brand-JAE2, para. 77. Menachem Bader claims to have hidden the cable from Brand to spare him further stress: Bader, *Sad Missions*, 101. Obviously, this is incorrect. See also Avriel, *Open the Gates!*, 181. Neither Bader nor Avriel mentions the signature code or the statement about large camps in Germany.
11. Brand-JAE2, paras. 75–76; Brand-SIME1, para. 170.
12. Brand-JAE2, para. 78. There is an innocent explanation for the failure to answer Brand's queries: Kasztner and Hansi Brand were in Hungarian custody from May 27 to June 1.

13. Longerich, *The Unwritten Order*, 210–11.
14. Braham, *The Politics of Genocide*, Vol. 1, 673.
15. Minutes of the Jewish Agency Executive meeting, May 25, 1944, CZA. Ben-Gurion did not specify his reason for imposing secrecy, but obviously his concern was to avoid the public exposure and ruin of the proposed Goods for Blood deal.
16. On the disastrous aversion of the Labor Zionists to publicity in matters of rescue, see Shabtai Beit-Zvi, *Post-Ugandan Zionism on Trial: A Study of the Factors That Caused the Mistakes by the Zionist Movement during the Holocaust* (Tel Aviv: privately printed, 1991), Vol. 2, 100–2, 111–13.
17. David S. Wyman, ed., *America and the Holocaust, Vol. 8: War Refugee Board—Hungary* (New York: Garland Publishing, 1990), 64–65.
18. NARA, RG 65, Folder 47826-249: FBI Intelligence Report, *SS Organization in Hungary Responsible for Jewish Persecution* (May 17, 1945), para. 7. Kasztner's confederate Biss peddled a similar falsehood: "When Brand failed to return within a fortnight, Himmler no longer believed in getting anywhere through us, and Eichmann was given a free hand to resume the deportations, which involved 10–15,000 people daily." Andre Biss, "The Deportations from Hungary, 1944," *Wiener Library Bulletin*, July 1963.
19. "DICTIONARY: Information about the UK and Eire: Interrogation No. 25," TNA KV 2/965, para. 37. Naturally, this had the support of Himmler; as Veesenmayer informed his colleagues, "The offer was the result of a secret order of the *Reichsführer-SS*." Veesenmayer to Foreign Office, July 22, 1944, Kasztner Trial prosecution exhibit 8.
20. Saul Friedländer, *The Years of Extermination: Nazi Germany and the Jews, 1939–1945* (New York: HarperCollins, 2007), 622.
21. On the reasons for Brand's decision to travel to Aleppo and the circumstances of his ensuing arrest, see Yehuda Bauer, "The Mission of Joel Brand," in *The Holocaust in Historical Perspective* (Seattle: University of Washington Press, 1978), 119–28; Friling, *Arrows in the Dark*, Vol. 2, 13–15.
22. Brand, Kasztner Trial testimony, April 1–2, 1954; Weissberg, *Desperate Mission*, 163–5. Grosz was arrested several days before Brand and held until the end of the war.
23. *New York Times*, May 21, 1964.
24. Brand-SIME1, para. 195. On the German attempt to split the Allies, see para. 197. See also the analysis of the US vice-consul in Istanbul, Leslie Albion Squires, "Activities of André Antal Gyorgy and Joel Brand," June 4, 1944, in Mendelsohn, *Relief in Hungary*, 110.
25. Brand-SIME1, para. 142.
26. Eichmann Trial exhibits T/1194 and T/1195; Eichmann Trial verdict, ss. 113, 116.
27. Randolph Braham, "Rescue Operations in Hungary: Myths and Realities," *Yad Vashem Studies* 32 (2004): 45–48. See also Shlomo Aronson, *David Ben-Gurion and the Jewish Renaissance* (Cambridge: Cambridge University Press, 2010), 139–40.
28. Martin Gilbert, "While the Allies Dithered, a Million Died," *Jewish Chronicle*, September 18, 1981. See Gilbert's detailed analysis in his *Auschwitz and the Allies* (London: Mandarin, 1991), 201–61 *passim*.

7

The Kenyérmező Deception

Eichmann and his aides had prepared the deportation and destruction of Hungary's Jews down to the smallest detail. Their master plan divided the country into six territorial zones. The mass deportations had started in Zone 1 (Subcarpathia) and Zone 2 (North Transylvania).

Central to Eichmann's operation was the deception of the victims. The Jews boarding the trains were meant to know nothing of their impending fate in Auschwitz. Instead they were to be told that they were being resettled for agricultural labor elsewhere in Hungary.

After the war, Kasztner was relatively frank about the deception of the Hungarian Jewish masses. He explained:

> The Germans used deception to hide the plan of extermination. By various ways and means they spread rumors nationwide that the Jews remained in the country. The Hungarian authorities issued decrees implying that the Jews were not being deported across the Hungarian border—this was among the German deceptions—and there were additional deceptions. At first they tried these deceptions on us, but we disbelieved them from the outset.[1]

How is it possible that hundreds of thousands of Jewish men, women, and children were rounded up and sent to their deaths by means of deception when the head of the Jewish rescue operation knew where the trains were really taking them?

Kasztner's defenders have assumed that Kasztner was blamed for "not providing Hungarian Jews with the information [about the Final Solution],"[2] for "failing to warn others of the fate awaiting them,"[3] or for "not informing Hungarian Jews of the real destination of the deportation trains."[4] In other words, they have claimed that Kasztner was faulted for his *omissions*. In contrast, many Hungarian Holocaust survivors insisted that Kasztner was complicit in the Nazi deception. These accusers did not blame him just for omissions, but also for his *actions*.

Which side in this dispute has a better understanding of Kasztner's deeds and motives?

Kasztner on the Deception

Kasztner's closest link with any provincial town during the Nazi occupation was his connection to Kolozsvár, the North Transylvanian capital city. He had visited the Jewish community twice before the end of the local ghetto drive; the city's *Judenrat* was led by his father-in-law, his brother, and his friends; and he was in regular telephone contact with his father-in-law, József Fischer, during the deportations from the Kolozsvár Ghetto to Auschwitz. Kasztner summarized these conversations as follows:

> He asked me over the telephone whether or not it was possible to save some of the Jews there. We didn't discuss the list [of emigration candidates] but rather the issue of saving some of the Jews in Kolozsvár. We discussed it 10 times. . . . I first spoke to him in mid-May. . . . He used every opportunity to call me.[5]

The period of Kasztner's telephone conversations with Fischer was the period in which the Jewish population peacefully boarded the death trains, believing that they were being taken for work elsewhere in the country. Kasztner was asked:

Q: Didn't your father-in-law tell you on the phone that there were positive rumors about the labor camp in Hungary?
A: Deportation and the destination—that wasn't a subject of our conversations. I didn't dare and he didn't dare to discuss it . . .
Q: So why didn't you tell the Jews of Kolozsvár everything you knew?
A: I did tell them everything I knew while I was in contact with them. Later I was only in contact with my father-in-law. I only dared to give him a clear hint, which I gave him: he must have known there was deportation and perhaps there was also extermination.
Q: So why didn't all the Jews in Kolozsvár know this?
A: Your Honor, are you asking my opinion? I think that my friends in Kolozsvár, including my father-in-law, didn't do everything they could and should have done.[6]

Thus Kasztner tried to exonerate himself by accusing his friends and his own father-in-law. However, in addition to being denied a warning, the victims were *actively deceived* by their community leaders, who were in regular contact with him in Budapest.

It is not surprising that Kasztner "didn't dare" to give Fischer more than a "clear hint" in these conversations, which were of course monitored by the Nazis. But that merely provokes the question: why did the Nazis place the head of the Jewish rescue committee—who knew their genocidal plans—in contact with the head of the Jewish community in North Transylvania's capital city as the plans were carried out?

If the Nazis had merely wanted to silence Kasztner, the phone calls would not have been permitted in the first place. The fact that they facilitated direct communications between Kasztner and Fischer—not just once, but ten times—suggests a more disturbing answer. The suspicion is reinforced by the eye-witness testimony of Holocaust survivors.

Auschwitz Survivors on the Deception

On May 25, 1944, the first train from the Kolozsvár Ghetto left for Auschwitz, carrying 3,130 Jewish men, women, and children. Among them were Yechiel Shmueli and his family. He testified about his deportation:

Q: How many people were on guard in Kolozsvár?
A: 20 policemen.
Q: How many people were in the Jewish community?
A: 18,000–20,000.
Q: When you entered the train, did you resist?
A: No. We entered normally.
Q: Why did you enter normally?
A: Because we were told that we were going to Kenyérmező. There was the ghetto leader Dr. Endre Balázs—a Jew—who said: "Brothers! Know that the Hungarian government has decided to evacuate the population of the town of Kenyérmező, and all Hungarian Jews will be interned there until the end of the war. Accept it calmly, because you'll be living together with your family."

Balázs, the head of the Jewish ghetto administration, was a relative of Fischer, Kasztner's father-in-law. Shmueli was asked:

Q: Was Fischer a respected Jew?
A: Yes, he was the head of the community.
Q: If Fischer had told you that you were going to Auschwitz, would you have taken it seriously?
A: Yes, he was a serious person.
Q: Did you all enter the train voluntarily—or rather, without resistance—because you thought that you were going to Kenyérmező and that you would have better conditions there?
A: We thought we would at least survive.
Q: This leader, Dr. Endre Balázs: was he sent to Auschwitz?
A: No.
Q: Where to?
A: To Switzerland on the Bergen-Belsen train.

On arrival at Auschwitz, Shmueli was separated from his wife, his mother, his daughter, and his grandchild; he was sent for slave labor in Warsaw. Only there did he learn that Auschwitz was a death camp and that his loved ones had been murdered.[7]

On the same train was David Rosner, a Labor Zionist who had been drafted into one of the Hungarian army's forced labor units. He had returned to Kolozsvár while on leave just before the ghetto was established at the beginning of May:

> Q: Did the people in Kolozsvár know anything about Auschwitz and about extermination?
> A: No.
> Q: Could you have left Kolozsvár if you had wanted?
> A: Yes, my mother lived in Turda [in Romania], 5 km from Kolozsvár.
> Q: Could you have gone over to her?
> A: Yes.
> Q: Could you also have gone back to your labor unit if you had wanted to?
> A: Yes. When the people were being loaded into the wagons I was put in charge of a wagon, and I had the chance to get out to bring water. . . . I was escorted by a Hungarian policeman who went with me to fetch water. The policeman told me: "Don't return to your wagon, because you belong in the labor unit." He knew that I was in the labor service from the insignia on my arm and head.
> Q: So what did you do?
> A: I told the policeman that we were allowed to go to Kenyérmező, and so I returned to the wagon.

This survivor relinquished a chance to avoid Auschwitz because he had been deceived about the destination. He was asked for further details:

> Q: What did you hear in the ghetto about Kenyérmező?
> A: I heard that in Kenyérmező there was an estate belonging to a landowner and I heard that the men would work and the women wouldn't.
> Q: Have you heard the name [Sámuel] Kohani?
> A: Yes. He stood on a platform the day before we were sent to Auschwitz and asked each of us to be obedient in the ghetto because the *Judenrat* promised the ghetto residents that they would be taken to Kenyérmező.
> Q: Was he speaking on behalf of the *Judenrat*?
> A: Yes.

Rosner was asked about the role of Kasztner:

> Q: Did you hear about him in the ghetto?
> A: Yes.
> Q: And what did you hear?
> A: That he was in control of the [local] *Judenrat*.

Rosner testified about a fellow Auschwitz inmate:

> Dr. Elkes was a neurologist in the Jewish hospital. When I was loading water into the wagon, I asked him: "Doctor, why do you have to go on the first train?" He answered: "We're preparing the health system in Kenyérmező and the first to go will get the best places...." When we were putting on prisoners' clothes together in Auschwitz, I said to him: "Doctor, you told us that we were going to Kenyérmező." Then he replied: "We were deceived."

In Auschwitz, Rosner and his family underwent the "selection" before Dr. Mengele. He was chosen for slave labor; his wife and child were sent to the gas chambers.[8]

Back in the ghetto, the deception of the Jewish masses continued without a pause. Jacob Freifeld, another Holocaust survivor, described what followed the first deportation:

> Kohani read out a letter saying that the first group had arrived in Kenyérmező, families would stay together, the old people were taking care of the children, the younger people were being sent to work. Housing and living conditions were decent compared to conditions in the ghetto.... He had some sort of paper in his hand. No-one knew what was written there, but he read from it. Next to him were the leaders of the *Judenrat*.

Freifeld, who had served in the Hungarian forced labor units, asked another ex-conscript for advice. It was the local manager of Kasztner's rescue committee:

> Since I had served for 18 months alongside Hillel Danzig, I approached him as a comrade.... I told him beforehand: "You're well aware that I just returned because I was sick and I wouldn't survive another ordeal like that." I asked him to tell me if there was any serious evidence for this letter. He replied that there was evidence and advised me to go, saying: "We know you'll be able to manage and you'll be able to rest." On this assurance, I left with the third train even though [as an ex-conscript] I would have had the right to leave with the final group.[9]

Freifeld joined his family on the deportation train, expecting to live in Kenyérmező; they too arrived in Auschwitz.

Danzig categorically denied Freifeld's allegation against him. But he confirmed that the spokesman of the city's *Judenrat*, Kohani, had spread the Kenyérmező story in the Kolozsvár Ghetto:

> I actually heard the Kenyérmező rumor many times. But I didn't confirm or try to confirm its accuracy to anyone. I'm quite careful to avoid spreading rumors when their accuracy isn't fully clear. I don't recall a meeting or a conversation, or even seeing Freifeld in the Kolozsvár Ghetto. His whole story that I advised him to hurry because we had learned a bitter lesson from our experience [as Hungarian labor conscripts] in Russia is totally incredible. I never expressed such a view.

According to Danzig's testimony, Kohani first heard the Kenyérmező story from a pair of Hungarians who called him to the ghetto fence under the watchful eye of a Hungarian gendarme; they were later identified as government agents. But this does not explain why Kasztner had been seen peddling the hoax on his May 3, 1944, visit. Nor does it account for the fake Kenyérmező letter that Kohani read out to the ghetto population.

Freifeld agreed that Danzig did not himself know the truth when he gave advice to board the death train. Danzig's account indicates that he too was a victim of deception:

> Q: Did you receive information from Fischer that the trains were heading for extermination?
> A: No.
> Q: Or that the trains were heading for Auschwitz?
> A: No. I remember the exact moment when the whole truth was revealed to me. ... The first person I met on reaching Budapest's Columbus Camp was [Kasztner's aide] Ernő Szilágyi. I asked him about the fate of my family, my parents and sisters [who had been held in a different ghetto]. He told me that they had all been sent to extermination in Auschwitz.[10]

It was Kasztner's aide in Budapest who had to enlighten the local manager of Kasztner's committee from Kolozsvár about the fate of the manager's family in Auschwitz.

The effects of the Kenyérmező deception on the victims were also witnessed by Levi Blum. He was waiting at a railway station when a train with thirty to forty wagons arrived from Kolozsvár:

> Suddenly a train full of people—children, old people, youngsters— pulled in. It was barred: each wagon had a gendarme, in other words a guard. ... I asked them: "Where are you heading?" They

answered: "We're going to Kenyérmező." I asked them: "How do you know that?" They replied: "We know that the ghetto personnel received postcards from Budapest. We're going to Kenyérmező to settle good sites for the others."[11]

Learning that his family members were still awaiting their departure from Kolozsvár, Blum decided to take advantage of the "opportunity" to travel with them to "Kenyérmező." He absconded from his labor unit—and hastened to enter the Kolozsvár Ghetto, where he would share their destiny.

Whenever doubts arose about the official line on the purpose of the trains, the leaders did their best to counter them. Anna Kőpich, a doctor, was deported to Auschwitz with her mother, her sister, and her child. Uncertain about the rumors disseminated by the authorities, she approached the ghetto commander Balázs and begged him to tell her the truth so that she could decide what to do. Balázs admitted that he did not really know the fate of the Jews boarding the trains—but promised her that whatever happened, she would still be able to work as a doctor. Based on this information, Dr. Kőpich made her "fateful mistake": she abandoned any thought of escape.

> The idea that our family would stay together gave me so much comfort that Balázs' version that the doctors would go to the great hospitals had become a certitude for me. And yet, the day our turn came, I was suddenly panic-stricken: what if everything was just a lie?

At this point Dr. Kőpich approached Balázs again and asked him to delay her departure from the ghetto:

> Then the knave read me a lecture about ethics, about the high mission of a physician. . . . "How could I let a whole transport [go] without medical assistance?" I felt ashamed and I no longer insisted. . . . The bastard . . . he knew he was sending us to death. . . . He was preaching about humaneness while he had his "passport" for Switzerland in his pocket. He was concerned with one thing alone: to evacuate the ghetto as quickly as possible and see himself in a train bound to the West.[12]

On arrival at Auschwitz, Dr. Köpich was separated from her mother and child, who were sent to the gas chambers. When she discovered their fate, she tried to commit suicide by throwing herself against the camp's electrified fence. Other inmates restrained her at the last moment.[13]

Paul Gross was sent to Auschwitz with eighty-seven family members, five of whom survived. Even when boarding the very last train from the Kolozsvár Ghetto, he and his loved ones were oblivious to the horrors awaiting them:

> Q: Did you hear about Kenyérmező?
> A: Only about Kenyérmező.
> Q: From whom did you hear officially?
> A: There was one man named Kohani. . . . When we were together in the ghetto, we heard from him that a postcard had arrived and he read it to the various groups in the camp; this postcard came from Kenyérmező. There was also a [Hungarian] gendarme, Urbán, who was an officer in charge of the ghetto; he told us officially to be quiet and obedient because we were being transported to Kenyérmező.

To encourage Jews to board the trains, the Hungarian gendarmes made sure that living conditions in the ghettos were intolerable. The overcrowding, starvation rations, and unsanitary environment were conducive to the spread of disease. In Kolozsvár, the outcome was an epidemic of typhus. As a member of the Jewish ghetto administration, Gross was in a position to observe the flurry of activity that ensued:

> After typhus broke out, the head of the city health department. . . gave instructions to stop the trains and quarantine the camp. I heard [Urbán] whispering to Balázs and was able to overhear part of the conversation. When Urbán said that there was a quarantine, Balázs replied: "The trains must go on, since we [i.e., the Kasztner Train group] can't proceed with our journey before that."[14]

The prerequisite for boarding the Kasztner Train was the smooth evacuation of the ghetto population on the "Kenyérmező" trains. Kasztner's colleagues were so committed to this task that when the non-Jewish city health inspector used the pretext of an epidemic to halt the deportation, the Jewish ghetto leader successfully lobbied the Hungarian authorities to thwart the rescue attempt.[15] And so the trains to Auschwitz continued.

What is the explanation for these shocking actions? Did the community leaders in Kolozsvár decide to hasten the deportation of eighteen thousand Jewish men, women, and children to "Kenyérmező" on their own initiative? Or were they following the instructions of their "rescuer" in Budapest?

"Eichmann Wanted No Fuss"

The original 1946 version of Kasztner's book-length report, the *Bericht*, includes an important passage. Describing his negotiations with Eichmann about the Kolozsvár Ghetto, Kasztner explained that he wanted to leave the compilation of the Kasztner Train group to the local *Judenrat*. However, Eichmann objected:

> *He said that this would lead to murder in the ghetto. He wanted no fuss*, otherwise "it's impossible to hold up the notion of a 'Zionist conspiracy' [i.e., the German pretext for the Kasztner Train] to the Hungarians." So a list had to be drawn up. [Emphases added.]

Thus Eichmann informed Kasztner that the precondition of their agreement was avoiding "murder in the ghetto" by making sure that there would be "no fuss." And what was Kasztner's response to this demand? Explaining how the list was compiled, Kasztner adds the following apologetic remark:

> The accusation that mostly the rich were saved, because they could afford their rescue, is totally false. *Only a few people in Klausenburg [Kolozsvár] knew how and why they came to be in a special transport. The "rescue secret" had to be kept.* [Emphases added.][16]

The meaning of the final sentences is horrendous. Kasztner is confessing here that he obeyed Eichmann's orders to prevent "murder in the ghetto" and to guarantee that "no fuss" would occur there.

The admission that "the 'rescue secret' had to be kept" is the smoking gun that proves Kasztner's complicity in the deception of the Jewish population of Kolozsvár. If the candidates for the "special transport" could not be allowed to learn that they were being rescued (or given a temporary reprieve) from destruction in Auschwitz, then the ordinary Jews in the ghetto could not be allowed to learn that they were being condemned to destruction in Auschwitz. If Kasztner had to mislead the hostages about the fate of the murder victims, then he also had to mislead the murder victims about their fate. It was impossible to deceive the few while informing the many: the deception had to be total. Otherwise, the fury and despair of those destined for the gas chambers would have provoked violent struggles for places on the Kasztner Train—"murder in the ghetto," in Eichmann's words. Keeping the rescue secret meant keeping the extermination secret and deceiving the entire population of the Kolozsvár Ghetto about the purpose of the deportations to Auschwitz.[17]

Kasztner fulfilled his commitment to Eichmann. After the war, his friends among the Jewish leadership in Kolozsvár insisted that they had not perceived the "special transport" as a rescue train while they were in the ghetto. Kasztner had told them that it was simply a vehicle for those holding British entry certificates for Palestine. In the words of Dezső Hermann, the deputy secretary of the city's *Judenrat*:

> The idea of deportation to Auschwitz never occurred to us and the danger of the destruction of Hungarian Jewry never crossed my mind, so I didn't join the escape. Our thoughts weren't about destruction and crematoria but about the ordeal of labor units. In our eyes the transport wasn't for rescue but for *aliya*, so we wanted to join it in order to make *aliya* to Palestine via Spain. In those days an opportunity for *aliya* was very attractive given the cruel conditions we were living under. . . . So the decision wasn't whether to rescue 380 out of 18,000 but whether to take them for *aliya*, because there was no perception of destruction, there was a perception of danger but no perception of destruction.[18]

In other words, candidates for the Kasztner Train in the Kolozsvár Ghetto were told that the purpose of the transport was immigration to Palestine, not salvation from the gas chambers of Auschwitz. Kasztner had been repeatedly informed by the Nazis that Jewish emigrants from Hungary could go almost anywhere *except* Palestine. But he had to create the illusion of a "Zionist transport" in obedience to the SS demand to prevent "murder in the ghetto." The "rescue secret" had to be kept so that the deportations would proceed with "no fuss," as stipulated by Eichmann.

It is therefore clear that when the Nazis arranged on ten occasions for telephone contact between Kasztner and Kolozsvár, his mandate was to ensure the efficient liquidation of the ghetto. Whether or not Kasztner told his father-in-law the truth about the death trains (a core issue of the Kasztner Trial) is immaterial: what is important is that Kasztner knew the truth and that he told his (witting or unwitting) accomplices on the scene to prevent panic during the deportation. If Fischer, Balázs, and colleagues believed the Kenyérmező fiction, then they had every reason to ensure the peaceful transfer of the masses and then proceed on their own expected journey to freedom. If, on the other hand, they knew or suspected the awful truth[19]—and Kasztner's remark that "only a few people" in Kolozsvár understood the "rescue secret" implies that he did not keep *all* of the community leaders in the dark—then they knew that missing the Kasztner Train would be a death sentence. The action of Balázs, the ghetto leader, in overcoming the suspension of the death trains due to medical quarantine shows the extent of his determination to send other people to "Kenyérmező" so that he could avoid going there himself. But whatever was in the minds of Kasztner's minions in Kolozsvár, one point is certain: Kasztner himself obeyed Eichmann's instructions to facilitate the deportation of the city's Jewish population to Auschwitz.

The Rescue Leader's Collaboration

If a few of Kasztner's contacts in Kolozsvár *knowingly* deceived their fellow Jews at his behest, it was only because the lives of their own families were at stake. These men were desperate and they fought for themselves and their loved ones without ethics or scruples. The totalitarian system did not allow them the moral "luxury" of choosing between good and evil. Instead they had to choose between different evils: they could either sacrifice their community to save their families or sacrifice their families to save part of their community. In a criminal trial, they could undoubtedly have raised the defense of duress. Is the same type of mitigation available to Kasztner?

It is important to distinguish Kasztner's actions from those of his agents or dupes on the scene. Kasztner was in charge of the national rescue committee. In that capacity, he had built close relations with the SS from the beginning of the occupation, despite his anticipation (soon reinforced by concrete evidence) of the impending fate of the Jewish masses. He converted the rescue committee from an under-ground network into a client institution under the official protection of the murderers. From the outset he disobeyed the Jewish Agency's orders to lead an information and resistance campaign—and when the Zionist youth continued their illegal missions regardless, he did his best to neutralize their efforts. He preferred to bargain with the *Eichmann-Kommando*. His "negotiations" were ideal for the Nazi project of destroying the Jewish population under the camouflage of rescue opportunities. If Kasztner's men in Kolozsvár were under duress, he was the vehicle for the duress. Whatever mitigating factors arise in their case do not apply to his deeds.

Kasztner sabotaged rescue opportunities in the Kolozsvár Ghetto and abetted the mass murder of its Jews in two ways: by paralyzing the escape effort with disinformation about the reinforcement of the guard at the border; and by encouraging the ghetto leaders to reassure the victims with lies about resettlement inside Hungary. The result of these actions was the efficient deportation of eighteen thousand innocent people to Auschwitz. There the vast majority were murdered on arrival. This included all those judged unfit for slave labor: children, their mothers, pregnant women, the elderly, the sick, and the disabled. Many of the able-bodied adults who survived the initial "selection" were systematically worked to death or murdered by other means.

The Auschwitz inmates from Kolozsvár soon realized that they had been betrayed. Otto Kornis described their reaction as the final deportation train from the ghetto reached the death camp. There was outrage when it was discovered that the Jewish VIPs who had encouraged them to hurry to "Kenyérmező" were not on board:

> Where did those people go?
> The internees shouted angrily, clenching their fists:
> "We'll show them after the war!"
> "They made a deal with the murderers!"
> "So they knew what was expecting us. We've been tricked."
> "The bastards!"[20]

The survivors did not forget. As soon as they returned from the camps, they demanded the prosecution of Kasztner and the former ghetto leaders as war criminals.[21]

But Kasztner was nowhere to be found. With the murderers defeated at the end of the war, neither Kasztner nor his accomplices ever again set foot in Kolozsvár.

Notes

1. Kasztner Trial testimony, March 2, 1954.
2. Bauer, *Jews for Sale?*, 151.
3. Shlomo Aronson, "Israel Kasztner: Rescuer in Nazi-Occupied Europe, Prosecutor at Nuremberg and Accused at Home," in *The Holocaust: The Unique and the Universal: Essays Presented in Honor of Yehuda Bauer*, eds. Shmuel Almog, David Bankier, Daniel Blatman, and Dalia Ofer (Jerusalem: Yad Vashem, 2001), 2.
4. Bilsky, *Transformative Justice*, 21–22.
5. Kasztner Trial testimony, March 1, 1954.
6. Kasztner Trial testimony, September 16, 1954.
7. Kasztner Trial testimony, June 13, 1954. For similar recollections of the speech by Balázs, see Sámuel Sámuel, "Útunk Auschwitzba [Our Journey to Auschwitz]," in *Memorial Volume for the Jews of Cluj-Kolozsvár* (New York: Moshe Carmilly-Weinberger, 1970), 241; Oliver Lustig, *Blood-Bespotted Diary* (Bucharest: Editura Ştiinţifică si Enciclopedică, 1988), 312.
8. Kasztner Trial testimony, June 18, 1954.
9. Kasztner Trial testimony, June 28, 1954.

10. Kasztner Trial testimony, August 15, 1954.
11. Kasztner Trial testimony, June 25, 1954.
12. Lustig, *Blood-Bespotted Diary*, 215–16.
13. Ibid., 218.
14. Kasztner Trial testimony, June 21, 1954.
15. According to another ghetto inmate, "[the] leaders of Kasztner's group . . . were afraid that they would not be able to get to Budapest on time to make their Swiss connection. Therefore, they persuaded the competent people to lift the quarantine." Nussbächer, *Sentenced to Live*, 29.
16. Kasztner, *Bericht*, 46. The location of this passage implies that Eichmann issued the instructions on or shortly after June 3, but Kasztner is dissembling here: if Eichmann had to prevent "fuss" in the ghetto, he had to do so throughout its existence. He probably made his wishes known to Kasztner in one of their first private meetings during the week of May 20–26. Kasztner's final testimony at the Kasztner Trial on September 16, 1954 ("I learned the whole truth at the end of May from Eichmann") suggests that the crucial discussions took place in that week: there were no meetings during May 27–June 1, 1944, as he was under arrest by the Hungarians.
17. For elaboration of this point, see Kasztner Trial verdict, ss. 43–44, 59; Beit-Zvi, *Post-Ugandan Zionism on Trial*, Vol. 2, 115. Judge Halevi thinks that Eichmann made his terms explicit; Beit-Zvi disagrees.
18. Kasztner Trial testimony, March 15, 1954. See also Hermann's interview with Braham on October 8, 1972, cited in Braham, "What Did They Know and When?", 32, 46n32.
19. Fischer, Hermann and Danzig were aware of the Holocaust before the Nazi occupation of Hungary. Danzig admitted his awareness of Auschwitz but claimed that he fell for the Kenyérmező hoax anyway: see his Kasztner Trial testimony, August 15, 1954. Hansi Brand found it "inconceivable" that they were fooled: see Braham, "What Did They Know and When?", 46n33.
20. Lustig, *Blood-Bespotted Diary*, 200. In addition to the Auschwitz survivors who described the role of the Kolozsvár *Judenrat* in spreading the Kenyér-mező deception, a ghetto inmate who later joined the Kasztner Train mentions it: Ladislaus Löb, *Dealing with Satan: Rezső Kasztner's Daring Rescue Mission* (London: Jonathan Cape, 2008), 48.
21. Yosef Krausz, Kasztner Trial testimony, June 17, 1954; David Rosner, Kasztner Trial testimony, June 18, 1954.

8

Sabotaging Rescue
in the Ghettos

The Nazis were eager to use their methods of deception in ghettos all over Hungary. To do this, they had to prevent the activation of the Zionist rescue network that had been built up so carefully before the occupation.

The most straightforward way to neutralize the Zionists was to arrest or kill the core rescue activists in the capital. The Nazis did indeed capture many young Zionists who set out to warn the provincial Jewish communities or smuggle people across the borders.[1] Also caught in the dragnet were high-ranking figures such as Moshe Schweiger, who had been appointed by the Jewish Agency to plan resistance to the Germans.

Total suppression of the rescuers, however, would merely have driven them underground. Far more promising than seeking to crush the rescue operation was the strategy of co-opting its leader. In this way the SS could abort illegal activity at the embryonic stage. The impact of this policy on the struggle to save Jews in Subcarpathia and North Transylvania was tragic.

Kasztner on Illegal Rescue

For hundreds of thousands of ordinary Jews in the provinces—those not selected for the Kasztner Train—the sole hope of survival lay in illegal rescue actions: warning the victims and provoking mass flight. What was Kasztner's attitude to such actions? On this point we have his answers under cross-examination in Jerusalem:

> The *Judenrat* body handling the provincial towns was a Zionist body working in connection with us. . . . The body, which the [rescue] committee was involved in creating, served as a telephone link to other places as far as possible. . . .[2] It's true that the issue of being able to make a telephone call was just a technical question. I couldn't impose it on a committee member who was less busy, so we created the body to maintain contact with the provincial towns.

Kasztner elaborated:

> Censorship permitting, we could have a telephone conversation between the body and the provincial towns. . . . I didn't because I didn't have time as I was busy. . . . Besides Kolozsvár, I didn't personally telephone any of the provincial towns.[3]

So Kasztner insisted that he had been too busy to make any phone calls. This was in spite of the fact that on ten occasions he found the time to receive calls from his father-in-law in Kolozsvár.

What about visiting the provinces in person? Kasztner's testimony on this point is no less instructive:

> Besides Kolozsvár, I did not visit the provincial towns. . . . It was forbidden for a Jew to travel at the time. For Kolozsvár I received special permission. . . . *I could request such permission to go to other provincial towns* [emphasis added]. . . . I don't remember if any other committee members visited other provincial towns.[4]

Just as he could have used the telephone, Kasztner could have visited the provincial Jews with permission from his Hungarian opposite numbers.

Kasztner failed to tell Jews in the ghettos about Auschwitz and arrange their escape—and he tried to prevent others from doing so. As Zionist youth leader Rafi Benshalom explained, even before the deportations Kasztner was already "opposed in principle" to illegal rescue missions to the provinces.[5] Once the deportations were under way, he issued an ultimatum to the activists:

> Following our first successes, the *"tiyul"* [cross-border flight] had hit a sandbank and many members [of the youth movements] were lost. The question then arose whether we would be better off rejecting the *"tiyul"* issue and sending our people via groups of emigrants [under the deal with the SS]. *Kastner demanded we make a decision* [emphasis added]. Nevertheless, we remained constant and were never taken in by the "wider concept" [of negotiations with the SS].[6]

Benshalom records a significant fact: at the height of the deportations, when thousands were being sent to Auschwitz each day, Kasztner attempted to stop the illegal Zionist rescue missions.

Sabotaging the Zionist Warnings

When Kasztner failed to halt the illegal rescue missions altogether, he still found ways to limit their scope and effectiveness. The most important was ensuring that the activists had no actual information to impart if they tried to motivate the victims to flee. Here the central factor was Kasztner's suppression of the Auschwitz news.

Some of the young Zionists who embarked on missions to the provincial towns were aware of the fate of Jews under Nazi rule in Poland and elsewhere. From this they inferred that the fate of Jews under Nazi rule in Hungary would be similar. But this only gave rise to a plausible *opinion*; it was not *information*.

In contrast, weeks before the mass deportations began, Kasztner had concrete information about the Nazi plans for Hungarian Jewry, including an eye-witness warning (conveyed from Bratislava) that the deportees would be gassed in Auschwitz and the news that thousands of deportees (from the Kistarcsa and Topolya camps) had already been sent there. These facts could and should have been shared with the rescue activists before they traveled to the provinces. Instead they were deprived of information.

The Zionists who arrived in the provincial communities displayed no knowledge of the evidence already available to the head of the rescue committee. Their postwar accounts do not even mention the Auschwitz Protocols—the eye-witness account of the escapees Rudolf Vrba and Alfred Wetzler—let alone instructions to spread the news in the ghettos.[7]

This was a tragic missed opportunity. According to David Gur, a specialist on the rescue efforts of the Hungarian Zionist youth movements, during the first months of the Nazi occupation "at least 55 emissaries visited 97 cities and labor camps. All told—104 missions."[8] Lacking solid information, these messengers could only hazard their opinions on the likely fate of the Jewish masses—opinions based on the precedents in the other Nazi-occupied countries.

Immediately before deportations began in Kassa (now Košice), for example, a Zionist messenger addressed a group of young people in the ghetto:

> I warn you that at this very moment, Jews are being deported from other ghettos in the country. They are being taken *probably to Germany or possibly to occupied Poland* [emphasis added], where death or slave labor awaits them. . . . The camp at Kenyérmező is a fiction, but your parents would never listen to me. . . . Those who have Zion in their hearts will take the chance on freedom instead of sure slavery or death.[9]

For all his courage and sincerity, this messenger was unable to accomplish his mission because he had no actual information. He understood that the destination of the trains was not Kenyérmező, but he did not know that it was in fact Auschwitz. His warning lacked credibility because it was an expression of opinion—not information. That night, the ghetto authorities issued an announcement of their own:

> Tomorrow morning you will be transferred to Kenyérmező, which is good news. . . a false rumor appears to have been spread saying that you will be taken out of the country. This is a Zionist lie. They are the ones who take Jews out of the country, not us. Do not listen to them, and do not try to escape from the factory. From now on, anyone who approaches the fence will be shot without warning by the gendarmes on patrol.[10]

For tormented young people who were being urged to abandon their families and brave the wrath of the authorities by fleeing the ghetto, the difference between "probably" or "possibly" being taken to Germany or Poland and the *factual certainty of being delivered to the gas chambers of Auschwitz* proved decisive. Of course, inmates who had not heard the messenger's opinion were even less inclined to defy the gendarmes, especially after postcards from "Kenyérmező" began to arrive in the ghetto.[11] As a result, they obediently entered the trains that carried them, unawares, to their deaths.

As the last Jews were being deported from Kassa, two more Zionist messengers arrived from Budapest. They learned that the ghetto was being liquidated and the people transferred to an "unknown destination." Finding a deportation train still waiting near the station, the rescue activists opened several wagons and exhorted those inside to flee. The results were disheartening: the victims refused to panic, since they expected to be taken "to live in a new place." The two Zionists became increasingly desperate:

> "Save yourselves! Whoever escapes has a chance to live! In many places Jews have escaped and they are hiding in special shelters. You must understand that they are taking you to your death!" we shouted, but saw that our words fell on deaf ears, perhaps on hearts bursting with fear. In addition to the despair, we sensed anger from the leaders of the community who had over the last months ignored the warnings and had instructed the masses of Jews to believe in false promises.

In spite of their apprehensions, the activists were too uninformed even at this late stage to enlighten the victims about the "unknown destination." Finally, someone—probably one of the Jewish leaders—emerged from a wagon and ordered the Zionists to close the doors and leave; otherwise he would call the guards.[12] Thus the rescue mission ended in failure—not least because the activists had been given none of the specific facts that might have dispelled the optimistic beliefs of the public. Of twelve thousand Jews deported from Kassa to Auschwitz, only four hundred and fifty returned after the war.[13]

One of these Zionist messengers also traveled to Dés (now Dej) in order to rescue a colleague's mother and sister. In the ghetto he urged the women to escape immediately because they were in "real danger." His warning contained no news about Auschwitz or gas chambers. His mother and sister chose to share the destiny of the other Jews. Next the messenger proceeded to a nearby collection camp. In this camp (it "was not fenced and there were no guards to be seen") he told the inmates:

> I have come from Budapest. I am a representative of the Zionist Movement. Real danger awaits you. At any moment you may be sent to *an unknown destination*. It's *doubtful* if you'll return alive [emphases added]. It's possible for you to escape. I brought you documents and money. The moment you reach the capital, we will help you find shelter. Many others have escaped, you are not the first.

The response to this warning was equally predictable: "Everyone says that we are going to be taken to a work camp." The Zionist insisted that it was a hoax. He added: "We already know what has happened to Jews in countries that were captured by the Germans." But this merely provoked the complaint that "you're bringing danger to all of us." The Zionist returned in a state of despondency to Budapest, where his fellow messengers reported similar experiences. They soon heard that the Jewish population of Dés had been loaded onto trains and sent to "an unknown destination."[14] In total, more than seven thousand seven hundred Jews were deported from this ghetto to Auschwitz.

Another Zionist activist traveled to Nyíregyháza in northeast Hungary, bringing false identification papers and money to facilitate flight from the ghetto. Apparently, this messenger was just as ignorant as his counterparts elsewhere in the country with respect to the impending slaughter of the Jews. A young woman who heard what the messenger had to say later recalled:

> The transports started to leave. We did not know that it meant total physical extermination. We knew that it meant an ordeal, but escape also posed many difficult dangers, and we preferred to be in the ordeal together.[15]

In other words, having encountered the rescue activist from Budapest, this ghetto inmate was none the wiser about the Nazi plans. Instead of using the false papers and funds to escape with her family, she decided to join them on the deportation train. More than fifteen thousand two hundred Jews were concentrated in Nyíregyháza before the ghetto population was sent to Auschwitz.[16]

These examples show that the Zionist messengers to the ghettos were told nothing about the Auschwitz Protocols or the destination of the trains. Although they expressed their *opinions* based on events in the surrounding countries, none of them had concrete *information* about the Nazi plans for Hungarian Jewry. Yet the vital information (the messages from Bratislava) had been available to Kasztner for weeks.

An inadvertent confession by Kasztner that he not only failed to keep the rescue activists informed but also allowed them to be misled by Nazi disinformation is found in his Israeli trial testimony. He suddenly made an astonishing claim:

> In Budapest we heard the rumors circulated by the Hungarians and the Germans, we heard slightly later and tried to check the rumors. *Komoly wrote in his diary that the Kenyérmező news was apparently confirmed: he wrote this around mid-June* [emphasis added]. It's just typical of the atmosphere of false rumors and speculation that we had.[17]

No such entry can be found in Komoly's diary, but the comment is revealing nonetheless. If Kasztner let the chairman of his own committee believe that the Jews gassed in Auschwitz were alive and well in Kenyérmező—which even the uninformed Zionist messengers had identified as a fiction—then this in itself is enough to establish his role in disrupting the warning effort.

Case Studies in Deception

While the head of the rescue committee did his best to stop illegal rescue missions and suppressed information that might have rendered warnings credible, the deception of the victims proceeded without hindrance. In countless ghettos, the SS and the gendarmes spread rumors about "resettlement inside the country for work." Meanwhile local Jewish leaders tried to prevent panic.

Claims have been made that the Jewish masses in the Hungarian ghettos were fully informed about the Final Solution but refused to believe it.[18] Such arguments are contradicted by the testimony of members of the rescue committee. Brand, for example, mentioned the matter to his British interrogators at the height of the deportations in June 1944: Hungarian Jews, he explained, "thought that deportation meant just another place of work; they would not realise that it meant death."[19] Kasztner made the same point in a letter he wrote in July 1944, just days after the suspension of the deportations: "the hundreds of thousands went to Auschwitz in such a way that they were unaware until the last moment of what it meant and what was going on. We, who knew it, tried to stop it," but were unable to achieve much.[20] Kasztner repeated this conclusion in his postwar report, the *Bericht*, where he noted that in every ghetto the Jews were convinced until the last moment that the trains would not leave Hungary.[21] In short, the Jewish masses were not informed that ghettos meant deportation, and that deportation meant death. Indeed, Holocaust testimonies from Hungary are full of accounts of victims who lost the chance to flee because they were misled about their fate.

The largest Jewish community in the provinces was Nagyvárad (now Oradea). Béla Zsolt, a famous Jewish intellectual who was already familiar with the realities of the Holocaust, commented on the remarkable success of the deception scheme in this ghetto:

> Surprisingly, the majority of the people believed the rumour, spread by the ghetto command with calculated malice, that we would be taken to a labour camp near Lake Balaton to drain swamps and help with the harvest. Very few here knew where we were really going.[22]

When the deportation commenced, the victims actually struggled for the best places on the train, such was their ignorance of the true destination:

> [The Jews] charged the wagons, pushing and shoving desperately, as though they were absolutely determined not to be left behind. . . . The gendarmes, who had been prepared to force the Jews into the wagons, stood behind them with their hands on their hips, watching in motionless amazement as they filled the wagons of their own accord.[23]

Yosef Katz, a lawyer, was one of tens of thousands deported from this city to Auschwitz. He described the deception of the population by means of rumors that were endorsed by the local *Judenrat*:

> After three weeks [in the ghetto], when the trains started leaving, it was said that people were now going to Kenyérmező, that there was a big camp, and that all the Jews would stay there until the end of the war—and there was no-one who said otherwise. . . . I had been in labor

camps, and I was familiar with the Nazis' methods and their lies. So I said: "You must not believe this lie!" And there was someone there from the Jewish leadership who said that I was inciting the public and they would have to report me to the authorities.

Katz was warned to stop his "incitement," put under guard by the *Judenrat*, and taken for interrogation by the gendarmes. Similar treatment was meted out to any other Jew who questioned the Kenyérmező hoax and tried to warn people. Katz described the orderly deportation from his community:

> The people thought they were going to Kenyérmező, where they would stay until the end of the war. Even those who had doubts didn't know exactly. . . . I hid a small saw in my bread with three other Jews. When I boarded the wagon I was told by the man in charge: "What do I say in Kenyérmező if I'm missing three Jews?"[24]

The Jews of Nagyvárad were confined to two ghettos. According to Katz, they were guarded by forty to fifty gendarmes. Yet these ghettos imprisoned a total of thirty-five thousand people.[25] As a result of the deception policy, the authorities were able to carry out the deportation at minimal cost in manpower.

The disinformation had similar effects in many other communities. In Ungvár (now Uzhhorod), seventeen thousand Jews were held. Martin Földi, a member of the ghetto's administrative committee, was personally assured by the Gestapo that people would be taken to work in normal conditions and that families would remain together. He then received instructions from the local *Judenrat* to draw up a list of transferees, who were expected to volunteer for the first train:

> Inside the ghetto there was a loudspeaker and we requested those persons who wished to leave together to come to the office to register. Whole families reported, or one member of a family who gave us a list of all the members of the family, their relatives and friends. There was an official there, he was also a Jew and in fact one of us, who recorded and drew up the list. On the following day there was a roll-call and all the people were divided into sections of 50 or 52 persons—approximately 1,500 to 2,000 people in all.[26]

These Jews, needless to say, were all deported to Auschwitz. The impact of the deception on members of the Jewish public is recorded in a typical survivor account:

> [In the ghetto] rumour had it that we would be taken to work, and now our greatest worry was to remain together with our families.

I do not know of anyone who attempted to escape from the ghetto [emphasis added]. . . . [When the deportations began] they announced through a microphone the names of heads of families, and these people had to be ready with their families by the following day. . . . They said that we would stay within Hungary, also the officials said the same.[27]

This ghetto had an underground courier service to send news to the Jewish leadership in the capital; presumably, the couriers could have brought back accurate information and warnings *from* the capital.[28] In spite of that fact, the deception effort in this community was so effective that, apparently, local Jewish leaders were induced to participate in organizing the deportations.

In Felsővisó (now Vişeu de Sus), twelve thousand Jews had been concentrated on the pretext of relocation for work. Here, as elsewhere, the victims had never heard of Auschwitz. After the first train left, there was a temptation to flee the ghetto, but the local *Judenrat* insisted that everything was "under control" and that the people were being taken to a site inside Hungary. The assurance was reinforced by the standard Nazi postcard deception. Among those deported on the third train were Rudolph Tessler and his family:

In [Felsővisó] we were told that the card was confirmation of what the [*Judenrat*] elders had been telling us. But, as we would soon find out, it was not true . . .

Ironically, the member of the *Judenrat* who had shown us the postcard was taken to Auschwitz on the fourth transport. He tried to kill himself when he found out what was happening. He took cyanide but was saved and carried to Auschwitz on a stretcher. He realized that he could have saved us by letting us run away.[29]

Tessler was deported along with his parents, brothers, sisters, aunts, uncles, and cousins. Not until they reached the border junction and the train turned toward Poland did the deportees from this ghetto understand that they had been deceived. But it was impossible to escape from the sealed wagons.

In Máramarossziget (now Sighetu Marmaţiei), another twelve thousand Jews were confined. Among them were the young Elie Wiesel and his family. After the departure of the first train, their non-Jewish servant successfully infiltrated the ghetto and beseeched them to escape to a shelter that she had prepared. The Wiesel family debated the options.

In their eyes, the choice was not between life and death but between abandoning the community and sharing its destiny:

> We surely would have accepted her offer had we known that "destination unknown" meant Birkenau—or even simply that we would be deported from the country. But we didn't know. All we knew was what we had been told: that the convoys were headed for the interior. "Well-informed" Jewish notables in Budapest had given clear assurances on this point.

As usual, the rumors disseminated inside the ghetto alleged that the Jews would be sent to a labor camp inside Hungary where families would stay together. Accordingly, the Wiesel family decided to reject the offer of shelter. Their would-be savior had infiltrated the ghetto in vain.[30] Wiesel, his parents, and three sisters were deported to Auschwitz; his mother and youngest sister were immediately sent to the gas chamber and his father died on a subsequent death march.

In Marosvásárhely (now Târgu Mureş), over seven thousand Jews had been concentrated. One of them, Lajos Erdélyi's father, managed to find his way out of the ghetto:

> he ducked under the barbed wire unnoticed by his dozy guards, and brought me three yellow dandelions to mark my birthday. A horrible thought: one might risk the barbed wire for three little flowers—and nobody during three weeks of ghetto living even attempted an escape, to flee from our approaching tragedy. We believed the lies of being taken to a town called Kenyérmező . . .[31]

The deception not only endangered those able-bodied adults who might have escaped; it also amounted to a death sentence on the weakest. In this ghetto, a policeman approached a Jewish family and offered to protect and raise one of the children as his own. Unaware of the Nazi plans, the family decided not to part with the seven-year-old—who died in the gas chambers a few weeks later.[32]

Was Kasztner involved in spreading Nazi disinformation in these ghettos? Did he organize the distribution of fake letters and postcards to substantiate the reassuring lies of the authorities? There is every reason to believe that Eichmann's injunction to ensure "no fuss" in the ghettos and Kasztner's policy of keeping the "rescue secret"—hence the extermination secret—applied throughout the provinces. On this point there is some second-hand evidence. Dr. Lily Zamir's father was concentrated in Huszt (now Chust) with another eleven thousand

Jews; from the ghetto, he succeeded in contacting Kasztner (either by courier or by telephone). According to Dr. Zamir,

> forty-eight hours before being deported from Huszt to Auschwitz, he consulted Kasztner about whether to escape to Romania through the Carpathians. The answer was: "As sure as the sun shines every morning, no harm will come to you, the worst is behind us." My father, his first wife and their 9-year-old daughter did not run away and two days later they were on the train to Auschwitz.[33]

Another fact is suggestive: the "Kenyérmező" letters were not only sent to the provinces but also received by deportees' relatives in Budapest.[34] Here the ban on Jewish travel was no barrier to spreading the truth; yet in spite of his knowledge that the letters were part of the deception, Kasztner made no effort to discredit them. It is worth recalling his admission (quoted earlier) that even though he knew the truth, he allowed the chairman of his own rescue committee to believe in the Kenyérmező deception as late as mid-June 1944.

Human Costs of Rescue Sabotage

During the deportations from Subcarpathia and North Transylvania, two more Jews, Arnost Rosin and Czesław Mordowicz, escaped from Auschwitz. Like Vrba and Wetzler before them, the pair fled to Slovakia, where they contacted Jewish leaders. They reported that since mid-May, thousands of Hungarian Jews had been arriving at the death camp every day. Only 10 percent of these Jews were registered as inmates; the other 90 percent were murdered on arrival. "Never," they stated, "had so many Jews been gassed since the establishment of Birkenau." Although the ovens "worked day and night" to dispose of the bodies, these were inadequate for the purpose, so pits measuring 30 m long and 15 m wide had been dug in the nearby forest and the corpses burned in them. Thus the "exterminating capacity" of the camp had become "almost unlimited."[35]

There is no way to calculate exactly how many of these Jewish men, women, and children might have survived but for Kasztner's interference with the rescue campaign. He was certainly to blame for the collapse of the escape effort in Kolozsvár on the day of the ghetto's formation; and he helped to spread false rumors there during the deportations to Auschwitz. It is a fact that he did his best to prevent efforts to expose the deception in the other ghettos; and after failing to stop the warning missions altogether, he rendered them ineffective by withholding his vital information from the messengers. There is also the suspicion that he organized the distribution of fake letters and postcards to several ghettos from Budapest. Given the proximity of these communities to the border, the existence of the smuggling network in Romania, and the limited time and manpower available to Eichmann's SS unit, the preventable losses were probably substantial.

It is not unthinkable that tens of thousands of lives in the border areas would have been saved by an underground Zionist campaign coordinated by the rescue committee in Budapest. This is consistent with the accounts of Holocaust survivors. Concerning the Kolozsvár Ghetto, Paul Gross asserted:

> If we had known that we weren't going to Kenyérmező . . . and if we had known that we were being sent to Auschwitz for extermination, then more than half of the 18,000 [in the Kolozsvár Ghetto] could have survived. The city of Turda was just a few kilometers from us; the Romanians were there; and in that case we could have saved people.[36]

Eliezer Rosenthal came to a similar conclusion about the Nagyvárad Ghetto:

> The border was 3, 4, 5 km away . . . . There were families who asked to have the children sent to them [in Romania], but the mothers took the children with them into the ghetto. I have personal knowledge of countless cases. But they missed the opportunity . . . . There was a big sewer passing through the ghetto area and many succeeded in escaping through this sewer. I don't want to exaggerate, but if we had known the fate awaiting us, many thousands could have escaped this way because the sewer exit was in the direction of the forest.[37]

Escape opportunities existed in other communities near the border. Arnold Dávid Finkelstein, the rescue activist who organized the cross-border smuggling of hundreds of Hungarian Jews, recalled various spontaneous escape efforts from North Transylvania. He described how a single Jew from Szatmárnémeti (now Satu Mare) moved his own family to Romania and then returned three times in order to smuggle another thirty-eight Jews from this town. According to Finkelstein, nine out of every ten escapees managed to cross the border safely, without being intercepted by guards.[38]

Kasztner's own beliefs about the human costs of the deception can be ascertained from his words at the time. In the second half of June he was approached by two Zionist paratroopers sent from Palestine to organize Jewish resistance to the Nazis. The surviving paratrooper, Yoel Palgi, remembered Kasztner's description of the deportations:

> He spoke of things done here that made my hair stand on end. *Hundreds of thousands of Jews were led astray* by the words of their leaders who promised them that they were being taken to labor camps inside Hungary's borders with decent conditions [emphasis added]. These leaders knew full well the fate awaiting those taken, but hoped to save their own lives in this way. So the Hungarian Jews went to the slaughter without even raising their voices in protest.[39]

The significance of this statement lies not in Kasztner's charges against the local Jewish leaders (which may well have been an unfair generalization from the record of his agents in Kolozsvár) but in his estimate of the numbers who perished because they did not know the truth.

The "Paradoxical Protection" of the SS

The importance that the Nazis attached to Kasztner's committee was underlined by an incident that began on May 27. On that day, the Hungarian secret police raided a print shop and two apartments used by the Zionist underground, seizing foreign funds and identity papers forged by the Zionist youth for the purpose of smuggling refugees. They promptly arrested the Zionist smuggling operatives as well as Kasztner, Hansi Brand, and several members of their committee. Hansi Brand was confronted with the printer of the forged papers, who had been beaten almost beyond recognition; then she too was tortured by interrogators bent on discovering the truth about her husband's mission to Istanbul. In spite of her ordeal, she did not reveal the "Reich secret" of the Jewish rescue committee's negotiations with the Germans behind the back of the Hungarian regime.

What followed was a concerted Nazi campaign to secure the release of Kasztner and his colleagues. First Krumey appealed to the Hungarian secret police on behalf of the *Eichmann-Kommando*. Clages also intervened on behalf of the Gestapo. Finally, all other means having failed, Ambassador Veesenmayer, Hitler's representative, contacted Prime Minister Sztójay on June 1 with a single demand: free Kasztner's committee.[40]

While the Zionist youth activists vanished into the black hole of the secret police prisons, the committee members were released forthwith. Kasztner reflected on the meaning of the top-level Nazi campaign to secure his freedom: the connection with the *Eichmann-Kommando*, he explained, afforded the committee members protection from the German and Hungarian secret police. If important Nazis were willing to make small concessions to them, and even to lobby the Hungarian government on their behalf, then the negotiations had to be sponsored by a higher German authority.[41]

No doubt there was a reason for what Kasztner terms the "paradoxical" protection of the SS. But it was not, as he speculates, the desire to ensure the success of the Goods for Blood deal: a similar episode occurred in late July, after the Brand Mission was rejected by the British. As Freudiger observed, throughout the Nazi occupation, whenever Kasztner was arrested by the Hungarians, the SS "delivered him again and again."[42]

Another detail of the six-day detention is noteworthy. The imprisoned Zionists had endured the typical methods of the secret police: Hansi Brand, for example, was beaten so savagely that she was unable to walk for several weeks. Kasztner would later allege that the order to free him came just as he was receiving the first punches and kicks from his interrogators.[43] But this was a fiction. Contrary to his postwar claim, he was not beaten at all by his captors; he emerged from the secret police prison unscathed.[44] Kasztner, it seems, was the only Jewish rescue activist who was seen as untouchable by the destroyers of the Jews.

On emerging from Hungarian custody, Kasztner discovered that his position was dire. While he had diligently executed his mandate to prevent any "fuss" during the liquidation of the ghettos, Eichmann had broken his side of the bargain by murdering as many as possible of the "rescue candidates." There was not a single survivor from any of Kasztner's lists for the ghettos of Subcarpathia.[45] As for North Transylvania, Kasztner learned that up to half of the Kolozsvár Ghetto inmates on his original list had been sent to Auschwitz.[46] Most of the Jews from these areas—designated Zones 1 and 2 in the Nazi deportation plan—had already been sent to their deaths, but not one of the "rescue candidates" had been moved to the capital. The deal with the SS had not yielded even the *appearance* of saving a single life.

Fortunately—or so Kasztner thought—messages had arrived from Istanbul during his imprisonment. Brand reported that a draft interim agreement on the Goods for Blood offer was on its way to Budapest (the interim agreement was in fact a bluff devised by the rescue activists in Istanbul in order to gain time).[47] On June 1, straight after his release, Kasztner rushed to Eichmann with the cables and requested a suspension of deportations until the arrival of the agreement. Much to his consternation, Eichmann replied that it was out of the question: "On the contrary, I'll proceed full steam ahead."[48]

Kasztner did not stop the talks. He merely requested the transfer of his VIP "emigration candidates" to the capital, as agreed. Eichmann promised; Kasztner's microscopic "rescue deal" was intact—at least, for those VIPs who were still alive.[49]

"Roulette with Human Lives"

Two days later, on June 3, Eichmann tried to strike the death-blow to Kasztner's hopes. He summoned the head of the rescue committee and announced that he would not bring the "rescue candidates" to Budapest after all. So the surviving Jews on Kasztner's original list of VIPs would be delivered to Auschwitz as well.

Kasztner was horrified. Fuming outside Eichmann's office, he assessed the results of his "rescue negotiations" with the Nazis: hundreds of thousands of Jews had already been sent to Auschwitz, but not even *one* of the few hundred people on his lists had been saved. It was unacceptable.

Kasztner rushed to see Krumey and Clages. He warned them that if Eichmann did not relent, he would inform the Jewish Agency (hence the West) of the futility of any diplomatic contact with the Nazis.[50]

After lobbying Krumey and Clages, Kasztner returned to Eichmann's office. He was kept waiting outside for half an hour. When he entered, Clages had just left the room; obviously, he had intervened on Kasztner's behalf. Krumey, Wisliceny, Hunsche, and Novak were all standing behind Eichmann. Kasztner was offered a chair. Eichmann exploded in a frenzy of rage. Having concluded his outburst, he began to bargain:

> EICHMANN: What do you really want?
> KASZTNER: I must insist that our agreements be carried out. Will you bring the people we chose from the provinces to Budapest?
> EICHMANN: When I say no, it means no!
> KASZTNER: Then for us there's no point in negotiating further.

Kasztner pretended to stand up and leave.

> EICHMANN: Your nerves are overstretched, Kasztner. I'll send you to recover in Theresienstadt. Or would you prefer Auschwitz?
> KASZTNER: That would be useless, no-one would replace me.

115

The exchanges continued for an hour. Throughout the argument, according to Kasztner, Eichmann's aides listened quietly. Eichmann repeatedly appeared to be on the verge of giving in, only to erupt again. "I can't play the Jew-rescuer here," he roared, "I promised László Endre that no Jew would return to this country alive!"

Finally, salvation came from an unexpected source. Wisliceny interjected: he had informed the Hungarians that the Nazis had uncovered "a dangerous Zionist conspiracy." The Zionist conspirators had to be isolated, and this could be a pretext for bringing a group of Jews from Kolozsvár to Budapest. At last Eichmann caved in.[51]

On a superficial reading of his account, Kasztner appears to have displayed great tenacity and courage in the face of an adversary who held all the power in his hands and who could have had him killed at any moment. But a careful study suggests otherwise.

To begin with, Kasztner had already appealed to Clages, a Gestapo/SD officer close to Himmler. Before entering the room, he spent half an hour waiting outside while Clages pressed Eichmann on his behalf. A small detail illustrates where the balance of power really lay: as soon as Kasztner entered the room, Eichmann offered him a chair; Eichmann then *kept his own officers standing* while the argument raged for over an hour.

Eichmann's furious outbursts and his threats against Kasztner were the tactics of a bully who knew that he had to back down. If Eichmann had really believed, following the intervention of Clages, that he could still get away with breaking the agreement, he would not have wasted a moment on the meeting. Kasztner's threat to stop the talks and thus sabotage the diplomatic initiative in Istanbul—an initiative begun by Eichmann on orders from Himmler—ruled out any possibility of canceling the deal; and his quick dismissal of Eichmann's threat to send him to Auschwitz betrayed his awareness that the matter had already been settled in his favor.

All that remained was for Wisliceny to offer his master a face-saving exit; hence the fiction of the "Zionist conspiracy" disclosed to the Hungarian government. Eichmann grasped at this straw as soon as it was offered to him. But when Kasztner left the room, his frustration boiled over. In his postwar testimony, Wisliceny described what happened next: Eichmann "again threw a fit of rage, saying that I had stabbed him in the back in the presence of that 'Jewish swine.' More and more he saw through my 'tricks,' soon I would go too far, and so on." Wisliceny was ordered to bring five to ten people from each ghetto to Budapest, but "not to find" the other Jews on Kasztner's lists.[52]

What Kasztner's account of the June 3 confrontation actually reveals is not a Jewish leader who single-handedly overwhelmed the orchestrator of the Final Solution in Hungary, but a Jewish collaborator who understood his indispensability to the plans of the Nazis and knew how to exploit personal and bureaucratic divisions in their ranks. Not Kasztner but Eichmann was the isolated party in this confrontation. On Kasztner's side were Clages, who was in touch with Himmler; Krumey, to whom he also appealed before the meeting; and Wisliceny, who had discussed a postwar alibi with him when they met in Kolozsvár a month earlier.

The most striking aspect of Kasztner's account was his analysis of the situation in the first few minutes of the confrontation with Eichmann:

> If Eichmann could not be made to back down here and now, then the committee, which in the game of roulette with human lives had placed its money on the German number, would be a loser no less naive than so many of its predecessors in occupied Europe. . . . The loser in this game would also be called a traitor.[53]

Kasztner's confession that he had gambled the outcome of his policy on "the German number" proves that his deal meant stopping all rescue activities not authorized by the killers. Under the deal, the operations of the Jewish rescue committee were placed under Nazi control. Here is the reason for Kasztner's previous actions to block any real hope of rescue for the provincial Jewish masses: keeping the "rescue secret" to prevent a "fuss" in the ghettos during the deportations; spreading the hoax about resettlement inside the country; opposing the missions of the Zionist youth to the provincial communities; and depriving these rescue activists of any concrete information that might have enabled them to start a panic.

Kasztner had won a small victory against Eichmann: a few hundred Jews had been transferred from the provinces to a Nazi-controlled camp in the capital. Meanwhile, hundreds of thousands of men, women, and children, ignorant of their impending fate, had been sent to a terrible death. The Nazis proceeded with their mass deportation plan—and they continued to enlist the aid of the head of the Jewish rescue committee.

Notes

1. For numerous examples, see Cohen, *The Halutz Resistance in Hungary*, 106–27.
2. This Zionist body was the central *Judenrat*'s information service, staffed by Jenő Kolb, Miklós Buch, and Sara Friedlander, among others. Another Zionist institution, the *Judenrat*'s provincial department, led by Moshe Rosenberg and Lajos Gottesmann, was responsible for sending underground messengers to several ghettos, as discussed below.
3. Kasztner Trial testimony, March 2, 1954.
4. Ibid., March 3, 1954.
5. Benshalom, *We Struggled For Life*, 35.
6. Ibid., 62.
7. See the testimonies of key activists Moshe (Pil) Alpan, Efra Teichmann-Agmon and David Gur: ibid., 40–53, 123–34, 135–59. For another example of a messenger who arrived with no news, see Teréz Mózes, *Staying Human Through the Holocaust* (Calgary: University of Calgary Press, 2005), 66.
8. David Gur, "Missions of the Zionist Youth Movements in Hungary to the Provincial Cities in 1944," *Yalkut Moreshet* 2 (Winter 2004): 80–82.
9. As witnessed by ghetto inmate Mordecai Hauer: see Roger Cohen, *Soldiers and Slaves: American POWs Trapped by the Nazis' Final Gamble* (New York: Knopf, 2005), 61–62. The date of this incident is uncertain. It allegedly occurred during Eichmann's visit in late April; but according to this account, the deportations were already under way elsewhere in the country and deportations from the ghetto commenced the next day, indicating mid-May.
10. Ibid., 62–63.
11. Ibid., 59. For more on the deception in this ghetto, see, for example, Zahava Szász Stessel, *Wine and Thorns in Tokay Valley: Jewish Life in Hungary, The History of Abaujszanto* (Madison, NJ: Fairleigh Dickinson University Press, 1995), 211; idem, *Snow Flowers: Hungarian Jewish Women in an Airplane Factory, Markkleeberg, Germany* (Madison, NJ: Fairleigh Dickinson University Press, 2009), 46–47.
12. Arányi, *One Eye Cries While the Other Laughs*, 134–7.
13. Braham, *The Politics of Genocide*, Vol. 1, 600.
14. Arányi, *One Eye Cries While the Other Laughs*, 124–8. These incidents must have taken place in the first week of deportations, as Arányi was captured on May 23 and imprisoned and tortured for a month.
15. Avihu Ronen, *Ha'kerav al ha'hayim: Ha'shomer ha'tzair be'Hungaryah, 1944* [*The Battle for Life: Hashomer Hatzair in Hungary, 1944*] (Givat Haviva: Yad Ya'ari, 1994), 102, quoting Hannah Fuchs (Nissman), herself a former Zionist youth activist who had left Budapest for Nyíregyháza at the beginning of the Nazi occupation.
16. Braham, *The Politics of Genocide*, Vol. 1, 602.
17. Kasztner Trial testimony, September 16, 1954.
18. For example, Bauer, *Jews For Sale?*, 151, 160. Bauer distinguishes *information* from *knowledge*. Although "most" of the Jews in Hungary had the necessary information, "they did not believe it, or refused to act on it, or did not see any way to act on it." His evidence is unpersuasive. He claims, without citations, that the BBC's Hungarian Service carried news of the genocide in June, July and December 1942: ibid., 150. In fact the British Foreign Office

determined in early 1942 that the BBC's Hungarian Service should ignore Jewish matters. This policy continued until the Nazi occupation. See Gabriel Milland, "The BBC Hungarian Service and the Final Solution in Hungary," *Historical Journal of Film, Radio and Television* 18, no. 3 (1998): 354–5. The suppression was also reviewed in *The BBC and the Hungarian Holocaust*, BBC Radio 4, November 12, 2012, 8pm. See "Could the BBC Have Done More to Help Hungarian Jews?" at http://www.bbc.co.uk/news/world-europe-20267659 (accessed November 13, 2012).

19. Brand-SIME1, para. 34(b).

20. Kasztner to Schwalb, July 12, 1944, Haganah Archive, 80/p187/32.

21. Kasztner, *Bericht*, 35. Kasztner also found that Hungarian Jewish deportees who had been diverted to Austria "have little idea of the fate of the deportees to Auschwitz, or how lucky they are to have escaped themselves": ibid., 156.

22. Béla Zsolt, *Nine Suitcases* (London: Pimlico, 2005), 44.

23. Ibid., 207–8.

24. Kasztner Trial testimony, June 17, 1954. See also Mozes, *Staying Human Through the Holocaust*, 77–79. The local *Judenrat* leader, Alexander Leitner, admits that he "communicated quieting news with our people" at the behest of the gendarmes. He considered it his duty not to foster panic. The next day he was told that he was exempt from deportation: Leitner, *The Tragedy of the Jews in Nagyvárad (Oradea)*, CZA S26/1564, 113, 118.

25. Braham, *The Politics of Genocide*, Vol. 1, 642.

26. Eichmann Trial testimony, May 25, 1961. Földi himself was later deported with his family members, who were murdered.

27. DEGOB, Protocol 174. See also Protocol 699: "We heard that they were going to take us away for work but we were not going to leave the borders of the country but would stay in Western Hungary." And Protocol 2385: "They told us that we were going towards Western Hungary to work but when we arrived at the border we realised in dismay that we were heading towards Poland." Földi (*supra*) was apparently one of the officials who thought that the destination was a work site in Germany, for he received a postcard from "Waldsee" after the first transport; in Auschwitz he was in turn forced to write such a postcard.

28. Braham, *The Politics of Genocide*, Vol. 1, 594.

29. Rudolph Tessler, *Letter to My Children: From Romania to America Via Auschwitz* (Columbia: University of Missouri Press, 1999), 46, 54.

30. Elie Wiesel, *All Rivers Run to the Sea* (New York: Schocken Books, 1995), 69–70. See also DEGOB Protocol 91: "In general we were told that we would be taken to work. A gendarme colonel . . . gave his word that we would not be taken out of the country, only to Hortobagy [in Hungary] to work. We believed it, since we wanted to believe it. As far as I know a few people tried to escape from the ghetto."

31. Not until the second day on the deportation train was it clear that Kenyérmező was a hoax: see Lajos Erdélyi's account at http://www.iremember.hu/text/erdelyilajossurvivalengl.html (accessed July 17, 2010).

32. Recounted in Agnes Kadar, "Historical Position of the Hungarian Jewry and Untold Ghetto Accounts," in *Life in the Ghettos During the Holocaust*, ed. Eric Sterling (Syracuse, NY: Syracuse University Press, 2005), 48.

33. Email from Lily Zamir to Eli Reichenthal, January 14, 2011. Dr. Zamir is head of the Department of Adult Education and director of the Center for Women and Gender Studies at David Yellin College, Jerusalem. Both of her parents lost their first families in the Holocaust.

34. Stessel, *Wine and Thorns in Tokay Valley*, 211.

35. Mordowicz-Rosin Report, in Swiebocki, ed., *London Has Been Informed*, 282–3.

36. Kasztner Trial testimony, June 21, 1954.

37. Kasztner Trial testimony, July 15, 1954.

38. Kasztner Trial testimony, June 25, 1954.

39. Yoel Palgi in *Magen Baseter* [*Secret Shield*], ed. Zerubavel Gilad (Jerusalem: Jewish Agency, 1948), Kasztner Trial defense exhibit 40, 416. Palgi disavowed this chapter in the Kasztner Trial as it had been ghostwritten for him. Since he had issued no such repudiation in the six years between its publication and his testimony as a government witness, it is reasonable to treat it as an accurate statement of his recollections.

40. Kasztner, *Bericht*, 40–41; Biss, *A Million Jews to Save*, 49–51; Weissberg, *Desperate Mission*, 223–4. Biss observes, "The Germans did everything to find the prisoners and secure their liberation." In fact they were only interested in Kasztner and his committee; they did not try to free the Zionist youth captives.

41. Kasztner, *Bericht*, 47–48.

42. *Freudiger Report*, 49.

43. Kasztner, *Bericht*, 40.

44. Szamosi, *Rudolf Kasztner in History, in Testimony and in Memory*, 157n342, citing interview with Hansi Brand.

45. Kasztner, *Bericht*, 41. Kasztner writes, inaccurately, that all Zone 1 Jews had already been deported.

46. Kasztner Trial testimony, March 1, 1954.

47. For Brand's messages, see Szamosi, *Rudolf Kasztner in History, in Testimony and in Memory*, 104. For the text of the "interim agreement," see Paul Lawrence Rose, "Joel Brand's 'Interim Agreement' and the Course of Nazi-Jewish Negotiations, 1944–1945," *The Historical Journal* 34, no. 4 (1991): 911–12. The text did not reach Budapest until July 7, after the destruction of the provincial Jews.

48. Kasztner, *Bericht*, 41.

49. Ibid. Eichmann only promised to bring the (surviving) candidates from the North Transylvanian ghettos; it was too late for those in the Subcarpathians.

50. Kasztner, *Bericht*, 42.

51. Ibid., 43–44.

52. Wisliceny's commentary on Kasztner's *Bericht*, March 25, 1947, Eichmann Trial exhibit T/1116, 10–11.

53. Kasztner, *Bericht*, 43.

9

The Strasshof Deal

By the second week of June 1944, the regions of Subcarpathia and North Transylvania (designated Zones 1 and 2 by the SS) were almost *judenrein*. Over 289,000 Hungarian Jews had boarded the trains to Auschwitz in the belief that they would be resettled with their families in locations such as Kenyérmező. Another 388 Jews had boarded the train from the Kolozsvár Ghetto to an SS hostage camp in Budapest in the expectation that they would be allowed to immigrate to Palestine. All of these Jewish men, women, and children—murder victims and terrorized hostages alike—were victims of deceptions by Eichmann's SS unit.

The Nazis now turned to the destruction of the Jews in northern Hungary (Zone 3). The head of the Jewish rescue committee understood all too well that he would be branded a traitor unless he could show concrete achievements from his "negotiations." At the same time, he knew that the killers were completely devoted to their mission.

Kasztner's next "rescue deal" with Eichmann—the transfer of around fifteen thousand Hungarian Jews for slave labor in Austria rather than instant death in Auschwitz—must be seen in this light. Kasztner's version is as follows. On June 13, 1944, he offered 5 million Swiss francs to Eichmann in return for keeping one hundred thousand Jews in Hungary for the Goods for Blood deal. Eichmann was unwilling to delay the deportation of one hundred thousand Jews, but within twenty-four hours he agreed to move thirty thousand Hungarian Jews to the Strasshof labor camp in Vienna instead of Auschwitz. Half would be removed from the provinces and half from the capital. Eichmann not only wanted the SF5 million fee but also ordered the rescue committee to cover all of the Strasshof group's living costs.[1] Some fifteen thousand to eighteen thousand provincial Jews were actually delivered to Strasshof; the Budapest Jews were never sent because the mass deportations ended in early July 1944. The Strasshof group included children, pregnant women, and old people, all of whom would have been gassed immediately had they been sent to Auschwitz.

In assessing Kasztner's version, we must ask these questions: Was it Kasztner who persuaded Eichmann to divert these deportees to Austria? Did Kasztner believe at the time that he had persuaded Eichmann? And what price did Kasztner have to pay Eichmann for the Strasshof deal?

To anticipate what follows, the answers to these questions are (respectively): Eichmann diverted fifteen thousand Jews to Austria on orders from his superiors; Kasztner knew at the time that the Strasshof transports had nothing to do with him; and Eichmann's price for allowing Kasztner to take credit for these transports was two-fold—(a) deceiving the Jewish rescuers abroad about the Holocaust in Hungary and (b) helping to organize the deportation of scores of thousands of Jews to Auschwitz.

The proof is found in documentation submitted at Nuremberg and in Kasztner's own statements.

Kaltenbrunner's Orders to Eichmann

On June 7, 1944, Ernst Kaltenbrunner, head of the SS Reich Security Main Office (RSHA), was asked to send several thousand Jews to Austria for slave labor. The request had been made by Austrian industrialists, including Karl Blaschke, the mayor of Vienna. Accordingly, Kaltenbrunner sent Eichmann direct orders to divert several trainloads of Hungarian Jews from Auschwitz to the Strasshof labor camp in Vienna.

Kaltenbrunner's orders were in no way intended to spare the lives of these Jews. On the contrary, in his letter informing Mayor Blaschke of the forthcoming slave labor transports, Kaltenbrunner wrote:

> For the special reasons cited by you I have in the meantime given orders to ship several evacuation transports to Vienna-Strasshof. . . . At the present, 4 shipments with approx. 12,000 Jews are pending . . .

> According to previous experience it is estimated that 30% of the transport will consist of Jews able to work (approx. 3,600 in this case), who can be utilized for the work in question, whereby it shall be understood that they are subject *to be removed at any time*. It is obvious that only a well guarded, enclosed place of work and a large camplike billeting arrangement can be utilized and this is an absolute prerequisite for making these Jews available. Women unable to work and children of these Jews who are all kept in readiness for special action [*Sonderaktion*] and therefore one day will be removed again, have to stay in the guarded camp also during the day . . .

> I hope that these transports will be of help to you in carrying out these urgent work details of yours.[2]

The term "special action" was Nazi code for gassing and burning in the death camps. Kaltenbrunner's instructions to Eichmann thus specified the temporary diversion of several thousand Hungarian Jews for slave labor in Austria and stipulated that later these Jews—especially the women and children—would be sent to their deaths in Auschwitz.

Based on evidence such as this letter, Kaltenbrunner was convicted of crimes against humanity in the trial of the major Nazi war criminals at Nuremberg, sentenced to death, and executed.[3]

In other words, the Strasshof operation was not a result of negotiations conducted by the Jewish rescue committee, as Kasztner asserted at the time and afterwards: it was a result of the Nazi demand for slave labor, and it included a plan for mass extermination. This conclusion was established beyond all doubt at the Nuremberg Trials, the Kasztner Trial, and later the Eichmann Trial.[4] And since the Strasshof operation was based on instructions from Kaltenbrunner—instructions that Eichmann could not ignore—Kasztner deserves no credit whatsoever for the diversion of these Jews from Auschwitz.

When Kasztner and his defenders claimed after the war that the Strasshof scheme was a Jewish rescue achievement—and some of these defenders are still echoing this claim[5]—they unwittingly exonerated Eichmann's superior Kaltenbrunner from one of the war crimes that led to his conviction and execution at the Nuremberg Trials.

The chain of command in the Strasshof plan extended not from Kasztner to Eichmann to Kaltenbrunner, but from Kaltenbrunner to Eichmann to Kasztner.[6] But if so, what was Kasztner's role? Did he understand *at the time* that he was not taking part in a rescue deal?

What Did Kasztner Know?

The truth can be divined from Kasztner's own account. According to the *Bericht*, the Strasshof negotiations began in a private meeting with Eichmann on June 13.

Kasztner protested that the extermination of the Hungarian Jews in Auschwitz had placed his committee in an impossible position vis-à-vis world Jewry and the Allies. "Our moral credit is gone," he explained. "No-one abroad still believes that the Germans ever took the rescue plan seriously."

"What do you imagine?" screamed Eichmann. "Maybe you believe that the Reich has enough food to feed hundreds of thousands of Hungarian Jews for months, or staff and doctors to treat the sick?" By implication, it was more efficient to kill them.

Kasztner claims that he asked what Eichmann would do if a Goods for Blood deal now came from Istanbul. If all the deportees had been gassed, what "merchandise" would the Nazis have to trade for the trucks? It was at this point that Kasztner supposedly offered to pay for the lives of one hundred thousand Jews.[7]

Kasztner wants his readers to believe that he raised the expected failure of the Goods for Blood plan as an argument against further deportations. But both sides knew that the plan had no chance of succeeding. Kasztner had considered the odds "very slim" from the start, while Eichmann had amply displayed his determination to murder Hungary's Jews. Kasztner's purported bluff was therefore futile.

The true meaning of this exchange is quite different: Kasztner was explaining that his services to the Nazis would be worthless if he lost credibility on the Jewish side. His declaration to Eichmann on June 13 ("Our moral credit is gone") was an overt expression of his private thoughts during their previous clash on June 3 ("The loser in this game would also be called a traitor"). No traitor can function if his people see him for what he is. Kasztner was begging Eichmann to grant him at least the *appearance* of a rescue achievement—in order to rebuild his own "moral credit."

Kasztner's prayers were answered almost immediately. The next day—probably on the night of June 13–14—he was privately informed by Wisliceny that the *Eichmann-Kommando* wanted to divert some of the deportees to Austria. And on June 14, Eichmann confirmed that thirty thousand Jews would be kept "on ice" in Austria.[8] Did Kasztner—who had struggled for weeks to persuade the SS to transport three hundred Jewish hostages from Kolozsvár to Budapest—really imagine that in a mere twenty-four hours he had persuaded the same Nazi officers to divert no fewer than thirty thousand Jewish deportees from Auschwitz to Vienna? Did he think that overnight his bargaining power had multiplied by a factor of one hundred (from three hundred to thirty thousand Jews)?

Kasztner's account implies that the German side initiated the Strasshof operation. He grasped the opportunity and offered to assist the *Eichmann-Kommando*'s scheme in exchange for receiving the "moral credit" for the "rescue" of Strasshof deportees. The Nazis responded with their own set of demands, including funds for the Strasshof group's living expenses (other, more sinister demands will be examined later). Kasztner may even have realized from the outset that the Strasshof Jews were scheduled for destruction in Auschwitz. The documentary evidence for this version of events is not lacking.

First, there is Kasztner's testimony in the Jerusalem libel trial. While insisting that *he* had initiated the Strasshof plan—proof of Kaltenbrunner's instructions to Eichmann notwithstanding—Kasztner nevertheless made some revealing statements. He began:

> It occurred to us that the talks in Istanbul would not produce actual results and we sought an alternative based on Hungarian Jewish assets that were doomed to be lost anyway.... We offered to pay SF5 million to the Germans for the departure of a group of 600 to Spain and for the transfer of 100,000 Jews to Austria instead of Auschwitz, without undergoing selection. [Eichmann] agreed to send 30,000 instead of 100,000 as above: about 15,000 from the provinces and about 15,000 from Budapest, including 7,000 children (among the 15,000 from Budapest).[9]

This account differs from the previous version in the *Bericht* in several respects:

1. Kasztner says that at the time of the Strasshof deal, he had already lost all hope for the Brand Mission; his alleged bluff vis-à-vis Eichmann was thus doomed to fail. Kasztner could not have imagined that he was extracting real concessions from Eichmann by means of this bluff.
2. Kasztner states that he specifically asked Eichmann to send the Jews to Austria for labor. Was it simply an amazing coincidence that Eichmann had already been ordered to send Hungarian Jews to that very place for that very purpose? Did Kasztner spontaneously think of a "rescue deal" that just happened to be identical to the instructions already given to Eichmann? If Kasztner really had been ignorant of Kaltenbrunner's plan, surely he would not have asked Eichmann to deport Hungarian Jews to the Reich as slave labor. Kasztner must have known what Eichmann had already been ordered to do with these Jews.
3. Kasztner does not say what fate he anticipated for those of the deportees who were incapable of work (such as the "7,000 children"). If he thought that the able-bodied deportees would be kept alive solely for the purpose of slave labor, then he could not have entertained such hopes in respect of the children, the pregnant women, the sick, the disabled, or the elderly. He must have understood that the Nazis were likely to murder these nonworking Jews. Not only was he aware of

Kaltenbrunner's request for slave labor, but he also knew at the time (or at least drew a well-founded inference) about Kaltenbrunner's proviso regarding the "special action" (*Sonderaktion*) for the nonworking majority.

The suspicion that Kasztner volunteered to collaborate with Kaltenbrunner's slave labor and mass murder operation, in return for the opportunity to take "moral credit" for this pseudo-rescue plan after the fact, is reinforced by his answers under cross-examination:

> Usually I didn't believe Eichmann. *I had no confidence that the 15,000 wouldn't be sent to extermination*, but I had hope, Eichmann himself offered me inspection. *In the first stage I had no possibility of inspecting. The first stage was one or two months.* [Emphases added.][10]

This means that for the sake of restoring his "moral credit," Kasztner agreed to an operation that meant dispatching Jews on trains which—for all he knew—would carry them straight to the gas chambers. He agreed to it on the strength of Eichmann's promises, even though he would have no chance in the short term to find out where the Jews were being sent or what was being done to them. Here was another example of his propensity to play "roulette with human lives" for the sake of self-aggrandizement.

How Did Kasztner's Colleagues React?

It therefore comes as no surprise that Kasztner's colleagues did not see the new deal with Eichmann as a magnificent "rescue achievement." On the contrary: since there was no reason to expect that the fate of the Jews sent to Strasshof would differ from that of the other deportees, some of his colleagues ignored the deal completely.

In his diary entries from the first ten days after the Strasshof deal, Ottó Komoly, the chairman of the rescue committee, mentioned a few meetings with Kasztner and the topics discussed. These included the difficulties of compiling the passenger list for the Kasztner Train; the ordeals of Jews forced to surrender their homes to Christians whose houses had been hit in air raids; the bombing of industrial sites in Budapest by the Allies; the suicide of the prominent Revisionist Zionist Imre Varga when the *Judenrat* rejected his plea for resistance to the deportations; and trivialities such as winding up his clock. The Strasshof deal was not mentioned. One would expect the chairman of Kasztner's rescue committee to mention the potential rescue of thirty thousand people. Obviously, Komoly would have recorded this achievement (or at least hinted at it) if he had taken it seriously. The lack of any reference to the Strasshof deal by June 24—ten days after the agreement with Eichmann—suggests that Komoly regarded it as just one more deportation, which would end in the same way as the other deportations.[11]

Hansi Brand, Kasztner's closest aide in the rescue committee, did not refer to the Strasshof deal during her Kasztner Trial testimony. She remembered delivering suitcases filled with valuables to the Nazis as ransom for the Kasztner Train passengers (who were then sent to a concentration camp) but she did not mention the issue of payment for the Strasshof Jews.[12] At the Eichmann Trial, she testified that Eichmann promised "in the end" that he would "finally" send fifteen thousand Jews to Austria, which suggests that initially she did not believe his promises to Kasztner. In her assessment, the fact that Jews were actually transferred to Strasshof was "a success of the subsequent negotiations conducted with Becher."[13] Those talks did not begin until June 20—a week after the deal between Kasztner and Eichmann. It seems that Hansi Brand, in spite of her loyalty to Kasztner, did not regard the deal as a *bona fide* rescue operation.

Moshe Krausz, head of the Palestine Office in Budapest, also heard nothing at the time about the mass "rescue" of Jews in Strasshof. During the Kasztner Trial he testified that throughout Kasztner's negotiations with Eichmann, the rescue committee members did not refer to any concessions by the Germans other than sparing the Kasztner Train hostages.[14] This testimony is corroborated by Krausz's contemporary statements. His letter to his Geneva counterpart Chaim Posner on June 19 mentioned no successes by the rescue committee; its July 13 sequel expressed grave fears for the fate of the Kasztner Train but gave no hint of the rescue committee's supposed role in saving Hungarian Jews through transfers to labor camps in Austria.[15]

Yoel Palgi, a Zionist fighter from Palestine sent to prepare resistance to the Nazis, conferred with Kasztner in Budapest on June 21 or 22. He heard a lengthy and boastful account of Kasztner's talks with Eichmann, the Goods for Blood plan, and the Kasztner Train. Not once did Kasztner mention the Strasshof deal or arrangements for "rescue" shipments to Austria. Neither Palgi's post-mission debriefing, nor his postwar memoirs, nor his Kasztner Trial testimony contains any reference to this alleged achievement by the Jewish rescue committee.[16]

There is no credible evidence that Kasztner's colleagues in Budapest saw the Strasshof plan as a genuine rescue operation at the time of his deal with Eichmann. Some of them attached so little importance to the agreement that they did not mention the transfers to Vienna at all.[17] But if Kasztner had failed to impress most of his colleagues in Budapest with the news of his latest "rescue achievement," he did not hesitate to transmit his version to the rescue activists abroad. For one of the Nazi conditions for restoring his "moral credit" was his further assistance in deceiving the free world about the ongoing massacre of Hungarian Jewry.

Notes

1. Kasztner, *Bericht*, 49–50. These meetings probably took place on June 12–13, not (as Kasztner writes) on June 13–14.
2. Kaltenbrunner to Blaschke, June 30, 1944, NCA, Vol. 6, 3803-PS, 738, emphasis in original.
3. IMT, Vol. 22, 538.
4. Ibid.; Kasztner Trial verdict, ss. 71–74; Kasztner Appeal, Agranat verdict, 2046, Silberg verdict, s. 33; Eichmann Trial verdict, s. 116(a).
5. For example, Porter, *Kasztner's Train*, 176–9, 180–1, 190–1. Remarkably, Porter gives Kasztner the "credit" for this action even as she concedes that "Eichmann had little choice but to comply" with his superior's orders. She also falsely attributes the Strasshof news to Krumey, making liberal use of invented quotations.
6. Kasztner Trial verdict, s. 71.
7. Kasztner, *Bericht*, 48–49.
8. Ibid., 49.
9. Kasztner Trial testimony, February 19, 1954.
10. Kasztner Trial testimony, March 2, 1954.
11. *Komoly Diary*, June 14–24, 1944. These were the first ten days of the Strasshof plan, according to Kasztner's *Bericht*.
12. Kasztner Trial testimony, March 31, April 1, 1954.
13. Eichmann Trial testimony, May 30–31, 1961.
14. Kasztner Trial testimony, July 2, 1954.
15. Krausz to Posner, June 19, 1944, YVA, P 12; Krausz to Posner, July 13, 1944, Kasztner Trial prosecution exhibit 123.
16. *Palgi Report 1*; *Palgi Report 2*; Yoel Palgi in *Magen Baseter* [*Secret Shield*], ed. Zerubavel Gilad (Jerusalem: Jewish Agency, 1948), Kasztner Trial defense exhibit 40, 416; Yoel Palgi, *Into the Inferno: The Memoir of a Jewish Para-trooper Behind Nazi Lines* (New Brunswick, NJ: Rutgers University Press, 2003), 90–91; Palgi's Kasztner Trial testimony, March 16–18, June 4, 1954.
17. Only Fülöp Freudiger, the Orthodox representative on the *Judenrat*, believed that Eichmann's shipments to Austria had been kept "on ice" for the sake of the Goods for Blood negotiations: *Freudiger Report*, 37. But Freudiger had no independent information and simply took Kasztner's word for it: see his Kasztner Trial testimony, August 13, 1954. Freudiger did not mention any payment made by Kasztner's committee to the Nazis for the Strasshof deal.

10

Deceiving the Outside World

Testifying in Jerusalem in 1954, Kasztner denied that he and his committee had ever been expected to collaborate with the Nazis. Eichmann, he insisted, had never demanded anything of the kind. Eichmann "did not dare to demand anything about [influencing] the mood of Hungarian Jews," declared Kasztner. Moreover, "He did not demand that we spread good propaganda abroad. Becher did not demand this either."[1]

That Eichmann wanted "no fuss" in the provincial ghettos has already been demonstrated. We have also examined Kasztner's response. But did Eichmann try to spread Nazi disinformation abroad as well? Was the Jewish rescue committee expected to comply? The answer is found in Kasztner's communications about the Strasshof deal.

At the beginning of June 1944, Moshe Krausz had sent his own summary of events in Hungary to the Jewish Agency. His message, which was seen by the Red Cross, offers an appropriate benchmark for comparison. Krausz wrote that one hundred and seventy thousand Hungarian Jews had already been sent to the Auschwitz death camp, while another one hundred and thirty thousand were in the process of being deported. Another two hundred thousand Jews in the provinces were confined to ghettos pending deportation to Auschwitz; and it was clear that three hundred thousand Jews in the capital would also be sent there. The entire Jewish population of Hungary would be wiped out by the end of the month, according to Krausz's projections. The only hope was intervention by neutral diplomats to save women, children, and the elderly, preferably by arranging their emigration.[2]

Tragically, this message—in which Krausz reported that the Nazis were sending all Hungarian Jews to perish in Auschwitz—never reached its intended recipients. Meanwhile, Kasztner and Hansi Brand sent their own cable to Istanbul. They declared that deportations were continuing, but said nothing about the destination or fate of the deportees. Instead they stressed the fury of the Nazis at the lack of response to their offer

and the urgency of setting up negotiations between a Jewish representative and the Gestapo/SD agent Laufer.[3]

Thanks to Kasztner's communications and the Brand Mission, the
activists and decision-makers of the Jewish Agency were now thoroughly confused about the situation of Hungary's Jews. Their disori-
entation was evident in the debate held in the JAE on June 11, 1944.

Yitzhak Grünbaum, head of the Zionist rescue committee in Palestine,
began the discussion by announcing that he had appealed to the
Americans to bomb Auschwitz. The Nazis, he explained, were deporting twelve thousand Jews per day from Hungary to Poland, where
thousands were being murdered on a daily basis. But his colleagues
were not so sure. Ben-Gurion replied: "We do not know the truth
concerning the entire situation in Poland, and it seems that we will be
unable to propose anything concerning this matter." Other participants
agreed, rebuking Grünbaum for proposing to bomb Auschwitz—which
contained "a large labor camp"—and other sites where Jews were
being held.[4] The JAE members did not accept Grünbaum's assessment of the fate of the Hungarian Jews. Apparently they believed—
or at least hoped—that many of the Jews sent to Poland had been
kept alive.[5]

This confusion was exacerbated by another meeting that took place
on the same day. It was the belated encounter between Moshe Shertok,
head of the Jewish Agency's political department, and Joel Brand, who
had been arrested by the British in Aleppo in Syria. Asked if the deportations from Hungary had been halted for the duration of the Goods
for Blood talks, Brand gave three different answers.[6] The difficulty was
compounded when Shertok asked Brand what would happen if he either
returned to Budapest with a rejection of Eichmann's offer or failed to
return at all. Brand predicted that in the event of the offer's rejection,
"wholesale extermination will start at once," and that in the event of
his failure to return, "all Jews will be slaughtered."[7] The implication was
that extermination had *not* yet started and that Hungary's Jews were
not yet being slaughtered.

Shertok was completely misled by Brand's mistaken assumptions
about the events in Hungary. On June 15, having returned to Palestine,
he accompanied Ben-Gurion to a meeting with the British High
Commissioner, Sir Harold MacMichael. Shertok reported that Eichmann's
offer was serious: the Nazis had decided "to defer the killings" in Hungary.
He added that "many Germans and their wives seemed genuinely full
of compassion," though "this might be spurious." Ben-Gurion conceded

the likelihood that "the whole business was a trick," but he did not challenge Shertok's claim that the massacre of Hungary's Jews had been postponed.[8]

The confusion of the Jewish Agency's decision-makers regarding the fate of Hungarian Jewry was a product of the Nazi deception surrounding the Goods for Blood offer. The deception was furthered unwittingly by Brand and knowingly by Kasztner. The next phase of this effort involved a series of letters about the Strasshof plan that Kasztner sent to his foreign Jewish contacts. Each of the letters repays careful examination.[9]

Letter No. 1: June 13

Kasztner's first message was sent on June 13, the day he learned of the Strasshof plan. He immediately composed a long letter to Joseph Schwartz, the European head of the JDC:

> I have just been told that in a few days the names will be announced of the camps where the first 30,000 should be sent. Since this means only unemployable people (children, women, the sick and the elderly), maintenance of the camps prior to transport of these people to Spain will need to be provided for . . . a monthly sum of $860,000 should be available . . . for only in this manner can it be hoped that at least part of the Jews still existing here will stay alive.

After a detailed and mostly accurate account of the stream of antisemitic decrees and the concentration of the provincial Jews in ghettos, Kasztner suddenly inserted the following remarks:

> Out of about 1 million souls, about 400,000 have been deported up to the present date and further transports are in preparation. . . . Secretary of State Endre plans to make all of Hungary Jew-free by the end of August. . . . The first reports from the deportees have already arrived: *employable people were in part taken to Waldsee near Ludwigshafen; about 750,000 postcards have come from there. Unfortunately, the announcements about the fate of the rest are not gratifying.* [Emphases added.]

Kasztner addressed the Brand Mission and the German conditions for the emigration of Hungarian Jews:

> It entails *the rescue of people in the form of a deportation.* The Germans want to bring people to Spain, naturally (as you know) in return for appropriate consideration . . .

131

It should therefore be arranged urgently that: (1) reception camps will be available for 5,000–6,000 per week; (2) they will be transported further by ship to Palestine each week. On point (1), note that the 6,000 number is not fixed but could be 3–4 times higher [i.e., 18,000–24,000 per week]. . . . On point (2): if Palestine cannot admit 30,000–50,000 people at once, North Africa or another country should be ready to host the people temporarily, in case Spain refuses their temporary stay. Indeed, once this aspect of the question is resolved, the first transport could be sent immediately. *This would generally mean that the people are deported, since the Germans insist on it and always speak to the Hungarians of a deportation.* [Emphases added.]

To cover the living expenses of these emigration candidates, the letter urged the JDC to provide $500,000 at once, over and above the monthly payments of $860,000.

In this letter, Kasztner "informed" the JDC that several hundred thousand Jewish deportees from Hungary were alive and well in "Waldsee." But he had known for weeks that Waldsee was a Nazi camouflage for Auschwitz.

It is important to recall his exchange with Krumey on May 2. The context of that exchange was Krumey's pretense that a train had gone to Waldsee, when Kasztner already knew that it had traveled on the route to Auschwitz. Kasztner had told Krumey: "there's no point in playing hide-and-seek."[10] He had seen that Krumey was dissembling and that Waldsee was a Nazi fiction designed to conceal deportation to Auschwitz.

Moreover, on the very day of his letter to the JDC, June 13, Kasztner had revealed what he knew of the deportees' fate during his clash with Eichmann; and Eichmann had admitted that the deportees were no longer alive.[11] So contrary to what he wrote in his letter of June 13, Kasztner had no doubt that the deportees had been taken not to Waldsee for labor but to Auschwitz for death.

Besides claiming that the able-bodied deportees were in Waldsee when he knew that they had been sent to Auschwitz, Kasztner's letter of June 13 stated that news of the treatment of the nonworking deportees was "not gratifying." Obscured by this murky expression was his certainty that they had been gassed.

In his June 13 letter, Kasztner also tried to persuade the JDC to accept the Nazi formula of "rescue in the form of a deportation." This condition had been imposed by the SS at the beginning of the negotiations: the obvious aim was to obtain Jewish consent to the deportations by disguising the transports to Auschwitz as a rescue operation. As an incentive, Kasztner even raised the prospect of the mass emigration of as many as twenty-four thousand Jews each week to Palestine—knowing that this destination had been ruled out by Eichmann.[12]

While hundreds of thousands of Hungarian Jews were being gassed in Auschwitz, Kasztner did not imagine that they were being held at Waldsee pending their departure to Palestine at the rate of up to twenty-four thousand per week. Nor did he believe in the principle of mass rescue "in the form of a deportation" by the Nazis. The only conclusion to be drawn from these falsehoods is that by sending reassuring news of imaginary "rescue operations" to Jewish organizations in the free world, he was helping the Nazis to conceal the ongoing massacre of the Jews of Hungary.

A nearly identical letter was dispatched on the same date by the JDC's delegate in Budapest, Joseph Blum. If the letter was Nazi disinformation, the SS would have had it sent by two Jewish sources in order to bolster its credibility. Blum did not negotiate with Eichmann; he would have relied on Kasztner for his information.[13]

Letter No. 2: June 14

Kasztner's second letter was sent the next day to Nathan Schwalb, one of the top Zionist rescue coordinators in Europe; a copy went to Saly Mayer of the JDC. The letter began with what seemed to be a despairing description of the plight of Hungarian Jewry:

> In the hour of writing these lines the deportation is in full swing; and if this terrible process cannot be stopped or slowed at the last minute by an unexpected twist or perhaps through an action of ours, Hungary will be entirely de-Judaized [entjudet] in a few weeks.

> So far the countryside is already de-Judaized, while our brethren still remaining here are fully concentrated in camps and ghettos. . . . Based on the current position, the deportation from Budapest can be counted on in the first half of the month of July.

> That is the dry and bitter reality.

Thus Kasztner directed the reader's attention to the Hungarian deportations instead of the Nazi killings. He did not refer to Auschwitz or gas chambers. At best the letter gave hints, as in a passage blaming the situation on Brand's failure to return from Istanbul:

> it is far from me to seek to judge our friend Joel. I will only say this much: that every hour of delay can claim hundreds of Jewish lives.

This is all the sadder as his cabled news is quite promising. But now I must await the hour of his return to Budapest; and only then will I have a complete picture.

Kasztner's next paragraph again only hinted at the true destination and treatment of the deportees:

In spite of this *fatal* delay, in recent days I have been able to arrange that the transports leaving in the next few days will be divided into two parts. A total of 20,000–30,000 Jews are expected to go to Austria, *instead of Poland as at present,* and there [i.e., in Austria] they will temporarily be subject to special treatment. Hopefully, these Jews can be rescued later in the framework of Joel's negotiations and will eventually be directed for emigration. [Emphases added.]

Kasztner discussed the transfer of the hostages from the Kolozsvár Ghetto to the SS "preferred camp" in Budapest: "The rescue of these people was the first promise made to me," he explained, "and the fact that this commitment was kept convinced me that I can rely on similar concrete promises." He requested large amounts of aid for the Jews "temporarily housed" in Austria, adding that they would probably leave for Palestine. And he declared that his latest deal with the Nazis had already yielded results: "yesterday evening we gave food to the first 300 rescued from the first three deportation trains."[14]

In this letter, Kasztner continued his obfuscations about the destination and fate of the deportees. Instead of stating clearly that hundreds of thousands of Jews were being delivered straight to the "selection" for the gas chambers in Auschwitz, he wrote that the deportees were being sent to Poland and gave hints that their lives were in danger unless Brand returned to Budapest.

The impact of the news about the deportations to Poland was further softened by Kasztner's claim that the next deportees from Hungary would be sent to relative safety in Austria. So Schwalb and the other Zionists had to devote their efforts to pursuing rescue negotiations based on the Brand Mission. No less misleading was Kasztner's suggestion that the Jews taken to Austria would eventually be allowed to immigrate to Palestine—an option already excluded by the Nazis.

Nowhere in his letter did Kasztner tell the awful truth: that the extermination of the deportees in Auschwitz had not been postponed for a single day, let alone until Brand's return from his mission.

Letter No. 3: June 15

On June 15, the head of the Jewish rescue committee dispatched his third letter in as many days. It was passed to Eliahu Dobkin, a member of the JAE in Palestine.[15] Whereas the previous letters had advocated "rescuing" the victims by funding their deportation, all of a sudden Kasztner held out the prospect of keeping the Jews in Hungary:

> In connection with the negotiations conducted by Joel Brand, we have assumed the obligation to deliver to the authorities charged with Jewish affairs certain quantities of goods. These goods are to be repaid with human lives, i.e., the deportations are to be stopped.

How did Kasztner achieve this retreat by the Nazis? According to his letter, as there was no sign of Brand and no news about his negotiations for trucks from the West, Jewish leaders in Budapest had devised a contingency plan involving the purchase of alternative civilian goods (e.g., medicines) in Axis territory:

> Our efforts in this matter . . . are likely to be successful. . . . The lot of the Jews will be alleviated by our partners in proportion to the amount of the goods which we will provide. Many hundreds of thousands have to be saved from deportation and from its consequences; we must accordingly be helped to carry out this operation.

The letter demanded an immediate contribution of SF8 million (possibly by the Zionists) in addition to $10 million from the JDC. These sums would be handled as loans, repayable after the war and "guaranteed by the whole property of the Jewish community of Budapest, which possesses, in real estate alone, much more than $50–60 million." In effect, the Jews would buy their rescue by mortgaging their assets. Kasztner concluded on an optimistic note: "It is as yet possible to help and to save the lives of many hundreds of thousands of Jews, no time must be lost, do everything necessary for the success of this endeavour."

Here was a radical new idea that seemed to augur the salvation of Hungarian Jewry. Was it genuine?

From the first meeting with Wisliceny to the multiple encounters with Eichmann, the SS had insisted that the precondition for any "rescue deal" was the deportation of the Jews from Hungary. Eichmann himself had stated that he would only "sell" Hungarian Jews once they were on German soil. Nowhere did Kasztner's other letters that month even hint at the possibility of halting deportations. Nowhere does Kasztner's

Bericht refer to any Nazi agreement that month to stop deportations under any circumstances. If such an offer had been made, then surely it would have been mentioned in his postwar account, as a justification for continued negotiations.

As for the substance of the proposal, Kasztner did not explain why the Germans needed to use Jews to procure goods already available in their own territories. Nor did he mention an insurmountable obstacle to his mortgage scheme. As outlined in his previous messages, Jewish assets in the capital (and in the provinces) had been expropriated by the Hungarian authorities; restitution was most unlikely. Kasztner wanted to borrow against fictitious collateral. His plan entailed acquiring goods that the Germans could easily obtain on their own, using outside funds borrowed against property the Jews had already lost. Such a scheme—essentially a vast mortgage fraud against world Jewry—could not have saved the Jews in Hungary.

Although the Germans had no intention of halting the deportations or sparing the lives of Hungary's Jews, they were most anxious to open contact with the West and were naturally seeking a substitute for the stalled missions of Brand and Grosz. In addition, the German and Hungarian authorities were competing to steal Jewish assets. Even if the Germans could not take physical possession of the real estate, they could still realize its monetary value by mortgaging it—at the expense of world Jewry. Complicity in the SS plunder effort, rather than a nonexistent offer to stop the deportation, is the likely explanation for Kasztner's June 15 letter.

Letter No. 4: June 18

When Kasztner sent his fourth letter several days later, a dramatic change was under way in Budapest. The *Judenrat* leaders, having observed the deportation of the provincial communities in Zones 1–3, now understood that only immediate action would prevent the total destruction of Hungary's Jews (followed by their own deaths). They had reversed their previous decision to handle news of the slaughter confidentially and had begun to circulate the eye-witness Vrba–Wetzler report—the Auschwitz Protocols—among the Hungarian elite.[16] It was now inevitable that information about the genocide would reach the outside world; indeed, by June 18, Krausz was in possession of both the Auschwitz Protocols and a summary of the horrors of the deportations, which he was able to forward to Switzerland the next day. Kasztner's letter of June 18, which was probably sent to the Zionist rescue activists in Istanbul, must be seen in that context.

The letter opened with what purported to be a factual description of the events in Hungary. It did not conceal the progress of the deportation and it acknowledged that most of the Jews were no longer in the country:

> Up to today 400,000 people have been deported and it is stated explicitly that the full cleansing of provincial Hungary is inevitable, as this is a foregone conclusion.

> For Budapest it is said that no decision has been made about its fate, but we are not deceiving ourselves with hopes and we expect the worst here.

Kasztner continued (underlining in original):

> It is already admitted openly by the Germans that a selection of the deported human materials is taking place as follows: (1) employable men; (2) employable girls and childless women; and (3) the unemployable and children. The first two groups are allocated for various work as promised; group three is <u>exterminated</u> in the infamous Auschwitz. These are the <u>bare</u> facts.

Here, for the first time during the deportations, Kasztner stated that some of the deportees would be sent to the death camp at Auschwitz and not to an imaginary labor camp at Waldsee.

After repeating the details of the Brand Mission, Kasztner wrote that Brand's failure to return to Budapest with a written agreement on Goods for Blood was a disaster for the rescue effort. He speculated (correctly) that Brand had not returned because he was being held against his will. But in the meantime, twelve thousand Jews were being deported each day. Kasztner summarized the state of the negotiations:

> what was previously current is no longer negotiable and there can be no more discussion of ending deportation in general. What can be negotiated is the rescue of a small fraction of the unemployable adults and children, plus the alleged guarantee that nothing will befall the employable Jews, who will receive provisions just like the other categories of workers there. We must be satisfied with these meager guarantees and devote all our effort to safeguarding at least bare survival along this line.

Kasztner outlined his substitute for the failed Brand Mission:

> In Germany three camps will be established for 10,000 people each in this unemployable category; but these must be founded and maintained solely by us or by foreign Jews (for termination in Auschwitz would cause the Germans no other expenses than the gas costs, and they cannot and will not overpay). These camps have the purpose of becoming transit camps, with the target of letting these people leave for Spain or Portugal and enabling them to proceed to Palestine, Africa or overseas if emigration permission is granted and ships made available.

Kasztner exhorted the rescue activists to work with the JDC to arrange visas and interim accommodation for the thirty thousand Jews in Spain. He urged them to enlist the assistance of the Red Cross and perhaps even Allied governments, arguing that "all these people will proceed as soon as possible [from Spain] to Palestine because the majority have [British entry] certificates." Proving to the Nazis that the effort was being taken seriously was the best way to persuade them to keep some of the nonworking Jews alive in transit camps. Kasztner encouraged the activists to devote themselves to his plan for the thirty thousand Jews.

Kasztner turned to the challenge of providing for the Jews in the transit camps. He asserted that the first twelve thousand "unemployable" Jews were due to leave that very week from four ghettos: Miskolc, Győr, Komárom, and Érsekújvár (now Nové Zámky). The transit camps were almost bare, so a substantial aid operation was required:

> You must handle medicine, vitamins, etc., etc., and perhaps send these with Red Cross assistance. The matter is extremely urgent because, as stated, the first transports are ready to leave for these camps this week (of [June] 15). Set up a special committee for this purpose, it is worthwhile in order to save children's lives.

The cost of maintaining these transit camps would amount to SF500,000 per month, by Kasztner's estimate.

Kasztner's letter of June 18 revealed for the first time that some of the deportees were destined for the death camp in Auschwitz. The admission was unavoidable because the Auschwitz Protocols were now circulating in Budapest; but it disguised yet another of his distortions. Kasztner listed three categories of deportees: (1) employable men; (2) employable women; (3) unemployable adults and children. He then reported as fact the Nazi claim that the first two categories would be used for work, when he knew that the vast majority of the deportees had been gassed. Thus he insinuated that although the Nazis intended to transfer some of the deportees to Auschwitz, *most of the deported Hungarian Jews had not been killed.*

The subtle distortions in this letter were meant for the foreign rescue activists; but a recent scholar also seems to have been misled. Shlomo Aronson has written:

> one of the things you find in that correspondence is that Kasztner, yet in June–July 1944, assumes that some of the deportees to Auschwitz were not sent to their death but rather put to work . . .

> That means that to the question whether Kasztner know [*sic*] already in April 1944 that Auschwitz meant death for all those who were sent there, one of the answers is that, *bona fide*, he did not.[17]

Contrary to Aronson's argument, Kasztner certainly knew at the time that deportation to Auschwitz was a death sentence; he even said so after the war. At Nuremberg he declared that Eichmann "had the Hungarian Jews brought to Auschwitz gassed at once."[18] In the Kasztner Trial he testified that when the expulsion of the Hungarian Jews began, he "knew then the meaning of deportation to Auschwitz."[19] Likewise, his confederate Andre Biss recalled begging the SS "not to send these deportees to Auschwitz. We knew . . . that there they would be immediately sent into the gas-chambers—with the exception of a few who were picked out as soon as they reached the camp."[20]

It is understandable that Aronson would argue that Kasztner did not know the whole truth at the time. For if he did know, only one explanation remains: the June 18 letter was Nazi disinformation, written to disguise the fact that most of the Jews from the provinces were already dead. Another of Aronson's observations is relevant here: in this letter, Kasztner was "beyond despair and yet still businesslike, almost imitating the typical Nazi jargon."[21] This probably refers to the words "deported human materials" (*deportierten Menschenmaterials*) appearing in the second paragraph. A more plausible explanation for Kasztner's imitation of "the typical Nazi jargon" in this letter is that the text was prepared or dictated by the Nazis.

Parallel to his pretense that most of the Hungarian Jews were still alive, Kasztner insisted that the only possibility of rescuing any of them was via his dealings with the Nazis. For the purpose of his latest plan, three camps would be established in Germany for a total of thirty thousand unemployable Jews; and these would proceed from Spain to Palestine, since "the majority have certificates" allowing them entry. This may seem to resemble the Strasshof plan, but it is nothing of the kind. The Strasshof plan concerned the transport of fifteen thousand Jews from the provinces and another fifteen thousand from Budapest to Austria for slave labor and then extermination; to fulfil their purpose, these transports had to include large numbers of adults fit for labor, not just the unemployable. Furthermore, the Nazis had ruled out sending any of the Jews in their hands to Palestine, so there was no basis for Kasztner's pledge that "all these people will proceed as soon as possible to Palestine because the majority have certificates."

Most intriguing of all was Kasztner's claim that "the first transports" were due to leave Hungary that very week. Supposedly, the trains were to depart from four ghettos: Miskolc, Győr, Komárom, and Érsekújvár. But this was impossible: for *all of the Jews in all four ghettos had already been sent to Auschwitz*. The last deportation trains from Miskolc and Érsekújvár had crossed the border on June 15, and the last deportation trains from Győr and Komárom on June 16.[22] By June 18, the date of Kasztner's letter, the Jews on these trains had reached Auschwitz and undergone the "selection" for the gas chambers.

There are only two possible explanations for Kasztner's statement in his letter. One is that he already knew that these Jews had been gassed when he wrote that they were about to be spared, in other words, that he was lying. The other is that he did not yet know it, but chose to raise unjustified hopes among his rescue contacts that these Jews would be spared—in spite of the fact that he had every reason to expect that any Jews boarding a Nazi train would be sent to die in Auschwitz. Whatever the explanation, Kasztner's account of his rescue efforts in this letter was intentionally misleading.

The Information Debacle

The disinformation communicated by Kasztner was consistent with the confusion of the official Zionist leadership at this time. The extent of that confusion can be gauged from an address by Chaim Weizmann on June 18. Speaking to the Board of Deputies of British Jews, Weizmann referred to the dangers facing Hungarian Jewry: "The first batches of these people have already gone to this place of extermination, to this mass grave of Jews, to Poland—and others may follow them." Weizmann expressed the hope that his fears would turn out to have been exaggerated, especially as the facts were "not so easily ascertained," but stressed that his remarks were based on "trustworthy sources."[23] More than a month after the Nazis had begun the full-scale extermination of Hungarian Jewry, the president of the World Zionist Organization thought that only the "first batches" of deportees had been sent to die and worried that "others may follow them"—essentially the "information" that had been communicated to the JAE at the beginning of the Brand Mission. And Weizmann was unable to say for certain that even these facts were not exaggerated.

The next day occurred two events that soon transformed the Zionist leadership's perception of the situation in Hungary. The first was the dispatch of a letter from Richard Lichtheim, the Jewish Agency's representative in Geneva, to his superiors in Jerusalem, informing them of the reports of the Auschwitz escapees Vrba, Wetzler, Mordowicz, and Rosin; these had just come to his attention.[24] Lichtheim wrote that there were "specially constructed buildings with gas-chambers and crematoriums" in Birkenau (information from the Vrba–Wetzler report) and added the crucial point that "12,000 Jews are now deported from Hungary every day. They are also sent to Birkenau" (information from the Mordowicz–Rosin report). Of the Jews transferred to this destination from all over Nazi-occupied Europe, it was believed that "90% of the men and 95% of the women have been killed immediately."[25]

The importance of Lichtheim's summary of the Auschwitz reports lay in the clear confirmation to the JAE that nearly all the Jewish deportees from Hungary were being gassed—and not kept in labor or transit camps, as suggested in Kasztner's messages.

The second decisive event was the dispatch of a message from Moshe Krausz in Budapest. From his base in the Swiss consulate, Krausz was able to pass a letter and two documents to a visiting Romanian diplomat for delivery to the Jewish Agency's Palestine Office in Geneva. The first document was a comprehensive description of the savagery of the concentration and deportation process in the provincial ghettos. The second document was an abridged version of the Vrba–Wetzler report on Auschwitz.

Although Krausz did not have a copy of the Mordowicz–Rosin report describing the fate of the deportees, his covering letter left no room for doubt: "approximately 90%" of them had been taken "to Poland, Auschwitz-Birkenau," and "the whole Jewish race in Hungary is condemned to death." Krausz wrote that all efforts to help those in the ghettos had failed; that almost all of the provincial communities had been liquidated; and that the Jews of Budapest were now concentrated in special houses pending their deportation. As for negotiating with the killers, "The German authorities make promises, but do not keep them."

Krausz believed that a few thousand might be saved in the capital by distributing entry certificates to Palestine and passports to neutral countries, but he saw no other opportunity for rescue. He nevertheless requested the publication of his letter and the enclosed documents "either now or at a later date, so that the world may learn of the cruelties committed in the 20th century in so-called civilised countries."[26]

Krausz's material was passed not only to its intended recipient, Chaim Posner of the Jewish Agency's Palestine Office, but also to George Mantello, a Jewish businessman and rescue activist from Transylvania working at the Salvadoran consulate in Geneva. As requested by Krausz, Mantello published the information at once and started an international publicity campaign to halt the massacre of Hungary's Jews—a campaign that would play a vital role in preventing the mass deportation of the Jews of Budapest.

It is instructive to compare the messages to the outside world from Krausz and Kasztner during this period. Krausz's first letter to the Jewish Agency had fallen into the hands of the Red Cross by June 6, but was never forwarded or published; the second was sent on June 19 and resulted in worldwide publicity. Both of these letters stated that hundreds of thousands of Hungarian Jews were being sent to their deaths in Auschwitz. In his second letter, Krausz also pointed to the futility of negotiations, declaring that the Germans were bargaining in bad faith.

Kasztner's letters were sent to the JDC and the Zionists abroad in the space of five days, from June 13 to June 18, and all of them reached the relevant Jewish organizations. While Kasztner stressed that hundreds of thousands of people were being deported, he systematically camouflaged their fate. At first he pretended that most of these Jews were alive and well in Waldsee. Later on, when the Vrba–Wetzler report began to circulate in Budapest and it seemed likely that it would reach the outside world, he only conceded that a minority of "unemployable" Jews were dying in Auschwitz. His final letter appears to have been written specifically in order to defuse the foreign impact of the Vrba–Wetzler report.

Whereas Krausz dismissed the Nazi promises as worthless, Kasztner encouraged the Jewish rescue activists in the free world to devote all their efforts to a Nazi-sponsored "rescue" operation and to accept the Nazi formula of "rescue in the form of a deportation." Whereas Krausz mentioned the possibility of saving small numbers by issuing Palestine entry certificates in Budapest, Kasztner claimed that the Nazis would agree to the transfer of up to twenty-four thousand Jews per week to Palestine. Other aspects of Kasztner's letters, such as the Nazi jargon ("deported human materials"), reinforce the suspicion that they were part of a Nazi disinformation campaign.

The only remaining question is whether Kasztner participated in this campaign voluntarily. Were his letters written under duress? Or were they perhaps doctored without his knowledge?

Duress may appear to be a plausible excuse: after all, Kasztner was living and working under Nazi protection and several of his relatives were being held hostage in a Nazi "preferential camp" in Budapest. The problem is that nowhere in the *Bericht*, in his postwar correspondence, in his interrogations and affidavits at Nuremberg, or in his testimony during the Kasztner Trial did he even hint at such an excuse. The leaders of the Jewish Working Group in Slovakia, Rabbi Weissmandel and Gisi Fleischmann, were also living under the Nazi jackboot, and they too chose to negotiate with the killers; but in their messages to the outside world, they reported the truth about the death camps, demanded the bombing of the railway lines to Auschwitz, and exposed the hoax of the Waldsee postcards.[27] If Kasztner—unlike Weissmandel, Fleischmann, or Krausz—found himself in a master–servant relationship with the SS, it was a relationship he had entered of his own free will.

The possibility that Kasztner's letters abroad were doctored by the Nazis without his knowledge has not been mentioned by his defenders. In any case, there was nothing covert in the transmission of these letters. Until May 1944, the rescue committee had relied on couriers from German military intelligence; but days before the beginning of the full-scale deportation, these military agents had been arrested and their functions, including courier services, had been taken over by the SS. Kasztner acquiesced in this arrangement.[28] Since he had already accepted SS control of his committee's communications with the outside world, there is no reason to believe that he wrote anything that the SS had to alter without his knowledge. If Kasztner had really wanted to send out accurate news of the murder of Hungary's Jews in Auschwitz, he could have turned to neutral consulates or sympathetic foreign diplomats—which is how Krausz dispatched the Vrba–Wetzler report to Switzerland.

Only one possibility remains: the letters examined above were tools in a systematic effort, undertaken with Kasztner's knowledge, to mislead his Jewish contacts abroad—and through them, the outside world—about the state of the negotiations, the prospects for rescue, and the fate of the Hungarian Jewish deportees. Just as Kasztner aided the Nazis by misleading the victims in the ghettos, so he aided the Nazis by deceiving the would-be rescuers in the free world.

Notes

1. Kasztner Trial testimony, March 3, 1954.
2. Edouard de Haller to Max Huber, June 6, 1944, quoted in Arieh Ben-Tov, *Facing the Holocaust in Budapest: The International Committee of the Red Cross and the Jews in Hungary, 1943–1945* (Dordrecht: Kluwer Academic Publishers, 1988), 149–50.
3. Kasztner and Hansi Brand to Pomerantz, June 6, 1944, Kasztner Trial prosecution exhibit 27. Laufer's alias, Schröder, was used in the cable.
4. Meeting of the Jewish Agency Executive, Jerusalem, June 11, 1944, in *The Bombing of Auschwitz: Should the Allies Have Attempted It?*, eds. Michael J. Neufeld and Michael Berenbaum (Lawrence: University Press of Kansas, 2000), 252–3.
5. The Zionist press reported that the "initial transports" of Hungarian Jews had "begun to arrive" in Poland, "indicating the first phase of the liquidation of Hungarian Jewry." See "7,000 Czech Jews Murdered in Gas Chambers," *Palestine Post*, June 11, 1944.
6. Brand-JAE2, para. 36. First Brand cited Eichmann's claim that although deportations would go on, the deportees would not be killed before the reply to the Goods for Blood offer was received. Next he mentioned Krumey's assurance that the deportations would stop as soon as news of the success of his mission reached Budapest. Finally he referred to the Gestapo agents Clages and Laufer: initially they had denied that any deportations were taking place; but subsequently they had admitted that the deportations were under way, and had insisted that the treatment of the deportees "would not be too harsh."
7. *Shertok Report*, 6; Brand-JAE2, para. 39.
8. For MacMichael's summary of the meeting, see High Commissioner to Colonial Office, June 15, 1944, TNA FO 371/42758.
9. The letters—dated June 13, 14, 15 and 18—are held at the Haganah Archive, Division 80/p187/32.
10. Kasztner, *Bericht*, 31.
11. Ibid., 48.
12. Ibid., 50–51.
13. Compare my analysis of this letter with the brief summary in Aronson, *Hitler, the Allies and the Jews*, 260–1, which omits the most important point: Kasztner's lie about the Waldsee postcards. Aronson does mention the Waldsee issue at ibid., 266, but there he attributes the same letter to Blum.
14. A copy of this letter sent to Saly Mayer refers not to three hundred but to three thousand saved from the deportation trains: Kasztner to Schwalb, June 14, 1944, JDC Archive, New York, Saly Mayer Collection, file 20(2).
15. British intelligence intercepted a copy sent to Dobkin: TNA KV 2/132, item 15(a). The British analyst correctly identified the author as Kasztner but misdescribed him as head of the Palestine Office (a position held by Krausz).

16. On the secrecy decision, see the eye-witness testimonies of Thomas Edmund Konrad and Andrew Elek (Samu Stern's grandson), Letters, *AJR Journal* (Association of Jewish Refugees, UK), November 2008 and January 2009, respectively. On the belated circulation of the Auschwitz Protocols, see Braham, *The Politics of Genocide*, Vol. 2, 828.
17. Aronson, "New Documentation on the Destruction of Hungarian Jewry and the Rescue Attempts," 140.
18. Kasztner, Interrogation No. 1581a, 6.
19. Kasztner Trial testimony, March 1, 1954.
20. Biss, *A Million Jews to Save*, 64.
21. Aronson, *Hitler, the Allies and the Jews*, 258.
22. Braham, *The Politics of Genocide*, Vol. 2, Appendix 6: Deportation Trains Passing Though Kassa in 1944: Dates, Origins of Transports, and Number of Deportees, 1403–5.
23. *The Letters and Papers of Chaim Weizmann, Series B—Papers, Vol. II: December 1931–April 1952* (New Brunswick, NJ: Transaction Publishers, 1984), 536.
24. The Vrba–Wetzler report had reached Nathan Schwalb on May 17 and he had forwarded it to the JAE's Eliahu Dobkin two days later: David Kranzler, *The Man Who Stopped the Trains to Auschwitz: George Mantello, El Salvador, and Switzerland's Finest Hour* (Syracuse, NY: Syracuse University Press, 2000), 70. Apparently Schwalb did not show his copy to Lichtheim, whose June 19 letter indicates that he had only just read the report. Another copy reached Jaromir Kopecky, the Geneva representative of the Czech government-in-exile, on June 10, and its contents were summarized in a BBC broadcast on June 18. The BBC broadcast, which reflected Kopecky's concern to prevent the imminent gassing of several thousand Czech Jews, said nothing about Hungary: Linn, *Escaping Auschwitz*, 29–30.
25. Lichtheim to Grünbaum, June 19, 1944, in *Archives of the Holocaust, Vol. 4: Central Zionist Archives, Jerusalem, 1939–1945*, ed. Francis R. Nicosia (New York: Garland Publishing, 1990), 125–7.
26. Krausz to Posner, June 19, 1944, YVA, P 12; for the modified version circulated by George Mantello and his supporters, see Kasztner Trial defense exhibit 126.
27. For example, Weissmandel's letters of May 16 and 31, 1944, in *Min ha'meitzar*, 103–11, 182–9. Unfortunately, these letters took several weeks to reach their intended recipients.
28. Kasztner, *Bericht*, 36.

11

The Strasshof Operation

In his messages to Jewish rescue activists in the free world about the Strasshof deal, Kasztner claimed that he had saved Jews from four provincial ghettos, when in fact they had already been sent to Auschwitz. This could be seen as evidence that his entire involvement in the shipments to Vienna was an invention. Perhaps Kasztner had nothing to do with the Strasshof operation. The falsehoods in his messages do point to such a conclusion.

That conclusion is mistaken. It is true that the Strasshof operation was *initiated* by the Nazis and not by Kasztner. Nevertheless, Kasztner did play a role in *organizing* these transports. As he explained in the *Bericht*: "the committee sent a letter to the rabbis or other personalities of the chosen ghettos, establishing the said principles for selecting the Jews to be sent to Austria. I then gave the lists and letters to Wisliceny," and "it was up to him to decide from which ghettos trains should leave for Austria."[1]

This account provokes important questions. Eichmann's SS unit had been instructed to send thousands of Hungarian Jews to Austria. The transfers to Austria were to take place regardless of anything that Kasztner said or offered, and the choice of ghettos lay with the SS. So what was the point of involving Kasztner, who did not initiate the scheme and was not in control of its execution? Why did the SS take lists and letters from the head of the Jewish rescue committee to the ghettos in question?

The answer is suggested in an observation by the Kasztner Trial judge, Benjamin Halevi, about the lists of VIPs for the Kasztner Train: "Everywhere the Nazis used the rescue plans and lists . . . as an incentive for the Jewish leaders to co-operate in the full-scale deportation process."[2] Arguably, the rescue committee's instructions to draw up the lists of deportees to be transferred to Austria had the same effect: these instructions induced the local *Judenrat* leaders to comply with the deportation plan and to prevent any disruption of the transports to Poland. Kasztner's role in the operation, on this view, was to ensure an orderly process of deportation.

Is Halevi's comment on the VIP lists true of the Strasshof lists as well? Did Kasztner actually agree to use the Strasshof operation as a means to pacify the remaining provincial ghettos? It is important to bear in mind his testimony in the Kasztner Trial:

> Usually I didn't believe Eichmann. I had no confidence that the 15,000 wouldn't be sent to extermination, but I had hope, Eichmann himself offered me inspection. In the first stage I had no possibility of inspecting. The first stage was one or two months.[3]

According to his own account, Kasztner had no reason to believe that he was involved in a rescue action or that any Jews would be kept "on ice," as Eichmann promised. He sent letters urging local *Judenrat* leaders to draw up lists of deportees in compliance with the deportation plan, but he suspected that all of these deportees would be sent to Auschwitz. And in the first week of the operation, *all of the deportees were indeed sent to Auschwitz*. Kasztner's treatment of this dismal fact is instructive.

The relevant section of the *Bericht* is entitled "Two Trains Were Exchanged." Kasztner tells the following story. Some three thousand Jews from the ghettos of Győr and Komárom had been selected for transfer to Strasshof. But thanks to an oversight by the SS escort, their train was misdirected to the border of Slovakia. As three thousand terrified human beings waited—trapped in the railway wagons—the SS escort cabled Eichmann for instructions; and Eichmann decided that since the train was already *en route* to Auschwitz, it would proceed all the way to the extermination camp. As Kasztner put it, three thousand Jews had been "chosen by fate" for death. But Eichmann—so says the *Bericht*—"compensated" the rescue committee for the disaster by sending a trainload of deportees from the city of Debrecen to Austria. "Fate," remarked Kasztner, "goes its own way."[4]

Such is Kasztner's version. The truth was still more horrible. To begin with, the Győr/Komárom train departed on June 16, but the first train from Debrecen to Strasshof departed on June 26.[5] Whereas Kasztner led his readers to believe that the two trains were switched *at the same time* as an outcome of a tragic confusion, there was in reality a ten-day interval between them. During that time, all that Kasztner knew was that three thousand Jews had entered a deportation train with the rescue committee's encouragement and had perished in the gas chambers as a result. Meanwhile the other Jews from Győr and

Komárom had obediently boarded the death trains as well. There is no reason to believe that one of the subsequent trains to Strasshof was intended as "compensation" for the train that had been "misdirected" to Auschwitz—and there is no evidence that Kasztner did believe this at the time.

Nor is there any evidence for the tale that the Győr/Komárom train was originally heading for Strasshof but was redirected to Auschwitz through misfortune. Indeed, there is evidence against it. In his June 18 letter to the JDC, Kasztner wrote: "The first of these transports [to Austria] will leave this week from Miskolc, Győr, Komárom, Érsekújvár, comprising 12,000 people in the unemployable category." In fact, all twelve thousand—not just the three thousand on the Győr/Komárom train—had already been sent to Auschwitz. Yet Kasztner boasted that all twelve thousand were part of his "rescue operation." Whether or not he was already aware of their fate when he wrote his letter to the JDC is immaterial here: the key points are his confession that he did not trust Eichmann's promises; that he had no way to verify the destination of the trains; that he suspected that the trains would go to Auschwitz; and that he nevertheless wrote to local Jewish leaders with instructions for organizing the deportees—and the fact that all of the Jews from these ghettos were indeed deported to the death camp.[6]

As an indication of the rescue options that existed in some of these communities, one inmate of the Miskolc Ghetto heard the local Zionists urging the ghetto's *Judenrat* to gather weapons. The leaders of the *Judenrat* threatened to betray the Zionists to the Nazis if they tried to organize resistance. This inmate obtained false identity papers, disguised herself with a crucifix, and walked out of the ghetto unchallenged.[7]

Himmler's Blackmailer

By the third week of June, over fifty thousand Jews had been transported from northern Hungary (designated Zone 3 by the SS) to Auschwitz. In total, 340,000 Jews had boarded the death trains.[8] Not a single Hungarian Jew had gone to a labor camp in Strasshof. The extravagant rescue claims in Kasztner's messages to his Jewish contacts abroad served to camouflage this human catastrophe.

The deportations then came to a standstill as the *Eichmann-Kommando*'s allies in the gendarmerie began the ghetto drive in southern Hungary (designated Zone 4 by the SS). Until June 16, the forty-one thousand Jews in these provinces had not yet been concentrated and it was by no means impossible to instigate a mass flight to neighboring Yugoslavia and Romania. It took the gendarmes until June 20 to move these Jews into ghettos. The fact that the concentration and deportation plan had to be carried out in geographic stages—region by region—explains why the *Eichmann-Kommando* was so determined to prevent panic and unrest among the victims.

As soon as the concentration in Zone 4 was completed, Kasztner received another "promotion" from the Nazis: on June 20, Eichmann introduced him to Becher, head of the Waffen-SS economic staff in Hungary. Kasztner now had a liaison to Himmler. In the *Bericht* he justified the relationship with two arguments: Becher was the *eminence grise* behind Eichmann's concessions; and Becher, as Himmler's appointee, was in a position to exert a positive influence on SS policy toward Hungarian Jews.[9]

The first argument is demonstrably false. Eichmann had granted no concessions to Kasztner, beyond allowing him to take credit for the survival of a few hundred hostages who were under SS control in Budapest. No one had been sent to Austria. Kasztner had not even earned the *appearance* of rescuing people under the Strasshof plan. Indeed, his growing desperation to regain his lost "moral credit" (and so avoid suspicion of treason) may have been one reason for his evident relief at Becher's intervention in the talks. In any case, neither Becher's self-serving statements at Nuremberg nor Kasztner's affidavits on his behalf refer to his supposed role in the Strasshof deal.[10] Since Becher's life was at stake during the Nuremberg investigations, he surely would have mentioned this "rescue operation" if he had indeed tried to save many thousands of lives this way.

The absence of concessions from Eichmann also illuminates the second point: that Becher had some power over Nazi Jewish policy in Hungary. What had been the results of Becher's influence so far? The ghetto concentration and the deportations to Auschwitz had been accomplished on schedule. Hundreds of thousands of Jews had been massacred in record time and with extreme cruelty. To the extent that Becher played a role in these events, it was not positive but negative. As Kasztner expressed it, there was "exemplary teamwork" between the SS departments: Eichmann's unit "liquidated," while Becher's economic staff "cashed in."[11] If Eichmann was Hitler's butcher, then Becher may be classified as Himmler's blackmailer. In the context of the Holocaust, the success of the blackmailer depended on the work of the butcher.[12]

Since Kasztner himself called Becher an extortionist, it is all the more remarkable that Becher never attempted to collect the sums that Kasztner had supposedly promised to pay the SS for the Strasshof deal. According to the *Bericht*, the Strasshof "rescue" fee of $1.5 million ($100 per head for fifteen thousand Jews) "never came to payment."[13] This fact is yet more evidence that there never was such a rescue deal. In truth, Kasztner learned of the planned shipments of Jewish slaves from Hungary to Austria and hastened to collaborate in further deportations, with the aim of taking credit for supposedly saving Jews. And the price for preserving his new-found status was paid not in money or valuables delivered to Becher, but in the lives of tens of thousands of victims deported by Eichmann.

Organizing the Deportations

By the time of Kasztner's meeting with Becher, not one Jew had been transferred to Strasshof. Every deportation train from Hungary had been routed to Auschwitz. Kasztner had repeatedly wagered that one or another ghetto transport would end up in the labor camp instead of the death camp—and each time he had bet on the wrong number. In his letters abroad, he had even gone to the lengths of naming four ghettos from which twelve thousand Jews had been saved, only to learn that they too had perished in the gas chambers. Like a desperate and losing gambler, he reacted by doubling his bets. If Jews had not been taken to Vienna from Zone 3, surely they would be taken there from Zone 4. All he had to do was to send instructions from the rescue committee to a few more ghettos. This time, he would definitely win back his "moral credit."

Kasztner's position was reinforced by the support he received from Becher, who (according to the *Bericht*) "encouraged Eichmann to keep our train-for-train agreement" (meaning that Eichmann had not kept it so far). Eichmann, in response, "demanded that I provide assistance in organizing the transport to Austria."[14] Since Kasztner had no power to transport Jews or determine their destination, this demand had but one meaning: he had to earn his "rescue achievement" by ensuring an efficient deportation from the ghettos—whether the trains were directed to Strasshof or to Auschwitz.

On June 20, after eight thousand six hundred Jews had been concentrated in the Szeged brick factory, an SS *Hauptsturmführer* arrived with a letter from Kasztner's aide Szilágyi to the Jewish leaders. One of those leaders, Dr. Leopold Löw, left a detailed account of what followed:

> In this letter Szilágyi approached us as his old friends, telling us that he was going to ease the condition of the Jews of the country. . . . Szilágyi's mission was to select 3,000 Jews from the camp according to the following criteria: 1. families with many children; 2. families of labour servicemen; 3. members of the families of those who prominently participated in the religious bodies of the Jews. . . . [The SS officer] expected us to keep everything in absolute secret, this is why he did not allow me to translate Szilágyi's letter into Hungarian so that no bystander [in the brickyard] could understand it.[15]

Löw and his colleagues set to work compiling the secret list of three thousand Jews according to the criteria set out by Szilágyi. The SS then arbitrarily reduced the numbers on the list to two thousand four hundred and specified that only children under twelve and adults over fifty were to be included.[16] The community leaders had to set to work all over again—this time deleting names from their original list.

Although there was a brief outbreak of panic when the SS insisted on conducting a head count of those on the list, the Jews were reassured by the standard rumor—spread by the Germans—that all transports leaving the brickyard would remain within Hungary. On the deception of the Jewish leaders in Szeged, Löw had this to say:

> Naturally, as members of the committee we had no idea that the selection was a decision between life and death. We did not know either about the death camp in Auschwitz, or that our brothers in Szeged were going to be transported there, or that the people on the list would be sent to Austria . . .

Such was the lack of information in Szeged that when the deportations commenced, there were Jews who hastened to join the first transport so that families could stay together or because they expected to rejoin their relatives elsewhere in the country. All these Jews—more than three thousand in total—were sent to Auschwitz.[17] Only after their orderly deportation were two more trains, carrying over five thousand Jews, dispatched to Austria. The fact that more than twice as many were sent to Strasshof as were named on the list prepared by Löw and his colleagues shows that the list procedure was not necessary for the operation. Its real purpose, from the standpoint of the SS, was to distract the Jewish leaders and to integrate them into the deportation system.

In Szolnok, four thousand six hundred Jews were concentrated in a sugar factory in the open air. The selections for Strasshof were carried out by the community leaders according to the same list procedure. It was described by one of the ghetto inmates:

> The Jewish Council was asked to organize the people in the camp into two groups, A List and B List. The lists were widely distributed throughout the compound. We were on the B List. My grandmother noticed that all the wealthy people in the town were on the A List. . . . The people on the A List were loaded onto one train, and the people on the B List were loaded onto the other. The train carrying the A List went to Strasshof. . . . The train carrying people on the B List headed for Auschwitz.[18]

From this account it is obvious that the masses were told nothing about the purpose of the lists, while the leaders believed that the A List was a guarantee of preferential treatment. Other eye-witness accounts confirm that the victims had no information at all about the destination of the trains.[19] In Szolnok (as in Szeged) the lists procedure meant helping the authorities to organize the Jewish public for the deportations.

In Kecskemét over five thousand four hundred Jews had been concentrated. Here too, lists were drawn up on the assumption that people would be sent to Austria. But the information turned out to be false. Two deportation trains left this ghetto, but neither was destined for Strasshof. According to a survivor of the second transport:

> we were lodged and informed that the next morning we would be set off. The destination, of course, was unknown to us. *The Kecskemét Jews asserted that we were bound to Austria, since 2,000 of them had been already selected for being taken there* [emphasis added]. As we travelled towards Hatvan, we realised that our destination was Poland. Auschwitz yet was an unknown location to us. We arrived in Auschwitz in the evening after three days of travel.[20]

The Strasshof plan had been used to deceive the entire Jewish population of the ghetto. The Jews of Kecskemét expected to be taken to Austria but they were all deported to Auschwitz. This fact proves what Kasztner's postwar account implied: he had the rescue committee's instructions to compile the lists distributed to the ghettos indiscriminately, encouraging the *Judenräte* to facilitate the deportation plan when he knew that in many of these ghettos the entire population was doomed to die in the gas chambers.

Eichmann wanted "no fuss" in the ghettos. By using the rescue committee to send instructions to the local Jewish leaders about drawing up the lists, he brought them into compliance with the deportation system. The execution of the Strasshof operation belies Kasztner's postwar denial that the provincial *Judenräte* had to help assemble transports to Auschwitz.[21] The *Judenräte* were indeed made to participate—albeit unknowingly—in organizing people for deportation to the extermination camp. In selecting some Jews for preferential treatment (the A List), they were unwittingly selecting other Jews for death (the B List). And the list procedure that made them participate in the SS deportation system was the direct result of Kasztner's decision to "provide assistance in organizing the transport" that Eichmann had been ordered to send to Austria.

Kasztner's Changing Story

The deportations from Zone 4 were carried out during June 25–28. Over four days, twenty-six thousand Jews were sent to Auschwitz. Since Eichmann could no longer delay providing the manpower required by the authorities in Vienna, he transported the remaining fifteen thousand Jews in these ghettos to Austria. The trains to Vienna departed from four sites: Debrecen, Szeged, Szolnok, and Baja.[22]

The Strasshof slave labor camp was under the command of Krumey, Eichmann's right-hand man, who was dispatched to Vienna for the purpose. Under his management, about a quarter of the inmates died or were killed in various ways—a death rate of 25 percent in the space of a year.[23] Krumey had people transferred from Strasshof to Auschwitz for "breaches of discipline" such as possession of money. His last act before evacuating the camp at the end of the war was to burn the comprehensive card index of its population, which would have revealed the exact number of Jews he had deported from the site to their deaths.[24]

During and after the war, Kasztner provided multiple versions of his "rescue" deal with Eichmann. He kept changing his story with respect to the number of Jews taken to Strasshof and the timing and content of the bargain. For instance:

- On July 12, 1944, Kasztner wrote that four trains containing "about 5,000" Jews had been sent to Strasshof instead of Auschwitz.[25] Perhaps he made a typographical error and meant to write "about 15,000." Or perhaps he still did not know how many Jews on the various lists had been transferred to Austria, as promised, and how many had been deported to Auschwitz.

- On October 21, 1945, Kasztner wrote that he had reached a provisional agreement with Eichmann after the public British rejection of the Goods for Blood offer: under this agreement, fifteen thousand Jews were in fact taken to Austria; another fifteen thousand were meant to be taken there from Budapest, but Hungarian Regent Miklós Horthy's veto of deportations from the capital made it superfluous.[26] This version was chronologically impossible, since the British did not publicly reject the Goods for Blood offer until *after* Horthy's veto.
- In December 1946, Kasztner submitted his comprehensive report, the *Bericht*, to the Zionist Congress. There he described an agreement with Eichmann, concluded *during* the Goods for Blood talks, to send fifteen thousand Jews from the provinces and fifteen thousand from Budapest to Austria. He asserted that six trains, carrying eighteen thousand Jews, had actually arrived in Strasshof.[27]
- On July 18, 1947, Kasztner told an interrogator at Nuremberg that, as a result of his negotiations, "about 17,000 Jews were taken from the provinces to Austria," and "about 15,000 Jews were removed from the provincial ghettos by the SS and taken to Budapest."[28] On this occasion, Kasztner claimed to have saved no fewer than thirty-two thousand Jews from the provincial ghettos by means of the Strasshof deal.

From these examples it is apparent that Kasztner could not make up his mind whether the Strasshof deal had been reached during or after the Goods for Blood talks; whether it included Jews from the provinces and the capital or from the provinces alone; or whether the total number of Jews transferred was five thousand, fifteen thousand, eighteen thousand, or thirty-two thousand. If Kasztner had really initiated the Strasshof operation and if he had really played a legitimate role in its implementation, then he would not have found it so difficult to remember the basic facts. The multiple contradictions in his accounts, and the obvious inaccuracy of some of them, discredit them all. The reason for these inconsistencies is that he was anxious to disguise his actual role in the operation—and to invent one or more fictitious versions that would enable him to appear before the bar of history as a "rescuer."

The truth about the Strasshof operation is as follows. Eichmann had been ordered to send several thousand Hungarian Jews to Vienna for slave labor before their eventual extermination. Kasztner was informed of the plan, either by Eichmann or by Wisliceny, and agreed to collaborate. He sent a series of messages to foreign Jewish organizations in which he conveyed the news of his impressive "rescue operation" while camouflaging the mass murder of hundreds of thousands in the gas chambers. He also helped Eichmann to organize the deportations from several ghettos by instructing the local *Judenräte* to make the selections for the transports.

Kasztner's aim was to restore his "moral credit" vis-à-vis the Jewish organizations abroad by misrepresenting the Nazi scheme as his own large-scale "rescue operation." If any of the Jews in Strasshof survived, they would be living proof of his achievement. The Nazis' aims were to deceive foreign opinion about the extermination campaign, to extort money or goods from world Jewry if possible, and to keep order in the remaining ghettos before sending the Jews to their deaths. In this episode, the needs of the collaborator dovetailed with the interests of the mass murderers. Meanwhile the destruction of the Jewish population of Hungary proceeded according to plan.

Notes

1. Kasztner, *Bericht*, 53.
2. Kasztner Trial verdict, s. 61.
3. Kasztner Trial testimony, March 2, 1954.
4. Kasztner, *Bericht*, 55.
5. Braham, *The Politics of Genocide*, Vol. 2, 723–4.
6. The populations of the four ghettos were Miskolc—13,500, Győr—5,635, Komárom—5,040, Érsekújvár—4,843. Total—29,018. Source: Braham, *The Politics of Genocide*, Vol. 1, 690.
7. Yehudi Lindeman, ed., *Shards of Memory: Narratives of Holocaust Survival* (Westport, CT: Praeger, 2007), 15.
8. Veesenmayer to Foreign Office, June 30, 1944: NMT Vol. XIII, NG-2263, 359.
9. Kasztner, *Bericht*, 52.
10. For example, Kasztner Trial defense exhibit 107 (Becher affidavit), prosecution exhibit 73 (Kasztner affidavit).
11. Kasztner, *Bericht*, 62.
12. For elaboration, see Kasztner Trial verdict, ss. 115–16; Kasztner Appeal, Silberg verdict, s. 38.
13. Kasztner, *Bericht*, v.
14. Kasztner, *Bericht*, 52.
15. DEGOB, Protocol 3618. The city's Neolog rabbi, Dr. Jenő Fränkel, also recorded the day's events. He too wrote that the letter containing the instructions to draw up the lists was signed by Szilágyi: Kasztner, *Bericht*, 54.
16. DEGOB, Protocol 3618.
17. Ibid.
18. Quoted in Agnes Kadar, "Historical Position of the Hungarian Jewry and Untold Ghetto Accounts," in *Life in the Ghettos During the Holocaust*, ed. Eric Sterling (Syracuse, NY: Syracuse University Press, 2005), 51–52.
19. For example, Zvi Nassi, *Ha'Haglayah: eduyot megurashim me'Hungaryah le'Ostriyah bi'tekufat ha'Shoah [The Exile: Testimonies of Deportees from*

Hungary to Austria During the Holocaust] (Jerusalem: Achva College of Education, 1995), 102ff, 114ff. I am grateful to Eli Reichenthal for this source.

20. DEGOB, Protocol 3192. At the beginning of June, the Jews of Kecskemét had received postcards from Waldsee. Moshe Sanbar witnessed the result: "It is impossible to describe the effect these cards had on the Jews.... The postcards acted as a sleeping drug, coming just at the right time ... to remove any thought of revolt or escape.... As far as I know nobody fled." Moshe Sandberg (Sanbar), *My Longest Year: In the Hungarian Labour Service and in the Nazi Camps* (Jerusalem: Yad Vashem, 1968), 18.

21. Kasztner, *Bericht*, 68.

22. Szita, *Trading in Lives?*, 103, gives this breakdown: Debrecen—6,641, Szeged—5,239, Szolnok—2,567, Baja—564. Total—15,011.

23. Braham, *The Politics of Genocide*, Vol. 2, 736.

24. Kasztner, *Bericht*, 152, 171.

25. Kasztner to Schwalb, July 12, 1944, Haganah Archive, 80/p187/32.

26. Kasztner to JAE, October 21, 1945, Kasztner Trial defense exhibit 142.

27. Kasztner, *Bericht*, 50.

28. Kasztner, Interrogation 1581a, 6–7.

12

Gestapo Informer

If Kasztner could not allow anyone to spread panic in the ghettos, still less could he support attempts by the Zionists to organize resistance and espionage.

On the contrary, Kasztner's dependence on SS patronage—his unique negotiating position, his freedom from detention, his privileges such as exemption from the Yellow Star, and his right to arrange the departure of a select group of Jews—required him to undermine resistance plans; and hence Kasztner's role in the betrayal of Zionist paratroopers from Palestine.

During the latter stages of the war, the Jewish Agency sent several volunteers to Europe to organize resistance and rescue attempts.[1] In January 1944, the agency made plans to send three such agents to Budapest. The plans came to fruition when the British army agreed to parachute three Zionists into Yugoslavia on a military mission to smuggle radio transmitters into Hungary for espionage purposes.

The first paratrooper, Hannah Szenes, crossed the Hungarian border on June 9 and was immediately captured with her escorts and radio. Unaware of this calamity, the other two, Yoel Palgi and Peretz Goldstein, crossed on June 19, prudently leaving their radio at the border with instructions to forward it to them later. Arriving in Budapest, they contacted Kasztner, their former Zionist youth instructor in Kolozsvár.

The head of the rescue committee was most alarmed to see Palgi and Goldstein. He saw their arrival as a direct threat to himself, his committee, and his deals with the Nazis. Soon after meeting these two paratroopers, he informed his Gestapo/SD contact, Gerhard Clages, that he was in touch with them. Remarkably, he then persuaded Palgi to report to the Nazis in the guise of a Jewish Agency rescue negotiator. Palgi was arrested within days. Meanwhile Goldstein was hidden among the Kasztner Train candidates in Columbus Street—until Kasztner induced him to surrender. Thus both paratroopers who had contacted Kasztner fell into enemy hands, and their mission was sabotaged.

The outcome of the paratroopers' mission to Hungary raises several issues. Did Kasztner have any legitimate reason for informing the Gestapo that he was in contact with Palgi and Goldstein? What did he hope to achieve by sending Palgi to report to the Nazis? What was his role in Goldstein's surrender? These issues were examined in detail at the Kasztner Trial—with unfortunate results for Kasztner—and can now be revisited in light of subsequent evidence.

The information about Kasztner's treatment of the paratroopers Palgi and Goldstein comes from several sources. These are problematic, to say the least.

Kasztner's various accounts manipulated dates and facts and were full of evasions and contradictions, all calculated to sanitize his role in the affair. These were exposed during the Kasztner Trial and helped to turn public opinion against him. In his main trial testimony, for example, he did not mention two central facts that emerged under cross-examination: that he had informed the Gestapo of his contact with Palgi and Goldstein; and that he had then persuaded Palgi to report to the Gestapo headquarters in person and thereby abandon the paratroopers' military mission.[2]

Palgi himself made a formal complaint against Kasztner to the Zionist movement in December 1946.[3] But his Mapai superiors soon persuaded him to hide his suspicions from the public, and a year later he wrote an adulatory article for the party newspaper upon Kasztner's arrival in Palestine.[4] At the Kasztner Trial, this balancing act fell apart; after describing Kasztner as a hero, Palgi was forced to admit to "deliberately lying" in the original edition of his memoirs in order "to protect Kasztner."[5] The revised edition, issued in 1977, provided a much more damaging description of Kasztner's role.

Similar problems plague the testimonies of Hansi Brand and the Zionist youth leaders, all of whom were concerned to exculpate Kasztner for reasons of personal and political loyalty. Hansi Brand, for example, appears to have coordinated crucial elements of her testimony with Kasztner.[6]

Nevertheless, there is enough consistent evidence in these accounts to lead us to the truth about Kasztner's treatment of Palgi and Goldstein—and to document his activities as a high-level informer for the Gestapo.

Kasztner's Greeting

Kasztner explains in the *Bericht* that the Jewish Agency in Palestine had made plans to dispatch three agents on a dual mission: sending intelligence to the Allies and preparing Hungary's Jews for resistance to a Nazi occupation. "In the whirl of events," he writes, "we had long since abandoned hope for the arrival of our three comrades."[7] The words "abandoned hope" imply that he had been looking forward to the arrival of these Zionist agents from Palestine. His reaction to the appearance of Palgi and Goldstein at his home, on June 20 or 21, 1944, told a different story. As Palgi recalled, Kasztner became agitated and turned pale upon recognizing him. His first words were: "Are you mad? How did you get here?"[8]

At a second meeting the next morning, Kasztner told Palgi all about his talks with the *Eichmann-Kommando* and the fate of Hungary's Jews. Kasztner later described the general situation at the time: every day, thousands of people were being sent in cattle cars to Auschwitz. The provincial communities had been almost wiped out. Jews in Budapest had been transferred to specially marked houses so that they too could be deported to their deaths. "Everything, but everything, seemed lost," Kasztner wrote in the *Bericht*.[9]

But this is not what he told the two paratroopers. According to Palgi, Kasztner credited himself with single-handedly saving the Jews of Budapest and claimed that many of the provincial Jews were also alive. All of this, allegedly, was thanks to his dealings with the *Eichmann-Kommando*. Palgi summarized what he heard from Kasztner:

> The Germans believe in [Goods for Blood] and it's good that they believe in it. . . . Its initial success: a quarter of a million Jews had not yet been deported from Budapest, their fate hanging on the outcome of the negotiations. Tens of thousands or perhaps hundreds of thousands of Jews were in the death camps. But a specific command to put them to death had not yet been given.[10]

But by the time he met Palgi in the second half of June 1944, Kasztner knew that the Germans did *not* believe in any mass rescue deal, as they had no intention of sparing the Jews; that the deportation from Budapest to Auschwitz had *not* been suspended thanks to his talks with the Nazis, but was in fact imminent; and that there were *not* hundreds of thousands of provincial Jews alive in the death camps, because orders had already been given to put them to death.[11] Most important, since the deportation from Budapest was already in preparation, he knew that his continued talks with the *Eichmann-Kommando*, and his vain promises of a negotiated rescue, were gaining time not for the Jews but for the Nazis.

Palgi's account of Kasztner's words mirrors what Kasztner was then telling the outside world (unbeknownst to Palgi) in his letters to Jewish rescue activists. It reflects a pattern of deception by Kasztner in relation to the fate of Hungary's Jews as they were being annihilated. Here the misrepresentations served a specific purpose: convincing the paratroopers—who had come to further the British war effort and to organize Jewish resistance—not to undermine his relations with the Nazis.

At this meeting, Kasztner began to weaken the paratroopers' commitment to their mission by offering a fictitious account of the Goods for Blood proposal. Palgi described his performance:

> Kasztner's eyes burned with a flame of faith when he spoke of it. . . . Both the Nazis and Kasztner were waiting impatiently for Brand's return. *Eichmann promised that for the time being they wouldn't destroy any Jews, but keep them "on ice," as he put it* [emphasis added] . . . .

> "We'll save hundreds of thousands!" Kasztner cried, with shining eyes.[12]

This too was a litany of falsehoods. A week before the paratroopers reached him, Kasztner had warned Eichmann that the gassing of Hungary's Jews in Auschwitz had ruined his "moral credit" because no one thought that the Nazis took the negotiations seriously; and Eichmann had shouted in reply that Germany did not have the resources to keep the deportees alive.[13]

Thus before Palgi and Goldstein had even had the chance to acquaint themselves with the Zionist youth movements they were to organize in their resistance mission for the Jewish Agency, and before they had obtained the radio transmitter to be used in their espionage mission for the British army, Kasztner was already demoralizing them with disinformation. He falsely advised them that the gassing of the provincial Jews and the deportation of the capital's Jews had been postponed thanks to his negotiations, implying that pursuing either of the paratroopers' missions would risk Jewish lives.

But the Zionist paratroopers were unpersuaded by Kasztner's words.[14] Kasztner's efforts to frustrate their mission now moved into higher gear.

Informing the Gestapo

After the morning encounter with Kasztner, the two paratroopers were to attend a third meeting, this time with the Zionist youth leaders, at the Jewish community building. But as they arrived for this meeting the next day, Palgi and Goldstein noticed that they were being followed. To evade their pursuers, they split up.

According to Palgi's main report to his British military superiors, the paratroopers soon found each other again and went to see Kasztner. But Kasztner had shocking news: in the meantime, assuming that both had been arrested as British spies by the Hungarians, he had decided to approach the Germans "in order to save them." Kasztner told the two paratroopers that he had visited "the German security branch of the Gestapo, and told them that two envoys had arrived in connection with the negotiations on behalf of the Jews for the Brand case." The Germans had "advised" him "to bring these two Jews to them," on the assurance that "all necessary steps" would be taken to free the paratroopers from captivity.[15]

Kasztner's account in the *Bericht* differed slightly: there he stated that Palgi soon contacted the rescue committee and was hidden in a private apartment, but nothing was heard from Goldstein. Fearing that Goldstein had been arrested, "we approached Clages, informed him that the two were our colleagues, and requested his intervention." Clages allegedly promised to investigate; he learned that the Hungarians were handling the case and that Goldstein had not been caught.[16] Kasztner elaborated during his trial testimony:

> We went to inform German counter-espionage of the two paratroopers' arrival; the authorities had known of their presence in the country right from the start. . . . The practical and ethical dilemma was whether to try to protect them and ourselves by going to the Schwabenberg [i.e., the SS headquarters] and informing about their presence. The decision was made after Goldstein had vanished; we were afraid that he had fallen into the hands of the Hungarian authorities.[17]

Nowhere does Kasztner refer to a crucial fact recorded in Palgi's mission report: Clages ordered Kasztner to bring both paratroopers to the Gestapo.

In Kasztner's various statements, the decision to inform the Gestapo about his contact with the paratroopers entailed, on the one hand, a humble request to the Nazis to save the paratroopers from the Nazis' Hungarian quislings; and on the other, a devious ploy to mislead those same Nazis about the reason for the paratroopers' arrival and to conceal the truth about their military mission.[18] So two questions arise: Did Kasztner really try to obtain Gestapo protection for the paratroopers? And did he really try to fool the Gestapo with a false alibi for the paratroopers' arrival?

As he explained it to the paratroopers, and as he described it in the *Bericht* and in his trial testimony, Kasztner's motive for informing Clages was to save the paratroopers from the Hungarians. Kasztner purportedly believed that one or both of the paratroopers had been captured and that approaching the Gestapo with the false alibi that they were on a secret diplomatic mission was the only way to free them.

But a request for German protection for the paratroopers would have been logical only on the assumption that the Hungarians were hunting them without the consent of the Nazis. This assumption is belied by Kasztner's own trial testimony, in which he pointed out that the manhunt "was a joint one by the Hungarians and Germans, who cooperated . . . the Germans were following these paratroopers."[19] If he already knew that the Germans were aware of the paratroopers' presence and had instigated the manhunt for them, how then could he have imagined that the Germans would protect the paratroopers from the Hungarians who were obeying their orders? It must have been obvious to Kasztner that the sole aim of the Nazis and the Hungarians alike was to capture these Jewish agents, interrogate them under torture, and, in all probability, execute them. This casts doubt on Kasztner's claim that he was trying to protect Palgi and Goldstein when he informed the Gestapo of his contact with them.

In any case, in the aftermath of the war Kasztner gave a very different explanation of his motive for informing the Nazis. To his friend Hillel Danzig he wrote:

> We asked ourselves what would happen if our connections to these two British officers became clear to the Gestapo. . . . What would have happened to you, staying in the Columbus Camp, if the Germans had linked us, the other party to the agreement, to supporters of sabotage and espionage? And it was not just you. In those days there was a transport of 15,000 Jews from the provincial towns to Austria. . . [and] another 15,000 had to be chosen for forced labor and were to be sent to Austria. We therefore decided on a "pre-emptive remedy" of informing Clages (you remember the Gestapo officer with whom we were in contact) that Peretz [Goldstein] had disappeared and that Peretz and Yoel [Palgi] were [our] close associates . . .[20]

Here Kasztner does not say that he meant to save the paratroopers from the Hungarians. Instead he claims that he meant to save the Columbus and Strasshof Jews from the wrath of the Nazis. Yet *nowhere does he assert that any threat to harm these Jews in reaction to the presence of the paratroopers was made before he disclosed his contact with them.*

It was Kasztner himself who revealed his connection with Palgi and Goldstein to the Nazis and so created the possibility of pressuring the rescue committee by threatening the Columbus and Strasshof Jews. Far from explaining his conduct, the safety of these Jews would have been a compelling reason for him *not* to inform the Nazis about meeting the paratroopers.

So the true reason for Kasztner's decision to inform Clages about his contact with Palgi and Goldstein stemmed neither from his concern for these paratroopers nor from his concern for the fate of Hungarian Jews. Kasztner's claims along these lines were simply false. A process of elimination reveals that his motive was not to protect others, but rather to protect *himself*—by maintaining good relations with the Nazis. This explains why he did not wait to find out if Palgi and Goldstein had really been captured and why Clages was confident that he would deliver the paratroopers to the Gestapo.

What of Kasztner's supposed false alibi for the paratroopers? Did he really try to fool Clages with this ruse? His explanation of the alibi shifted from one version to another in his postwar statements. In his apologetic letter to Hillel Danzig, written in February 1946, he briefly mentioned telling the Gestapo that the paratroopers "had come to assist us in the preparations and the selection of the list of candidates for the [Kasztner] train."[21] As far as is known, he never repeated that particular version of the alibi. In the *Bericht*, his formal report to the Zionist Congress later that same year, he said nothing about introducing the paratroopers as rescue operatives of any kind.[22] But in his final trial testimony in March 1954, Kasztner offered this explanation of the false alibi:

> If we informed about the arrival of two emissaries of the Yishuv [i.e., the Jewish community in Palestine] who had come from Istanbul to negotiate rescue matters . . . if we argued that the manner of their arrival was the only feasible one and that they had left their radio at the border, then perhaps we could secure a kind of immunity for both of them.[23]

This version was rejected by the court as an insult to its intelligence, and it is not hard to see why. Did Kasztner really try to convince Clages that the only "feasible" way for Jewish Agency negotiators to make contact with the Germans was to parachute into Yugoslavia on a British plane, cross the Hungarian border illegally, make preparations to smuggle a radio transmitter into the country for military espionage purposes, enter Budapest under false identities, and hide themselves from the Germans? For Clages to have been misled by such a tale would have required profound personal stupidity.

In his trial testimony, Kasztner discussed this supposed deception of his Gestapo/SD contact and admitted that Clages was *not* misled regarding the paratroopers' mission. His remarks on this point are telling:

> I don't think [Clages] believed it wasn't espionage. He knew it was espionage but he played along. There were some people who were interested in helping us and Clages was one of them; otherwise he would have arrested us at once. . . . He was one of the people who were interested in helping us. . .[24]

Plainly Clages, the Gestapo/SD officer, was not interested in helping the Hungarian Jews. When Kasztner asserted that Clages was "interested in helping us," what he really meant was that Clages was interested in helping him and his committee. The remark "[Clages was] interested in helping us" betrays the existence of a patronage relationship between the Gestapo/SD officer and the head of the Jewish rescue committee.

The inescapable conclusion is that Kasztner never tried to fool Clages with the tale of "Jewish Agency negotiators" sent to Budapest in the guise of British paratroopers. When he informed Clages of his contact with Palgi and Goldstein, he was ordered to turn them in, so he concocted this story as a pretext for delivering them to the Gestapo without arousing the suspicions of his colleagues. In this affair, Kasztner did not deceive Clages. He deceived Palgi and Goldstein—in collusion with his Gestapo/SD patron Clages.

Sending Palgi to the Nazis

Following his instructions from Clages, Kasztner now set about persuading the paratroopers to report to the Gestapo. The decisive step took place during a meeting in the apartment of Dr. Erzsebet Kurcz, an associate of the rescue committee, on June 23. This meeting was attended by Kasztner, several Zionist youth leaders, and one or both paratroopers; Kasztner claimed that Palgi was present and that Goldstein was still missing, presumed captured.

According to Kasztner's postwar account, he warned Palgi that the arrival of the paratroopers in Budapest was a threat to the safety of the rescue committee and to the success of its rescue operations. His evidence was that his building had been searched by detectives on the hunt for two young men fitting their description.[25] Moreover, Goldstein had fallen into Hungarian hands and could only be freed through Nazi intervention. The only solution was for Palgi to report to the Gestapo, to identify the paratroopers as Jewish Agency rescue negotiators, and to request German protection, starting with the immediate release of Goldstein. Kasztner subsequently explained his reasoning:

> We assumed that Goldstein had been caught, in which case the rescue committee members would also be arrested in the next few hours or days. We were willing to take this chance out of respect for the emissary of the Yishuv. But we gave Palgi the right to decide. . . . Palgi made his decision: he told me to inform the Gestapo headquarters at Schwabenberg of the arrival of the two emissaries and to ask the Germans to free Goldstein, who was a victim of the Hungarian authorities.[26]

So Kasztner's postwar justification for urging Palgi to report to the Gestapo hinged on his claim that Goldstein was nowhere to be found and was believed to have been captured by the Hungarians. Kasztner claimed that in reporting to the Gestapo, Palgi was trying to save Goldstein. However, multiple testimonies prove that Kasztner's justification was a lie. Goldstein reappeared before the end of this meeting (at the very latest)—and Kasztner nevertheless urged *both* paratroopers to present themselves before the Nazis.

Palgi gave several different versions of what transpired in the fateful meeting, but one element was consistent: Kasztner knew that Goldstein had eluded capture and his demand to report to the Nazis was addressed to both paratroopers.

- The most reliable of his accounts are his mission reports to the British, which were not intended for public consumption. Palgi's main report stated that before the meeting he found Goldstein at the agreed *rendezvous*; when they arrived at the meeting together, Kasztner "was amazed to see them because he had been informed that they had been arrested."[27] In his other report, Palgi indicated that both of them were meant to report to the Gestapo and explained that he ordered Goldstein not to accompany him.[28]
- In the first edition of his memoirs, Palgi gave his reasons for objecting to Goldstein's participation: if both paratroopers reported together, as Kasztner was demanding, they would undergo separate interrogations and the Nazis would manage to unravel their alibi.[29]
- Palgi repeated this point in another account published not long afterwards, noting that compliance with Kasztner's demands meant "turning ourselves over to the Gestapo, who would harshly interrogate and even

torture us." For this reason, Palgi instructed Goldstein not to join him ("I at least wanted him to be saved").[30]

- Testifying at the Kasztner Trial, Palgi tried to shield Kasztner by denying Goldstein's presence at the Kurcz apartment meeting, but he added that Goldstein had reappeared soon afterwards and had strongly opposed the idea of reporting to the Nazis.[31]
- Finally, in the revised edition of his memoirs, Palgi repeated that Goldstein had been at the Kurcz apartment meeting and offered his most damning account of Kasztner's methods of persuasion:

> Suddenly, Kasztner quietly said, "I informed them that you were coming."
>
> Peretz and I leaped from our places as though stung, and our shouts came simultaneously. "What have you done?"

Kasztner's protestations of good faith were not too convincing to Palgi, who "felt like a hunted animal and saw no escape. What could be done? Should we kill him and run?" Palgi felt that he had no alternative to reporting, as Kasztner demanded, in the guise of a Jewish Agency rescue negotiator. This, he thought, was a "dreadful mission" with almost zero chance of success. So he decided to go by himself, and instructed Goldstein to leave the country at the first opportunity.[32]

Whichever version of Palgi's reminiscences one chooses to believe, it is clear that saving Goldstein was not the reason why Kasztner ordered Palgi to present himself before the Nazis; on the contrary, Kasztner made this demand to *both* paratroopers and Palgi considered the idea so dangerous that he forbade Goldstein to join him.

There is no need to rely on Palgi's veracity to prove this fact. Other witnesses confirm that Goldstein was not missing at the time, as Kasztner claimed. One of the Zionist youth movement leaders at the Kurcz apartment meeting was Peretz Révész. During the Kasztner Trial he stated repeatedly under oath that Goldstein had been at the meeting.[33] Kasztner's closest aide at the time was Hansi Brand. She testified that Kasztner had told her about the meeting within hours of its conclusion. By the time he sent Palgi to see the Gestapo, "Kasztner already knew that Goldstein had been found."[34]

Kasztner's postwar rationale for sending Palgi to the Gestapo must therefore be discounted as an outright fabrication. Far from persuading Palgi to risk himself in order to save Goldstein from danger, he wanted to send *both* paratroopers into the jaws of the beast. Only Palgi's good sense saved Goldstein from arrest—for the moment.

Kasztner's demand that Palgi and Goldstein report to the Gestapo was a demand to abandon their true mission and turn themselves over the Nazis. When Palgi presented himself at the SS headquarters the next day, he had to give the address of his hiding place—Brand's former apartment.[35] There he was arrested on June 27 by Hungarian agents under Gestapo supervision. Under interrogation, he was tortured so savagely that he tried to commit suicide. He was shown his captured radio and forced to confess the truth about the "Jewish Agency negotiations" ruse and his military mission for the British. He was then handed over to the Gestapo.[36]

The behavior of Clages after Palgi's arrest reinforces the conclusion that the "negotiations" ruse was simply Kasztner's pretext—agreed in advance with Clages—for delivering the paratroopers to the Nazis. Unable to resist the tortures of his interrogators, Palgi broke down and confessed that the whole story about traveling to Budapest under British military cover to further the rescue negotiations was a ploy devised by Kasztner to mislead Clages. Yet Clages, once in possession of this information, neither withdrew his protection from Kasztner's rescue committee nor punished Kasztner in any way—as he surely would have done if Kasztner had really tried to deceive him about a British military operation in Budapest.[37]

Delivering Goldstein to the Hungarians

Palgi had agreed to report to the Gestapo, sacrificing his mission and risking his life, on condition that his young comrade Goldstein would be spirited out of the country as quickly as possible. Goldstein's flight was important not only for humanitarian reasons but also because he was the operator of the radio transmitter that the paratroopers had planned to smuggle over the border. If Goldstein and the radio were captured, he could be forced to reveal his transmission codes, enabling the Hungarians to send disinformation to the British.[38] Kasztner did not yet know (unless it had been divulged to him by Clages) that the radio had already been captured. But having surmised that the paratroopers had been under surveillance from the outset, he had reason to expect that the radio would be intercepted sooner or later. To prevent a serious blow to Allied espionage in Hungary, it was essential to save Goldstein from falling into enemy hands.

With Palgi in Hungarian custody, there was now the obvious danger that he would be used as a hostage to secure Goldstein's surrender. Naturally, the Hungarians could use the rescue committee to convey a message informing Goldstein that Palgi would be killed unless Goldstein turned himself in. To avoid this, Kasztner and his colleagues had to be able to tell the authorities, truthfully, that they did not know Goldstein's whereabouts, and so could not contact him in order to pass along official threats. All this underlined the urgency of supplying false identity papers to Goldstein and ordering the Zionist youth to smuggle him out of the country at once.

The Hungarian authorities did indeed secure Goldstein's surrender by threatening to kill Palgi. Their task was simplified by the fact that Kasztner did not keep his pledge to smuggle Goldstein over the border, but instead "concealed" him in a predictable location in the heart of Budapest—one that was surrounded by SS guards.

In light of Palgi's decision to report to the Gestapo, Goldstein had chosen to flee to Romania. However (as he would later disclose to Palgi in prison), the people in charge of arranging his flight (i.e., Kasztner and the rescue committee) "put me off with all sorts of excuses."[39] Hearing of Palgi's arrest, Goldstein again made plans to leave the capital and cross the border. But then he consulted Kasztner, who convinced him not to escape but to hide in the Jewish camp on Columbus Street. Accordingly (as Goldstein told Palgi in prison), "Kasztner drove me to the camp run by the SS."[40]

Why did Kasztner frustrate Goldstein's escape and instead "conceal" him in the Columbus Street camp? In his conversation with Goldstein and in his postwar accounts, Kasztner argued that his aim was to reunite the young paratrooper with his parents (who were housed in Columbus Street) and then send the whole family out of Hungary in the Kasztner Train.[41] Overlooked in Kasztner's explanation was the pertinent fact that once inside the camp, Goldstein had no escape and could be required to surrender at any time. He could not disguise himself, as the residents included hundreds of his former friends and neighbors from Kolozsvár, some of whom were bound to recognize him; he could not slip away, as all the exits were guarded by the SS; and he could not refuse to surrender, as he was vulnerable to threats against his parents (as well as Palgi). When Kasztner escorted him to the Columbus Street camp, Goldstein's fate was sealed.

The suspicion that Kasztner took Goldstein into the camp on false pretenses is reinforced by his conduct when the time came for the Kasztner Train to leave Budapest. At this point, Kasztner returned to Columbus Street and informed Goldstein that joining his parents on the transport was not such a good idea after all. In Kasztner's words:

> We decided to advise him to stay because we weren't confident that the Germans wouldn't search the train passengers and find him. There was no other way for him to leave the country. Maybe I told Goldstein this. I didn't impose it on him but I advised him after the rescue committee's decision.

Why did Kasztner reverse his previous advice to Goldstein and urge him to remain in the camp after the transport's departure?

> Maybe one of our considerations was that by doing so we could show him to the Gestapo and convince them that he hadn't run away, he had come for the reasons explained by the rescue committee to the Gestapo, meaning for rescue purposes.[42]

Goldstein had to remain behind, the better to deliver him to the Gestapo.

On July 1, hours after the Kasztner Train's departure, Kasztner and several of the rescue committee members were arrested by Hungarian counter-espionage and questioned about Goldstein's whereabouts. The interrogators threatened to execute Palgi unless Goldstein turned himself in. They also told Kasztner that the radio transmitter had fallen into their hands.[43] That put an end to the paratroopers' meager chances of obtaining Gestapo protection as "Jewish Agency rescue negotiators."

Kasztner's account of the interrogation and the consequent surrender of Goldstein changed radically over time. In his postwar letter to Hillel Danzig, he generously placed the blame on Hansi Brand, who "promised the five detectives that she would lead them to Peretz."[44] But during the libel trial several years later, when it became clear that Hansi Brand was not prepared to volunteer as his scapegoat, Kasztner finally confessed the truth. He admitted to approaching his interrogator and asking for permission to leave the Hungarian prison with some colleagues to look for Goldstein.[45]

Kasztner claimed that he just wanted to talk to the young paratrooper, to explain the situation to him, and to offer him a free choice between escape and surrender. But the circumstances of their final meeting in Columbus Street leave no doubt that surrender was Goldstein's only option. The camp was under SS control and the rescue committee members were escorted there by Hungarian counter-espionage agents. Goldstein could not run away—and if he refused to come out, the Hungarian agents would simply ask the SS to deliver him by force. When Kasztner informed Goldstein that Palgi's life was at stake, the outcome was a foregone conclusion. For good measure, Kasztner did *not* tell Goldstein that the radio transmitter had been captured, which meant that the paratroopers' cover story vis-à-vis the Gestapo had been exposed and that Goldstein could expect to be tortured and executed as a British spy.[46]

To summarize: Kasztner originally tried to persuade *both* paratroopers to report to the Gestapo in the guise of rescue negotiators. Palgi, knowing that he had little chance of survival, agreed to report on his own—provided that Kasztner would smuggle Goldstein out of the country. Kasztner promised to do so; but after Palgi's arrest, he took Goldstein to Columbus Street on the pretext of joining his parents on the Kasztner Train. When the transport was due to leave, Kasztner urged Goldstein not to join his parents after all and told him that he too should report to the Gestapo, with the same transparent cover story that Kasztner had given to Palgi. Hours after the transport's departure, Kasztner returned to Columbus Street, informed Goldstein that Palgi's life depended on his surrender to the Hungarian agents waiting outside, but did not disclose that the paratroopers' cover story was now useless.

It is hard to avoid the conclusion that events were manipulated by Kasztner to ensure that Goldstein ended up in a prison cell alongside Palgi. Kasztner was certainly acting under duress by the time he escorted the Hungarian agents to Columbus Street, but the same cannot be said of his prior obstruction of Goldstein's flight from Hungary and his decision to move the paratrooper to an SS-controlled hiding place in Budapest. The facts tend to support Palgi's own assessment: "technically, Dr. Kasztner turned Goldstein over to the enemy."[47]

Conclusion

The significance of the Palgi/Goldstein episode does not lie in the possibility that the two paratroopers might have organized resistance or other rescue activities if they had avoided capture. There was no prospect of an effective Jewish uprising in Budapest at the time, and the paratroopers' mission could not further the nonviolent rescue efforts of the Zionist youth. In addition, the paratroopers were under Hungarian surveillance soon after they crossed the border,[48] and they might well have been caught even without Kasztner's intervention.

What is revealing about the Palgi/Goldstein episode is not the capture of the paratroopers, but rather Kasztner's conduct: he acted as a Gestapo informer.

It is tempting to accept the excuse that Kasztner's priority was to protect the Jews in Columbus Street and that he resorted to informing the Gestapo only out of concern for their safety. That temptation should be resisted. Before Kasztner informed Clages of his meetings with Palgi and Goldstein, the arrival of the paratroopers had yet to provoke a single threat against the Columbus Street Jews or the Kasztner Train deal. But as soon as Kasztner announced the link between his committee and the paratroopers, Clages ordered him to deliver them to the Gestapo; thereafter, the Kasztner Train deal really did hang in the balance. The threatened cancellation of this deal was not the *motive* but the natural *result* of informing Clages. It was a danger incurred by Kasztner's own actions.

Kasztner saw the arrival of the paratroopers as a threat to his position as a Nazi-protected Jewish leader. The head of the Jewish rescue committee had not been granted unique privileges by the Nazi security apparatus so that he could shield Jewish resistance organizers and British military spies. Even knowing of such subversives without telling his protectors would have been regarded as major insubordination. He had to prove his obedience by thwarting any activities liable to displease the Nazis.

By the first week of July 1944, all three Jewish paratroopers sent to Hungary—Szenes, Palgi, and Goldstein—were undergoing systematic torture in the interrogation chambers of the security services. At this time Kasztner's ties with the commanders of these bodies—József Garzoly of Hungarian counter-espionage and Gerhard Clages of the Gestapo/SD—were remarkably close. Both of them, according to his testimony, were anxious to assist him in liberating the paratroopers:

> Garzoly said that with all of his desire to help, he dared not do it as the Germans knew about the episode.... Those who wanted to help [the paratroopers] included Garzoly and the Hungarian government.... Some people were interested in helping us and Clages was one of them.[49]

As the Kasztner Trial judge, Benjamin Halevi, mordantly observed, it was with the "help" of Garzoly and the "help" of Clages that the captured Jewish paratroopers were being beaten to a pulp.[50]

If Clages, Becher, and other top Nazis "wanted to help" Kasztner, it was because they expected Kasztner to help them in return. The ordeal of the paratroopers indicates what kind of help the Nazi security services expected to receive—and did receive—from the head of the Jewish rescue committee.

Notes

1. On the Zionist paratrooper missions to Nazi Europe, see Yoav Gelber, "The Mission of the Jewish Parachutists from Palestine in Europe in World War II," *Studies in Zionism* 7, no. 1 (Spring 1986): 51–76; Judith Tydor Baumel-Schwartz, *Perfect Heroes: The World War II Parachutists and the Making of Israeli Collective Memory* (Madison: University of Wisconsin Press, 2010).
2. See Kasztner Trial verdict, s. 81.
3. Palgi, *Into the Inferno*, 259–61.
4. Palgi, "Le'vo Yisrael Kastner," *Davar*, December 11, 1947, Kasztner Trial prosecution exhibit 39.
5. Kasztner Trial testimony, March 17, 1954.
6. See Kasztner Trial verdict, s. 92, noting that Kasztner first named Hansi Brand as the Gestapo's informant but then switched to the rescue committee's treasurer, Sándor Offenbach—testimony corroborated by Hansi Brand on the witness stand in spite of the fact that Offenbach had no contact with the Gestapo at the time.
7. Kasztner, *Bericht*, 70.
8. Yoel Palgi, *Ruach gedolah ba'ah* [*A Great Wind Came*] (Tel Aviv: Ha'Kibbutz Ha'Meuchad, 1946), 110; his Kasztner Trial testimony, March 16, 1954; *Into the Inferno*, 86.
9. Kasztner to Danzig, February 6, 1946, Kasztner Archive.
10. Palgi, *Ruach gedolah ba'ah*, 114; also his Kasztner Trial testimony, March 16, 1954 ("the deportation had not yet started in Budapest itself. Kasztner claimed that it had not started thanks to his negotiations.... I remember him telling me that the deportation had stopped because of his negotiations."); *Into the Inferno*, 91 ("Tens, perhaps hundreds of thousands of Jews were in death camps. Perhaps there was truth in Eichmann's words to Kasztner that he was keeping these Jews alive for the exchange [with the trucks].")
11. Kasztner had heard from Eichmann himself at the end of May 1944 that "hundreds of thousands of Jews were being taken and destroyed in cold blood": Kasztner Trial testimony, September 16, 1954.
12. Palgi, *Into the Inferno*, 90; cf. Palgi, *Ruach gedolah ba'ah*, 113–14.
13. Kasztner, *Bericht*, 48.
14. *Palgi Report 2*, 9; Palgi, *Ruach gedolah ba'ah*, 116.
15. *Palgi Report 2*, 9. The assumption that the paratroopers had been caught seems hard to reconcile with the demand by Clages that they report to him, for how could Kasztner bring them to see Clages if they were in Hungarian custody? It is possible that Kasztner went to Clages assuming that the paratroopers had been arrested, but Clages replied that this was not so and then demanded that Kasztner deliver them to him.
16. Kasztner, *Bericht*, 71.

17. Kasztner Trial testimony, February 28, 1954.
18. Kasztner Trial verdict, s. 91.
19. Kasztner Trial testimony, February 19 and 28, 1954.
20. Kasztner to Danzig, February 6, 1946.
21. Ibid.
22. Kasztner, *Bericht*, 71–72.
23. Kasztner Trial testimony, March 8, 1954.
24. Ibid.
25. For Kasztner's contradictory accounts of the search, see Kasztner to Danzig, February 6, 1946; *Bericht*, 71; his Kasztner Trial testimony, February 19, February 28 and March 8, 1954. Cf. *Palgi Report 2*, 10, Palgi's Kasztner Trial testimony, March 16, 1954; *Into the Inferno*, 95, 100. Kasztner variously asserted that the search took place an hour after the initial meeting with the paratroopers, or not long before the Kurcz apartment meeting; that the detectives questioned the owner of his building and warned her not to tell him about it, or that they questioned him directly; that there were three civilian detectives, or five Hungarian and German agents; and so on. For analysis, see the Kasztner Trial verdict, s. 97, where Judge Halevi concludes that Kasztner simply invented the search as a tool of emotional blackmail against the paratroopers.
26. Kasztner Trial testimony, March 8, 1954.
27. *Palgi Report 2*, 9.
28. *Palgi Report 1*, 2. Here Palgi omits Kasztner's role in persuading him to report.
29. Palgi, *Ruach gedolah ba'ah*, 123–5.
30. Palgi's account in *Magen baseter [Secret Shield]*, ed. Zerubavel Gilad (Jerusalem: Jewish Agency, 1948), Kasztner Trial defense exhibit 40, 417.
31. Kasztner Trial testimony, March 16, 1954.
32. Palgi, *Into the Inferno*, 101–3.
33. Kasztner Trial testimony, March 30, 1954.
34. Kasztner Trial testimony, March 31, 1954.
35. Hansi Brand's Kasztner Trial testimony, March 31, 1954. Palgi expressed uncertainty on this point in his testimony. Palgi reported not to Clages but to the latter's subordinates.
36. *Palgi Report 1*, 2–3; *Palgi Report 2*, 11–13; *Magen baseter*, 418; *Into the Inferno*, 117–31. Kasztner testified that "Hansi and I ran to Clages, informed him of Palgi's arrest by the Hungarians and begged him to have him released. He promised this." As Judge Halevi observed, "Kasztner tells us this whole story with a straight face," as if Clages could have been expected to rescue the paratroopers from the Hungarians acting on his orders. See Kasztner Trial verdict, s. 91.
37. As noted in Beit-Zvi, *Post-Ugandan Zionism on Trial*, Vol. 2, 116. NB the comment by Hecht, *Perfidy*, 125: "Now revealed as the 'base' of the enemy spy operations, Dr. Kastner remained the trusted pal of the SS Nazis and Hungarian gendarmes who continued to help him 'save Jews.'"
38. *Palgi Report 2*, 14; Palgi, *Into the Inferno*, 129, 137.
39. Palgi, *Into the Inferno*, 176; also *Ruach gedolah ba'ah*, 204; *Magen baseter*, 474.
40. Palgi, *Into the Inferno*, 176.

41. Kasztner to Danzig, February 6, 1946; Kasztner, *Bericht*, 71.
42. Kasztner Trial testimony, February 28, 1954. Under re-examination on March 8, Kasztner pretended that not he but Offenbach had advised Goldstein to stay behind. Cf. Palgi, *Into the Inferno*, 177–8, which offers a confused account of this episode, as related by Goldstein in prison. Palgi's rendition of Goldstein's words conflates two separate events: (i) Kasztner's advice *before* the train's departure to stay behind and report to the Gestapo; and (ii) Kasztner's advice *after* the train's departure to surrender to the Hungarians.
43. Kasztner Trial testimony, March 8, 1954.
44. Kasztner to Danzig, February 6, 1946.
45. Kasztner Trial testimony, March 8, 1954.
46. Kasztner Trial verdict, s. 102.
47. Kasztner Trial testimony, March 18, 1954.
48. Palgi testified that while he and Goldstein were awaiting a train to Budapest, their guide was approached at the station by a Hungarian man. Palgi gave no thought to the incident at the time, but later realized that the mission was probably already doomed at that point: Kasztner Trial testimony, March 16, 1954.
49. Kasztner Trial testimony, March 8, 1954.
50. Kasztner Trial verdict, s. 91.

Hungarian Jews arriving at Auschwitz. Most of the Jews from the train were sent to the gas chambers after this photograph was taken.

A Hungarian Jewish family about to be murdered in Auschwitz.

Rezső Kasztner, head of the rescue committee in Budapest. During the Nazi occupation of Hungary, he became the only Jewish leader allowed to negotiate with the SS.

Joel Brand, member of the rescue committee
in Budapest. He received Adolf Eichmann's
Goods for Blood offer and was sent on a
disastrous mission to Turkey.

Rudolf Vrba, Slovak Jewish escapee from
Auschwitz. With his fellow escapee
Alfred Wetzler, he coauthored an eye-witness
report, the *Auschwitz Protocols*, which
was instrumental in ending the full-scale
deportation from Hungary.

Moshe Krausz, head of the Palestine Office in Budapest, who sent the *Auschwitz Protocols* to the free world. He was also behind large-scale rescue operations that saved tens of thousands of Jews from the fascist terror. Credit: Beit Ha'edut, Nir Galim, Israel.

Yoel Palgi, Zionist paratrooper sent to Hungary
on a military mission. After being captured
and tortured, he later escaped.

Peretz Goldstein, Zionist paratrooper sent to Hungary
on a military mission. After being captured and
tortured, he died in a concentration camp.

Hannah Szenes, Zionist paratrooper sent to
Hungary on a military mission. She was
captured, tortured, and executed.

Shmuel Tamir, defense counsel in the Kasztner Trial, who exposed
Rezső Kasztner's activities during the Holocaust in Hungary.
Credit: Shmuel Tamir's family.

13

Sabotaging Rescue in Budapest

On June 24, 1944, as the Nazis were preparing to destroy the Jewish population of Budapest, two important incidents took place. One was to ignite a firestorm of worldwide publicity. The other was intended to be a closely guarded secret—and so it has remained until now. One was the product of the determination of a Jewish rescuer. The other was the action of a Jewish leader who pretended to be a rescuer.

The background to both incidents was the distribution of the Vrba–Wetzler report, or Auschwitz Protocols, a detailed description of the Nazi extermination process. Several days earlier the report had been forwarded by Moshe Krausz to Switzerland. There it had been handed to George Mantello, an official at the Salvadoran consulate in Geneva. With a record of unorthodox and often illegal activities to rescue people from the clutches of the Nazis, Mantello immediately understood what had to be done: the curtain of secrecy and deception surrounding the mass murder of the Hungarian Jews had to be rent asunder and the news of the crime publicized far and wide.

Mantello distributed copies of the Vrba–Wetzler report to the Swiss government and foreign office, to all Jewish organizations, and to the Papal Nuncio. He also took the information to Walter Garrett, director of the Exchange Telegraph, a British wire service. At Mantello's behest, Garrett summarized the facts in a four-part press release, which he personally delivered to the main Swiss and foreign newspapers and cabled to President Roosevelt, Prime Minister Churchill, and the Archbishop of Canterbury, as well as the Queen of Holland and other figures in the free world. The first newspaper article based on the Vrba–Wetzler report appeared in Switzerland in the *Neue Zürcher Zeitung* on June 24: it was the beginning of Mantello's international press campaign to stop the massacre of Hungarian Jewry—a press campaign that would generate no less than fifty-three articles in the space of two weeks.[1]

Since the Vrba–Wetzler report was now being published abroad, it must have been apparent to the Nazis that immediate action was needed to defuse the situation. The Nazis had to create enough confusion to buy time for their remaining operations. Sure enough, there occurred a second intervention on June 24: Kasztner dispatched a detailed letter to the Zionist rescue activist Nathan Schwalb, who—like Mantello—was based in Geneva. A copy was sent to Saly Mayer of the JDC. After giving an accurate summary of the horrors of the ghettos and deportations in the provinces, Kasztner inserted the crucial item of disinformation:

> The flow of trains to Auschwitz could be neither halted nor contained. Many of the deportees who were sent to work have already given signs of life. All these cards are dated from Waldsee and report that those concerned are fine. A few thousand of these postcards have arrived recently.[2]

Knowing that the destination of the trains could no longer be hidden, Kasztner was now asserting that not all of the deportees had been put to death in Auschwitz: for substantial numbers, according to him, the last stop was not the crematoria at Birkenau but the non-existent work site at Waldsee. Here it must be repeated that—by his own admission in the *Bericht*—Kasztner had been familiar with the purpose of the Waldsee hoax since his deal with Krumey at the beginning of May.

Kasztner's attempt to neutralize the effects of the Auschwitz information abroad did not succeed. Within twenty-four hours, Horthy received a personal appeal from the Pope to end the deportations. And the next day, June 26, he was given an ultimatum by President Roosevelt, who warned that unless the deportations were halted, "Hungary's fate will not be like that of any other civilized nation." Horthy acted at once: he convened his Crown Council to register a protest against the anti-Jewish campaign. In the meeting he urged the Sztójay government not to deport the Jews of Budapest and requested the removal of Baky and Endre from their posts. But he did not try to enforce his wishes, and Sztójay disregarded them. Instead, the country's diplomats were instructed to reassure the Allied and neutral powers that the deportees had been "sent to Germany for work" and that "the Jews' willingness to work diminishes when they are separated from their families," who were therefore accompanying them.[3]

"Kasztner Brought the Postcards"

Since the Sztójay regime had successfully resisted Horthy's half-hearted effort to rein in the anti-Jewish terror, the Nazis were able to proceed with their plans unhindered. Kasztner described the *Eichmann-Kommando*'s next move in the *Bericht*. Eichmann, according to this source, stated that he was about to deport the Jews of Budapest, which would leave thirty thousand Jews in western Hungary. These thirty thousand Jews were not "ethnically valuable material," so Eichmann was willing to move them all to Austria in readiness for an agreement from Istanbul. Kasztner replied that deporting the Jews of Budapest would simply convince the Allies to stop negotiating.[4]

If this version is to be believed, it would appear that Eichmann was offering to spare the lives of another thirty thousand Hungarian Jews, *in addition* to the fifteen thousand already on their way to Strasshof. And it seems that Kasztner, according to his own account, casually dismissed the opportunity to save those Jews—all of whom were subsequently deported to Auschwitz. But Kasztner had learned from bitter experience that Eichmann's promises were not to be trusted. He also knew that whether Hungarian Jews were sent to Austria—where there was an ongoing demand for slave labor[5]—or to Auschwitz was wholly unrelated to his dealings with the SS. Unfortunately, whatever his objections to additional deportations, Kasztner did nothing to disrupt Eichmann's plans for the Jewish population of the capital. On the contrary.

At this point the Nazis resumed their attempts to mislead the Jews of Budapest by distributing postcards allegedly sent from Waldsee, but actually written under duress by Jews arriving at Auschwitz. In Budapest, as in the provincial ghettos, the postcards were used to reassure the victims in advance of their deportation to the death camp. The Nazis had the messages distributed through official Jewish channels. Moshe Krausz, testifying at the Kasztner Trial, described an incident involving three hundred to four hundred postcards:

> By coincidence, I was in the *Judenrat* office and they showed me the postcards. They said that Kasztner had brought them from the Germans. I read a few, then Kasztner came in. . . . When Kasztner arrived, I asked him: "Why did you order the *Judenrat* to distribute the postcards? Have you read the contents? One can see that the contents of the postcards are each identical; that the people wrote them under duress; that the style is the same as well." . . . But Kasztner

insisted that they had to be distributed. Then he left. The *Judenrat* said that since the Germans had sent them via Kasztner—and since Kasztner had said that they should be distributed—they couldn't take it upon themselves not to distribute them, and they would do as Kasztner said.[6]

Krausz repeated his account under cross-examination:

> I entered the *Judenrat*, I found the postcards and started reading them. Meanwhile Kasztner came in. . . . [*Judenrat* leaders] Dr. [Samu] Stern and [Károly] Wilhelm were there. . . . [The Nazis] wanted the whole *Judenrat* to see the postcards, to deceive not just the recipients but perhaps the entire Jewish community. . . . I thought that maybe it would be better not to distribute them, so that fewer Jews would be deceived. The people there didn't want any arguments and they took the postcards from Kasztner. . . . Straight away I asked: "How did these postcards come into your hands? There are no stamps, nothing." And [one of them] said: "Kasztner brought them from Schwabenberg [Eichmann's headquarters]." Perhaps Kasztner didn't bring them himself—maybe he brought them through an aide—but they told me that Kasztner had brought them. All communication [with the Nazis] was via Kasztner.[7]

Although this testimony was uncorroborated at the time, there is no longer any doubt that Krausz was telling the truth about Kasztner's role: we have already seen Kasztner spreading the Waldsee hoax abroad in his messages to Jewish rescue activists in the free world. And he certainly understood that the purpose of the hoax was to facilitate the Nazi extermination campaign by camouflaging the fate of the deportees.[8]

That Kasztner organized the distribution of the postcards in the capital also points to his responsibility for the fake letters and postcards delivered to Jewish leaders in Kolozsvár and other provincial communities. If he forced the functionaries of the central *Judenrat* to spread Nazi disinformation among the Jewish public in Budapest, then it is unlikely that he behaved any differently with respect to the Jewish masses in the ghettos.

The Hostage Train

Aside from delivering the Zionist paratroopers Palgi and Goldstein to the Gestapo and organizing the distribution of the Waldsee postcards to families that were about to be deported to their deaths, the focus of Kasztner's activities during the Nazi preparations to destroy the Jews of Budapest was making the final arrangements for the departure of the Kasztner Train.

Explaining how the candidates for the train had been gathered, Kasztner remarked that after June 10, Eichmann suddenly started to keep his promises: further, albeit smaller, groups from various ghettos continued to arrive in Budapest.[9] In addition to the 388 Jews transported from Kolozsvár, he estimated that two hundred to four hundred were subsequently removed from other ghettos, notably Szeged, Debrecen, Bácsalmás, Szombathely, and Székesfehérvár.[10] The number of Kasztner Train passengers from the provinces thus amounted to six hundred to eight hundred. After Eichmann's decision to enlarge the quota of places on the transport to one thousand three hundred, there were some five hundred to seven hundred seats to be allocated to Jews in Budapest.

The final arrangements made in Budapest for the Kasztner Train became highly controversial. Here a number of issues will be addressed: What were the terms agreed between Kasztner and Eichmann concerning the direction of the train and the fate of its passengers? What were the passengers themselves told about their fate? Who selected the passengers and what criteria were used? Most important of all, why did the Nazis agree to the train's departure from Budapest?

The conditions for the departure of the transport were hammered out in a series of meetings between Kasztner and Eichmann. The product of these negotiations, according to Kasztner, was a memorandum setting out the following terms: (a) the route would pass via Nazi Germany and occupied France to a neutral country; (b) beforehand the group would spend "a few weeks" in the Strasshof camp in Vienna; (c) the one thousand three hundred passengers would travel in thirty-five railway carriages and would take up to 80 kg of personal luggage each; (d) during their stay in the Reich, they would receive preferential treatment, including the same food rations as German civilians, exemption from the Yellow Star, and exemption from forced labor; (e) their food provisions would be carried on the same train; (f) food provisions for the thousands of Hungarian Jews already deported to Strasshof would also be taken on the train.[11]

In payment for these terms, the Jewish side had to deliver a ransom of $1,000 per head. This fee was personally stipulated by Himmler, thus resolving a dispute between Eichmann (who demanded first $200, then $500 per head) and Becher (who would accept no less than $2,000 per passenger).[12] Because the final number of passengers was 1,684—several hundred Jews managed to board the train without permission at the last moment—the Jewish rescue committee ultimately handed over $1,684,000 in money and valuables to the SS. In addition, the committee produced evidence of the opening of a letter of credit for the price of thirty tractors (instead of trucks) in Switzerland. And it actually delivered 15,000 kg of coffee.[13]

The most significant point in the agreement between Kasztner and Eichmann was the stipulation that after leaving Hungary, the group would be kept waiting for "a few weeks" in a transit camp at Strasshof in Nazi Vienna. This meant that the passengers would remain in the grip of the SS when the time came to deport the Jewish masses from Budapest to Auschwitz. From this fact alone, it is quite obvious today—and it must have been just as obvious to Kasztner then—that Eichmann planned to use the alleged "rescue candidates" as hostages to ensure the obedience of the Jewish leadership as he completed the destruction of Hungarian Jewry.

Other facts lead to the same conclusion. Kasztner led the passengers to expect that the transport would make a "short stop" in Strasshof before proceeding to the Spanish border, whereupon the passengers would make *aliya* to Palestine.[14] In his contemporary correspondence, as in his postwar *Bericht*, the train is defined as an "*aliya*" or as a "Palestine transport." Yet the Palestine Office in Budapest, managed by Krausz, had denied Kasztner the use of the original six hundred Palestine entry certificates—which would not have sufficed in any case for the number ultimately accepted by Eichmann. Moreover, the SS had firmly denied permission to leave for Palestine, insisting that the passengers would have to go somewhere else. Why, then, did Kasztner maintain the charade of a "Palestine transport"? What was the purpose of deceiving the "rescue candidates" in this way? After all, there was no need to motivate Zionists to join the "*aliya* to Palestine." All Jews in Budapest were now desperate to escape the Nazi terror, and no one would have declined a place on the train merely because its destination was not the Jewish homeland.

So the reason for Kasztner's deception was quite different. It virtually leaps out of a passage in Kasztner's *Bericht*, where he explains that the transport involved "*aliya* in the form of deportation." Hundreds of passengers, perhaps the majority, had not yet been locked up in ghettos, yet they were expected to board this train voluntarily. The Jewish refugees from Poland were especially opposed to the plan. They saw the idea of "*aliya* in the form of deportation"—based on trusting the promises of the SS—as "insane."[15]

If the prospective hostages were suspicious when they nevertheless believed that they had official entry permits for Palestine, how would they have reacted if they had realized that the alleged destination was a fraud and that they would be held in the Third Reich for "a few weeks" at the very least? Knowing this, how many of the passengers—who were desperate to escape the terror of the SS—would have accepted Kasztner's invitation to trust the promises of the SS?

Hansi Brand's Eichmann Trial testimony stressed the fears of the train candidates and unwittingly confirmed this explanation of Kasztner's reason for deceiving them:

> People did not believe us—they did not seriously believe that the transport would really reach a neutral foreign country . . . it had never happened that Jews reached a neutral foreign country. It had never happened. . . . People were very sceptical, very mistrustful. Even the refugees, who were already living illegally, said no, we will remain in our bunkers, we will not go to Columbus [Street], because we do not see any guarantee that it really is true that people will reach a neutral foreign country. They were simply afraid.[16]

The fiction of "*aliya* to Palestine" by means of a journey to a neutral country was needed because not many would have trusted the promises of the SS otherwise. The deliberate deception about the final destination of the transport is the second sign that Kasztner was aware of the hostage-taking plans of the SS.

Choosing the Hostages

One of the most controversial issues surrounding the Kasztner Train's departure was the allegation of favoritism in the choice of passengers. According to his accusers, Kasztner controlled the selection for the transport and he was guilty of unjustly preferring his relatives and friends, his townspeople from Kolozsvár, his fellow Labor Zionists, and/or wealthy and important Jews.[17] Kasztner and his defenders maintained that he did not draw up the passenger list but delegated the task to others; that most of his relatives did not escape on the train but perished in Auschwitz; and that the final passenger list was representative of the Hungarian Jewish community.[18] The truth lies in between these opposite poles.

It appears that while Kasztner established the basic guidelines for the composition of the passenger list, he did not choose the names personally. Undoubtedly he exercised the greatest influence in arranging the inclusion of several hundred people from his home city: under his original deal with Krumey, two hundred "emigration candidates" were to be removed from Kolozsvár and one hundred more from all the other provincial communities in Hungary. The initial list for Kolozsvár was drawn up by the former head of the city's Orthodox community, Zsigmond Léb, in Budapest; allegedly, the price of admission was $12,000.[19] It was sent back and forth several times and was completed by the *Judenrat* in the ghetto. The lists for the other ghettos were compiled by Kasztner's rescue committee colleagues Komoly and Szilágyi.[20] These lists typically became useless, since Eichmann liquidated most of the ghettos without making any exceptions for individuals, and the rescue committee then had to choose other names in the communities that remained.

As for the capital, Kasztner again delegated the selection of passengers to Komoly and Szilágyi.[21] His own preference, it seems, was to include the "intellectual élite" of the Jewish population—writers, scientists, doctors, and artists—but many were reluctant to "trust the promises of the SS" and declined the offer of places on the transport. By the end of June, Kasztner had relinquished the last vestiges of his control over the allocation of seats, and each faction of Budapest Jewry had been given its own quota of candidates to fill: Orthodox Jews were nominated by Freudiger; Neolog figures were added by Stern; a list was submitted by the foreign refugees; and activists were recommended by all of the Zionist groups.[22] To meet the $1,000 per person fee for the train's departure, 150 places were sold to the rich.

Did Kasztner, as is often alleged, give preferential treatment to his relatives? He later claimed that whereas twenty-one members of his family were on the transport, more than one hundred others were deported to their deaths.[23] A plausible case can be made that the Kasztner family members on the passenger list were included not because of their connection to him but because they were themselves prominent figures: his father-in-law, for example, had been the most important Jewish leader in North Transylvania, while his brother and other relatives had held official positions in the local Zionist movement.[24]

If Kasztner was not "guilty" of favoritism toward his own family, did he give special consideration to his party colleagues or to members of the Zionist movement in general? According to his testimony at the Kasztner Trial, "Most of the Zionist leaders left Budapest on the Bergen-Belsen train."[25] These included Ernő Szilágyi of the far-left Hashomer Hatzair and the right-wing Revisionist leader Lajos Gottesman; there were also about two hundred and fifty activists from the Zionist youth movements—a significant proportion of the membership.[26] In total, the list of passengers included one hundred and ninety-nine Zionists from North Transylvania and two hundred and thirty from Budapest. But although Zionists gained a substantial share of the places on the final list, the overwhelming majority of seats were allocated to others; most of the passengers were Neolog Jews, and there was also an Orthodox group with one hundred and twenty-six members.[27] This group included fervent anti-Zionists such as the Satmar Rebbe and his entourage. Indeed, when Kasztner's actions were investigated in Kolozsvár after the war, one of the chief accusations against him was that he had discriminated *against* local Zionists by transferring Palestine entry certificates—and thus places on the transport—to people who were not entitled to them.[28]

If places on the Kasztner Train were not granted on the basis of family or political loyalty, were they given on the basis of wealth? The organizers never hid the fact that one hundred and fifty seats were sold in order to finance the rest. There was also a group of fifty Jewish passengers who had paid Becher for special protection passes. But there is also no doubt that there were many people of modest means on the train. The passenger list included several hundred such individuals: students, employees, merchants, dressmakers, workmen, tailors, nurses, engineers, gardeners, secretaries, and others.[29] If no more than two hundred of the five hundred to seven hundred seats allocated in Budapest went to people who had paid the rescue committee or Becher's staff for their places, then a further three hundred to five hundred seats were given to Jews who had not made payments. It would therefore be inaccurate to say that the train was simply a procession of the rich.

If the convoy was not composed exclusively of Kasztner's friends and relatives, of Zionists, or of the rich, what were the criteria of distribution? The answer is that there was a definite bias in favor of those sponsored by influential elements in the Jewish community. Kasztner stated this clearly.[30] Likewise, Freudiger recalled that while many people "cried, threatened and implored to be allowed to depart," ultimately "nearly all prominent Jews as well as the majority of the valuable personalities of the conservative Hungarian Jewish community were included in this transport."[31] The picture painted by Kasztner and Freudiger is one in which all sections of the Jewish leadership vied to gain appropriate representation for their favored groups. Each lobby frantically pressured the Zionist rescue committee to include as many of its members as possible. Kasztner hailed the result of this unseemly procedure as a "Noah's Ark" of Hungarian Jewry.

Why the Nazis Agreed to the Train's Departure

The result of the system for populating the Kasztner Train was stark. While the Nazis were completing the deportations from the provincial towns and preparing the final blow, the deportation from Budapest, the community leaders devoted all their time and efforts to squabbles over the composition of the special transport. Instead of concentrating on the central mission—warning the general Jewish population of what was in store; saving lives through bribery, organizing individual escapes, and finding hiding places; and seeking the aid of foreign consulates in granting diplomatic protection to as many Jews as possible—they gave their attention to infighting over the prospect of saving themselves and their preferred groups. In particular, Kasztner's colleagues on the rescue committee, who should have been coordinating the rescue drive in Budapest with the aid of the Zionist youth, were instead adjudicating the claims of various parties for inclusion in the transport. In Freudiger's words, these colleagues "furnished superhuman efforts, working day and night to get through the material."[32] All of this was very convenient for the Nazis.

Also ideal from the Nazi point of view was the fact that each section of the Jewish leadership nominated those individuals that it valued the most. Orthodox and Neologs, Zionists and anti-Zionists—all provided lists of their most prominent representatives. It would have been impossible to conceive of a more efficient procedure for gathering hostages for the Nazis.[33] As Freudiger noted, "the transport by right was called by the Germans a 'parade of prominent Jews.' In other words, it practically served as a sample collection."[34] Once the chosen passengers had been assembled, the Nazis could threaten them at will. Any disobedience on the part of the Zionist rescue committee or the Jewish leaders remaining in Budapest and any obstruction of the final Nazi measures to destroy the Jewish masses could be countered by a threat to liquidate the chosen passengers of the Kasztner Train at a moment's notice.

The Kasztner Train was thus well suited to the interests of the Nazis. Kasztner had already agreed that the transport would spend crucial weeks in the Reich before departing. It was obvious that the convoy's stay in the Reich would coincide with the planned deportation of the Jews of Budapest. So Kasztner must have understood that the passengers would be hostages during the deportations.

To say that Kasztner was aware of Eichmann's and Becher's hostage-taking scheme is not to say that he welcomed it, let alone that he wanted any harm to befall the hostages. On the contrary, Kasztner was most anxious that the hostages should eventually be freed. He sought guarantees from his Nazi contacts: Becher, Clages, and Wisliceny all assured him that the continuation of the group's trip after a "brief stay" in the Reich had been approved by Himmler.[35] For Kasztner, who had long since renounced the option of illegal rescue actions conducted against the will of the Nazis, the special transport was the final test of his leadership of the rescue committee. Having lost his "moral credit" vis-à-vis the Jewish rescue organizations abroad and having gambled the entire outcome of rescue on the deal with the Nazis, Kasztner certainly hoped that at some point the Jews on his special transport would be allowed to leave Nazi-occupied Europe.

Eichmann, in turn, was aware of Kasztner's total dependence on him, and—after the train's departure from Budapest on June 30—he used various techniques of mental torture to press home his advantage. At one point in the journey, he cabled that the transport should proceed to the holding center at Auspitz in the Sudetenland. His instructions were immediately leaked to the passengers, who concluded that they were heading for Auschwitz and sent a desperate message to the rescue committee in Budapest. Kasztner confronted Eichmann and was told that the site of Auspitz had been judged unsuitable and that the convoy would travel by a different route. Not long afterwards, the train reached Linz in Austria, where the passengers were ordered to take a shower. Panic ensued because the Jews thought that they were being taken to a gas chamber like those in Auschwitz.[36] By such tactics, Eichmann was able to subject the group to the greatest possible distress and to dramatize Kasztner's complete subordination to the Nazis.

So the train's circuitous journey continued until its arrival on July 9, not at the agreed destination of Strasshof, but at the hostage camp at Bergen-Belsen.[37] Meanwhile, events were unfolding in Budapest that held life-and-death importance for the hundreds of thousands of Jews awaiting deportation and destruction.

The Struggle over the Capital

At 9 AM on July 2 began a four-hour bombing raid against Budapest by American planes. Whole residential areas were the targets. The raid inflicted thousands of civilian casualties. Leaflets dropped on the city by the bombers detailed the disastrous war situation facing the Axis powers and added a clear threat to the Hungarian regime. The American government demanded to know "whether there is to be deportation to Poland or to any other place and/or adoption of any measures . . . tantamount to mass execution." The American government was closely watching the persecution of the Jews and reminded the Hungarian authorities that all those involved in the anti-Jewish drive would be "dealt with" in line with previous public warnings.[38]

Elsewhere in the country, the death trains were still rolling. Between July 4 and July 6, Eichmann accomplished the deportation of the Jews of western Hungary, designated Zone 5 in his extermination plan. A total of 29,556 Jews were packed into ten trains and dispatched on the journey to Auschwitz.[39] As in the other Hungarian provinces, the deportation was carried out with utter ruthlessness. In Zalaegerszeg, the Hungarian forces tortured the Jews so savagely in their search for valuables that dozens of victims needed medical help, others died, while others went insane or killed themselves.[40] In the Sárvár internment camp, it was discovered after the departure of the trains that several infants and children had been left behind; these youngsters were promptly delivered by the local Hungarian authorities to the Nazis "for labor in Germany."[41]

Meanwhile thousands of Hungarian gendarmes had converged on the capital. Their official task was to move the city's Jews into buildings marked by the Yellow Star. But rumor had it that they were also at the disposal of Eichmann's ally László Baky, who intended to carry out a coup against Horthy and to install an outright fascist regime. Intelligence about the coup attempt contributed to Horthy's reservations about the deportation policy. In a meeting with Hitler's representative Edmund Veesenmayer on July 4, the Hungarian Regent harshly criticized Baky and his partner-in-crime Endre. Horthy added that on a daily basis he was being bombarded with pleas from the Pope, the King of Sweden, the International Red Cross, and the Swiss, all urging him to stop the deportations of Jews.[42] No doubt the American air raid on Budapest two days earlier had also influenced his judgment, as had the Allied military advances in Europe.

Horthy had to act. He arranged for an "air-raid alarm" as camouflage, summoned a loyal armed regiment to his aid, and ordered Baky's gendarmes out of Budapest. So ended (for the moment) Eichmann's ability to put into effect the planned mass deportation from the capital.

On July 6, Veesenmayer had a detailed discussion with Hungarian Prime Minister Sztójay. In this meeting, Sztójay confirmed that Hungary had decided to stop the deportations. He gave several reasons: the antisemitic measures that the Nazis were demanding of Hungary were harsher than the policies of their satellites in Romania and Slovakia; the Nazi deal allowing the emigration of the Weiss-Manfréd family of Jewish industrialists had led to considerable publicity; enormous foreign and domestic pressure to stop the deportations had been brought to bear on the Hungarian regime; reports about the fate of the deportees were circulating among leadership circles in Budapest; and intercepted messages sent by American and British diplomats in Switzerland to their respective governments had urged reprisals against Hungary for its treatment of its Jewish minority. Sztójay read from one such communication, which gave exact addresses of Hungarian government buildings in Budapest for the purpose of bombing raids. Another of the messages named seventy Hungarians and Germans believed to be responsible for the deportations. Sztójay feigned indifference to such personal threats, claiming that he did not care what happened to the Jews in the event of an Axis victory, and that he would be executed anyway in the event of an Axis defeat—but Veesenmayer sensed that the intercepted messages had affected his attitude to the deportations.[43]

Judging from Horthy's and Sztójay's remarks to Veesenmayer, the worldwide publicity about the gassing of the Jews in Auschwitz and the resulting international uproar and reprisal threats had been a major influence on the Hungarian government's decision to spare (for the time being) the Jewish population of Budapest. This publicity was the direct result of Moshe Krausz's decision to forward the Vrba–Wetzler report about Auschwitz to Switzerland, where the diplomat George Mantello had alerted the media. As Mantello later pointed out, had the report been sent several weeks earlier, "perhaps we could have put a stop to the [previous] deportations, since we would have started a big press campaign in Switzerland and abroad."[44]

The Hungarian prime minister's concerns notwithstanding, the mass deportations continued for three crucial days. Now it was the turn of the Jews living in Budapest's suburbs: Zone 6 in Eichmann's plan. The victims, who had already been forced into local ghettos or Yellow-Star houses, were then moved to the brickyards of Budakalász, northwest of Budapest, and Monor, southeast of the capital. These Jews—24,128 souls in total—were deported to Auschwitz in eight trains.[45] The cruelty of the Hungarian authorities' tactics was undiminished. Jews who ventured outside the capital for the funerals of relatives in the suburb of Rákoskeresztúr were allowed to attend the burials, then arrested upon leaving the cemeteries and deported to their deaths.[46]

By this point all of the provincial Jewish communities in Hungary had been destroyed. Veesenmayer reported to the German Foreign Office that 437,402 men, women, and children had been dispatched to their fate in eight weeks.[47]

The Collaboration Continues

Horthy officially vetoed further expulsions from Hungary on July 7. The mass deportations actually ended on July 9—the day of the Kasztner Train's arrival in Bergen-Belsen. The time frame of negotiations concerning the VIP transport and its journey to Bergen-Belsen had covered the whole of the mass deportations, from the remotest provincial town to the suburbs of Budapest. Now the Kasztner Train's passengers were being held hostage in a Nazi concentration camp. Kasztner therefore had no choice but to strike yet another deal with the SS, and this is precisely what he did.

Kasztner explained his new bargain as a "precaution" in case the mass deportations resumed. The terms of the deal, which he arranged with Eichmann and Becher, were as follows. First, another trainload of one thousand five hundred Jews would be sent to Bergen-Belsen "for emigration." Second, on top of the fifteen thousand Jews already sent to Strasshof from the provincial towns, another fifteen thousand Jews (including seven thousand children) would be sent there from Budapest. Of these, one-third would await their transfer in the rescue committee's preferential camps in the capital, where they would not have to endure the torturous methods of the Hungarian gendarmes.[48]

Asked about this new deal during the libel trial in Jerusalem, Kasztner gave a frank reply:

> According to our evaluation, although the deportations had stopped on reaching Budapest itself, the battle for Hungarian Jews had not yet ended. Therefore we continued with precautions, we also made a deal with Eichmann in case the Germans prevailed over Horthy's will.[49]

The bargain outlined by Kasztner would not have saved lives. The one thousand five hundred to be sent to Bergen-Belsen and the fifteen thousand destined for Strasshof would have been left in the hands of the Nazis; these Jews would have been put to death at a time of the Nazis' choosing after the remainder of the Jewish population of Budapest had been gassed. If the deportations had resumed, Kasztner's rescue committee would have been locked into another arrangement with the SS while hundreds of thousands of Jews were being delivered to Auschwitz. Striking such a deal with Eichmann and Becher had a clear implication: neither Kasztner nor anyone under his influence would do anything likely to provoke the SS to renege on its commitments, such as warning Jews in Budapest about the gas chambers.

On July 12, Kasztner sent Schwalb a detailed letter about the "rescue negotiations" and their failure. "The dream of the big plan is finished," he wrote, referring to the Goods for Blood offer. By this point the fate of the Hungarian Jews could no longer be covered up: the deported Jews "went to Auschwitz in such a way that they were unaware until the last moment of what it meant and what was going on. We, who knew it, tried to stop it," but were unable to do much. Kasztner revealed that the "big plan" he had been negotiating entailed deporting the Hungarian Jews to Poland: at the time of Brand's departure, the Nazis said that "the selection [of Jews for emigration] would go ahead in Auschwitz" and that "the suitable people for the [Goods for Blood] plan would be kept there." But as it turned out, "Auschwitz was in full operation from the moment that the trains disgorged the Hungarian Jews"—something that Kasztner presented as a surprise, as if he had ever entertained any illusions about the purpose of the death camp.

Turning to his activities during the deportations, Kasztner painted a thoroughly misleading picture. He not only claimed credit for the trains diverted to Strasshof but also double-counted the "success" of his VIP train, mentioning about 1,000 Jews from the provinces who had been spared from deportation and moved to Budapest, as well as another contingent of 1,691 Jews to be delivered via Vienna to Bergen-Belsen for transfer to Spain.

Kasztner proposed alternatives for a meeting between the Nazis and Jewish representatives abroad: either he himself would travel with a "friend" of Eichmann's to see the JDC's Lisbon delegate Joseph Schwartz or the Gestapo/SD agent Laufer ("who has given us much help in our work") would go with Komoly to visit Schwalb and the JDC's Saly Mayer in Switzerland. Finally he remarked that the mistrust between the two sides had resulted in the death of half a million people—essentially blaming the catastrophe on the failure of the negotiations rather than on the bad faith of the Nazis.[50] In this letter Kasztner's willingness to manipulate facts in order to exonerate himself and to justify his dealings with the Nazis was on full display.

Kasztner's supine posture toward the SS is also visible in a document recording a conversation he had with Becher on July 15. The context of the meeting was the arrival just over a week earlier of the so-called interim agreement[51]—a fictitious offer devised by Brand and the Jewish Agency to convince the SS that the Western powers were serious about the Goods for Blood deal. Kasztner, of course, had never expected Eichmann's proposal to succeed[52]—indeed the British publicly rejected it soon afterwards—but he needed the SS to free the hostages now held in Bergen-Belsen.

Kasztner began the July 15 discussion with Becher by complaining that the SS negotiators had broken all their commitments to him. Regarding the deportations, "It was promised [by the SS] that the fit would be selected [for work] and the unfit would be kept on ice until a specific time, depending on the result of the negotiations, until it was established whether these had succeeded or failed. Instead the Auschwitz mill was set to work." Becher asked if Kasztner had informed the outside world of the exterminations. "No," replied Kasztner. But even though he had not done so, the truth would be known. He explained that Brand had done his best to conclude an interim agreement based on the Goods for Blood offer, but the conditions imposed by the SS had been unrealistic: "one couldn't expect that two weeks after Brand's departure, the British and American governments would already be loading goods onto ships, including trucks that will eventually reinforce the German war machine directly or indirectly." A meeting between German and Western representatives at "L"—presumably Lisbon—to further the negotiations would make sense only if the deportations came to an end, the gas chambers at Auschwitz were deactivated, and there were still some Hungarian Jews alive to exchange for the trucks. Kasztner also requested the release of the group from Bergen-Belsen. He assured Becher that he was not simply trying to secure the emigration of his own family. This led to a testy exchange:

KASZTNER:	I want you to know that what was done wasn't done on a family basis. I've wondered many times whether, instead of the negotiations, it wouldn't have been better to call on the Zionist youth and rally the people to active resistance to entering the brickyards and the wagons.
BECHER:	You wouldn't have achieved anything this way.
KASZTNER:	Maybe, but at least we would have kept our honor. Our people went into the wagons like cattle because we trusted in the success of the negotiations and failed to tell them the terrible fate awaiting them.[53]

Here Kasztner admitted that his policy of negotiating with the SS had not served the interests of the Jewish victims.

From this document, it is evident that by committing himself to a deal with the SS, Kasztner had abandoned any rescue option involving opposition to the concentration and deportation of the Jews. Instead he had chosen to rely on Eichmann's promise—and had he really believed this promise?—that the deportees would not be killed before the outcome of the Brand Mission was known. He had never expected an agreement to be reached on the terms set by the SS, as it was unrealistic to imagine that the West would assist the German war effort by supplying trucks. Nevertheless, even after finding out that the deportees from Hungary were in fact being gassed in breach of Eichmann's pledge, Kasztner had still refused to alert the outside world or the victims in the ghettos.

Kasztner's comments to Becher on July 15 were a partial confession of the consequences for the Jews of the negotiations pursued by the head of the rescue committee. But naturally he did not commit to paper the full extent to which he had become a tool of the Nazis. His actions thus far had included helping the SS to deceive the Jews of Kolozsvár into boarding the trains to Auschwitz; keeping the peace in several ghettos as a condition of taking credit for the Strasshof operation; actively misleading his foreign contacts by claiming that the deportees were alive in Waldsee when they had been murdered in the gas chambers; helping the SS to inflict the Waldsee hoax on the Jews of Budapest; knowingly delivering hostages to the SS on the pretext of departure to Palestine; and neutralizing his own rescue committee and the Zionist youth at the very moment when they were most needed to organize the rescue drive in Budapest.

In these circumstances, it was little short of miraculous that the Vrba–Wetzler report had been smuggled abroad and that the resulting international pressure had helped to prevent the deportations from the capital at the last moment. But Kasztner had not yet reached the limit of his willingness to collaborate. The ensuing months would reveal the distance he was still ready to travel in the service of the mass murderers.

Notes

1. David Kranzler, *The Man Who Stopped the Trains to Auschwitz: George Mantello, El Salvador, and Switzerland's Finest Hour* (Syracuse, NY: Syracuse University Press, 2000), 96–99, 123.

2. Kasztner to Schwalb (copied to Mayer), June 24, 1944, JDC Archive, New York, Saly Mayer Collection, file 20(2); a handwritten Hebrew translation is in the personal papers of Peretz Révész.
3. Braham, *The Politics of Genocide*, Vol. 2, 872–4.
4. Kasztner, *Bericht*, 58.
5. Szita, *Trading in Lives?*, 105.
6. Kasztner Trial testimony, July 2, 1954.
7. Kasztner Trial testimony, July 8, 1954.
8. Kasztner, London Affidavit, 6.
9. Kasztner Trial testimony, February 19, 1954.
10. Ibid., March 1, 1954. In fact, 154 out of the 200–400 had been transferred from two ghettos, Szeged and Debrecen: Kasztner, *Bericht*, 53. These 154 Jews were saved, not from Auschwitz, but from joining the 11,880 Jews deported from these two ghettos to Strasshof in Vienna.
11. Kasztner, *Bericht*, 60–61.
12. Ibid., 59. On the circumstances of the delivery, which was made at the end of July or the beginning of August, see the statement of the rescue committee treasurer Sándor Offenbach, Budapest, January 25, 1946, CZA, S53/2128.
13. Kasztner, *Bericht*, 75–76.
14. *Freudiger Report*, 37, 39. See also Löb, *Dealing With Satan*, 98: "Our greatest comfort, of course, was the hope of soon being in Spain or Portugal and then on our way to Palestine."
15. Kasztner, *Bericht*, 59.
16. Eichmann Trial testimony, May 30, 1961. Hansi Brand added: "At that time it was not widely known that the entire Weiss family was already safe in Portugal. That was not general knowledge in Budapest." In fact, several family members were being held hostage by the Nazis in order to deter their liberated relatives from "slandering Germany" abroad: Szita, *Trading in Lives?*, 129.
17. For example, Malkiel Grünwald's bulletin, reproduced in Shmuel Tamir, *Ben ha'aretz hazot* [*Son of This Land*] (Tel Aviv: Zemorah-Bitan, 2002), Vol. 1, 292–5.
18. For example, Kasztner, *Bericht*, 61–63; Ann Pasternak-Slater, "Kasztner's Ark," *Areté*, 15 (Autumn 2004), 12–16; Löb, *Dealing With Satan*, 115–18.
19. Szita, *Trading in Lives?*, 69n24. Irena Hirsch testified that her son was refused a place on the transport and subsequently deported to his death in Auschwitz because her family could not afford the fee: see her Kasztner Trial testimony, June 14, 1954.
20. *Komoly Diary*, May 2, 1944.
21. *Freudiger Report*, 38.
22. Kasztner, *Bericht*, 61.
23. Kasztner Trial testimony, March 1, 1954. Of these, nineteen were selected in the Kolozsvár Ghetto and two more (his wife and mother) in Budapest.
24. Kasztner Appeal, Agranat verdict, 2101. According to another source, Fischer chose no fewer than thirty-two family members in the Kolozsvár Ghetto: G. Z. (Zoltán Glatz), *Der Judenrat des Bergen-Belsen Transportes*, Geneva, February 10, 1946, YVA, M 20. This source also asserts that Fischer was well aware that the deportation trains were not taking the Jewish masses to Kenyérmező.

25. Kasztner Trial testimony, March 9, 1954.
26. Cohen, *The Halutz Resistance in Hungary, 1942–1944*, 101–3, 263–4n27. Among these *halutzim* were twenty-three Ihud (Mapai) activists from the Kolozsvár Ghetto.
27. Löb, *Dealing With Satan*, 117–18.
28. Yosef Krausz, Kasztner Trial testimony, June 17, 1954, summarizing the allegations of Jewish survivors before the postwar People's Tribunal of Cluj; Zoltán Glatz, *Der Judenrat des Bergen-Belsen Transportes*, accusing the Jewish leaders in Kolozsvár of showing favoritism toward their non-Zionist relatives.
29. Pasternak-Slater, "Kasztner's Ark," 13–14; Löb, *Dealing With Satan*, 117.
30. Kasztner, *Bericht*, 61–62.
31. *Freudiger Report*, 38–39.
32. Ibid., 38.
33. On arrival in Bergen-Belsen concentration camp, the Kasztner Train passengers "heard that other groups, too, had been assured of leaving within a fortnight and were still here eleven months later." Löb, *Dealing With Satan*, 114.
34. *Freudiger Report*, 39.
35. Kasztner, *Bericht*, 60.
36. Ibid., 63. Unlike Hungary's Jewish masses, the Jewish leaders in Budapest were aware of the Final Solution and the purpose of Auschwitz. Since several of these leaders, especially Zionist leaders, were on the Kasztner Train, their panic is not surprising.
37. Freudiger claims that the Kasztner Train was re-routed to Bergen-Belsen because the Strasshof camp commander refused to accept the transport: *Freudiger Report*, 39.
38. Zvi Erez, "Hungary—Six Days in July 1944," *Holocaust and Genocide Studies* 3, no. 1 (1988): 38.
39. Braham, *The Politics of Genocide*, Vol. 2, 775.
40. Ibid., 773.
41. Ibid., 769.
42. Erez, "Hungary—Six Days in July 1944," 46.
43. Document 187: Telegram from Veesenmayer to Ribbentrop Concerning a Discussion with Sztójay on the Cessation of the Deportations, in Braham, *The Destruction of Hungarian Jewry: A Documentary Account*, Vol. 2, 425–9.
44. Mantello to Vrba, May 18, 1964, quoted in Erich Kulka, "Five Escapes from Auschwitz," in *They Fought Back: The Story of the Jewish Resistance in Nazi Europe*, ed. Yuri Suhl (New York: Crown, 1967), 217–18.
45. Braham, *The Politics of Genocide*, Vol. 2, 779.
46. *Freudiger Report*, 33.
47. Document 193: Telegram from Veesenmayer to the Foreign Office Reportng on the Completion of the "Action" in Zone V, in Braham, *The Destruction of Hungarian Jewry: A Documentary Account*, Vol. 2, 443. For comparison of Ferenczy's and Veesenmayer's deportation figures, see Braham, *The Politics of Genocide*, Vol. 1, 674, Table 19.1.
48. Kasztner, *Bericht*, 65.
49. Kasztner Trial testimony, February 19, 1954.
50. Kasztner to Schwalb, July 12, 1944, Haganah Archive, 80/p187/32.

51. For the text of the "interim agreement," see Paul Lawrence Rose, "Joel Brand's 'Interim Agreement' and the Course of Nazi-Jewish Negotiations, 1944–1945," *The Historical Journal* 34, no. 4 (1991): 911–12. The text reached Budapest on July 7.

52. Kasztner writes, "The failure of this [Goods for Blood] plan was to be expected": *Bericht*, 73.

53. Kasztner-Becher minutes, July 15, 1944, Dinur Archive. I am grateful to Eli Reichenthal for translating this document. Yad Vashem, in the appendix to its translation of Kasztner's *Bericht*, purports to reproduce this document in its entirety, but omits the passage just quoted. See Rezső Kasztner, *The Kasztner Report: The Report of the Budapest Jewish Rescue Committee, 1942–1945*, eds. László Karsai and Judit Molnár (Jerusalem: Yad Vashem, 2013), 331–3.

14

Pseudo-Rescuer

Horthy's veto of the deportation from Budapest was a last-minute reprieve for the remnants of Hungarian Jewry, but there was no such interlude for the head of the Jewish rescue committee. All that Kasztner had to show for his months of "negotiations" with the Nazis was the removal from the country of 1,684 Jews, who had been delivered, not to freedom, but to a concentration camp in the Third Reich.

In these circumstances, the slightest deviation from total obedience to the Nazis risked not only the withdrawal of his official protection but also the execution of the hostages. Yet according to Kasztner, the next phase of his campaign to save the Jewish population from the Nazis was crowned with unprecedented success.

This chapter will review Kasztner's various claims about his rescue efforts in this period. These efforts allegedly involved preventing renewed mass deportations from Budapest to Auschwitz; intervening to liberate the three imprisoned Zionist paratroopers; stopping the Death March from Budapest to the Reich; halting the use of gas chambers in Auschwitz; and preventing the destruction of the Budapest Ghetto.

A pattern emerges. In each case, Kasztner masked his obedience to the Nazis by advancing bogus assertions about saving or trying to save Jewish lives. His *modus operandi* was to serve the murderers under the cover of saving the victims—a policy that could be called *pseudo-rescue*. It was the only sort of "rescue" that could be pursued by someone living and working under the killers' protection and dependent on their mercy.

The Race to Murder the Jews of Budapest

The Nazi plan to massacre the Jews in the capital had been frustrated by Horthy's intervention. But the Nazis were undeterred. On July 17, 1944, Ribbentrop outlined Hitler's demands of Horthy:

> The Führer expects that now the measures against the Jews of Budapest be taken without any further delay, with the exceptions ... granted to the Hungarian government [a reference to Horthy's offer

to allow about 7,000 Jews to emigrate]. However, no delay in the implementation of the general Jewish measures should occur as a result of these exceptions. Otherwise, the Führer's acceptance of these exceptions will have to be withdrawn.[1]

Eichmann was not prepared to tolerate the escape of even the few thousand Jews covered by Horthy's offer. He announced his intention to execute the operation against the Jews of Budapest so quickly that the victims would be loaded onto deportation trains before any of the Jews with permission to emigrate could obtain a travel document or foreign visa.[2] To underline his resolve, he deported two thousand seven hundred Jews from the Kistarcsa and Sárvár internment camps in defiance of Horthy's instructions.

Nor were Hitler and Eichmann alone in their determination to murder the rest of Hungary's Jews. On July 31, Himmler wrote to a Nazi *Gauleiter*:

> With regard to the Jewish Question in Europe, we just finished sending off 450,000 Jews from Hungary and are beginning to transport the second half. Be sure that I do possess at this decisive moment of the war, as I did before, the requisite toughness.[3]

Himmler repeated his assurances during an inspection visit to Auschwitz. "Eichmann's program," he declared, "will continue to be carried out and will be intensified month by month."[4]

Details were given to the German Foreign Ministry on August 19. It was explained that the concentration of the victims would be carried out by the Hungarian gendarmes from the date of August 25. The first deportation convoy of twenty thousand Jews would leave two days later; then eighteen thousand Jews would be deported every day until the Jews of Budapest were no more.[5]

Fortunately, these terrible plans were never put into effect. Some maintain that the last-minute cancellation of the scheduled deportations from Budapest to Auschwitz was due to Kasztner's dealings with the Nazis.[6] Is there any factual basis for this argument?

After the Brand Mission was exposed and rejected by the British on July 19–20, Kasztner continued his efforts to arrange negotiations between the Nazis and the West. His persistence paid off: the first meeting was held on a bridge at the Swiss–German border on August 21. On the Nazi side were Becher and an SS colleague, accompanied by Kasztner. Their opposite number was Saly Mayer of the JDC, acting with the tacit support of the US War Refugee Board.

Introducing himself as Himmler's envoy, Becher repeated the Goods for Blood offer and referred to the impending deportations from Budapest. When Mayer appealed to humanitarian considerations, Becher gave the terse reply: "I cannot negotiate on this basis."[7] The message was clear: unless his terms were accepted, hundreds of thousands would die. It was agreed to continue the talks, but the meeting was otherwise fruitless. The deportations from Budapest to Auschwitz had not been averted.

Meanwhile, the Nazis freed 318 Kasztner Train passengers and took them to Switzerland as a show of "good faith." Since the Nazis were about to complete the massacre of Hungarian Jewry, freeing these hostages merely served as a diversion from the next phase of the Holocaust in Hungary. In addition to disguising the Nazi plans, such an act of "rescue" facilitated a postwar alibi: if the Jews of Budapest were killed, Becher could blame Saly Mayer's intransigence for the victory of SS "extremists."

The Nazi deportation plan came to a sudden end early on the morning of August 25, when a cable from Himmler prohibiting deportations of Jews reached Otto Winkelmann, supreme SS commander in Hungary.[8] Did the Kasztner-initiated meeting between Becher and Saly Mayer play a role in the decision? Later that day, Becher cabled Himmler about the meeting:

> The other side announced that if further deportations to the Reich now take place, the negotiations will not be regarded as serious by the decisive authority [in the West] and will therefore be unsuccessful. *In the meantime the relevant order of the* Reichsführer *has arrived here* [emphasis added].
>
> Requesting permission to continue [the talks] in the spirit described [i.e., in line with Himmler's prohibition of deportations].[9]

Since Becher sent his report about the meeting *in response* to Himmler's order, Becher's report cannot be the explanation for Himmler's order.

Historian Yehuda Bauer has nonetheless argued that the talks were at least partly responsible for the decision to suspend the deportation. He tentatively cites Becher's postwar claim that he went straight to Germany to report to Himmler face to face and persuaded him to stop the deportation.[10] But this is refuted by Kasztner himself, who says that after the meeting on the Swiss–German border, he and Becher returned at once to Budapest. In other words, Becher did not go straight to see Himmler in the Reich.[11]

In addition to the nonexistent Becher–Himmler meeting, Bauer has offered his "conjecture" (on the basis of "SS usage") that Becher "probably" reported to Himmler by phone as well.[12] If true, this would place Himmler's awareness of the outcome of the talks before his prohibition of deportations from Budapest. However, Becher mentioned no such phone conversation in any of his postwar interrogations and affidavits. It is inconceivable that he would have forgotten such a decisive phone call, which supposedly saved hundreds of thousands of lives, had it taken place. So Bauer's conjecture is false. Becher did not inform Himmler about the progress of the talks, either in person or by phone, before Himmler's order prohibiting the deportations from Budapest.

It is therefore impossible to accept Bauer's claim to have "proved that the fact that the 200,000 Jews of Budapest were not deported in August 1944... was due directly to these negotiations" between Becher, Kasztner, and Mayer.[13] The prohibition of the deportations had nothing to do with those negotiations.

In reality, Himmler's order was provoked by an entirely different turn of events. On August 23, Romania changed sides and declared war on Germany. Having lost access to one of their primary sources of oil, the Nazis were now dependent on Hungary for oil supplies. The next day, Hungary's Interior Ministry informed Eichmann of Horthy's decision that the Jews of Budapest would be concentrated in camps outside the city, but would not be deported. An indignant Eichmann asked his superiors to withdraw his unit from Hungary, as its presence there was now useless.[14] Himmler was faced with Horthy's sudden refusal to countenance renewed deportations.

According to the postwar testimony of Otto Winkelmann, overall SS commander in Hungary, after the loss of Romania's oil, Himmler was reluctant to provoke Hungary by forcing a resumption of deportations.[15] This is consistent with Kasztner's version. On the evening of August 25, according to the *Bericht*, Wisliceny requested a meeting, at which he announced the departure of the *Eichmann-Kommando*. Himmler, taking account of Romania's defection, thought it unwise to annoy the Hungarians any further and had therefore ordered Eichmann and his unit out of Budapest.[16]

It seems odd to give Kasztner credit for "rescue" achievements that he did not even claim for himself.

Did Kasztner Try to Save the Paratroopers?

Throughout these events, the Zionist paratroopers Palgi and Goldstein, whom Kasztner had betrayed to the Gestapo, were undergoing interrogation and torture in the prison cells of the authorities. Their comrade Hannah Szenes, who had preceded them across the border and had been captured before them, endured the same brutality. It is quite possible that Kasztner did not learn of her imprisonment until some point in August. When he did find out, what did he do to save her? His testimony is instructive:

> To the best of my recollection, we did find her a defense attorney, a Hungarian lawyer, a young military man. *I don't remember* his name. . . . *I don't know* whether he called Hannah. . . . *I don't know* whether or not he visited her. . . . Offenbach [the rescue committee's treasurer] told me that the lawyer had visited her. *I didn't ask* how many times and *I didn't ask* when. . . . *I didn't ask* what Hannah had asked the lawyer to tell us. *I didn't ask* what she said or when she had reached Hungary. *I didn't ask* him what Hannah had said about her situation or whether or not she had food to eat. *I didn't ask* Offenbach if she was being tortured. [Emphases added.][17]

Thus Kasztner testified that he had found a lawyer to defend Szenes against charges of military espionage and had taken no further interest in her case.

Kasztner's protestations that he had at least hired a lawyer became a liability for him after being contradicted by Katerina Szenes, Hannah's mother. For three months (June 17–September 11, 1944) Katerina Szenes was held alongside her daughter in an effort by the Hungarian authorities to break the paratrooper. When Hannah remained obdurate,[18] her mother was freed and began a desperate struggle to save her daughter's life.

Katerina Szenes gave a harrowing description of her efforts to contact the head of the rescue committee. First she approached one of Kasztner's aides, a man named Grossman:

> I told him I had visited Hannah and she was requesting a lawyer. He said to me: "Why do you need a lawyer? It isn't necessary, everything is under control and she'll be released maybe tomorrow or the day after, maybe even today. Go home, I think she'll be home already." I ran home but she wasn't there.

> Every day I went to Grossman. . . . Meanwhile friends asked me, why Grossman and not Kasztner? Kasztner was the man who could help me and I had to appeal to him. I told Grossman that I wanted to speak to Kasztner. He said: "It's impossible as he's very busy; he's not at home now"—he always said something . . .

> With every day that passed, I was tormented that I still hadn't hired a lawyer. . . . [Grossman] said: "There's no need for a lawyer: everything

is already fixed. We already know that one person costs 15,000 *pengős*. We must free eight of these people, which means we need 120,000 *pengős* . . . do you have 15,000 *pengős*?" I said: "I have nothing at the moment but it won't be a problem . . . just tell me when to bring the money. . . ."

But I said that I had a food parcel for Hannah. . . . I said: "I'll get a lawyer anyway; at least he'll bring her the food parcel." So he said: "That's why you're getting a lawyer? Dr. Kasztner has permission to enter the prison." I asked: "Then why doesn't he go? Can we speak to him?" I asked for Kasztner's address. He said: "Impossible, I can't give it."[19]

From this account it is obvious that Kasztner and his representative did not hire a lawyer for Hannah Szenes and made every effort to discourage her mother from doing so. This was inadvertently confirmed by Hansi Brand in her testimony.[20]

Katerina Szenes testified that she visited Kasztner's office for three or four days in a row to arrange a meeting; each time she spoke to Kasztner's personal secretary. On October 12, she discovered that working in the same building was a family friend. It was the chairman of Kasztner's committee, Ottó Komoly:

I decided to approach Komoly. If I couldn't talk to Kasztner, then I would talk to Komoly. . . . I said to him: "I'm asking you to tell me the truth about Hannah's case. Every day they promise: they tell me they'll do everything, I must not appoint a lawyer, she'll be released and perhaps she has already been released. Tell me the truth!"

He looked at me and said: "What? Hannah is here?" I told him: "Don't you know that there are emissaries of the Yishuv here? There are two young men here [i.e., Palgi and Goldstein] as well as Hannah." He said: "I knew this, but I didn't know that Hannah was one of them. I'm hearing it for the first time. I promise you that we'll do everything we can, but get a lawyer today—right away."[21]

Komoly's ignorance of Hannah's imprisonment suggests that Kasztner did nothing to help her. Worse still, the experience of Katerina Szenes at the hands of his representatives indicates that he tried to *prevent* any constructive action from being taken to lessen her ordeal.[22]

Was Kasztner simply too busy with other concerns to address the fate of a single Jew, however horrible? This question is hard to reconcile with the one action he did take in respect of the three paratroopers—an action that falls squarely into the category of *pseudo-rescue*.

On October 14, the day before the Horthy regime was deposed in a coup by the Arrow Cross, Kasztner met three top Hungarian officials: József

Garzoly, head of the Hungarian counter-espionage agency holding the three paratroopers; Ottó Hatz, a Hungarian army officer; and István Oláh, director of Hungary's Defense Ministry. Also present was the Red Cross delegate Friedrich Born. At this meeting, according to Kasztner, it was agreed that all three paratroopers would be released under the auspices of the Red Cross.[23] So it seems that Kasztner was not indifferent to the fate of the paratroopers: even if he did little to help them on a day-to-day basis, he still took action at the political level to save them.

In this case, however, appearances are deceiving. By that date, it was common knowledge in informed circles in Budapest that Horthy was on the verge of announcing a ceasefire and withdrawing from the Axis. Kasztner himself admitted that he was aware of this prospect at the time; otherwise he could not have concluded a political deal with such high-level government representatives.[24] The imminent prospect of Hungary's defection from the Axis had important implications for the deal. If Horthy's attempt succeeded, all Allied POWs in Hungary, including the paratroopers, would be freed automatically, and Kasztner's deal with the government officials would be superfluous. But if Horthy's move was foiled by the Nazis and their fascist quislings, Kasztner's deal to free the paratroopers would be worthless.

In the circumstances, Kasztner must have realized that his "political" intervention to free Szenes, Palgi, and Goldstein was futile. So what did he hope to achieve? Presumably, his reason for staging this pseudo-rescue deal was the same as that of the government officials for cooperating. All of them had interacted with the Nazi occupiers and all of them could expect to fall under suspicion if Hungary switched sides. The sham agreement to release the paratroopers was an alibi tailored to the needs of all parties.[25]

The fate of the three paratroopers was tragic. On October 15, Horthy's defection attempt was crushed and the Arrow Cross seized power, initiating a new reign of terror against the Jews. Within two weeks, Hannah Szenes was tried before a military tribunal. She was executed by firing squad on November 7, as her mother waited in the same building to visit her. Around November 13, Peretz Goldstein was sent to Oranienburg concentration camp in Germany, where he perished. Ten days later, Palgi was also placed on a train to the Reich, but he managed to escape and return to Budapest, where he found refuge. Thus only one of the three Zionist paratroopers sent to plan Hungarian Jewish resistance to the Nazis survived the war.

Zionist Rescue without Kasztner

While Kasztner was leaving the paratroopers to their fate, his Zionist colleagues devoted themselves to genuine rescue activities. The most productive in this regard was undoubtedly Moshe Krausz. In his capacity as head of the Palestine Office, Krausz had smuggled the Vrba–Wetzler report on Auschwitz to the West, triggering the events that brought an end to the mass deportations. He also befriended the diplomat Carl Lutz, who was in charge of the foreign affairs section at the Swiss consulate. In partnership with Lutz, Krausz was now able to accomplish some of the most dramatic feats of rescue in Nazi-occupied Hungary.[26]

Most importantly, they won official Hungarian recognition for seven thousand eight hundred holders of Palestine entry certificates as British subjects. These certificate-holders were given Swiss diplomatic protection ("safety passes"). Another four thousand certificate-holders were placed under Swedish diplomatic protection, bringing the official total to almost twelve thousand.[27] But by misrepresenting the Palestine certificates as papers for whole families rather than for individuals, Krausz and Lutz managed to expand the number of Jews granted immunity to forty thousand.[28] The Zionist youth movements then multiplied this number again by forging safety passes in huge quantities. As a result, some eighty thousand to ninety thousand real and fake safety passes were circulated in Switzerland's name alone.[29] Although the Nazis and the Arrow Cross often disregarded the safety passes during their reign of terror, this rescue operation—initiated and managed by the Zionists—undoubtedly saved the lives of scores of thousands of Jews.

To protect the holders of real and fake safety passes, Krausz organized dozens of "protected houses" around the capital. Granted Swiss diplomatic immunity, these became refuges from the fascists. Some twenty-four thousand Jews found a measure of safety in homes with Swiss extraterritorial status.[30] Thousands more lived in buildings under the protection of other foreign missions.

The first and most famous protected house was the "Glass House" at 29 Vadász Street, where two thousand Jews received asylum after the Arrow Cross coup.[31] The building became the center of operations for Krausz and for a few hundred staff working under his supervision, who were recognized as Swiss employees and were exempt from wearing the Yellow Star.[32] The Glass House also became a base for the activities of the Zionist youth groups—activities (often conducted without Krausz's permission) that included forging and distributing safety passes, saving Jews from camps in Hungary, and smuggling Jews across the borders.[33] Of course, even the Glass House was never fully safe, and there were several attempted incursions by Arrow Cross thugs, who sometimes shot into the crowds of Jews in the courtyard.[34]

Krausz was not the only prominent Zionist who saved many Jewish lives during the Arrow Cross terror. Also active at this time was Ottó Komoly, the chairman of the rescue committee. Having ceded the initiative to Kasztner during the deportations from the provinces, Komoly now acted independently to save Budapest Jews, especially children. To that end he coordinated a special division of the International Red Cross, known as Department A and headquartered at 4 Mérleg Street. From there he recruited a staff of two hundred and fifty, including noted Zionists such as Hansi Brand and Zoltán Weiner.[35] Under Komoly's leadership, Department A set up dozens of children's homes with Red Cross extraterritorial status. In these homes a total of five thousand to six thousand children were sheltered from the depredations of the Arrow Cross.[36]

The establishment of the homes reflected the Zionist belief that "the children must be the first to be rescued."[37] Kasztner described the role of Zionist activists in bringing children to safety. They would break into the special Jewish houses, remove the children, and take them to the Department A homes. Sometimes they donned the uniforms of the Arrow Cross or the Hungarian paramilitary youth; on other occasions they disguised themselves as railway officials. They even forged Eichmann's signature; they also used cars with false German number-plates.[38]

Once living in the Department A homes, the children could be defended by armed members of the Zionist youth movements.[39] Komoly persisted in his campaign to save thousands of Jewish children after repeated arrests by the Hungarian authorities. He was murdered by the Arrow Cross before the end of the war.

All of these Zionist rescue operations took place without Kasztner's intervention. Krausz, who viewed Kasztner as a collaborator, refused to have anything to do with him. Apparently, Komoly and his staff saw no need to include Kasztner in their activities. Funding for Department A came from the *Judenrat* (reconstituted under new leadership) and not from Kasztner's committee.[40] Although Kasztner states in the *Bericht* that "our greatest worry was the Jewish children"[41] and although he notes the contributions of his rescue committee colleagues Offenbach and Hansi Brand to the work of Department A, he does not even hint at anything that he, personally, did to help them.

The organization of the safety passes, the protected houses, and the children's homes in the heart of Nazi-occupied Budapest serves as a shining example of what it was possible for even a few hundred dedicated and resourceful Zionists to achieve in this period without the patronage of the SS and without the dubious aid of Kasztner's dealings with Eichmann.

"The Faces of the Jews Light Up . . ."

On October 26, the Arrow Cross regime authorized the transfer of Jewish workers to the Reich, where they were to be used for work on fortifications. Tens of thousands of Jewish men from labor units, as well as women, were deported on foot on the road from Budapest to Vienna. What came to be known as the Death March officially commenced on November 8. The victims had to march in the winter weather without food or shelter. Those unable to keep up were shot by the Hungarian guards. As a result, the sides of the road were strewn with the corpses of Jews, which often lay out in the open for days.[42]

Although the forced marches were implemented by the Hungarians, ultimate responsibility lay with the Nazis. Eichmann personally demanded the delivery of fifty thousand workers and hoped to double that figure to one hundred thousand.[43] Also influential was Becher, whose position in the German evacuation command in Budapest gave him military-operational powers over the march.[44] Another of Kasztner's SS associates also played his part: the emaciated survivors who reached the borders of the Third Reich were handed over to Wisliceny for deployment as slave labor.

Kasztner provided a detailed account of the horrors in a letter sent to Saly Mayer. Just over half-way through his ten-page description, he saw fit to insert these lines:

> It is reported that at Hegyeshalom the convoys are taken over by Wisliceny. According to unequivocal reports from the border, the Jews are humanely received and treated by the German authorities. There they are washed and adequately provided for and sent onwards by train. As one of Eichmann's deputies explains, "The faces of the Jews light up when they reach the German border."[45]

This passage, contrasting the cruelty of the Hungarians with the kindness of the Germans, closely resembled the Nazi propaganda line. It amounted to a few sentences in a long and detailed factual account, so that the propagandist intent was not so obvious.[46] Doubtless, Kasztner did not spontaneously decide to disseminate such material; the natural inference is that elements in the SS were interested in exploiting the situation to establish a postwar alibi for themselves, with his assistance.

Since many of the deportees reaching the border were no longer in any condition to work, the bloody fiasco of the Death March was the subject of much discussion in the Nazi high command. It appears that Kasztner was privy to some of these exchanges. To Saly Mayer he wrote:

> On November 16, high-ranking visitors arrived in Budapest. They had seen the march of the deportees on the road from Budapest to Vienna. Possibly as a result, the deportation of women was stopped on November 17 and the deportation was stopped in general on November 18.[47]

Kasztner later identified the first visitor as Hans Jüttner, commander of the Waffen-SS. In the *Bericht* he gave credit to Jüttner for ordering the *Eichmann-Kommando* to stop the Death March within a day of his arrival. Thanks to Jüttner's intervention, he added, about seven thousand five hundred Jews were promptly rescued and returned to Budapest.[48]

Kasztner's assertions in the *Bericht* formed the basis of an affidavit he submitted to the war crimes investigators at Nuremberg in 1948. There he attributed the end of the Death March to Jüttner and Becher in no uncertain terms:

> On his arrival in Budapest, Jüttner protested against the conditions under which these deportations were proceeding to the chief of the SS and the German Police in Hungary Winkelmann asking that they be stopped.... In actual fact the "Death March" was halted later on, as I learned following the intervention of Becher and Jüttner with H. Himmler.[49]

In this statement, Kasztner did not claim that Jüttner had intervened directly with the *Eichmann-Kommando*. Rather, he asserted that Jüttner had overruled Eichmann by turning to Winkelmann and then Himmler.

In his initial testimony in Jerusalem, Kasztner repeated the story about Jüttner's orders to stop the Death March, albeit without specifying whether Jüttner had intervened with Eichmann or Winkelmann:

> When I came to Becher . . . I met two officers previously unknown to me: Jüttner and someone else. In the discussion they told me what they had seen on the road. . . . This is when Jüttner gave the order to stop the Foot March.[50]

Thus Kasztner suggested that Jüttner's orders were the result of a meeting in which he had participated. The implication was that Kasztner had helped to persuade Jüttner to halt the Death March. But under cross-examination he partially retracted this version, stating: "I met General Jüttner. . . . I don't know if my meeting with Jüttner produced results."[51] Apparently, Kasztner himself did not believe his claims in his letter to Saly Mayer, in the *Bericht*, and in his Nuremberg affidavit that Jüttner's orders had stopped the Death March. And there was reason for that skepticism: in his affidavit for the Eichmann Trial, Jüttner mentioned his protest to Winkelmann but did not even pretend that he had influenced the suspension of the Death March.[52]

Who was the second of the "high-ranking visitors" to Budapest in the meeting with Becher and Kasztner on November 16—the "someone else" mentioned in his original testimony? Kasztner answered this question in the *Bericht*: it was none other than the former commandant of Auschwitz, Rudolf Höss. The latter had come from Himmler's headquarters, where he had been informed of the *Reichsführer*'s "new line."[53]

During his trial testimony in Jerusalem, Kasztner was asked:

> Q: Did you meet SS *Obersturmbannführer* Höss?
>
> A: I did. I met him in the office of Dr. Billitz. Krumey was also there. I don't remember if Jüttner came in or not. They discussed the Foot March. Höss said it was swinish, what he had seen on the road between Budapest and Vienna. I confirmed it and gave him the details of how many of the marchers were dropping dead from it. He pretended to have already taken steps to end it. That's all. True, it was the commandant of Auschwitz. The man himself. Strange and tragicomic as it may seem, it's true.[54]

Why was the head of the Hungarian Jewish rescue committee granted the "honor" of an audience with Rudolf Höss, the former commandant of Auschwitz who had, just a few months earlier, orchestrated the destruction of Hungary's Jews? What are we to make of Kasztner's contention that this mass murderer was outraged at the methods employed in the Death March? Did the commandant of Auschwitz really help Kasztner to save Jews? And what was the "new line" that Höss had absorbed at Himmler's headquarters?

After his unprecedented "successes" at Auschwitz, Höss had been appointed to the SS Economic and Administrative Main Office (WVHA), where he was now in charge of the deployment of slave labor in the Niederdonau region of Austria.[55] It was in that capacity that he accompanied Jüttner to meet Becher in Budapest. Observing the horrors of the Death March on the Budapest–Vienna highway, the two Nazis were indignant, not for humanitarian reasons, but because the marchers had been reduced to such a state that they were plainly unfit for work.[56] Hence their expressions of dismay to Becher.

If Jüttner and Höss interfered with the march, it was not to save the victims but to ensure that Jews sent to the Reich were fit for slave labor. There remains the problem of explaining Kasztner's presence at the relevant meeting. In discussing the Death March with him, these Nazis were reviewing a matter of military importance—which was also a war crime—in front of a Jewish leader. That Jüttner and Höss were prepared to discuss such matters with him indicates how far Kasztner had been accepted by the inner circle of Nazi war criminals.

As for the mysterious "new line" that had been explained to Höss at Himmler's headquarters, this apparently meant the new *modus operandi* of exploiting any necessary interruption of the atrocities to establish postwar alibis. That is why the commander of the Waffen-SS and the former commandant of Auschwitz were anxious to display their "outrage" to the head of the Jewish rescue committee—who was trusted to describe their performance in a suitable fashion in his correspondence with Saly Mayer as well as in his postwar statements, culminating in an affidavit whitewashing one of these war criminals at Nuremberg.

The extent of Kasztner's integration into the SS anti-Jewish apparatus is betrayed by another of the revelations in his letter to Saly Mayer. There he explains what happened when Eichmann returned to Budapest on November 21 and learned of the protests about the unfitness of the Jews sent on the march. Eichmann's instant reaction was to demand Kasztner's assistance in rounding up some more suitable Jewish workers:

> He needed 65,000–70,000 Hungarian Jews at any cost; so far 38,000 had arrived at the German border. He needed another 20,000 Jews at any cost for fortification work. . . . He asked me if I was willing to find the 20,000 for him, in which case he would exempt dependents, etc., in which case the Swiss consulate along with the Swedes could grant 40,000 safety passes [to Jews in Budapest] and he would not disregard them. But if he did not get the 20,000 from me, then he would have to use the machinery of coercion.[57]

Kasztner, of course, was in no position to round up another twenty thousand Jews on Eichmann's behalf for slave labor. What is significant is that Eichmann made the request. This incident also illuminates Kasztner's earlier role in the slave labor transports from the provincial ghettos to Strasshof in Austria.

The Death March finally came to a halt at the beginning of December 1944.[58] This was due to several factors: notably, the Arrow Cross regime, in search of diplomatic legitimacy, was increasingly reluctant to comply with the Nazi demands; and almost all of the Jews in the category selected for deportation had already been sent on their way.[59]

As dictated by the requirements of Himmler's "new line," the Nazis tried to represent the end of the march as a humanitarian concession for which they were entitled to a reward from Saly Mayer. Kasztner was their tool for this. As Becher affirmed in his Nuremberg affidavit, "Halting the deportation by foot at the end of the November–December season was again regarded by Dr. Kasztner as a great deed performed by me and it was described accordingly in his announcement abroad."[60]

The essence of Himmler's "new line" was exploiting the ongoing destruction of Hungarian Jews to extort political and economic gains from the West. Whenever the Nazi machinery of terror confronted a setback or obstacle, it was now described in Kasztner's communications with Saly Mayer as a real humanitarian concession initiated by Becher and/or "high-ranking visitors" such as Jüttner and Höss. The "new line" was a policy of committing crimes while building alibis. Eichmann directed the crimes while Becher manufactured the alibis—using Kasztner, the pseudo-rescuer, as his instrument.[61]

Did Kasztner Stop the Gas Chambers of Auschwitz?

In his affidavit to Allied war crimes investigators in September 1945, Kasztner freely admitted that his life had been spared for the sole purpose of establishing postwar alibis for Nazis such as Becher. At the same time, he argued that in late 1944, Himmler had made a number of "concessions." He gave a dramatic example:

> According to Becher, Himmler issued instructions—on his advice— on the 25 November 1944 to dynamite all the gas chambers and crematoria of Oswiecim [Auschwitz]. He also issued a ban on further murdering of Jews . . .

Kasztner explained:

> In the hope of establishing contact with the Allies, Himmler made some concessions even without expecting economic returns. To this desire of Himmler may be ascribed the general prohibition

dated 25 November 1944, concerning the further killing of Jews. On 27 November 1944 Becher showed me a copy of Himmler's order on this subject. [E]ichmann at first did not obey this order.[62]

Thus Kasztner maintained that thanks to his dealings with Becher, Himmler was induced to dismantle the gas chambers in Auschwitz and to prohibit any further killing of Jews throughout Axis territory—this, in late November 1944. He even claimed to have seen Himmler's written instructions to that effect.

This story is called into question by the account in the *Bericht*, written a year later. There Kasztner did not claim to have seen a copy of Himmler's orders; he merely stated that the existence of the orders was later confirmed by "various sources" and was "more than a bluff." He also embroidered his account of Himmler's instructions: Himmler, he claimed, had ordered that Jewish workers in Germany were to receive the same provisions as other workers from the East; that sick Jews were to be given hospital treatment; and that all lower ranks of the SS had to put these measures into effect. Becher had allegedly passed the text of the orders to Kaltenbrunner.[63]

Further doubt was created by Kasztner's next detail in the *Bericht*: on November 27, the very day when he supposedly read the text of Himmler's orders ending the Final Solution and requiring all SS officers to comply, he was summoned by Eichmann. On the agenda was his next meeting with Saly Mayer. Eichmann announced that if no progress was made within twenty-four hours, he would eliminate the Jewish "dungheap" in the capital.[64] Or as Kasztner testified in the libel trial: "Eichmann declared that if a satisfactory answer was not received . . . then he would exterminate the Jews of Budapest."[65]

The inconsistency between Kasztner's version of Himmler's orders and the actual course of events—meaning the fact that Jews continued to be slaughtered until the last days of the Reich—was drawn to his attention during his cross-examination. Kasztner gave way: the order had not been carried out in full. Large numbers had been killed in concentration camps after this alleged order. Jews had been exterminated in the camps even at the beginning of May 1945.[66]

In fact Himmler could not have ended the killing without the permission of Hitler, who never relented in his commitment to the Final Solution. It is inconceivable that at this stage of the war, Himmler would try to end the Holocaust behind Hitler's back.[67]

The particle of truth in Kasztner's account is that at the end of November 1944, Himmler did order the destruction of the gas chambers in Auschwitz. But this was unrelated to the influence of Becher. It was also unrelated to the negotiations at the Swiss border, which had yielded nothing, as Eichmann's threats to Kasztner illustrate. And it was definitely unrelated to any decision to stop the murder of Jews, which continued (by means of starvation, slave labor, mass shootings, and death marches) until the end of the war. In January 1945, for example, orders were given for the evacuation of concentration camps in the East, with the stipulation that no survivors should fall into enemy hands; the ensuing death marches cost another quarter of a million lives.[68]

The final gassing at Auschwitz is believed to have taken place on October 30, 1944. Periodic small-scale killings occurred thereafter, but the camp's industrial murder functions had been completed. Orders to demolish the gas chambers and crematoria were delivered on November 24–25. The Birkenau death camp was merged with the main Auschwitz concentration camp, and the dismantling of the extermination facilities began at once.[69]

In other words, mass killings at Auschwitz ceased more than three weeks before the destruction of the killing installations. If the negotiations on the Swiss border had been linked in any way to the end of extermination at Auschwitz, Becher would have announced this development to Kasztner (and to Saly Mayer) in the first week of November. The decision that Becher revealed to Kasztner at the end of the month was not about halting mass murders in the camp but about destroying its installations, which had already fallen into disuse.

In reality, Himmler ordered an end to the exterminations at Auschwitz in the last days of October or the first days of November, the likely reason being the disastrous military situation, which meant that Soviet forces were advancing ever closer to the camp. At the end of November he ordered the eradication of the camp's gas chambers and crematoria.[70] Hearing of this second decision, Becher hastened to inform Kasztner, and the two of them turned it into the foundation for their self-serving invention about orders to halt the Final Solution in its entirety—orders supposedly issued thanks to their benign influence on the *Reichsführer-SS*.

Who Saved the Kasztner Train?

In the November 27 confrontation with Eichmann—which Becher also attended—Kasztner addressed another crucial issue in the talks with Saly Mayer: the fate of over one thousand three hundred Kasztner Train passengers still held hostage in Bergen-Belsen.

For weeks the Nazis had been promising to free the transport.[71] But the matter had just become acute owing to the arrival of a cable from Becher's representative at the Swiss border, Kettlitz, stating that he had been unable to contact Mayer for more than a week and saw no point in continuing the talks. It was in this context that Eichmann threatened to destroy the Jewish "dungheap" in Budapest.

At the meeting, Eichmann mentioned the impending departure of the remaining hostages from Bergen-Belsen and warned that Kasztner's family would be kept behind to guarantee his return from Switzerland. Kasztner replied that he would only travel to the Swiss border if his family left with the others; he promised to return to Budapest after their release. Becher, however, issued an ultimatum: unless he received SF20 million for the purchase of goods by December 2, *none* of the train passengers would be allowed to leave.[72] Becher never received the money, but the hostages were set free regardless. What is the explanation for this perplexing fact?

The notion that liberating the transport was an incentive for Saly Mayer to return to the talks can be discounted, for the release of the transport came after the resumption of negotiations. The next meeting on the Swiss border (which Saly Mayer did not attend) took place on November 29; Kasztner entered Switzerland for a private discussion with Mayer on December 1; and an official meeting with Mayer was held on December 5. The train did not leave German-controlled territory until the night of December 6–7.[73] Since negotiations resumed *before* the train was permitted to cross the Swiss border, renewing the talks could not have been the motive for freeing the train.

Another explanation for the train's release involves the private talk between Kasztner and Mayer on December 1. Kasztner had traveled to the border with Becher's warning that the train would not leave unless the money was paid by December 2. But the talks still had not produced results by December 1, when Kasztner met Mayer alone in a Swiss hotel and learned that he could pay only a fraction of the sum demanded. Kasztner claims that he prevailed upon the Nazi negotiators, Kettlitz and Krell, to send Becher a false message stating that SF5 million was available and that the chief obstacle to progress was the detention of the transport.[74] According to Bauer, this message had its intended effect: Becher sent a favorable reply on December 4, and 1,368 Jews crossed the Swiss border just days later.[75]

However, Bauer's claim is refuted by the chronology in Kasztner's *Bericht*. According to Kasztner, the false message to Becher was dispatched at 2 AM on December 2, but a cable from Berlin ordering the release of the train arrived on the night of December 1.[76] Since the false message to Becher was sent *after* the order to free the train, the former could not have caused the latter. So the machinations in Switzerland did not bring about the release of the Kasztner Train from Bergen-Belsen.

It is hard to avoid the conclusion that the decision to free the rest of the transport members was unrelated to the negotiations between Becher, his representatives, and Saly Mayer. Significantly, the order to free the train was sent from Berlin while Becher's ultimatum *delaying* its departure was still in force. This means that Becher was overruled by a superior, that is, by Himmler. The final order to free the transport seems to have been influenced by parties other then Becher.

One of those parties may have been Walter Schellenberg, head of SS foreign intelligence, who had been among the instigators of the Brand Mission and consistently supported peace feelers toward the West. Starting in October 1944, Schellenberg set up meetings between the *Reichsführer-SS* and Jean-Marie Musy, a right-wing Swiss politician working as intermediary for the Orthodox Jewish rescue activists Isaac and Recha Sternbuch; he also advocated the release of six hundred thousand Jews from Nazi territory to Switzerland. Himmler did not follow that advice, but Schellenberg's lobbying may have persuaded him not to detain the Kasztner Train hostages any longer. In January–February 1945, after these Jews left Bergen-Belsen, Schellenberg convinced Himmler to order the release of another transport of 1,210 Jews—the so-called Musy Train—from Theresienstadt to Switzerland.[77]

Perhaps Schellenberg was the decisive voice in persuading Himmler to free the remainder of the Kasztner Train hostages. What is clear is that the liberation of those hostages had nothing to do with any negotiations conducted by Kasztner in Switzerland.

Who Saved the Budapest Ghetto?

One of the first decrees of the Arrow Cross was the establishment of a ghetto in the capital. Jews lacking protective documents were forced to leave home and move to a small area around the Dohány Street synagogue. By December 2, about seventy thousand Jews had been concentrated in small apartments, with more than a dozen people living and sleeping in each room. The Red Army began its siege of the city on December 26, 1944; Pest was overrun on January 18, 1945; and Buda was conquered on February 13, 1945.

As they prepared to leave the capital, the Hungarian fascists decided to avenge their defeat by murdering all the Jews in the Budapest Ghetto. The massacre did not take place, and the seventy thousand Jews outlived the fascist terror.

According to Kasztner's postwar account, the rescue committee quickly learned of the imminent massacre. Kasztner was in Switzerland, but his colleague Andre Biss managed to alert Becher, who told Winkelmann, who forbade the Arrow Cross to commit the atrocity. Becher and Winkelmann then obtained Himmler's endorsement of their actions.[78] Kasztner's main Nuremberg affidavit for Becher stated that because of the SS officer's deeds, "about 85,000 Jews from the Budapest ghettos were neither deported nor exterminated during the months of November, December and January 1944–45."[79]

There is no doubt that Kasztner's account (seconded by Biss) is a fabrication from beginning to end. On July 7, 1947, Kasztner was allowed to participate in Becher's interrogation at Nuremberg. An exchange on the Budapest Ghetto proved frustrating for both parties:

> KASZTNER: Up until now the story of the Budapest Ghetto has been told in many different ways. Now I would like to hear your story, free from any external influence, then I am going to ask you some questions.
>
> BECHER: I need to be enlightened about the Budapest Ghetto. Do you mean Columbus Street?
>
> KASZTNER: No, I mean the ones whom Eichmann left behind in Budapest after the marches on foot. They were settled in a certain district of town . . .
>
> BECHER: Unfortunately, I do not know about this. Until this very moment, I did not know that these people had been ghettoized.
>
> KASZTNER: Pull yourself together, because this is a very important question. You will recall it.

The discussion continued in this vein:

> BECHER: Please point me in the right direction.
>
> KASZTNER: The foot marches were over. A certain number of Jews were allowed to stay in Budapest. I assume there was a reason why they stayed alive. Now the only question is whether these people had the Arrow Cross to thank for their lives?

BECHER: Obviously not.

KASZTNER: Don't you remember that in mid-December the Arrow Cross decided to exterminate any Jews still in Budapest and living in the ghetto? Wasn't this question ever presented to you?

BECHER: I have a vague recollection, but I cannot give a precise answer just yet.[80]

Kasztner's efforts notwithstanding, Becher did not remember doing anything to rescue the Jews in the Budapest Ghetto. Offered the chance to explain how he had helped to save seventy thousand lives, he was simply in the dark. Plainly Becher did not deserve the credit that Kasztner was trying to foist on him for the survival of these Jews.

In Kasztner's version, the Budapest Ghetto was saved on December 8, 1944. But the actual date of the rescue was January 16, 1945. By this point the Soviets were closing in. Pál Szalai, an Arrow Cross official who used his position to help Jews, described the events to the postwar People's Tribunal of Budapest. According to his testimony, he learned at the last moment that a force of seven hundred Germans and Hungarians was intent on "mass murder to be committed by machine guns that same evening." He promptly consulted the Swedish consulate and relayed a warning from Raoul Wallenberg to Gerhard Schmidhuber, one of the German military commanders: if Schmidhuber did not prevent the massacre, "he would be held responsible and would be called to account not as a soldier but as a murderer." Schmidhuber intervened at once to defend the ghetto, which was liberated soon afterwards. This account of the last days of the Budapest Ghetto was confirmed by Jewish community leaders.[81]

Becher's ignorance of his alleged actions to save the Budapest Ghetto proves that Kasztner's story was baseless. It was nothing but an attempt to supply a postwar alibi for the SS war criminal.

Summary

After the destruction of the provincial Jewish population, Kasztner was anxious to justify his ongoing relations with the top Nazis in Hungary by claiming credit for all kinds of rescue activities. Since the Nazis certainly would not permit any genuine efforts to save Jews, he had to be content with projecting the *illusion* of saving lives, or pseudo-rescue. His most significant efforts were arranging futile negotiations with Saly Mayer while the Nazis were preparing to deport the Jews of Budapest to Auschwitz; negotiating a bogus deal to release the three

Zionist paratroopers; claiming credit for the efforts of his Zionist colleague Ottó Komoly to rescue thousands of children; pretending to have halted the Death March with the aid of the commander of the Waffen-SS and the former commandant of Auschwitz; claiming credit for the dismantling of gas chambers and for nonexistent orders to end the Final Solution; and attributing the rescue of the Budapest Ghetto to his SS patron, Kurt Becher.

In some cases, Kasztner's rescue claims disguised his role in the Nazi apparatus of terror: during the Death March, for instance, he was not only allowed to participate in a top-level session with Jüttner and Höss but was also asked by Eichmann to round up tens of thousands of Jews. Kasztner played an integral part in the "new line" introduced by Himmler: a policy of inventing humanitarian "concessions" by the Nazis in order to camouflage their guilt and to solidify their postwar alibis. Hence his letter commending the treatment of the Death March victims by Wisliceny at the German border and his Nuremberg affidavit falsely attributing the end of the march to Jüttner and Becher.

The most effective pseudo-rescue operation was the release of the Kasztner Train hostages from the Bergen-Belsen concentration camp. These hostages were freed in two phases, in August and December 1944. In both cases Kasztner was given credit for self-serving decisions by Himmler. The release of the first three hundred and eighteen Jews in August 1944 was, as Becher explained to Saly Mayer, a display of "good faith"—a propaganda gesture—by the SS. Like the rescue negotiations on the Swiss border, it was a distraction from Himmler's plan to deport hundreds of thousands of Jews from Budapest to Auschwitz. The order to free the remaining hostages, overriding Becher's veto, was issued by Himmler at the beginning of December 1944, while the negotiations with Saly Mayer were frozen. This decision, like the release of the Musy Train weeks later, was a ploy to generate positive propaganda abroad.

If Himmler was prepared to send small groups of Jews from the concentration camps to Switzerland at this point in the war, it was solely due to his urgent need to create a good impression in the West. Yet Kasztner built his postwar reputation largely on the myth of his key role in "saving" the hostages released by the *Reichsführer-SS*.

The liberation of the Kasztner Train and the manifestations of the "new line" in Hungary were not the only alibi attempts made during the Nazi military collapse. Their sequels would take Kasztner to the very heart of the Third Reich.

Notes

1. Saul Friedländer, *The Years of Extermination: Nazi Germany and the Jews, 1939–1945* (New York: HarperCollins, 2007), 624.

2. Randolph Braham, "The Rescue of the Jews of Hungary in Historical Perspective," in *The Historiography of the Holocaust Period: Proceedings of the Fifth Yad Vashem International Historical Conference,* eds. Yisrael Gutman and Gideon Greif (Jerusalem: Yad Vashem, 1988), 465.

3. Himmler to Mutschmann, July 31, 1944: Rothkirchen, "The 'Europa Plan': A Reassessment," 16.

4. Rudolf Höss, *Commandant of Auschwitz* (London: Weidenfeld and Nicolson, 1954), 211.

5. Grell to Foreign Office, August 19, 1944, Eichmann Trial exhibit T/1218.

6. Bauer, *Jews for Sale?,* 221.

7. Kasztner, *Bericht,* 92.

8. Veesenmayer to Ribbentrop, August 25, 1944, Eichmann Trial exhibit T/1222.

9. Becher to Himmler, August 25, 1944, in Müller-Tupath, *Reichsführers gehorsamster Becher,* 157.

10. Bauer, *Jews for Sale?,* 221; Becher's Nuremberg affidavit, Kasztner Trial defense exhibit 107, 6–7.

11. Kasztner, *Bericht,* 92.

12. Yehuda Bauer, letter to *Yad Vashem Studies* 33 (2005): 481. Elsewhere Bauer writes: "the August 25 order preventing the deportation of the Jews of Budapest was almost certainly a consequence of the negotiations on the Swiss border." Yehuda Bauer, *American Jewry and the Holocaust* (Detroit: Wayne State University Press, 1981), 433.

13. Yehuda Bauer, "Book Review: Michael R. Marrus, *The Holocaust in History,*" *Holocaust and Genocide Studies* 3, no. 3 (1988): 346.

14. Veesenmayer to Foreign Office, August 24, 1944, Eichmann Trial exhibit T/1219.

15. Zvi Erez, "Why Were the Jews of Budapest not Expelled in August 1944?," *Yalkut Moreshet* 2 (2004): 33. On Himmler's reasoning, see Braham, *The Politics of Genocide,* Vol. 2, 916–17; idem, "Rescue Operations in Hungary: Myths and Realities," 31–32; Richard Breitman and Shlomo Aronson, "The End of the 'Final Solution'? Nazi Plans to Ransom Jews in 1944," *Central European History* 25, no. 2 (1993): 197–8; Richard Breitman, "Nazi Jewish Policy in 1944," in *Genocide and Rescue: The Holocaust in Hungary 1944,* ed. David Cesarani (Oxford: Berg, 1997), 83.

16. Kasztner, *Bericht,* 92.

17. Kasztner Trial testimony, February 28, 1954.

18. Over the years, some of Kasztner's less scrupulous defenders have falsely insinuated that Hannah Szenes betrayed her colleagues under torture. These reportedly included Hansi Brand, in an interview with Shlomo Aronson: *Hitler, the Allies and the Jews,* 265. A more infamous example was Motti Lerner's television play *Kastner,* which led to an action for (posthumous) libel by the Szenes family: see the Israeli Supreme Court's ruling in *Giora Szenes v. The Broadcasting Authority,* HCJ 6126/94 (1999).

19. Kasztner Trial testimony, June 14, 1954.

20. Hansi Brand recalled: "one of the *halutzim* [Zionist youth] told me that there was a third prisoner with Palgi and Goldstein and that they [i.e., the Zionist youth] had appointed a lawyer for her." Kasztner Trial testimony,

March 31, 1954. Obviously, the Zionist youth belatedly appointed a lawyer because Kasztner and his committee had not done so.

21. Kasztner Trial testimony, June 14, 1954.
22. Krausz also charged that Kasztner's committee refused his offer to secure assistance from the department in the Swiss consulate representing British POWs: Kasztner Trial verdict, s. 113.
23. Kasztner Trial testimony, February 19, 1954.
24. Kasztner Trial testimony, February 28, 1954.
25. See Kasztner Trial verdict, s. 107.
26. For a comprehensive analysis of Krausz's rescue operations, see Nedivi, *Ha-Misrad ha-EretsYisre'eli be-Budapesht*, especially chapters 7–10.
27. Ibid., 273.
28. Braham, *The Politics of Genocide*, Vol. 2, 1115–16.
29. Krausz, Kasztner Trial testimony, July 2, 1954.
30. Nedivi, *Ha-Misrad ha-EretsYisre'eli be-Budapesht*, 297.
31. Braham, *The Politics of Genocide*, Vol. 2, 1139.
32. Ibid., 1116.
33. Ibid., 1117, 1138.
34. Ibid., 1148.
35. Szita, *Trading in Lives?*, 187.
36. Robert Rozett, "Child Rescue in Budapest, 1944–5," *Holocaust and Genocide Studies* 2, no. 1 (1987): 56.
37. Cohen, *The Halutz Resistance in Hungary, 1942–1944*, 180.
38. Kasztner, *Bericht*, 108.
39. Szita, *Trading in Lives?*, 188.
40. Braham, *The Politics of Genocide*, Vol. 2, 1121.
41. Kasztner, *Bericht*, 108.
42. Kasztner to Mayer, November 26, 1944, Kasztner Trial prosecution exhibit 28, 6; Kasztner's London Affidavit, 9; his Veesenmayer Trial testimony, March 19, 1948, Kasztner Trial prosecution exhibit 4, 3628–9.
43. Veesenmayer to Foreign Office, October 18, 1944, Eichmann Trial exhibit T/1235.
44. Kasztner, *Bericht*, 115.
45. Kasztner to Mayer, November 26, 1944, 6.
46. Kasztner Trial verdict, s. 115.
47. Kasztner to Mayer, November 26, 1944, 1.
48. Kasztner, *Bericht*, 126.
49. Kasztner's Nuremberg affidavit for Hans Jüttner, April 30, 1948, Tamir Archive.
50. Kasztner Trial testimony, February 22, 1954.
51. Kasztner Trial testimony, March 4, 1954.
52. Jüttner's Eichmann Trial testimony, submitted to the Court of First Instance, Bad Tölz, June 15, 1961.
53. Kasztner, *Bericht*, 126.
54. Kasztner Trial testimony, September 16, 1954.
55. Kádár and Vági, *Self-Financing Genocide*, 222.
56. Höss announced that he would only accept men fit for work and below the age of forty, the unfit being an excessive burden: Veesenmayer to Foreign Office, November 21, 1944, Eichmann Trial exhibit T/1242.

57. Kasztner to Mayer, November 26, 1944, 3.

58. Kasztner gives the date of December 8 in his London Affidavit, 9.

59. For the various factors involved, see Kádár and Vági, *Self-Financing Genocide*, 223–5, which also details Becher's claims to have influenced Himmler to stop the Death March, noting that there is virtually no independent evidence for any of them.

60. Becher's Nuremberg affidavit, Kasztner Trial defense exhibit 107, 10.

61. As Kasztner explained in the *Bericht*, 62, Eichmann's unit murdered and Becher's unit profited from the murders.

62. Kasztner, London Affidavit, 13. For Becher's claims about inducing Himmler to order an end to the annihilation of the Jews even earlier, in September–October 1944, see IMT, Vol. 11, 334; also Kádár and Vági, *Self-Financing Genocide*, 225–6. Biss also claims that Clages informed him of such an order by Himmler on September 30: Biss, *A Million Lives to Save*, 119. In reality, the gassings in Auschwitz continued for a full month.

63. Kasztner, *Bericht*, 132.

64. Ibid., 133.

65. Kasztner Trial testimony, February 22, 1954.

66. Ibid., March 2, 1954. See Daniel Blatman, *The Death Marches: The Final Phase of Nazi Genocide* (Cambridge, MA: Harvard University Press, 2011), 135–6: "The extermination activity in the concentration camps in the weeks and days before the evacuations was an inseparable part of the death marches chapter that began in January 1945 in camps in Poland, continued in the camps in Germany, and was to end in April–May [1945]."

67. Breitman and Aronson, "The End of the 'Final Solution'?," 203.

68. Friedländer, *The Years of Extermination*, 648–9; Blatman, *The Death Marches*, 12, 80–81.

69. Kádár and Vági, *Self-Financing Genocide*, 228–30.

70. Bauer conflates the cessation of gassing with the order to dismantle the gas chambers several weeks later: *Jews For Sale?*, 229.

71. Löb, *Dealing With Satan*, 188, 194–5.

72. Kasztner, *Bericht*, 134.

73. Löb, *Dealing With Satan*, 203.

74. Kasztner, *Bericht*, 136; Biss, *A Million Jews to Save*, 157.

75. Bauer, *Jews For Sale?*, 229.

76. Kasztner, *Bericht*, 136.

77. On these negotiations, see Monty Noam Penkower, *The Jews Were Expendable* (Detroit: Wayne State University Press, 1988), ch. 9; Paul Lawrence Rose and Herbert Druks, eds., *Archives of the Holocaust, Vol. 12: Hecht Archive, University of Haifa* (New York: Garland Publishing, 1990); Shmuel Ben-Zion, "Rakevet Musy [Musy's Train]," *Dapim le'heker tekufat ha'Shoah* 8 (1990): 135–61.

78. Kasztner, *Bericht*, 145–6. Biss claims that Becher first informed Himmler, who ordered Winkelmann to prevent the massacre: *A Million Jews to Save*, 175–6.

79. Kasztner's affidavit for Becher, August 4, 1947, Kasztner Trial prosecution exhibit 73.

80. Becher's Nuremberg interrogation, July 7, 1947, in Mendelsohn, *Relief in Hungary*, 77–80; translation from Kádár and Vági, *Self-Financing Genocide*, 235–6.

81. Braham, *The Politics of Genocide*, Vol. 2, 1005–7, 1017-18n129. See also Krisztián Ungváry, *Battle for Budapest* (London: I. B. Tauris, 2003), 249; Paul A. Levine, *Raoul Wallenberg in Budapest: Myth, History and Holocaust* (London: Vallentine Mitchell, 2010), 367–8. Szalai, like Wallenberg, is recognized as a Righteous Gentile by Yad Vashem.

15

A Guest of the SS

The beginning of December 1944 found Kasztner in Switzerland, where he had been conducting the talks with Saly Mayer. There Kasztner stayed for a month, until the time came to decide whether to return to Budapest or to join Becher's new headquarters in Vienna. In Budapest the head of the Jewish rescue committee was urgently needed: tens of thousands of Jews were being massacred by the fascists of the Arrow Cross. In Vienna there were a few hundred local Jews remaining, plus the Hungarian Jewish survivors of the Strasshof operation.

Kasztner understood that his duty as head of the rescue committee in Budapest was to return to Budapest. He later claimed that he had set out for the Hungarian capital, but was unable to complete the journey because the Red Army had encircled the city.[1] Instead, he reported, he stopped in Vienna, where—"luckily for me"—Becher was awaiting him.[2] So, according to Kasztner's initial account, he had intended to rejoin the Jews in Budapest, and not the Nazi in Vienna, but circumstances beyond his control forced him to stay with the Nazi in Vienna.

Needless to say, if Kasztner had truly wanted to return to Budapest to help the Jews there, he would not have remained in Switzerland for almost a month, until the Red Army was besieging the city. At the Kasztner Trial in Jerusalem, he admitted that his real aim had not been to return to Hungary but to see Becher in Vienna.[3] He also admitted that even before leaving Switzerland, he had returned funds given to him by Saly Mayer for the benefit of Jews in Budapest, because he knew he would have no opportunity to distribute them in the Hungarian capital.[4] So it is clear that, contrary to his initial claims, Kasztner had decided to go to Becher.

Why did Kasztner choose not to return to Budapest, where he could have acted independently to rescue Jews, but to Vienna, where any "rescue" actions he performed would be dependent on Nazi permission? At this stage he did not yet know that he would be sent to visit Bergen-Belsen and other Nazi camps by Himmler, so he could not have expected to help the Jews in those camps. He did, however, know that Becher was most eager to develop an alibi and that Becher needed a Jewish witness for that alibi.

Kasztner in Nazi Vienna and Bratislava

On December 30, Kasztner arrived in Vienna. He stayed there not as a guest of the local Jewish community, as one might expect, but as a guest of the SS. Through Becher's intervention with Dr. Ebner, deputy chief of the Vienna Gestapo, he was given a room at the Grand Hotel and a German foreign passport.[5] The Grand Hotel in Vienna was at the time the main residence of SS officers in the city.

Kasztner was called to the Gestapo headquarters, where Ebner ordered him to stay away from Aryans, to avoid making acquaintances, and to let no one know that he was a Jew.[6] He whiled away the first few weeks in Vienna in meetings with Becher, Wisliceny, and Krumey (all of whom had relocated there), and he also took the opportunity to visit the surviving Hungarian Jews who had been sent to Strasshof instead of Auschwitz.

One incident that took place in this period is revealing. On January 19, 1945, Becher produced a copy of one of Kasztner's reports on the talks with Saly Mayer—a report that the Gestapo had managed to intercept. The report was written in code that had confused Becher's colleagues. Becher therefore asked Kasztner for a translation; and Kasztner complied—omitting, he claimed, to decode "the sensitive parts" of the report.[7] What this means is that Becher considered Kasztner sufficiently reliable to the Nazis that he expected Kasztner to reveal the secret codes used by the Zionists in their internal communications. These codes were used, of course, precisely so that the Nazis would not be able to decipher the correspondence. Even if we choose to believe Kasztner's claim to have omitted "the sensitive parts" of the report, the incident is remarkable because of Becher's confidence that Kasztner was more loyal to him than to the Zionist movement.

The highlight of Kasztner's stay in Nazi Vienna came on March 28, 1945. Kasztner described what took place:

> Himmler came to Vienna to take military measures for the defense of the city. They took me to the building where the meeting about the security of Vienna had convened, with Himmler presiding. I stood there in the corridor with Krumey and Becher. When Himmler came out, Becher approached him and pointed to me.[8]

Himmler was already familiar with Kasztner because of his role in arranging negotiations between Nazi Germany and the West (the talks with Saly Mayer, with the participation of the US War Refugee Board).

Kasztner had now been introduced to the commander of the Waffen-SS (Jüttner), to the former commandant of Auschwitz (Höss), and to the *Reichsführer-SS* (Himmler). He had been given a German passport and he had been housed in the main SS residence in Vienna. He had even been asked to decode internal Zionist communications for the benefit of the SS. Despite being a Jew, he was trusted by the SS inner circle.

The Nazis needed a trustworthy Jewish collaborator like him because they needed alibis for the expected postwar trials. The extent of Kasztner's complicity in the Nazi alibi efforts is illustrated by his activities in Bratislava during March 31–April 2.

Kasztner's version is as follows. Concerned about the ongoing Nazi hunt for hidden Jews in Bratislava, he prevailed on Becher to lobby Himmler for permission to save them. At the end of March 1945, Becher reported that Himmler had agreed to release four hundred hidden Slovak Jews on these terms: the Gestapo in Bratislava would be ordered to stop the hunt for hidden Jews; Krumey would accompany Kasztner to Bratislava to organize the transport, which would assemble by the office of Becher's staff in Bratislava; and Jews from the Nazi collection center in the city of Sered would be allowed to join the transport.[9] On March 31, Kasztner and Krumey arrived in the Slovak capital, with Red Army rapidly advancing. They contacted the local Zionist youth leader Juraj Révész, who agreed to approach some hidden Jews on their behalf. By April 2, Révész had gathered twenty-eight Jews, including the Slovak Working Group's leader, Rabbi Weissmandel. All these were taken by truck to Vienna.[10] The next day, the transport left for Switzerland, where it arrived safely several days later.

The reality of the operation becomes obvious on inspection. Bratislava at the time was being abandoned by the Nazis and was on the verge of liberation by the Soviets. The hidden Jews in the city were eagerly awaiting the arrival of the Red Army. If the Nazis wanted to perform a humanitarian act, all they had to do was to call off the hunt for hidden Jews. Instead they actively sought out hidden Jews with the professed aim of "rescuing" them—from whom? From the Red Army? The source of danger to the hidden Jews was, of course, the Nazis. Yet, with Kasztner's help, the Nazis pretended to be the rescuers. Plainly, the only true reason for persuading hidden Jews to surrender to the Nazis and to join a group transport to Switzerland was to manufacture a postwar alibi for the SS officers involved: Krumey, Becher, and ultimately Himmler.

With the Soviets about to take the city, the hidden Jews in Bratislava were understandably reluctant to entrust themselves to the tender mercies of the SS. As Kasztner observed, only twenty-eight people assembled for the journey. The rest refused to leave their hiding places.[11] Sensibly enough, they preferred to conceal themselves and await their liberators. Even Rabbi Weissmandel came, according to Kasztner, only because he wanted to search for his wife and children (who had in fact been deported to Auschwitz and gassed). Révész himself chose not to leave Bratislava with Kasztner and the Nazis.

At the Kasztner Trial in Jerusalem, Révész testified that Kasztner and Krumey had sought out his hiding place, taken him to the Bratislava railway station, and then waited outside while sending him to see the stationmaster. His mission was to stop a train carrying Jews from Sered to Theresienstadt. Révész was unable to do so because the train had been sent on another route.[12] Plainly, if Krumey had really wanted to stop the train from Sered, he could have done so on his own authority. The only reason for asking Révész to meet the stationmaster was to use him as an alibi witness.[13]

The Bratislava incident was just one of a series of operations designed to secure alibis for Becher, Krumey, and (through them) Himmler. The next stage of the campaign was the mission to the concentration camps.

Origins of the Mission to the Camps

In his search for an alibi, Himmler needed to be seen as a moderate by the West; but at the same time he could not afford to antagonize Hitler, who had warned him against further negotiations with Jews.[14] In mid-March 1945, he commanded Oswald Pohl, head of the SS-WVHA with overall responsibility for the concentration camps, to order all camp commandants in Germany to stop killing Jews and to keep them alive. Pohl conveyed the instructions to Buchenwald, Neuengamme, Dachau, and Mauthausen in person; he also informed Sachsenhausen and Ravensbrück.[15] But in fear of Hitler's reaction, Himmler soon changed his mind about several of these camps.

Himmler's orders to Becher were part of this ambivalent policy. On the one hand, he told Becher to prevent the liquidation of several camps, primarily Bergen-Belsen; this was contrary to Hitler's edict that concentration camp inmates were not to be allowed to fall into enemy hands alive. On the other hand, he warned Becher to remain obedient to Hitler. These inconsistent orders served Himmler's interests: if Hitler found out, Becher would get the blame; but if the camps were successfully handed over to the advancing enemy forces, Himmler would be able to tell the West that he had acted to save lives.[16]

Becher's intervention in the concentration camps at the end of the war was not the result of Kasztner's persuasive skills, let alone any sort of humanitarian effort; it was one of his tasks for Himmler and a ploy to set up his own alibi. In this operation, the orders were given by Himmler and not by Kasztner.

It is instructive to compare the accounts of the protagonists. Becher admitted at Nuremberg that the mission to the concentration camps was undertaken at Himmler's behest. As he described the course of events, the *Reichsführer-SS* reviewed the possible results of surrendering the camps to the Allied forces and gave him the responsibility for Bergen-Belsen. Becher then asked Kasztner to accompany him—and Kasztner agreed.[17]

Similarly, Kasztner's first affidavit for the Allied war crimes investigators in 1945 left no doubt about the reason for the journey to the camps. Himmler, wrote Kasztner, permitted the bloodless handover of Bergen-Belsen and Theresienstadt to the Allies, "which in his eyes and eyes of his colleagues was such a generous and colossal concession that he certainly hoped for some political concession in return."[18]

But two years later, Kasztner submitted his main Nuremberg affidavit exonerating Becher. There he maintained that the mission to the camps was initiated by Becher, who "strove with Himmler" to prevent SS radicals from murdering the inmates.[19] Testifying in Jerusalem in 1954, Kasztner changed his story again. Now he insisted that the mission had been his own idea, which Becher had adopted under his influence. In his words, "Becher took me to Bergen-Belsen because I told him that the task still facing him was to save the Jews still surviving in Germany. I asked to join his journey. I don't know why he agreed that I join."[20]

Needless to say, what Becher needed from Kasztner was a Jewish eye-witness to testify about his selfless display of "humanitarianism." On this point Kasztner remarked: "It seems plausible that he wanted me to witness the alibi and how he delivered the camp to the Allies." But had it seemed plausible to him at the time? Kasztner claimed not to remember.[21]

Kasztner in the Concentration Camps

As part of the alibi mission ordered by Himmler, Kasztner traveled to three Nazi concentration camps. Alongside Becher, he entered Bergen-Belsen (April 10–11) and Neuengamme (April 12). With Krumey and Hunsche, he made a tour of Theresienstadt (April 16). He then accompanied Krumey to the Swiss border (April 19). Becher, now on his own, traveled to Flossenbürg (April 17), Mauthausen (April 20 and 27), and Dachau (April 28).

According to Kasztner's postwar account, on April 10, Himmler reiterated his instructions to Becher to visit several camps, starting with Bergen-Belsen. Becher and Kasztner immediately drove to Eichmann's head office at 116 Kurfürstenstrasse in Berlin to ensure his noninterference with Himmler's directive. Becher entered alone and spoke to Eichmann, who was (according to Becher) outraged at the thought of "that scoundrel Kasztner" visiting the camps.[22] Kasztner relates that the two SS officers left the building together. In one of the strange details of his account, he adds, with a hint of umbrage, that Eichmann deliberately looked away from the SS Mercedes where he was sitting.[23]

Bergen–Belsen

Becher and Kasztner reached Bergen-Belsen in the evening. Kasztner described what happened next as follows. Becher spent an hour talking alone to Josef Kramer, the camp commandant. Kasztner was then invited to join them. Kramer explained that there had been a typhus outbreak among the remaining Jewish inmates, who were also dying of starvation at the rate of five hundred to six hundred per day. The guards had orders to defend the camp by force. Kasztner claimed that he convinced Becher to surrender the camp to the Allies at once and that they left without making an inspection. Outside the camp, they encountered a trainload of several thousand "preferred" Jews who were being sent to Theresienstadt in wretched conditions. Kasztner allegedly asked Becher not to let the train leave under such circumstances, but his request was denied.

The next day, according to Kasztner, Becher telephoned Himmler for permission to surrender the whole area to the British army. Kramer showed them around part of the camp, where thousands of inmates were no more than "living skeletons." Becher spent several hours convincing the local Wehrmacht commanders to surrender the camp to the British; by the evening, an army vehicle was ready to depart for the British lines.

On April 12, writes Kasztner, the two were in Hamburg when they heard that a British officer had arrived in Bergen-Belsen to negotiate its surrender. Becher wanted to handle the matter personally, but Himmler warned him to leave it to the Wehrmacht. Becher's intervention, concluded Kasztner, came too late to prevent the mass murders that had taken place over the previous weeks, but it did affect the fate of tens of thousands who might have been endangered by a battle for the camp.[24]

This account is misleading in several respects, all of them calculated to sanitize Kasztner's conduct at Bergen-Belsen and to exaggerate Becher's impact on its handover. The alibi character of the operation is evident from a letter that Kasztner wrote to Saly Mayer on April 11. There he claimed that Becher had not only persuaded the Wehrmacht to declare the Bergen-Belsen area a neutral zone but also arranged for the surrender of Buchenwald.[25] In reality, most of the Buchenwald inmates had already been sent on a death march—on Himmler's orders. Those left behind took control of the camp from the retreating SS and were liberated by the Americans on the day of Kasztner's letter.[26] This disinformation about Buchenwald indicates that Kasztner was already manipulating his account of the day's events in order to establish Becher's alibi.

Kasztner's account was also less than forthcoming about his activities in Bergen-Belsen. There Kasztner and Becher encountered the trainload of "preferred" Jews bound for Theresienstadt. Far from urging Becher to stop the transport, as he wrote in the *Bericht*, Kasztner encouraged the Jews to proceed to their destination without panic. Dr. Joseph Melkman, a Dutch Zionist who was one of the train passengers, remembered his words:

> [Kasztner] mentioned to me the names of two people whom I actually knew, one was Nathan Schwalb, who was in Switzerland, and Dr. Abeles [a Slovak Zionist leader], who was with us on the train, and he said: "I promise you that you are going to be sent to a good place."

Melkman was asked:

> Q: You were liberated in the train?
> A: Yes, on the train, for the train had not yet arrived at its destination.
> Q: Do you know where the train was bound for?
> A: People from Theresienstadt told us that gas chambers had been prepared for us there.[27]

The Theresienstadt administration had indeed begun to construct a gas chamber and other extermination facilities on the grounds earlier that year.[28] Aside from this project, which was never completed, the arrival of death marchers from other camps was by now turning the "model ghetto" into another nightmare of starvation and disease. Kasztner's advice to the "preferred" Jews not to panic on their way to this "good place" is eerily reminiscent of his deception of the Jewish masses during the deportations from Hungary.[29]

What actually happened at Bergen-Belsen was somewhat different from the self-serving alibi accounts of Kasztner and Becher. On April 12, the day after the pair left the camp, two representatives of the local Wehrmacht contacted the advancing British forces. They explained that the Wehrmacht had taken responsibility for Bergen-Belsen two days earlier, that is, on April 10. The German army had found that conditions in the camp were horrific; the emissaries emphasized the need to avoid a battle for the camp or the escape into the countryside of inmates carrying typhus. Therefore the army wanted to deliver the camp into British hands. During the negotiations, the Wehrmacht contacted Himmler's headquarters for approval of the handover decision. Meanwhile a British officer entered Bergen-Belsen, met commandant Kramer, and reported to his superiors about the situation of the inmates. British troops finally liberated the camp on April 15. As historian Richard Breitman observes, although undertaken with Himmler's consent, the peaceful surrender of Bergen-Belsen was the result of "a military initiative and military negotiations."[30]

The evidence shows that the contribution of Kasztner and Becher to these events was virtually nil. The Wehrmacht took control of the area on April 10, before or shortly after the pair arrived. Kasztner gave Becher credit for convincing the army to hand over the camp, but the Wehrmacht was in fact anxious to prevent a battle or typhus epidemic. Not Becher but Himmler was the key figure consulted by the army before the surrender decision. The story of Becher's role in saving tens of thousands of lives in Bergen-Belsen with Kasztner's aid is no more than a cleverly manufactured myth.

Neuengamme

During their journey to Hamburg, Becher and Kasztner stopped off at a second concentration camp: Neuengamme. The camp commandant informed them that he had just moved his Jewish inmates to Bergen-Belsen, while several thousand Norwegian and Danish prisoners in the camp were under the protection of Count Folke Bernadotte of the Swedish Red Cross. The highlight of this visit, it would appear, was a performance by the camp orchestra in Becher's honor.[31] Nowhere does the *Bericht* mention any attempt by Becher (or Kasztner) to arrange the surrender of the camp or otherwise save the inmates. Exactly one week after their visit, on April 19, the remaining prisoners in Neuengamme were either sent on a death march or murdered within the camp.[32]

On April 13, Becher took Kasztner on a tour of the bombed-out city of Hamburg. It was at this point, according to the *Bericht*, that he made an explicit request for a postwar alibi for himself and Himmler.[33] Kasztner does not quote his reply. The fact that he was kept alive indicates that it was positive.[34]

Becher proposed traveling together to a series of concentration camps, including Theresienstadt, Mauthausen, and Dachau. In reality, the pair now separated: Kasztner visited Theresienstadt without Becher, and then Becher visited Flossenbürg, Mauthausen, and Dachau without Kasztner.

Theresienstadt

On the morning of April 16, Kasztner left for Theresienstadt in the company of Eichmann's aides Krumey and Hunsche.[35] On arrival at the "model ghetto," they were treated to lunch in the SS staff dining room. Joined by the SS camp commandant, Karl Rahm, the trio were then given a guided tour of the "ghetto" by its Jewish "elder," Rabbi Benjamin Murmelstein. The sights included a barber's shop, a cafe, an orchestra, a public kitchen, a warehouse, a bakery, a hospital, a fire station, and homes for children and the elderly; there was also a public library of fifty thousand books, which was little-used, according to Rahm, because Jews prefer "loitering in the street" to reading. Kasztner was not fooled by any of these scenes; his *Bericht* described the stage-managed tour with the appropriate tone of skepticism. When Kasztner interrupted Murmelstein's rehearsed discourse on the history of the camp to ask if he could speak to various Zionist leaders known to be held there, he provoked the nervous response that only Leo Baeck was available—the obvious implication being that the others were dead.[36]

The visitors were joined by Rolf Günther, Eichmann's deputy from Berlin. Günther, remarked Kasztner, "does not shake my hand, just as his boss never did."[37]

The group proceeded to a theater performance of Smetana's *Bartered Bride*. The Nazis and their Jewish guest ended their tour in a cinema, where they watched an official propaganda film; this painted an idyllic picture of the "model ghetto" at Theresienstadt, complete with Jewish "extras" who had long since been deported to Auschwitz.[38]

Finally, Krumey passed on Himmler's orders for the surrender of the camp, which Günther promised to carry out personally. Krumey accepted Kasztner's proposal to call on the Red Cross to take charge.[39] Such, at least, is Kasztner's version.

This account of the visit to Theresienstadt is intriguing in many respects, but it does not explain the decision to capitulate peacefully. The truth is that Kasztner did not initiate the involvement of the Red Cross, whose members had been invited to visit some time before his own arrival. On April 6, after being escorted around the camp by none other than Eichmann, two ICRC delegates, Otto Lehner and Paul Dunant, expressed their approval of conditions there—not the first time that ICRC visitors to the camp had been fooled. On April 15, the day before Kasztner's tour, Jean-Marie Musy's son entered the camp and contacted Schellenberg about prisoners there. That same day, the Swedish Red Cross used buses to remove Danish Jews. On April 21, Dunant made another inspection and again concluded, absurdly, that nothing he saw was being orchestrated for his benefit. Over the following days, the authority of the SS collapsed owing to a typhus epidemic, and on May 2, Dunant assumed control on behalf of the Red Cross, pending liberation by Soviet forces a few days later.[40]

What this chronology reveals is that Theresienstadt was repeatedly inspected—by the ICRC, by the Swedish Red Cross, by Musy's son, and by Kasztner—during the weeks before its abandonment by the SS. Eichmann and his aides personally escorted visitors around the camp in an attempt to make a good impression. From the efforts undertaken to mislead these outsiders as to the true character of Theresienstadt, it is obvious that the SS killers wanted to use the inspections to camouflage their crimes against the Jews behind a thick layer of propaganda. It is also obvious that they would not have chosen the "model ghetto" as the site of this systematic alibi campaign if they had been planning to ruin their own alibis by slaughtering the remaining inmates.

The unavoidable conclusion is that Kasztner's tour of Theresienstadt did not stop any planned massacre of its population; moreover, since the SS, for propaganda purposes, had already decided to invite the involvement of the Red Cross, Kasztner's visit did not contribute to improving the awful conditions in the camp. Kasztner's presence was futile from a humanitarian point of view. But could he have known this beforehand? There is evidence that he did know. In Bergen-Belsen he had encountered a trainload of Jews about to leave for Theresienstadt and had reassured them that they were going to "a good place." If Kasztner thought at the time that there was a real danger of a bloodbath in Theresienstadt, then he lied to the Jews on this train in the belief that doing so amounted to sending them to their deaths. If, on the other hand, he honestly thought at the time that Theresienstadt was "a good place," then his April 16 visit was not intended to prevent a last-minute massacre of the inmates.[41]

What, then, was the true purpose of Kasztner's tour of Theresienstadt alongside Krumey and Hunsche? The key is to be found in the fact that Krumey delivered Himmler's orders for a peaceful handover to Günther—and in Kasztner's observation, in his 1945 affidavit, that Himmler "certainly hoped for some political concession in return" for the camp's surrender.[42] Himmler had already ordered the transfer of all Jews in camps in Germany to Theresienstadt. These Jews, writes historian Daniel Blatman, "were to serve as hostages and bargaining cards in the negotiations [Himmler] was then conducting."[43] The handover of Theresienstadt therefore amounted to a surrender of Jewish hostages in the expectation of political benefits.

The reason why Krumey and Hunsche accompanied Kasztner to the "model ghetto" is equally obvious. These two war criminals were anxious to build up their alibis by participating in a major "humanitarian" operation. Kasztner's role, as before, was to serve as a Jewish eye-witness confirming the praiseworthy conduct of the Nazis. The more handovers he witnessed, the more Jews he could claim to have saved. Krumey's and Hunsche's alibi was also Kasztner's alibi.

In the company of Krumey and Hunsche, Kasztner dined with the SS staff, embarked on a guided tour, watched a theater performance, and viewed an official propaganda film. These surreal incidents indicate how far he had been integrated into the everyday activities of his traveling companions. By this point he fully expected to be treated as an equal by the mass murderers. The wounded pride in his complaint that Eichmann and his deputy never shook his hand is consistent with his previous indignation at Eichmann's refusal to look him in the eye when he was waiting in Becher's Mercedes.

More Alibi Operations

While Kasztner was serving as a witness to the efforts of Krumey and Hunsche at Theresienstadt, Becher was fortifying his alibi by traveling to other camps. On April 17, he arrived at Flossenbürg, where he passed on Himmler's orders against evacuating the inmates on a death march. This was countermanded the next day when the camp received Himmler's cabled instruction that "no prisoner is to fall alive into enemy hands." The day after that commenced the evacuation of twenty-five thousand to thirty thousand inmates, who were sent on their way to Dachau.[44]

On April 20 Becher traveled to Mauthausen. There he gave orders to find and release Moshe Schweiger, Kasztner's friend and former colleague on the Jewish rescue committee, who had been arrested after the Nazi occupation of Hungary. His next order of business was to meet Franz Ziereis, the SS camp commandant. Ziereis gave him a cool reception, but—according to Becher's later account—admitted that he had been instructed to massacre tens of thousands of Jewish inmates by blowing them up in hillside tunnels. Becher supposedly tried to thwart the massacre by confronting Kaltenbrunner, whom he met overnight on April 25–26. He allegedly dissuaded Kaltenbrunner from carrying out a bloodbath and elicited a promise to surrender the camp peacefully, but returned to Mauthausen on April 27 only to find that Kaltenbrunner had given orders for one thousand executions per day. Becher—according to his own postwar account—prevailed on Ziereis not to carry out the new order.[45] Having—so he claimed—saved tens of thousands of inmates from certain death, he departed.

Such is Becher's version. In contrast to this account, there is the dying declaration by Ziereis (who was mortally wounded after firing on American troops). Ziereis stated:

> According to an order by Himmler, I was to liquidate all prisoners on behalf of SS Obergruppenfuehrer Dr. Kaltenbrunner; the prisoners were to be led into the tunnels of the factory Bergkristall and only one entrance was to be left open. Then this entrance was to be blown up by the use of explosives and the death of the prisoners was to be effected in this manner. I refused to carry out this order.[46]

Nowhere in this confession does Ziereis mention his encounter with Becher—as he surely would have done if Becher had really contradicted orders given to him by Himmler or Kaltenbrunner. From the confession it appears that Ziereis disregarded the orders on his own initiative, perhaps seeing no point in obeying when defeat was imminent. Whether or not this was the actual course of events, there is no evidence for Becher's claim—later seconded by Kasztner—that his intervention saved tens of thousands from extermination at Mauthausen.

On April 28, Becher proceeded to Dachau, supposedly having heard that Kaltenbrunner was concerned about Americans approaching the camp. According to Becher's self-serving account, he met the camp commandant Eduard Weiter, who was already on the verge of departing, and secured an offer of truce to the advancing forces. This account is equally untrustworthy.

In fact, an evacuation was already being attempted when Becher appeared; this was sabotaged by the inmates, so Himmler ordered their extermination. Fortunately, the Americans arrived just in time to save the camp population.[47] Therefore Becher's claim to have saved the inmates of Dachau was also false. It is noteworthy that not even Kasztner would later credit Becher as savior of Dachau. In his main affidavit in Becher's favor at Nuremberg, Kasztner hailed Becher as the guardian angel of Flossenbürg and Mauthausen, but he did not even mention Dachau.[48]

When Schweiger was finally brought to him several days later, Becher explained the reasons for his release. In Schweiger's words, "Kasztner had constantly pressed [Becher] to find and rescue me. . . . Becher told me he had promised to deliver me to Kasztner in Switzerland as a 'personal gift.'"[49] But personal generosity was not the only motive for Becher's action. There was also the matter of certain valuables in Becher's possession: the so-called Becher Deposit, the Jewish rescue committee's payment for the release of the Kasztner Train from Budapest. As Kasztner would later testify, he had named Schweiger "as the person to whom Becher should give the deposit."[50] Becher had then sought Himmler's permission to release Schweiger.[51]

While they awaited the Nazi surrender, Becher gave several suitcases full of the valuables to Schweiger, saying that he was designating them "for the Jewish people."[52] He also induced Schweiger to sign a letter praising him. Becher was arrested shortly afterwards, and Schweiger delivered the Becher Deposit to the Americans at Bad Ischl in Austria (it was ultimately retrieved by the Jewish Agency).

Clearly, Becher had ulterior motives for releasing Schweiger from Mauthausen. He could not afford to be caught with extorted Hungarian Jewish assets in his hands. His options were to hide the deposit, to give it to Kasztner, or to transfer it to another person chosen by one of them. Kasztner admitted that he was the one who nominated

Schweiger as the ideal recipient of the valuables. Becher admitted that he had obtained permission to use Schweiger from Himmler. The handover of the Becher Deposit was thus yet another alibi action by Becher that was coordinated with Kasztner and overseen by Himmler.

Summary

During the last months of the war, Kasztner was integrated into the inner circle of Nazi war criminals. Having previously been introduced to Waffen-SS commander Jüttner and former Auschwitz commandant Höss in Budapest, he was now taken to see *Reichsführer* Himmler in Vienna. He was given a Nazi passport and was housed in the SS officers' residence, where the deputy head of the Gestapo arranged for his room. He also took part in a systematic Nazi alibi campaign that had been ordered by Himmler himself. This included visiting Bratislava to "save" Jews by persuading them to leave their hiding places and surrender to the Nazis; traveling to a number of concentration camps at Himmler's behest; and arranging for the Becher Deposit to be delivered to his friend Schweiger in circumstances that would reflect well on Becher.

None of these deeds were *bona fide* acts of rescue. None of Kasztner's actions at this time saved lives, and (apart from the release of Schweiger) the same can probably be said of Becher's activities. But these events would now serve as the basis for Kasztner's most daring move yet: his interventions on behalf of SS war criminals at Nuremberg.

Notes

1. Kasztner, London Affidavit, 3.
2. Kasztner, *Bericht*, 147.
3. Kasztner, Kasztner Trial testimony, February 22, 1954.
4. Kasztner, Kasztner Trial testimony, March 3, 1954.
5. Kasztner, *Bericht*, 147.
6. Ibid.
7. Ibid., 157.
8. Kasztner, Kasztner Trial testimony, February 22, 1954.
9. Kasztner, *Bericht*, 168–9.
10. Ibid., 170–1.
11. Ibid., 171.
12. Révész, Kasztner Trial testimony, March 30, 1954.
13. Kasztner Trial verdict, s. 116.
14. Kádár and Vági, *Self-Financing Genocide*, 239.
15. Daniel Blatman, "The Death Marches, January-May 1945: Who Was Responsible for What?," *Yad Vashem Studies* 28 (2000): 184.
16. Kádár and Vági, *Self-Financing Genocide*, 240.
17. Becher's Nuremberg affidavit, Kasztner Trial defense exhibit 107, 13.
18. Kasztner, London Affidavit, 13.

19. Kasztner's affidavit for Becher, August 4, 1947, Kasztner Trial prosecution exhibit 73.
20. Kasztner, Kasztner Trial testimony, March 3, 1954.
21. Ibid.
22. Becher's Eichmann Trial testimony, submitted to the Court of First Instance, Bremen, June 20, 1961, para. 43.
23. Kasztner, *Bericht*, 173; Interrogation No. 1581a, 10.
24. Kasztner, *Bericht*, 173–5.
25. Kasztner to Mayer, April 11, 1945, in Dov Dinur, *Kastner: giluyim hadashim al ha'ish u'fo'olo* [*Kasztner: New Lights on the Man and His Deeds*] (Haifa: Gestelit, 1987), 91–93.
26. On the Buchenwald death march, see Blatman, "The Death Marches, January–May 1945," 187–91 (noting that Himmler's orders reversed his March 1945 decision). On the camp's liberation, see the eye-witness accounts in *1945: The Year of Liberation* (Washington, DC: United States Holocaust Memorial Museum, 1995), 125–7; and *Buchenwald Concentration Camp 1937–1945: A Guide to the Permanent Historical Exhibition*, ed. Gedenkstätte Buchenwald (Göttingen: Wallstein Verlag, 2004), 232–6.
27. Eichmann Trial testimony, May 10, 1961. See also Lindeman, *Shards of Memory*, 37–38; Esther Reiss-Mossel's recollections on Ynet, April 19, 2009: http://www.ynet.co.il/articles/0,7340,L-3702860,00.html (accessed January 4, 2011).
28. Frantisek Fuchs, "Building Gas Chambers in Terezin" and Arnost Weiss, "The Duck Pond," in *Terezin*, ed. Frantisek Ehrmann (Prague: The Council of Jewish Communities in Czech Lands, 1965), 300–5; Miroslav Karny, "Die Theresienstädter Herbsttransporte 1944," *Theresienstädter Studien und Dokumente* 2 (1995): 30.
29. As noted in Hecht, *Perfidy*, 262n69.
30. Richard Breitman, "Himmler and Bergen-Belsen," in *Belsen in History and Memory*, eds. Jo Reilly, David Cesarani, Tony Kushner and Colin Richmond (London: Frank Cass, 1997), 81–82.
31. Kasztner, *Bericht*, 175.
32. Peter Longerich, *Holocaust: The Nazi Persecution and Murder of the Jews* (Oxford: Oxford University Press, 2010), 418. On the fate of the evacuees, see Blatman, *The Death Marches*, 162–3.
33. Kasztner, *Bericht*, 176.
34. See Kasztner's London Affidavit, 3: "I escaped the fate of the other Jewish leaders . . . [partly] because SS Standartenführer Becher took me under his wings in order to establish an eventual alibi for himself . . . [Becher] endeavored consistently to furnish me with evidence that he tried to save the Jews."
35. Some sources wrongly state that Wisliceny accompanied them: Aronson, *Hitler, the Allies and the Jews*, 318; Porter, *Kasztner's Train*, 290.
36. Kasztner, *Bericht*, 178–9.
37. Ibid., 180.
38. Ibid. On this film, see Karel Margry, "'Theresienstadt' (1944–1945): The Nazi Propaganda Film Depicting the Concentration Camp as Paradise," *Historical Journal of Film, Radio and Television* 12, no. 2 (1992): 145–62.
39. Kasztner, *Bericht*, 180.

40. On the Red Cross inspections, see Jean-Claude Favez, *The Red Cross and the Holocaust* (Cambridge: Cambridge University Press, 1999), 268, 305–6; Livia Rothkirchen, *The Jews of Bohemia and Moravia: Facing the Holocaust* (Jerusalem: Yad Vashem, 2005), 262–3. For Benoit Musy, see Paul Lawrence Rose, "Introduction," in *Archives of the Holocaust, Vol. 12: Hecht Archive, University of Haifa* (New York: Garland Publishing, 1990), xvi.

41. It might be objected that Kasztner had to tell the train passengers that they were going to "a good place" because he was being watched by the Nazis. But the Nazis would not have understood his words because he addressed the passengers in Hebrew: Lindeman, *Shards of Memory*, 37.

42. Kasztner, London Affidavit, 13.

43. Blatman, *The Death Marches*, 144.

44. Ibid., 174.

45. Kádár and Vági, *Self-Financing Genocide*, 241–2.

46. Franz Ziereis, Confession, May 22, 1945, in Hans Marsalek, Affidavit, April 8, 1946, *Nazi Conspiracy and Aggression*, Vol. 6 (Nuremberg: International Military Tribunal, 1946), Document 3870-PS, 791.

47. Kádár and Vági, *Self-Financing Genocide*, 242.

48. See Kasztner, Affidavit, August 4, 1947, Kasztner Trial prosecution exhibit 73.

49. Schweiger, Kasztner Trial testimony, March 22, 1954.

50. Kasztner, Kasztner Trial testimony, March 4, 1954.

51. Becher's Nuremberg affidavit, Kasztner Trial defense exhibit 107, 18.

52. Schweiger, Kasztner Trial testimony, March 22, 1954.

16

Nuremberg

In April 1945, Kasztner and his wife went to live in a boarding house in Geneva. There they stayed until December 1947, when they immigrated to Palestine, then already engulfed in war between Arabs and Jews. During the three-year period 1945–48, Kasztner repeatedly traveled to London and Nuremberg for the Allied war crimes tribunal, submitting affidavits and taking part in interrogations. He was especially concerned to incriminate three figures: Kaltenbrunner, Eichmann, and the Mufti of Jerusalem, Haj Amin al-Husseini. He also took the witness stand, testifying against Hitler's former representative in Hungary, Edmund Veesenmayer.[1]

Kasztner's activities at this time have become notorious. But this is not because of what he said *against* men such as Veesenmayer and Kaltenbrunner (whom he never met) or Eichmann (who was not in custody). It is because of what he said *in favor* of another group of Nazis: those of his SS contacts who were in captivity and under threat of prosecution for their crimes.

Alibis

Even as they destroyed Hungary's Jews, some Nazi officers did not conceal their wish to save their own necks. For instance, at their meeting in Kolozsvár on May 3, 1944, Wisliceny was already discussing his postwar fate with Kasztner. Wisliceny complained that Eichmann "had sent him to do 'the dirty work' of overseeing the concentration of the Jews, so that, as he put it, he would be unable to build himself an 'alibi.'"[2] Krumey raised the same issue that month. As Brand was about to leave Vienna for Istanbul on May 19, 1944, a revealing incident took place:

> Shortly before we took off, Krumey led me aside and asked me not to forget him during my negotiations in Turkey. I was to let them know that the SS did not consist entirely of people like Eichmann but that it also contained honorable officers such as himself and Wisliceny. He for his part would do everything in his power to save the Jews.[3]

The search for postwar absolution was also implicit in Kasztner's later encounter with Jüttner and Höss during the Death March in Budapest. And a clear request for an alibi came from Becher during his evening walk with Kasztner in Germany on April 13, 1945. Becher joined his plea for himself with a plea for similar consideration for Himmler.[4]

If Kasztner did promise to provide postwar testimonials to his SS contacts in return for their cooperation, this is not in itself proof of perfidy. Jews had little bargaining power against Nazis, and the prospect of alibis was one of the few incentives that could be offered to SS war criminals. So it is no surprise that Zionists abroad suggested offering such inducements during the negotiations for the Kasztner Train. In July 1944, Jewish Agency officials Venia Pomerantz and Menachem Bader advised: "Try to convince your clients. . . . We will never forget those who have helped us." A month later, the Jewish Agency in Istanbul informed the rescue committee in Budapest: "We will not forget those who stand beside us today, and that is more important than money."[5]

The fact that alibis were an acknowledged currency in the process of bargaining with Nazis does not, however, explain Kasztner's postwar behavior at the Nuremberg Trials. These events are controversial not just because Kasztner chose to keep whatever promises he had made in wartime, but because he praised major war criminals for acts of rescue they had never undertaken.

Affidavits

On September 13, 1945, Kasztner submitted his main affidavit to the Allied war crimes investigators. The affidavit was his first major postwar statement on his role during the Nazi occupation. He made a significant admission:

> I escaped the fate of the other Jewish leaders because the complete liquidation of the Hungarian Jews was a failure and also because SS *Standartenführer* Becher took me under his wings in order to establish an eventual alibi for himself. He was anxious to demonstrate after the fall of 1944 that he disapproved the deportations and exterminations and endeavored consistently to furnish me with evidence that he tried to save the Jews. SS *Hauptsturmführer* Wisliceny repeatedly assured me that according to him Germany cannot win the war. He believed that by keeping me alive and by making some concessions in the campaign against the Jews he might have a defense witness when he and his organization would have to account for their atrocities.[6]

Thus Kasztner frankly admitted that he had been kept alive for the purpose of providing a postwar alibi for two SS officers: Becher and Wisliceny.

In stating that Becher had tried to show disapproval of the exterminations "after the fall of 1944," Kasztner was, of course, hinting that Becher had displayed no such qualms during the mass deportations of the provincial Hungarian Jews to Auschwitz in May–June 1944. And his information about the other SS officers was still more damning. Wisliceny ("according to his own admission") was responsible for deporting the Jews of Slovakia and Greece, while Krumey had "directed the work in Hungary, Austria and Poland."[7] Clearly, Kasztner understood that all three—Becher, Wisliceny, and Krumey—had the blood of countless Jews on their hands. Far from giving alibis to these Nazis, as he would later do, he painted them as high-ranking war criminals, committed to the Final Solution.

Things began to change within weeks. On October 21, 1945, Kasztner and Schweiger sent a letter to Yitzhak Grünbaum of the Jewish Agency. They commented favorably on Becher's wartime activities:

> You know that it was with the help of the same Kurt Becher that the Budapest Ghetto was rescued, two additional transports [i.e., the Kasztner Train] were brought to Switzerland, and the concentration camps of Bergen-Belsen, Mauthausen, Neuengamme and Theresienstadt were handed over to the Allies without battle. The transfer of the Jews who were in Austria [i.e., the Strasshof group] into the hands of the Allies took place in the same manner.[8]

Schweiger, of course, had no first-hand knowledge of any of these alleged activities but relied on what he had heard from Kasztner and Becher. In retrospect, it appears that Kasztner was already laying the groundwork for his later interventions on Becher's behalf at Nuremberg.

This impression is confirmed by the contents of the two affidavits submitted by Kasztner on January 20, 1946. The first affidavit claimed that Becher had "acted in the interests of the Jews," not just to gain an alibi, and that Becher had personally asked Himmler to halt the killings. It added that the Nazi officer had "never identified himself with Nazi methods." It also mentioned Krumey, who acted "in a comparatively humane way" and was partly responsible for the survival of the majority of the Strasshof Jews.[9] It would have been more accurate to say that Krumey was responsible for the fact that a quarter of the Strasshof group had died. Krumey's last act at that particular camp was to destroy the card index of the inmates, which would have revealed how many had been deported from there to Auschwitz.[10]

The second affidavit was devoted to Becher. It stated that Becher had "succeeded in obtaining from Himmler the exit from Germany of several groups of Jews" and "prevented the execution of almost 100,000 Hungarian Jews in the Budapest ghetto, etc." Describing how his rescue committee had used Hungarian Jewish valuables as a ransom, Kasztner claimed that Becher had agreed to treat it as a deposit, to be returned to the Jews at the end of the war rather than delivered to his SS superiors.[11]

A year later, Kasztner had raised his sights to another SS criminal. In reply to a letter from Krumey's wife, he wrote: "it is likely that soon I will go to Nuremberg and I will take this opportunity to testify in your husband's case before the appropriate authorities. On this occasion I shall not fail to point to the mitigating circumstances that exist in your husband's case." (He also offered to send a food package.)[12] Soon afterwards, Kasztner was in contact with Krumey himself: "I hope the steps that were taken will make it easier for you to regain your freedom and to begin your life on a new basis. As far as conditions permit, I will try to help you in this."[13] So as early as February 5, 1947—the date of this letter—Kasztner was already promising to help exonerate Krumey from all charges of war crimes.

By July 22, 1947, he was also intervening on behalf of Wisliceny. In a memo on possible indictments against Eichmann's SS unit, he demanded a separate trial for the Holocaust perpetrators. After mentioning Wisliceny and Krumey as possible candidates for such a trial, he added that the former was the only available member of Eichmann's staff who could give a full picture of the extermination policy and its perpetrators. Unless extradited, Wisliceny would probably be put to death in Slovakia, denying the world the benefit of his testimony.[14] Kasztner's call for a trial of Eichmann's staff was, in reality, a plea to save Wisliceny from the hangman's noose.

Kasztner's main affidavit for Becher was submitted a few days later, on August 4, 1947. "There can be no doubt about it," wrote Kasztner, "that Becher belongs to the very few SS leaders having the courage to oppose the program of annihilation and trying to rescue human lives."[15] What had Becher done to "oppose the program of annihilation"? According to Kasztner, he had released the Kasztner Train; secured Himmler's order in late 1944 prohibiting further exterminations of Jews; rescued Jews hidden in Bratislava; prevented the liquidation of the Budapest Ghetto; brought about the surrender of three concentration camps (Bergen-Belsen, Neuengamme, and Theresienstadt); and thwarted last-minute massacres at two more camps (Mauthausen and Flossenbürg).

Kasztner credited Becher with saving as many as 233,760 lives. On this accounting, the SS officer was one of the greatest humanitarians of the war. And the affidavit praised not only Becher's *actions* but also his *motives*. Kasztner concluded:

> Becher did everything within the realm of his possibilities and position to save innocent human lives from the blind fury of killing of the Nazi leaders. Therefore, even if the form and basis of our negotiations may be highly objectionable, I did not doubt for one moment the good intentions of Kurt Becher and in my opinion he is deserving, when his case is judged by Allied or German authorities, of the fullest possible consideration.

He professed to make these statements not only in his own name but also on behalf of the Jewish Agency and the World Jewish Congress.[16]

As if this affidavit was insufficient, Kasztner submitted two more declarations on Becher's behalf on April 30, 1948. The first affidavit related to the crushing of the Slovak national uprising and the subsequent liquidation of the remnants of Slovakia's Jews by the Nazis. Kasztner referred to three SS men: Becher, *Obersturmbannführer* Vitezka (head of the Gestapo in Slovakia), and *Obergruppenführer* Gottlob Berger (who was in charge of suppressing the revolt). He placed all the blame for the destruction of the Jews on Berger. Becher, he averred, had been eager to save lives and had lobbied Himmler in order to do so.[17]

The second affidavit concerned the Death March in Budapest. It noted that the commander of the Waffen-SS, Hans Jüttner, had "protested against the conditions under which these deportations were proceeding . . . asking that they be stopped." Furthermore, the Death March had actually been halted thanks to the intervention of Becher and Jüttner with Himmler.[18] In reality, Jüttner had been traveling with the former Auschwitz commandant Rudolf Höss, and the two had objected to the Death March, not on humanitarian grounds, but because the victims were unfit for slave labor. The affidavit did not mention Höss.

Next, on May 5, 1948, Kasztner submitted an affidavit for Krumey, fulfilling the promise he had made a year earlier. Conceding that Krumey had been "an important member" of the *Eichmann-Kommando*,

Kasztner took credit for the Strasshof operation and stated that Krumey had been responsible for the welfare of the fifteen thousand Jews in the Strasshof group:

> Krumey performed his tasks displaying remarkable good will towards those whose life or death depended to a great extent upon the way he understood how to implement his orders.... I put forward a number of proposals to Krumey aimed to alleviate the plight of this special group, and always I was met with full understanding and sympathy on his part.

Kasztner also gave Krumey credit for the survival of "29 Jews" taken from hiding in Bratislava and for counteracting orders to kill the thirty thousand inmates of Theresienstadt.[19] Thus Kasztner attributed the survival of no less than forty-five thousand Jews to Krumey.

Finally, Kasztner made a statement in favor of Wisliceny, who had been executed in Bratislava the previous day. As a result of the talks with Wisliceny, "the Germans made a number of concessions: 15,000 Hungarian Jews were sent to Austria and 1,700 Jews were permitted to leave for Switzerland." Wisliceny was "the first SS officer who obtained concessions, however minor, that breached the principle of total annihilation which was then in effect."[20]

Why Did Kasztner Help the Nazis at Nuremberg?

Of the statements Kasztner submitted about his Nazi contacts during the war, only the first depicted them accurately as war criminals.

It is important to contrast Kasztner's fulsome praise for Becher in his later declarations with the picture he had painted in his original London affidavit in September 1945. There Kasztner had described how Becher had protected him solely "in order to establish an eventual alibi for himself." The self-serving Nazi in this statement is hardly the benevolent Becher of the later testimonials. There is also a striking disparity between Kasztner's affirmation in September 1945 that Krumey was the murderer of the Jews of Poland, Austria, and Hungary, and his glowing commendations of Krumey in January 1946 and May 1948.

What accounts for this apparent change of heart? Several explanations have been proposed. Here we must bear the chronology in mind. The change in Kasztner's stated opinion of Becher occurred between his September 1945 affidavit and his letter to Grünbaum in October praising Becher as a rescuer. The change regarding Krumey came between the September 1945 affidavit attacking him as a mass murderer and the January 1946 affidavit alleging that he had acted "in a comparatively humane way."

Did Kasztner actually believe his statements on behalf of these Nazis? This possibility can be discounted. In September 1945, Kasztner accurately described the SS officers he would later defend as war criminals.

Psychological explanations have been proposed. It has been suggested that Kasztner, having promised alibis to his SS contacts in order to win their cooperation, felt honor-bound to keep his pledge.[21] This is substantiated by one of Becher's interrogators, Richard H. Gutman, who confronted Kasztner about his intervention for the Nazi:

> When I said to Kastner that I didn't understand his loyalty and concern for a man like Becher, he answered me, with a sentimental and far-away look in his eye, that when he once went into an SS office, he saw their belts hanging on the clothes rack. And on the belt buckles was inscribed the motto, *Meine Ehre ist Treue*—My Honor is Loyalty.[22]

The difficulty with this explanation is that it cannot account for Kasztner's initial condemnations of his Nazi contacts in his September 1945 affidavit. If he felt honor-bound to these SS officers, then why did he not provide them with alibis from the outset? Kasztner may have wanted others to believe that he was merely keeping a pledge to Becher, but this was not the actual reason for his conduct.

Another psychological explanation, the "megalomaniac theory," was advanced by Joel Brand. He argued that Kasztner's motive was a need to regain the sense of power he had enjoyed in wartime; supposedly, Kasztner felt that he could only become important again by exercising a life-or-death influence over Becher and colleagues.[23] Others have suggested that he was a victim of "cognitive dissonance," based on the need to create an acceptable image of his murderous interlocutors to justify his association with them in his own eyes.[24] But then we would expect to find a consistent approach in his affidavits, rather than a change from condemnation (in September 1945) to exoneration (January 1946 and after).

The most elaborate theory of Kasztner's conduct has been provided by Shoshana Barri, who makes a number of claims. First, she suggests that the Jewish Agency was aware of perhaps all of Kasztner's interventions for war criminals.[25] Second, she argues that his actions served the Jewish Agency's goals: the alibis for Becher and Jüttner were meant to help regain Hungarian Jewish assets and may have secured Becher's efforts as an intermediary in arms deals for the Israeli military; the memo seeking Wisliceny's transfer to US custody (to spare him from hanging) was an attempt to gain Wisliceny's assistance in locating Eichmann.[26] Third, she argues that Kasztner's actions could not have saved these criminals if the West had been committed to bringing Nazis to justice rather than to pursuing Cold War objectives.[27]

How accurate are these claims? First, the Jewish Agency surely knew of some of Kasztner's affidavits, as he himself told them what he was doing. But this does not prove that the agency either gave permission for these testimonies in advance or approved of them in retrospect. Here some weight should be attached to the Israeli diplomat Gideon Raphael's recollections. In 1994, Raphael said in an interview that he and Eliahu Dobkin of the Jewish Agency had been told by Kasztner of his plan to assist Becher, Krumey, and Wisliceny—and that both had strongly objected.[28] Equally illuminating is correspondence between Gerhart Riegner and Maurice Perlzweig of the World Jewish Congress at the time of the Kasztner Trial. Riegner wrote to Perlzweig: "It is, of course, clear that Kastner never got any authority from me nor you nor from the Agency to intervene on our behalf for Becher."[29] From these statements it is clear that the Jewish Agency knew of Kasztner's aid to war criminals, but did not approve of it.

On the second point, Barri offers evidence that Kasztner justified his interventions for Becher and Jüttner as attempts to regain Hungarian Jewish property. For example, in a letter to Israeli Finance Minister Eliezer Kaplan in July 1948, Kasztner referred to the Becher Deposit (the remnants of the valuables paid as ransom for the departure of the Kasztner Train) and to a sum of 163,000 Swiss francs that had been passed to Jüttner. So there is no doubt that regaining these assets was on Kasztner's mind at Nuremberg. Also, it is clear from his memo for Wisliceny that Kasztner wanted evidence that might assist a future prosecution of Eichmann. But the fact that Kasztner tried to provide these services to the Jewish Agency in no way establishes his *motive* for helping his SS contacts. Perhaps he decided to act on behalf of these war criminals for reasons of his own and then cited the regaining of Jewish assets and the hunt for Eichmann as his *justifications* to the Jewish Agency.

That the Jewish Agency's goals do not explain Kasztner's conduct at Nuremberg becomes clear when we turn to Krumey. As Barri admits, "There seems to be no evidence that the Jewish Agency had any need of Krumey's services," and so Kasztner's interventions on behalf of

Krumey "remain unexplained."[30] Yet Kasztner twice acted to help Krumey at Nuremberg.

Barri's third contention is equally unpersuasive. If the Allies had been looking for an excuse not to punish Kasztner's SS contacts, they would have welcomed his interventions on behalf of those contacts. But the opposite was the case. Nuremberg prosecutor Robert Kempner regretted inviting Kasztner to testify, since Kasztner had started roaming the detention center for Nazi officers looking for those he could help. "In the end," added Kempner, "we were very glad when he left Nuremberg."[31] Far from welcoming Kasztner's aid to his SS contacts as a pretext to avoid punishing them, the Nuremberg prosecutors found his behavior most offensive.

None of these theories explains the key facts: first, Kasztner's change of heart towards his former SS contacts between October 1945 and January 1946; and second, his decision to intervene in favor of Krumey. But there is another explanation that does resolve these issues. It is based on letters from Kasztner's private archive.

A Mystery Solved

From late October 1945, Kasztner was in the midst of a frenzied correspondence with his father-in-law József Fischer, the former leader of the *Judenrat* in Kolozsvár and the former head of the Kasztner Train group in Bergen-Belsen. At this time Fischer was already in Palestine, while Kasztner was still in Switzerland. The focus of the correspondence was the charge of collaboration that was being leveled against both of them by the Hungarian Jewish Holocaust survivors.

In a letter dated November 9, 1945, Fischer informed Kasztner about new arrivals to Palestine who had come directly from Kolozsvár (now renamed Cluj). The immigrants reported that the Auschwitz survivors who had returned to the city hated the passengers of the Kasztner Train. An investigation of the Kasztner group was taking place. In particular, "The old accusation is being raised that the people who were meant to go with the [Kasztner Train] group were accelerating the deportations of the rest [of the Jews in the Kolozsvár Ghetto]."[32]

In a letter sent on the same day (in reply to a previous letter), Kasztner provided more details of the situation in Cluj. He reported that the local Attorney-General was investigating the Kolozsvár *Judenrat*. The allegations were, first, that the local *Judenrat* leaders had "accelerated the deportations" so that they could escape on the Kasztner

Train; second, that only the rich were chosen for the Kasztner Train, while Zionists with Palestine certificates were rejected; and third, that the local *Judenrat* did not explain the meaning of deportation to the inmates of the Kolozsvár Ghetto.[33]

On November 12, Fischer wrote with more information. He informed Kasztner that yet another group of Hungarian Jewish survivors had arrived in Palestine making further claims against Kasztner. One of the rumors in circulation was that a letter had been found in Cluj in which Kasztner gave instructions for accelerating the deportation of the Jewish ghetto inmates to Auschwitz so that the Kasztner Train group could leave as soon as possible. Fischer also referred to the investigation being conducted by the People's Tribunal of Cluj.[34] In reply, Kasztner remarked that the allegation of his involvement in accelerating deportations "cannot be left unanswered."[35]

The context of Kasztner's change of heart toward his SS contacts was one in which Kasztner was under suspicion of collaboration. Allegations were being made against him both in North Transylvania and in Palestine. Kasztner was concerned about these charges. Even Ben-Gurion wrote in his diary on November 3, 1945, that "Kasztner, Brand's comrade in Switzerland, thinks he is being accused of having been a collaborator. . . . He is afraid to come to Palestine."[36]

It was in these circumstances that Kasztner was expected to testify in Nuremberg (an issue he mentions in the correspondence).[37] After submitting his September 1945 affidavit excoriating his SS contacts as war criminals, Kasztner discovered that he was under suspicion of collaborating with them. From late October 1945, he understood that anything he said against Becher, Krumey, and others might rebound against him. Only if he could demonstrate that he had substantial rescue achievements to his credit—and that his SS contacts had contributed to those achievements—could he hope to justify his dealings with them. So Kasztner could no longer afford to condemn his SS associates. He had to pretend that they had helped him to save large numbers of Jews.

The need to justify his wartime dealings against the background of charges of collaborating with the Nazis supplies a plausible explanation for the important facts already outlined: Kasztner's sudden change of heart in late 1945; his attribution of wholly fictitious mass rescue activities to Becher and Jüttner; his attempt to save Wisliceny from execution on the pretext of a trial of Eichmann's SS unit; and his decision to act in favor of Krumey in spite of the Jewish Agency's lack of interest in Krumey's "services." It explains why Kasztner told those who questioned his conduct in Nuremberg that he was only keeping his commitments to men who had helped him to save Jews. Kasztner's actions in Nuremberg were not the deeds of a person afflicted with megalomania or cognitive dissonance; they were not the deeds of a loyal and obedient servant of the Jewish Agency; they were the deeds of a suspected collaborator seeking to invent a plausible pretext for his dealings with the SS.

The Outcome

The results of Kasztner's efforts on behalf of Nazi criminals at the Nuremberg Trials were as follows:

- Kurt Becher was freed, as Kasztner later boasted, "thanks to my personal intervention."[38] After his release, Becher—the former aide to Himmler—became one of the most successful businessmen in West Germany. He built up a fortune that likely had its origins in looted Hungarian Jewish assets.[39]
- Hermann Krumey, Eichmann's deputy and the murderer of the Jews of Poland, Austria, and Hungary, was set free in 1948, soon after Kasztner's affidavit singing his praises. Later he was rearrested, and a West German court sentenced him to five years in prison—whereupon he was released again on the basis of time served.[40] Amid public uproar, the prosecution appealed, and he finally received a life sentence in 1969.[41]
- Dieter Wisliceny, the murderer of the Jews of Slovakia, Greece, and Hungary, did not benefit from Kasztner's intervention. After testifying as a prosecution witness at Nuremberg, he was sentenced to death by the courts in Czechoslovakia, where he was executed in 1948.
- Hans Jüttner, commander of the Waffen-SS, was sentenced to ten years in a labor camp, which was reduced to four years on appeal. At the time of the Eichmann Trial he was the proprietor of a sanatorium in Bavaria.[42]

Notes

1. Aronson suggests that Kasztner was instrumental in Kaltenbrunner's execution: *Hitler, the Allies and the Jews*, 326. For his campaign against Eichmann and Husseini, see ibid., 330. See also Kasztner's Veesenmayer Trial testimony, March 19, 1948, Kasztner Trial prosecution exhibit 4.
2. Kasztner, Kasztner Trial testimony, February 18, 1954.
3. Weissberg, *Desperate Mission*, 125.
4. Kasztner, *Bericht*, 176.
5. Löb, *Dealing With Satan*, 276.
6. Kasztner, London Affidavit, 3.
7. Kasztner, London Affidavit, 11.
8. Kasztner and Schweiger to Grünbaum, October 21, 1945, cited in Shoshana Barri (Ishoni), "The Question of Kastner's Testimonies on Behalf of Nazi War Criminals," *The Journal of Israeli History* 18, no. 2–3 (1997): 146.

9. Kasztner, Affidavit, January 20, 1946, cited in Barri, "The Question of Kastner's Testimonies on Behalf of Nazi War Criminals," 142–3.
10. Kasztner, *Bericht*, 152, 171.
11. Kasztner, Affidavit, January 20, 1946, CZA, S53/2128.
12. Kasztner to Margarete Krumey, January 16, 1946 [should read 1947], Kasztner Archive.
13. Kasztner to Krumey, February 5, 1947, quoted in Weitz, *The Man Who Was Murdered Twice*, 64.
14. Kasztner, "Possible Indictment Against RSHA IV(b)4," Memorandum, July 22, 1947, Tamir Archive.
15. Kasztner, Affidavit, August 4, 1947, Kasztner Trial prosecution exhibit 73.
16. Ibid.
17. Kasztner, Affidavit (re: Slovakia), April 30, 1948, Tamir Archive.
18. Kasztner, Affidavit (re: the Death March), April 30, 1948, Tamir Archive.
19. Kasztner, Affidavit, May 5, 1948, Tamir Archive.
20. Kasztner, Affidavit, May 5, 1948, quoted in Weitz, *The Man Who Was Murdered Twice*, 66. The CZA file reference given by Weitz is incorrect and the CZA staff could not locate this document, but I have no reason to doubt its existence. In addition, Weitz erroneously states that Wisliceny was executed in February 1948; in fact the execution took place on May 4, 1948.
21. See Aronson, *Hitler, the Allies and the Jews*, 326: "giving Becher his due at Nuremberg was a part of the rescue strategy itself. Those who saved Jews should have been acknowledged; otherwise, one could not have expected them to have done it to begin with."
22. Hecht, *Perfidy*, 266–67n134.
23. Joel Brand and Hansi Brand, *Ha'Satan veha'nefesh*, 110.
24. Weitz, *The Man Who Was Murdered Twice*, 63–64; Barri, "The Question of Kastner's Testimonies on Behalf of Nazi War Criminals," 141.
25. Barri, "The Question of Kastner's Testimonies on Behalf of Nazi War Criminals," 143, 145, 164.
26. On Becher and Jüttner, see ibid., 156–61, 163; on Wisliceny, ibid., 156, 163.
27. Ibid., 152–3, 163–4. See also Aronson, *Hitler, the Allies and the Jews*, 325: "at Nuremberg, Kasztner could have expected the Allies to leave Colonel Becher alone anyway because Becher's position and rank would hardly make him a worthy defendant. . . ."
28. Gideon Raphael, Interview, *Ha'aretz*, December 2, 1994. Barri summarizes Raphael's comments in "The Question of Kastner's Testimonies on Behalf of Nazi War Criminals," 151, but does not draw the obvious conclusion from them.
29. Riegner to Perlzweig, December 30, 1955, CZA, Z6/1117. Barri quotes part of this correspondence in a footnote, "The Question of Kastner's Testimonies on Behalf of Nazi War Criminals," 162–63n75.
30. Barri, "The Question of Kastner's Testimonies on Behalf of Nazi War Criminals," 163.
31. Joel Brand and Hansi Brand, *Ha'Satan veha'nefesh*, 107.
32. Fischer to Kasztner, November 9, 1945, Kasztner Archive. I am grateful to Eli Reichenthal for his translations of these letters.
33. Kasztner to Fischer, November 9, 1945, Kasztner Archive.
34. Fischer to Kasztner, November 12, 1945, Kasztner Archive.

35. Kasztner to Fischer, December 10, 1945, Kasztner Archive.
36. Weitz, *The Man Who Was Murdered Twice*, 33.
37. Kasztner to Fischer, November 9, 1945, Kasztner Archive.
38. Kasztner to Kaplan, July 26, 1948, Kasztner Trial prosecution exhibit 22.
39. For Becher's postwar biography, see Müller-Tupath, *Reichsführers gehorsamster Becher*; Kádár and Vági, *Self-Financing Genocide*, 249–60; Harold Serebro with Jacques Sellschop, *Beyond Redemption? The Nazi Colonel Who Saved Jews and Plundered Their Wealth* (Bath: Westmoreland and Trent Publishers, 2007).
40. *Jerusalem Post*, February 11, 1965.
41. *Jerusalem Post*, August 31, 1969.
42. Jüttner, Eichmann Trial testimony, May 31, 1961.

17

Kasztner in Court

At the end of the Holocaust, some of the few shattered survivors of Auschwitz returned to their former homes to search for loved ones and to seek a modicum of justice. In Kolozsvár—now renamed Cluj and ceded to Romania—the authorities quickly organized a People's Tribunal to punish the worst of the Hungarian torturers and killers. But the survivors were not satisfied. They also demanded a trial of the *Jewish* leaders who had assured them that the death trains were taking them to work in "Kenyérmező."

One of those survivors, Yosef Krausz, later recounted that the targets of the investigation were divided into three categories: the "Kasztner Group"; those who took orders from the "Kasztner Group"; and the ordinary passengers on the Kasztner Train. The ordinary Kasztner Train passengers, some of whom returned to the city, were allowed to go free. But the first two groups (twenty-five people in total) were to be prosecuted for war crimes. As for Kasztner himself, Krausz explained:

> Everyone in Kolozsvár wanted [a war crimes trial]: the representatives of the Jews and the Zionists. . . . Public opinion was that although the trial never took place, if Kasztner had turned up in Kolozsvár at that point, there wouldn't have been time to try him because he would have been torn to pieces on his way to the tribunal.

Krausz was challenged: surely the whole investigation had been organized as a communist show-trial of the Zionists? This suggestion was firmly rejected:

> It wasn't the Communist Party that started it. The Zionists started it: they said that Kasztner took the [Palestine] certificates, divided them among his friends and sent the Zionists to Auschwitz . . . . And I was now asking the question of whether other people and families had the same feeling as I did . . . the feeling of wanting to lynch Kasztner.

In fact these attitudes to Kasztner were far from unique:

> I heard it from hundreds of people. . . . He was accused by the public in Kolozsvár of not telling the population that the convoys were going to Auschwitz. On the contrary: they deceived the population by saying that they would be taken to Kenyérmező. The Romanian border at the time was a couple of kilometers from Kolozsvár and those who crossed it survived.[1]

Another of the survivors, David Rosner, testified along the same lines:

> Q: On your return to Kolozsvár, what did people think of Kasztner?
> A: The atmosphere towards Kasztner was very bad. If he had returned, he would have been killed in the street . . .
> Q: Why would they have killed Kasztner?
> A: Because he was the cause of the deception of the Jews . . .
> Q: Was that the public consensus?
> A: Yes.[2]

During the Nazi occupation, the head of the Jewish rescue committee in Budapest visited his home city twice with official permission. But matters changed after liberation. Neither Kasztner nor any of his accomplices ever returned to Kolozsvár.

In Hungary, charges of Kasztner's collaboration with the Nazis soon reached the national press. Kasztner himself gives examples in his *Bericht*. One Budapest daily stated that Kasztner had achieved great influence with Gestapo and had even left the country in the company of Gestapo officers, taking his ill-gotten gains with him. Another newspaper alleged that Kasztner had provided espionage services to the Gestapo, both in Hungary and abroad.[3]

Wherever Kasztner went, accusations of wrongdoing followed him. In March 1946, Moshe Krausz—having been dismissed from his position in the Palestine Office in Budapest—sent the Jewish Agency a report in which he blamed Kasztner for playing along with the Nazis' "rescue" negotiations.[4] At the 22nd Zionist Congress in Basel in December, Krausz submitted a complaint against Kasztner. The secretariat of Ihud Olami, the Labor Zionist world body, felt compelled to issue a statement praising Kasztner's "tremendous work during the war."[5] Kasztner in turn charged Krausz with defamation before the Zionist Congress's court of honor, but the case went nowhere. Kasztner also presented to the Congress his own detailed written report, the *Bericht*, in an attempt to justify his activities during the Holocaust in Hungary.

Even after he judged it safe to enter Palestine, Kasztner was dogged by suspicions. He was occasionally confronted by Holocaust survivors. For example, having endured slave labor in Hungary, Levi Blum immigrated to the new State of Israel. A public reception was held to honor the newly arrived Kasztner:

> It was too much for me. I jumped up and said: "You're making a big mistake here!" To Kasztner I said: "You're the only one who was Eichmann's close ally. You were a Quisling! You're a murderer!" I told him: "You can sue me, because I'm too poor to sue but I dare *you* to sue *me*. I know that you were responsible for the Jews of Hungary, including Kolozsvár, going to Auschwitz. You were the one who knew where they were going and what the Germans intended." Kasztner didn't respond. I asked him: "Why did you send the Kenyérmező postcards to Kolozsvár?" Someone in the audience shouted out: "It wasn't him—it was Kohani!" Kohani was embarrassed . . . . He wasn't comfortable denying it. So he said: "Yes, I received those postcards." So I asked him: "Who were they from?" He replied: "It's none of your business, I don't answer to you."

This was not Blum's last encounter with Kasztner:

> Suddenly, I saw the Mapai party's election candidate list for the Knesset. On it was "Dr. Israel Kasztner, in charge of rescue in Hungary." When I read this, the blood rose to my head.[6]

Such reactions had consequences for Kasztner. In 1950 the Israeli Knesset passed the Nazis and Nazi Collaborators (Punishment) Law, which carried the death penalty. Kasztner was summoned for a police interrogation, but he was not charged with any offense.[7]

"For three years now," wrote Israeli columnist Yoel Marcus in 1952, "many Jews from Hungary have been accusing a man in an official position of testifying on behalf of a Nazi war criminal, of dark dealings and fat profits at the expense of saving Jews."[8]

Background to the Kasztner Trial

By that time, Kasztner had secured a respectable status in Israeli political life. He was a senior government official, serving as the spokesman for the Ministry of Commerce and Industry. He was a journalist for the country's Hungarian-language newspaper *Új Kelet* and he was in charge of Hungarian-language broadcasts for the government's Kol Yisrael radio station. In national elections he had twice appeared on the candidate list of the ruling socialist Mapai party; sooner or later, he was likely to find his way into the Knesset.

The survivors' accusations finally caught the attention of the Israeli public in what became known as the Kasztner Trial. The case was sparked by the publications of Malkiel Grünwald, an elderly political pamphleteer who owned a boarding house in Jerusalem. Posing as a loyal supporter of the Orthodox-Zionist party Mizrachi, Grünwald had started to publish a regular bulletin in which he attacked establishment figures.

Grünwald's bulletin was distributed under the title *Letters to My Friends in the Mizrachi*. Issue number 17, circulated in August 1952, was devoted to Kasztner. It began by inciting his assassination ("My dear friends, the smell of a corpse fills my nostrils! This will be the finest funeral yet! Dr. Rudolf Kasztner must be eliminated!") and it continued with an avalanche of vilification. It accused Kasztner of saving fifty-two of his relatives as well as hundreds of rich Jews ("mostly converts"), while leaving thousands of veteran Zionists to their fate. Kasztner was—according to Grünwald—a Nazi collaborator, an "indirect" mass murderer of Hungarian Jewry, a Holocaust profiteer, and the savior of Kurt Becher, a Nazi war criminal.[9]

Grünwald's outburst quickly came to the attention of members of the Israeli government, who saw it as an opportunity to silence him for good.[10] Attorney-General Chaim Cohen informed the target of Grünwald's ire that he had to agree to a lawsuit or resign his government job. "If, as I presume, there is no truth in these accusations, the man printing them should [himself] be put on trial," wrote Cohen.[11] The government duly initiated a case of criminal libel, with Grünwald as defendant.

Grünwald searched for a lawyer. He found one of the most talented attorneys in Israel: Shmuel Tamir—scion of a Revisionist Zionist family, former deputy commander of the Irgun in Jerusalem, and supporter of the right-wing Herut party led by Menachem Begin. Tamir had a burning desire to expose what he saw as the abysmal record of the Zionist movement's leftist Mapai leadership during the Holocaust.[12] He resolved to turn the trial of Grünwald into a trial of Kasztner and of Mapai.

The Prosecution Case

The Kasztner Trial should have been an open and shut case. Legal observers were certain that Grünwald would lose. The case was allocated to Jerusalem District Court Judge Benjamin Halevi, who had a record of defending the interests of the state.[13] When the prosecutor, Amnon Tel, decided to put Kasztner on the stand, matters looked stark for Grünwald. Kasztner began to testify on February 18, 1954.

For days Kasztner boasted of his heroic battle against the Nazis. He explained how he had confronted the "monster" Eichmann, who gloried in the suffering of Jewish children; how he had cajoled Eichmann into allowing the exit of several hundred Jews on the special VIP train; how he had stood firm as Eichmann threatened to send him to Auschwitz; how he had induced Eichmann to send fifteen thousand Jews to Strasshof in Austria instead of to the gas chambers; how he had saved the Jews of Budapest by deceiving the Nazis; and how he had formed a fruitful working relationship with Becher. He denied outright that he had given any postwar testimony or affidavit in favor of Becher or that he had gone to Nuremberg in order to save Becher.[14]

The newspapers praised Kasztner to the skies. The judge was also impressed, asking Tamir if Grünwald was ready to change his plea to guilty. Grünwald refused.[15]

What followed was perhaps the most dramatic reversal in Israeli legal history. Kasztner had taken just four days to establish himself as the champion of Hungary's Jews. Tamir took seven more days to expose him as a liar and a Nazi collaborator. The prosecution had only itself to blame for this result: three times Tamir suggested abandoning the trial and putting the issue before an independent public inquiry, whose findings his client would accept; three times prosecutor Tel declined.

Kasztner's undoing came on February 25, 1954. On that date he was cross-examined about his denial that he had given any testimony or affidavit to help Becher at Nuremberg. "I tell you now," stated Tamir, "that Kurt Becher was released at Nuremberg thanks to your personal intervention." Kasztner exclaimed: "That's a dirty lie!"[16] Tamir then produced Kasztner's letter to Finance Minister Eliezer Kaplan of July 26, 1948, in which he had written that Becher had been freed "thanks to my personal intervention."[17] The letter had been submitted to the court by the prosecution on Kasztner's behalf. Tamir continued:

> Q: Do you admit to having written this letter?
> A: Yes.
> Q: A minute ago you said it was a lie that Becher was released from Nuremberg thanks to your personal intervention. Do you still stick to that statement?
> A: I stand by what I said in this courtroom.[18]

Kasztner now stood exposed before the judge as a perjurer who had helped a Nazi war criminal to escape justice. His credibility was shattered. He tried to free himself from the trap: "What I wrote to Kaplan was an exaggeration," he protested, "I'm allowed to tell you that it's a lie that he was released thanks to my personal intervention."[19] In other words, he was not lying to the court *now* because he had lied *then*, in his letter to Kaplan. For Kasztner, there was no escape.

Tamir persisted, day after day, in demolishing Kasztner's excuses. He accused Kasztner of betraying the Zionist paratroopers Palgi and Goldstein to the Gestapo.[20] He accused Kasztner of favoritism in selecting the VIP train passengers from Kolozsvár. He forced Kasztner to admit to receiving Yishuv leader Yitzhak Ben-Zvi's call on European Jews to resist the Nazis—which he did not convey to the Jews of Kolozsvár.[21] He forced Kasztner—who had taken credit for Himmler's instructions allegedly halting the Final Solution—to admit that the orders had not been carried out and that the mass murders had continued to the end of the war.[22] And he forced Kasztner to admit that he had been introduced to Himmler because the *Reichsführer-SS*, like Becher, wanted a postwar alibi from him.[23] As the cross-examination wore on, Kasztner began to complain of feeling ill, and the judge repeatedly halted the proceedings to let him recover.

When the trial resumed after a month-long postponement, Attorney-General Chaim Cohen took charge of the prosecution. All of Israel had been electrified by the charges against Kasztner, and Tel was widely perceived as inept.

On June 4, Kasztner returned to the witness stand. Recalling his prior testimony that he had submitted no affidavit in Becher's favor, Tamir produced a translation of Kasztner's August 4, 1947, affidavit in Becher's favor. The statement, given in the name of the Jewish Agency and the World Jewish Congress, pleaded that Becher deserved "the fullest possible consideration" by the Allied and German authorities. Kasztner had been caught red-handed again. "I regret it if I made a mistake," commented Kasztner on his previous perjured testimony.

Cohen tried to help: if Kasztner had to make the same statement about Becher today, would he still make it? "Yes," replied Kasztner, but he would do it without referring to the Jewish Agency and the World Jewish Congress. Any decent person would have done the same for Becher; moreover, he had given no testimony that could help any Nazi officer other than Becher.

At this point Cohen took out a sheaf of papers, intending to show that other Jews had also testified on behalf of Nazis. Suddenly he stopped. "Your honor," he exclaimed, "I'm afraid that I've misled the court. . . . I have here the original English version of the affidavit." Cohen had previously asserted that the original was missing.

The judge now began to question Kasztner, who conceded that he had promised to help several Nazis, but insisted—falsely, of course—that he had never actually done so; his promises had been purely tactical. He had felt a "moral obligation" to help Becher. As far as he knew, the Nazi had not taken part in the murder of Jews.[24]

The Defense Case

Tamir had unmasked Kasztner as a dissembler, guilty of intervening on behalf of a top Nazi at Nuremberg. It was time for the defense to make its case.

The first element in Tamir's defense strategy was to expose the sordid reality of the deportation from Kolozsvár: Kasztner's relatives and friends in the ghetto had calmed the Jews with tales about Kenyérmező after Kasztner visited the city in full knowledge of the imminent deportations to Auschwitz. A series of Holocaust survivors who had lost their families testified that the masses in the ghetto had known nothing of the Final Solution and had been misled by false rumors endorsed by the ghetto leadership. And these mutually corroborating statements by the witnesses from Kolozsvár were echoed by Auschwitz survivors from the even larger ghetto of Nagyvárad.

Attorney-General Cohen offered no challenge to the Hungarian survivors who testified for the defense. The evidence about the deception of the Jews in the ghettos before their deportation to Auschwitz could not be gainsaid. Nor could it be denied that the very Jewish leaders who had spread the false rumors had subsequently escaped on Kasztner's VIP train.

Tamir's second step was to dramatize Kasztner's betrayal of the Zionist paratroopers from Palestine. To this end he called Katerina Szenes, Hannah's mother. She gave a heartbreaking account of meeting her daughter in captivity and later seeking in vain to save her daughter's life. Her story cemented the status of Hannah Szenes as an Israeli heroine—and underlined Tamir's contention that Kasztner stood for the opposite of everything that Hannah represented.[25]

The third element of Tamir's defense strategy was to introduce his key witness: Moshe Krausz, former head of the Palestine Office in

Budapest and architect of the rescue of scores of thousands of Jews. Postwar the Jewish Agency had rewarded Krausz for his achievements by unceremoniously firing him from his post. He was now eking out a living as an office clerk.

For over a week Krausz detailed Kasztner's crimes. He explained how Kasztner, even before the deportations began, had agreed to the SS formula of "emigration via deportation"; how Kasztner had promoted "departure to Palestine" for Jews without Palestine entry certificates; how Kasztner had bargained for his VIP train while hundreds of thousands of Jews were being deported to their deaths; how Kasztner had organized the distribution of the Waldsee postcards even though he knew full well that the senders had been forced to write them before being gassed in Auschwitz; how Kasztner had continued his dealings with the SS even after the Hungarian government had halted the mass deportations; and how Kasztner had repeatedly interfered in genuine rescue operations. In Krausz's view, all these actions stemmed from Kasztner's thirst for power. In the cross-examination, Cohen tried again and again to undermine Krausz's credibility, but was unable to break him.[26]

Also on Tamir's witness list was Eliahu Dobkin, former member of the JAE. The purpose of calling Dobkin was to destroy Kasztner's claim that his affidavit for Becher had been submitted on behalf of the agency. Dobkin denied ever having given Kasztner permission to act on the agency's behalf or even having heard of Becher before the Kasztner Trial.[27] This denial was almost certainly untrue, as Kasztner now tried to point out in a sealed letter he submitted to the judge. The letter drew attention to several instances in which Dobkin would have encountered Becher's name. But Halevi, viewing Kasztner's intervention as improper, returned the letter unopened to Tamir and Cohen.[28]

With these and other witnesses, Tamir consolidated the attack on Kasztner he had begun during the prosecution case. But the trial was still not over. Hillel Danzig, former head of the rescue committee in the Kolozsvár Ghetto, close friend of Kasztner, and passenger on the VIP train, had written to the judge denying Holocaust survivor Jacob Freifeld's testimony that Danzig had given him false reassurance while the victims were being sent to Auschwitz. The court now called Danzig to the stand.

Danzig admitted to some awareness of Auschwitz before the Nazi occupation of Hungary, but denied having had any knowledge of a general extermination policy. No warnings about Auschwitz had been received in the ghetto. But after the VIP train candidates were moved to Budapest following the ghetto's liquidation, the first thing he learned was that the deportees had been sent to the death camp.[29]

Tamir cross-examined Danzig about his meeting with Kasztner when the latter visited the ghetto on May 3, 1944.[30] Had Kasztner warned him that the Jews of Kolozsvár would be sent to the gas chambers of Auschwitz? Danzig was evasive:

> Q: I will sum it up for you again: in other words, your conversation with Kasztner didn't leave you any the wiser about German intentions regarding the expected danger?
> A: I cannot confirm or deny this theory.
> Q: This is the language of the Ministry of Foreign Affairs, not an answer.
> A: It was a crisis point in the negotiations and Kasztner could not say anything concrete about German intentions. This is what I remember now.[31]

Thus even Danzig, who had done everything he could to back up his friend while on the witness stand, professed to be unable to recall a warning about the imminent mass murder from Kasztner.

Embarrassed by one of his closest allies, Kasztner had to be asked to clear up the confusion. Had he communicated the Auschwitz news to Danzig or anyone else in the Kolozsvár Ghetto? Kasztner was recalled to the stand one last time. After much ducking and weaving, he admitted that he had not given an explicit warning—and then he blamed his father-in-law and friends for not doing more to alert the Jewish masses. As for the Holocaust survivors from Kolozsvár who had testified about their deception by means of false rumors spread by the ghetto leaders, Kasztner added:

> I'm very sorry for the witnesses from Kolozsvár who appeared here. In my opinion, they don't represent the Jews of Kolozsvár. It's no coincidence that not a single public figure in Kolozsvár was among them. I understand their feelings after losing their loved ones, but to say they didn't know anything takes a little nerve.

This provoked the obvious retort:

> Q: It seems to me that the public figure Danzig said the same or almost the same.
> A: Danzig is still a public figure, and there are probably certain memory functions to repress what is unpleasant. I don't mean

to argue that he wasn't telling the truth here, but if he understood my words in Kolozsvár as he said here, then he must be an Englishman with "double understatement."[32]

Thus Kasztner attacked his own father-in-law, his friend Danzig, and even the victims themselves, for not knowing what he had refused to tell them. His insistence that he was unsure about what would happen to the ghetto inmates was contradicted by his own previous testimony that after meeting Eichmann's aide Wisliceny in the Kolozsvár police station, he had no doubt that extermination was the Jews' imminent fate.[33]

After Kasztner's final performance, Cohen and Tamir presented their summations and the judge retired to consider his verdict. Clearly, Kasztner had something to hide. There was (and is) no way of knowing whether Kasztner or Danzig was telling the truth about what had passed between them in the ghetto. But one thing was not in dispute: Kasztner had not warned the ordinary Jews of Kolozsvár during his visit on May 3, 1944—and afterwards his relatives and friends, instead of communicating news of the impending deportations to Auschwitz, had misled those Jews with tales about resettlement in Kenyérmező.

If the people of Israel were transfixed by the revelations in the Kasztner Trial itself, they were to be even more stunned by the judge's verdict.

Notes

1. Kasztner Trial testimony, June 17, 1954.
2. Kasztner Trial testimony, June 18, 1954.
3. Kasztner, *Bericht*, 187.
4. Miklós (Moshe) Krausz, *Memorandum über die Tätigkeit des Palästina-Amtes in Budapest in den kritischen Kriegsjahren 1941–45* (Budapest: March 4, 1946), Kasztner Trial prosecution exhibit 124, 3–5.
5. Weitz, *The Man Who Was Murdered Twice*, 52.
6. Kasztner Trial testimony, June 25, 1954.
7. Tom Segev, *The Seventh Million: The Israelis and the Holocaust* (New York: Owl Books, 2000), 258.
8. *Herut*, August 26, 1952, quoted in Weitz, *The Man Who Was Murdered Twice*, 88.
9. See the analysis of the bulletin in the Kasztner Trial verdict, ss. 2, 114.
10. Segev, *The Seventh Million*, 263.
11. Weitz, *The Man Who Was Murdered Twice*, 89.
12. See, for example, Tamir's column in *Herut*, March 16, 1951, and his two-volume autobiography, *Ben ha'aretz hazot* (Tel Aviv: Zemorah-Bitan, 2002).
13. Weitz, *The Man Who Was Murdered Twice*, 97–98, 99–100.
14. Kasztner Trial testimony, February 18, 19, 22, 23, 1954. For a condensed translation of Kasztner's main testimony, see Hecht, *Perfidy*, 59–62, 64.

15. Kasztner Trial proceedings, February 24, 1954.
16. Kasztner Trial testimony, February 25, 1954.
17. Kasztner to Kaplan, July 26, 1948, Kasztner Trial prosecution exhibit 22.
18. Kasztner Trial testimony, February 25, 1954, translation from Weitz, *The Man Who Was Murdered Twice*, 118.
19. Kasztner Trial testimony, February 25, 1954.
20. Kasztner Trial testimony, February 28, 1954.
21. Kasztner Trial testimony, March 1, 1954.
22. Kasztner Trial testimony, March 2, 1954.
23. Kasztner Trial testimony, March 4, 1954.
24. Kasztner Trial testimony, June 4, 1954.
25. Kasztner Trial testimony, June 14, 1954. Kasztner's supporters still resent the comparison: see, for example, Dan Laor, "Who is Hungary's Real Holocaust Hero? Israel Kastner vs. Hannah Szenes Debate Just Won't Die," *The Forward*, November 13, 2013.
26. Kasztner Trial testimony, June 25, July 1, 2, 4, 5, 8, 9, 10, 12, 1954.
27. Kasztner Trial testimony, June 28, 1954.
28. Weitz, *The Man Who Was Murdered Twice*, 157–8.
29. Kasztner Trial testimony, August 15, 1954.
30. Danzig was very confused about the dates, but from the context it is clear that May 3, 1944 was the date of their meeting.
31. Kasztner Trial testimony, August 19, 1954.
32. Kasztner Trial testimony, September 16, 1954.
33. According to Kasztner, Wisliceny's statements at their meeting on May 3, 1944 "meant not saving Jews but exterminating them, as one of the top murderers": Kasztner Trial testimony, March 2, 1954.

18

The Verdicts

It took Judge Halevi nine months to produce his decision. During that time, public opinion moved even further against Kasztner. As elections approached, the government increasingly saw him as a political liability. He lost his job at Israel's state radio and his name was removed from the Mapai candidate list.

When Halevi returned to the courtroom to deliver his verdict on June 22, 1955, no one knew quite what to expect. Tamir still had no idea if he had won or lost the case. Kasztner chose not to attend the session, waiting instead in a nearby boarding house. Halevi began to read passages from his massive verdict in a slow and steady voice. The reading took fourteen hours. As he made his way through the pages, a whisper ran through the packed room: "Kasztner will have to commit suicide."[1]

"Kasztner Sold His Soul to the Devil"

The verdict began with a summary of Grünwald's allegations against Kasztner, which Halevi divided into four counts: collaboration with the Nazis; "indirect murder" or "paving the way for the murder" of Hungarian Jewry; joint plunder of the victims with Becher, a Nazi war criminal; and saving Becher from punishment after the war.[2]

Turning to the first two allegations, Halevi explained the background of the Holocaust in the Hungarian provinces. Citing Kasztner's own words, he emphasized that Eichmann's success in destroying the provincial Jews, in spite of limited time and manpower, was due in no small measure to the strategy of deception. This was also clear from the "shocking" accounts of the victims on the witness stand.[3]

Based primarily on the eye-witness testimony of Holocaust survivors from Kolozsvár and Nagyvárad, Halevi ascertained the following facts: (i) The Jewish masses in the ghettos obediently entered the death trains because they knew nothing of Auschwitz and expected to be sent to Kenyérmező. (ii) The Nazis were successful in deceiving them because the disinformation was spread by the local Jewish leaders. (iii) Thanks to this deception, the ghettos were calm and there was no real opposition to the deportations. (iv) Thousands of Jews could have escaped from the ghettos in Kolozsvár and Nagyvárad alone, but they missed the opportunities because they had been deceived. (v) The Jewish leaders who disseminated the Kenyérmező rumors in these ghettos were spared from deportation to Auschwitz and were later sent to Switzerland on the Kasztner Train. Halevi set out to determine whether there was a causal connection between the deception of the victims in the ghettos (i–iv) and the departure of the Kasztner Train (v).[4]

The verdict then reviewed the background of Kasztner's rescue committee and the negotiations that led to his deal with the Nazis. Halevi drew attention to Kasztner's drive for power, which made him easy prey for the machinations of the Nazis.[5] Kasztner and Brand began the talks with the intention of making a deal to save all Hungarian Jews, but news of the creation of ghettos and accumulating evidence of the Auschwitz deportation plans soon made it clear that this was an impossible dream. At this point Krumey played his trump card: permission for the emigration of six hundred Jews selected by Kasztner.

Why had Krumey made this "concession"? Kasztner's committee was a threat to Nazi plans because it was expected to become the nucleus of the Zionist rescue and resistance effort. The committee had been ordered by several of the Zionist leaders in Palestine (Yitzhak Ben-Zvi, Moshe Shertok, Yitzhak Grünbaum) to prepare for self-defense against the Nazis. After the occupation, the Zionist youth in Budapest had organized their own illegal operations. Experience had taught the Nazis that everywhere the Zionists were the activist element in the Jewish population and would supply the leadership for anti-Nazi activities.[6]

The Nazis negotiated with Kasztner to forestall such underground operations. Halevi noted that almost as soon as the talks began, Kasztner and his committee were placed under Nazi protection. The reason was clear: "Nazi protection for Kasztner and his rescue committee, and exit permission for Kasztner's chosen 600 VIPs, were an integral part of the psychological warfare tactics for the extermination of the Jews."[7]

Having explained Krumey's motive for offering the "concession" to Kasztner, the verdict addressed Kasztner's motive for accepting it. In Halevi's words, "The temptation was great." When he accepted Krumey's offer on May 2, 1944, Kasztner was in despair because he had learned of the imminent deportations to Auschwitz. Here was an opportunity to save six hundred Jews—including his family, friends, and political colleagues—while justifying his contacts with the SS.

Surrendering to the temptation proffered by the SS on May 2, 1944, was a fateful decision:

> But *timeo Danaos et dona ferentes* ("I fear Greeks bearing gifts"). When Kasztner accepted this gift he sold his soul to the Devil.

> The instant result of the deal with Krumey was Kasztner's dependence on the will of the Nazis.

Before the deal, Kasztner was free to end the negotiations, renounce his Nazi protection, and take the Jewish rescue committee underground. After the deal, he had to satisfy the Nazis in order to save the six hundred Jews. Any disobedience or provocation on his part would bring about the cancellation of the deal and the extermination of the six hundred.[8] Krumey's "gift" was a trick designed to make it impossible for the rescue committee to go underground and organize the illegal rescue campaign feared by the Nazis. By accepting the "gift," Kasztner renounced illegal rescue methods and restricted his committee to Nazi-approved activities.[9]

Worse still, Halevi argued, the deal with Krumey bound Kasztner to secrecy. From the outset, the Nazis had insisted that the talks were a "Reich Secret" that could not be disclosed to the Hungarians. But Kasztner's deal for the Jewish VIPs was a secret that could not be revealed to ordinary Jews. As Halevi argued,

> If Kasztner was forbidden to reveal the "rescue secret," then logically he could not give away the extermination secret. . . . Kasztner was well aware that any leak of the extermination secret would endanger him and the whole rescue committee, and end the joint rescue plans. The negotiations with SS leaders, on which Kasztner had gambled the entire rescue outcome, forced him to withhold his news of the extermination plan from the Jewish masses in Hungary.[10]

To test this assumption, the verdict examined in detail the events in Kolozsvár, which Kasztner visited on May 3, 1944, the day after his deal with Krumey. If Kasztner really intended to warn the masses in defiance of the Nazis, then here was his chance to do it. But the two witnesses from the local Jewish leadership, Hillel Danzig and Dezső Hermann, were adamant that he had conveyed no such warning. Even Kasztner did not explicitly claim that he had told them his specific news about the imminent deportations to Auschwitz.[11]

Furthermore, by informing the Jewish leaders in Kolozsvár about the deal for their emigration while withholding his news of the imminent mass murder of their community, Kasztner simultaneously gave these leaders an incentive to keep order in the ghetto while distracting them from the consequences of doing so. It was this action by Kasztner that accounted for the facts outlined by Halevi at the beginning of his verdict: as the Jewish masses in Kolozsvár were being deported from the ghetto to Auschwitz, their leaders not only failed to organize escapes but also gave assurances about resettlement in Kenyérmező.[12] And the disaster in Kolozsvár served as a model for the other provincial ghettos. The deal for the emigration of six hundred VIPs created a "pyramid" of collaboration, with Kasztner at the "apex" in Budapest and the local Jewish leaders forming the "base" in the ghettos throughout Hungary.[13]

Thus Halevi concluded that Grünwald had been right in his first two allegations against Kasztner: collaboration with the Nazis and indirect murder of Hungary's Jews. He endorsed Krausz's argument that Eichmann's Goods for Blood offer, like Krumey's deal with Kasztner, was a ruse to buy time for the extermination plan.[14] He also found, after lengthy analysis, that Kasztner's dependence on the mass murderers had induced him to become a Gestapo informer in the case of the paratroopers Palgi and Goldstein and that he had obstructed the rescue of the third paratrooper, Hannah Szenes. He determined that Kurt Becher had been a war criminal and that Kasztner had saved him from punishment at Nuremberg in order to cover up their wartime collaboration. Only on the count of plundering the Jewish victims in Hungary did Halevi exonerate Kasztner. For this libel, Grünwald received a token fine of one Israeli pound.

At the core of Halevi's reasoning was the proposition that Kasztner's deal with the Nazis amounted to a contract in which each side accepted a known benefit and paid a known price: Kasztner gained the benefit of saving a chosen few and paid the price of ending illegal activities to save the masses; the Nazis gained the benefit of simplifying the mass murders and paid the price of sparing a chosen few.[15] Halevi's point about the *reciprocity* inherent in any contract is mistaken by some critics for an assertion that there was *equality of bargaining power* in this situation. For instance, Leora Bilsky writes: "The judge's willingness to find a valid contract at the root of the Kastner–Eichmann relationship lent a sense of formal equality to the two parties and obscured the radical inequality between them that resulted from the conditions of terror, deceit and uncertainty in which Kastner and the rescue committee operated."[16]

This criticism misses the actual reasoning in the trial verdict. Halevi's central claim was that through the deal with Krumey, Kasztner made himself and the Jewish rescue committee *dependent* on the will of the Nazis. Halevi repeatedly stressed that there was no equality of bargaining power between the two sides. In his view, Kasztner's deal with the SS entailed collaboration precisely *because* the relationship was so unequal:

> The Nazi partner, *unfathomably stronger than Kasztner* . . . swept its dependent "partner" into the whirlpool of blood. For the Nazis—and *they controlled the unequal partnership*—the extermination and "the rescue" were a single project: the rescue of a handful of Jewish leaders and their families, according to Kasztner's choice, was approved by Eichmann as an integral part of the plan for the extermination of 800,000 Hungarian Jews. [Emphases added.][17]

Halevi pointed out that as long as Kasztner wished to deal with the more powerful Nazis, he had to accept their terms: turning the rescue committee into an SS puppet institution; acquiescing in the full-scale deportation; concealing the "rescue secret"—and hence the extermination secret—from the Hungarian Jewish masses. And Halevi was, plainly, right about this.

But one point was indeed fatal to Judge Halevi's argument. This was his approach to the central accusation made by the Holocaust survivors: that Kasztner helped to deceive the victims into boarding the trains to Auschwitz. Halevi simply ignored this charge.

In his study of the "test case" of Kolozsvár, Halevi summarized the key fact: a whole community was deceived and sent to Auschwitz even though its leader, József Fischer, was in touch both before and during the deportation with Kasztner, who knew the Nazi plans. Halevi outlined the possible explanations: "Did Kasztner not reveal the information needed to stop the deception, or did Fischer not reveal the information he received from Kasztner to the victims of the Nazi deception? The trial testimony points to the former."[18] Although the trial testimony proved that the victims were deceived because their leaders *endorsed the Nazi deception* (an action), Halevi argued that the victims were deceived because their leaders *did not reveal information disproving the deception* (an omission). Halevi overlooked the possibility that the victims were deceived because Kasztner gave orders to deceive them.

The flaw in Judge Halevi's verdict was not the harshness of his condemnation of Kasztner but the fact that his condemnation was not harsh enough. Halevi ignored the survivors' claims that Kasztner had helped to deceive them and accused Kasztner instead of merely failing to do his duty. By softening the evidence in this way, he created an opening for others to overturn his verdict.

The Reaction

The result of the verdict was political chaos. Opinions divided along party lines; any sense of proportion was lost. "All those whose relatives were butchered by the Germans in Hungary know now clearly that Jewish hands helped the mass murder," proclaimed the communist newspaper.[19] Mapai members "in principle support collaboration with all occupiers, including the Nazis," thundered Herut.[20] For his part, Prime Minister Moshe Sharett (formerly Moshe Shertok) took to his diary to label the verdict as "a nightmare, horrible. . . . Strangulation for the [Mapai] party, the worst of the pogroms."[21]

In spite of the partisanship of much of the commentary on the verdict, voices of disquiet were heard even in pro-government circles. Moshe Keren of *Ha'aretz*, in one of a series of articles attacking the decision, nevertheless wrote that Kasztner "must be brought to trial as a Nazi collaborator," and that in such a trial, he "should defend himself as a private citizen, and not be defended by the Israeli government."[22]

Now that Kasztner had been accused of collaboration by an Israeli judge, it was the duty of the government to prosecute him under the Nazis and Nazi Collaborators (Punishment) Law of 1950. It was, no doubt, in order to avoid such an embarrassing turn of events that the government promptly announced its intention to appeal the verdict to the Supreme Court. The decision provoked one of the ruling coalition parties, the General Zionists, to abstain in a no-confidence vote, leading to the collapse of the Mapai government and new national elections—in which the Herut party almost doubled its Knesset representation.

If the government and Tamir were determined to make their respective cases in court, others were less restrained. Israel's far-right began to clamor for Kasztner's death. One of its most prominent ideologues, Dr. Israel Eldad, wrote in his journal *Sulam*: "Kasztner was a criminal according to the verdict given. Under Israeli law the crime is punishable by death."[23]

For Kasztner, the years between the verdict and the Supreme Court decision were dark. He was placed under police protection; he and his family became outcasts. Having left his government post, Kasztner earned a meager living as a journalist at the Mapai party's Hungarian-language newspaper. Early on the morning of March 4, 1957, as he was returning home, he was approached by a young man, who addressed him by name and shot him. Kasztner collapsed in a pool of blood and was rushed to hospital. There, after two operations, he died eleven days later.

It was not long before rumors of a high-level conspiracy began to spread. Kasztner's police protection had been withdrawn shortly before the attack. The security services quickly rounded up dozens of young members of Eldad's *Sulam* group. Two of them, Ze'ev Eckstein and Dan Shemer, admitted their guilt. Eckstein, who was accused of pulling the trigger, had been a government informant inside the far-right cell. Along with the alleged planner of the operation, Joseph Menkes, they were convicted of murder and jailed for life—but released on Ben-Gurion's orders after only six years.[24] It was suggested that covert forces in the government had organized the killing to silence Kasztner while casting the blame on its right-wing opponents.

As is true of many conspiracy theories, there were factors consistent with the allegation, but no real evidence to support it. There was, however, evidence against it. The withdrawal of Kasztner's police protection had been ordered by a security official who was a close friend of Kasztner and would not have tried to endanger him.[25] Unlike the government—which, far from seeking to bury the case, had thrown its resources into his exoneration—the circle surrounding the killers had openly incited Kasztner's death. And no investigation since has given any reason to believe in a government plot.[26]

The search for a hidden scandal surrounding Kasztner's murder merely distracts attention from another issue: the controversy over the findings of Israel's Supreme Court.

The Supreme Court

The Supreme Court's decision was handed down in January 1958 by a panel of five judges: Shimon Agranat, Moshe Silberg, Yitzhak Olshan, Shneur Zalman Cheshin, and David Goitein.

The finding that Kasztner had "paved the way" for the Holocaust in Hungary was rejected by all. The majority—Agranat, Olshan, Cheshin—also cleared Kasztner of collaboration. Goitein held that Kasztner's postwar aid to Becher supported the charge of wartime collaboration, but there was no sign of a financial motive as alleged by Grünwald, who was therefore guilty of libel. Only Silberg ruled firmly that Kasztner had collaborated in the deportations to Auschwitz. The judges unanimously condemned Kasztner for helping Becher at Nuremberg.

By far the most important verdict exculpating Kasztner was delivered by Agranat, who gave this summary of his views:

> (1) In this period [Kasztner] was motivated by the sole aim of saving Hungarian Jewry as a whole, i.e., saving as many as he thought it possible to save in the circumstances of time and place. (2) This motive was consistent with the moral duty of rescue that he had as head of the Relief and Rescue Committee. (3) Influenced by this motive he chose the policy of financial or economic negotiations with the Nazis. (4) This policy can pass the test of reason and prudence. (5) His conduct during and after his visit to Kolozsvár (May 3)—both in its active aspect (the "VIP" plan) and in its passive aspect (not disclosing the "Auschwitz news" and not encouraging acts of forcible resistance and escape on a large scale)—was consistent with his ongoing belief in the policy that he saw at all important times as the only chance of rescue. (6) Hence one cannot detect a moral fault in his conduct; one cannot discern a causal link between it and facilitating the deportation and extermination; it should not be seen as becoming collaboration with the Nazis.[27]

Essentially, Agranat argued that since Kasztner aimed not to help the Nazis kill Jews but to save as many lives as possible, and since Kasztner thought that negotiating with the Nazis was the best and only way to achieve this, nothing he did during those negotiations counted as collaboration.

The Israeli judges did not have access to all of the evidence set out in this book. They had not seen Kasztner's wartime letters claiming that the Jews who had been deported to their deaths in Auschwitz were actually alive and well in "Waldsee."[28] Nor were they aware of his postwar testimonies for Nazi mass murderers Wisliceny, Krumey, and Jüttner. But the evidence available even then was sufficient to prove that Kasztner had collaborated in deceiving the Jewish victims in the ghettos. To dispute this conclusion, the judges had to resort to peculiar modes of reasoning.

One of the issues before the court was the definition of collaboration. In the 1952 case of *Pal v. Attorney General*, Judge Olshan had ruled that a "collaborator" was anyone who intentionally assisted the Nazis in their crimes, whether or not he identified with their aims.[29] There was no need to show that an alleged collaborator actually intended or wished to help murder Jews; it was enough that he intentionally acted in the knowledge that his conduct would serve that end. But in the Kasztner appeal, Judges Agranat and Cheshin discarded that definition. "Let us not find fault with such a person," wrote Agranat, "merely because he knowingly performed an action that may have promoted the Nazis' objectives, if it becomes apparent that he did this out of worthy motives that are not morally questionable . . . "[30] According to Agranat and Cheshin, even though Kasztner's conduct had helped the Nazis to deport and exterminate the Jews, he was still no collaborator, as he had never intended or wished to cause the deaths of the victims. In Cheshin's view,

> Even if Kasztner imposed silence on himself knowingly, albeit in mute surrender to the aggressive will of the Nazis, in order to rescue a handful of Jews from the valley of death, there is still no evidence here that he stained his hands by collaborating with the enemies of his people in carrying out their plan to exterminate most of the Jewish community in Hungary, *even if through his actions—more accurately: omissions—the task of extermination was facilitated.* [Emphasis added.][31]

As Hemda Gur-Arie explains in her analysis of the case, in adopting such a stringent definition of collaboration—a Jew who knowingly helped the Nazis to kill Jews was not a collaborator unless he actually intended or wanted the Jews to be exterminated—the judges "emasculated the rationale underlying the criminal Nazis and Nazi Collaborators (Punishment) Law."[32]

Falsifying Evidence

Aside from their dubious legal reasoning, the Supreme Court judges also resorted to some creative interpretation of the evidence before them. Agranat's verdict contained numerous examples:

1. Agranat dismissed each new item of information about the Nazi murder plans that reached Kasztner as a mere "apprehension" that was not enough to convince him of the certainty of the extermination of the Jews or the futility of his negotiations with the SS:

> The result of examining the "Auschwitz news" . . . is that Kasztner was gravely apprehensive that deportation of Jews of the provincial towns, gathered in the ghettos, was a close possibility; but . . . *the news was not sufficiently certain or unquestionable* that it required him to abandon—already when conducting the conversation with Krumey on May 2—his chosen line of rescue to avert the Holocaust. [Emphasis added.][33]

Agranat's version may be contrasted with Kasztner's actual state of mind at the time, as he later described it in the *Bericht*: "All signs showed that deportation could be postponed no longer—except by a miracle." It was a question of weeks, or even days.[34] Contrary to Agranat's contention that Kasztner regarded the evidence available to him as insufficient even after his May 2, 1944, meeting with Krumey, Kasztner wrote that he sought the meeting *precisely because* he had amassed enough evidence of the Nazi murder plans to break off his "rescue negotiations" if he so chose.

2. Agranat expressed particular skepticism about Kasztner's knowledge of the fate of the Jews who were deported from the Kistarcsa detention camp to Auschwitz before the full-scale deportation began. He disputed Kasztner's account in the *Bericht* of his May 2 confrontation with Krumey about the Kistarcsa operation. According to the *Bericht*, when Krumey stated that the deportees had been sent to work in Waldsee in Germany, Kasztner replied: "there's no point in playing hide-and-seek."[35] Agranat maintained, in Kasztner's defense, that Kasztner's account of the confrontation was false. He denied that Kasztner had ever spoken these words or challenged Krumey about the Waldsee story. Agranat found it "inconceivable—given the prevailing reality of the Nazis at the time—that [Kasztner] dared to confront the German officer on whose good will the fate of Hungary's Jews depended with such clear and sharp words of indignation."[36] And if Kasztner had not rejected the Waldsee story, wrote Agranat, he was not yet certain at that time that the Jews from Kistarcsa had been gassed.

This objection had a fatal flaw: Kasztner stated in the *Bericht* that he knew for a fact, even before the meeting, that the deportation train from Kistarcsa had been sent to Auschwitz. This is because his Jewish contacts in Slovakia had seen the train *en route* to the death camp in Poland.[37] The train had *not* been observed *en route* to Germany. Since Kasztner knew that the Kistarcsa train had gone to Auschwitz, he could not have believed the pretense that the Jews aboard it were alive and well in Waldsee. Agranat's objection relied on the premise that Kasztner did not know what he explicitly said he did know.

3. On the basis of these misrepresentations, Agranat constructed his central thesis: since Kasztner was not yet sure that the Jews in the ghettos would be murdered, he was entitled to "conceal" the truth about the Holocaust from them.

Agranat reviewed Kasztner's state of knowledge at the time of his visit to Kolozsvár on May 3, 1944. He argued that the evidence was not conclusive: Kasztner could still have imagined that the Nazis were not about to kill the Jews there. But Kasztner's own trial testimony contradicted this claim.

During his May 3 visit, Kasztner went to see Wisliceny, who was in charge of driving the Jews into ghettos. According to Agranat:

> [Wisliceny] was pessimistic about the future of Hungarian Jewry and also informed the head of the rescue committee of the increased vigilance at the Romanian border . . . . With all this, it is clear that *at this point Kasztner still did not believe that all hope was lost and had not yet concluded that the deportations were inevitable* . . . . [Emphasis added.][38]

Agranat's assertion contradicted the following passage from Kasztner's testimony about the meeting in Kolozsvár:

> Wisliceny . . . had irritated Eichmann, who had sent him to do "the dirty work" of overseeing the concentration of the Jews, so that, as he put it, he would be unable to build himself an "alibi." He did not go into detail—but of course this meant not saving Jews but *exterminating them, as one of the top murderers* [emphasis added].[39]

Contrary to Agranat's thesis, Kasztner was in no way uncertain about the Nazi plans for the Jewish population of Kolozsvár. In his testimony, Kasztner stated the opposite: having met Wisliceny on May 3, he knew exactly what the Nazis had in store for the Jews. It is difficult to avoid the impression that Agranat was guilty of intentional falsification here.

4. Central to Kasztner's collaboration, according to the trial verdict, were his actions to prevent the mass escape of Jews. Especially damning was the proven fact that the escape operation in Kolozsvár had ended straight after Kasztner's visit. But Agranat purported to see no connection between Kasztner's presence and the end of the escape effort. He suggested that the escapes of Jews had stopped, not because of Kasztner's intervention, but because the local Jewish rescue activists had fled, and because the border patrols had intensified. Indeed, Agranat claimed that Kasztner had tried to *encourage* mass flight:

> on May 3, Kasztner did not give the concrete Auschwitz news to the community leaders in Kolozsvár, but on the other hand he gave a general warning of the gravity of the situation, *asked them to escalate the escape* and gave them money for this purpose [emphasis added].[40]

Here Agranat did not mention Kasztner's own testimony that he conveyed the news of increased border patrols to the local Jewish leaders on instructions from the Nazis to stop the escape effort ("I had to tell those who wanted to escape to Romania to be more careful and to use other ways"[41]).

In any case, Agranat was not too sure of his point that Kasztner had tried to encourage escape. Later in the verdict, he contradicted himself, justifying Kasztner's policy of "not encouraging acts of . . . escape on a large scale" during his visit to Kolozsvár.[42]

Thus Kasztner had and had not caused the end of the escape operation in Kolozsvár; and he had and had not encouraged the victims to escape from Kolozsvár. But whether he had or had not encouraged escape, his decisions were to be excused. No matter what Kasztner had said, no matter what Kasztner had done, Agranat could see no moral fault in his conduct.

5. Agranat argued that Kasztner was right to keep the "Auschwitz news" to himself rather than disclosing it to the Jews of Kolozsvár and other ghettos, because any other course of action would have undermined the Goods for Blood talks, which Kasztner viewed as the only way to save the Jewish masses:

> if Kasztner reasonably thought that delivering the "Auschwitz news" to the leaders in Kolozsvár and other towns would be useless in saving most of the Jews in the provincial towns and might, furthermore, ruin the negotiations conducted with the Nazis, which he saw as the only chance for most of Hungary's Jews to avoid the danger facing them, then there was no moral duty at all to do so [i.e., deliver the Auschwitz news] . . . [43]

Agranat's argument depended on the assumption that Kasztner believed in the possibility of a mass rescue deal as a result of the Goods for Blood proposal. But Kasztner had made it clear in his trial testimony that he believed no such thing. He had testified that he had entertained "no illusions about the realism of these [Nazi] demands," and that he had "estimated the odds as very slim."[44] Kasztner never imagined that the West could be persuaded to give the Nazis ten thousand trucks in exchange for the lives of the Jews. Instead he maintained that he had agreed to discuss Eichmann's offer solely as a delaying tactic—a rationale that made no sense when the extermination was already under way.

So Agranat, admitting that spreading the alarm was incompatible with Kasztner's dealings with Eichmann, nevertheless excused Kasztner's refusal to do so on the basis of an argument that had been contradicted by Kasztner himself.

6. Agranat justified Kasztner's deal with the SS as an attempt to stop the deportation trains: the VIP emigration plan, he asserted, was "a product of the negotiations to prevent the deportation of Hungarian

Jews in general."[45] But Kasztner had testified that the "rescue plan" that was the focus of his negotiations with the SS did *not* entail halting the deportations. Quite the opposite:

> Eichmann . . . was willing to release 100 Jews per truck from German-occupied territory. But he could do nothing for the Jews in Hungary. "I can only sell from Germany," he said. So he was starting with deportation of Jews to Germany.[46]

So Kasztner did *not* expect to stop the deportations by negotiating with the SS, as Agranat claimed. According to Kasztner's testimony, full-scale deportation of Hungary's Jews was a *precondition* of the Goods for Blood deal. Here as well, Agranat misrepresented facts.

As these examples indicate, Judge Agranat twisted the evidence before him, contradicting Kasztner's own statements in order to credit Kasztner with intentions that Kasztner did not have and hopes that he did not entertain. Agranat's purpose, it would seem, was not to discover the truth but to exonerate Kasztner.[47]

The Fundamental Flaw

If Agranat's version of the Kasztner issue was a travesty, all of the Supreme Court verdicts shared a common defect: they systematically misstated the claims made against Kasztner by the Holocaust survivors who had testified in the case.

The District Court had watered down the central allegation of the survivors. The survivors accused Kasztner of *helping to deceive* them about their terrible fate; but Judge Halevi's verdict had merely referred to Kasztner's *refusal to warn* them about it. The Supreme Court judges built on this flaw. All of them ignored Kasztner's acts of deception and considered only his sins of omission. Agranat wrote:

> the main issue here is whether Kasztner's *inaction* towards the Jews of Kolozsvár and other provincial towns—*not giving them the concrete "Auschwitz news,"* etc.—resembled abandoning most of these Jews to the Nazi murderer in order to save a few of them. [Emphasis added.][48]

Likewise, Olshan argued:

> I can understand someone saying that, when they saw that the deportations were continuing, Kasztner and his colleagues . . . *should have warned all the Jews* . . . . But this only means a difference in weighing the situation and in calculating the odds; and the worst that Kasztner can be accused of is his evaluation of the situation and his incorrect view of the issues. [Emphasis added.][49]

Cheshin agreed:

> *He did not tell Hungarian Jews of the danger* because he did not
> see the use, and because he thought that deeds resulting from the
> knowledge would do more harm than good. . . . What was the point
> of preaching and warning? [Emphasis added.][50]

Thus the Supreme Court majority concentrated on Kasztner's alleged silence about the impending destruction of the Jews. Then they tried to excuse his decision not to warn the victims. Their task in exonerating Kasztner would have been much more difficult if they had been compelled to address the real issue: his active role in helping to deceive the victims into boarding the trains to Auschwitz. Unfortunately, Silberg, the dissenter, did not hold his colleagues to account on this point. Instead he asserted that "Kasztner *did not tell* the ghetto leaders what he knew," and he referred to *"the silence and muteness that Kasztner imposed on himself."*[51] No trace remained of Kasztner's role in spreading false rumors about Jewish resettlement in "Kenyérmező."

In the Supreme Court decision, the allegation raised in the testimony of the Holocaust survivors was all but forgotten. Sanitizing Kasztner's conduct, instead of condemning his crimes, was a way to dampen the controversy and quieten the Israeli public. The alternative—rejected by the Supreme Court—was to tell the truth, the whole truth and nothing but the truth.

Notes

1. Gideon Dean, "The Kastner Affair II," *The Reconstructionist*, February 10, 1956, 17.
2. Kasztner Trial verdict, s. 1.
3. Ibid., ss. 3–5, 12.
4. Ibid., s. 14.
5. Ibid., ss. 16, 35.
6. Ibid., ss. 33–34.
7. Ibid., s. 36.
8. Ibid., s. 39.
9. Ibid., s. 40.
10. Ibid., s. 44.
11. Ibid., ss. 51–53.
12. Ibid., ss. 57–59.
13. Ibid., s. 61.
14. Ibid., s. 80.
15. Ibid., s. 63.
16. Leora Bilsky, *Transformative Justice: Israeli Identity on Trial* (Ann Arbor: University of Michigan Press, 2004), 51. See also Hemda Gur-Arie, "History,

Law, Narrative: The 'Kastner Affair'—Fifty Years Later," *Dapim Journal: Studies on the Shoah* 24 (2010): 256; Pnina Lahav, *Judgment in Jerusalem: Chief Justice Simon Agranat and the Zionist Century* (Berkeley: University of California Press, 1997), 134.

17. Kasztner Trial verdict, s. 67.
18. Ibid., s. 51.
19. *Kol Ha'am*, June 26, 1955, quoted in Szamosi, *Rudolf Kasztner in History, in Testimony and in Memory*, 188.
20. *Herut*, June 27, 1955, quoted in Yechiam Weitz, "The Herut Movement and the Kasztner Trial," *Holocaust and Genocide Studies* 8, no. 3 (Winter 1994): 357.
21. Yechiam Weitz, "Political Dimensions of Holocaust Memory in Israel During the 1950s," *Israel Affairs* 1, no. 3 (1995): 139.
22. *Ha'aretz*, July 14, 1955, quoted in Hecht, *Perfidy*, 184.
23. Quoted by Naomi Levitzky, *Koteret Rashit*, June 26, 1985.
24. Szamosi, *Rudolf Kasztner in History, in Testimony and in Memory*, 199. Kasztner's wife and daughter were approached for their consent. Only his daughter agreed, but the men were freed anyway: Segev, *The Seventh Million*, 309.
25. Szamosi, *Rudolf Kasztner in History, in Testimony and in Memory*, 196.
26. See *Koteret Rashit*, June 26, 1985, for one such investigation. For a denial of official complicity, by the former head of the security services, see Isser Harel, *Ha'emet al retsah Kastner: Terror yehudi be'Medinat Yisrael* [*The Truth about the Kasztner Murder: Jewish Terror in the State of Israel*] (Jerusalem: Idanim, 1985).
27. Kasztner Appeal: Agranat verdict, 2176–7.
28. These letters were concealed for many years by the Labor Zionist establishment in Israel, lest they be exploited by Kasztner's critics: Shlomo Aronson, "New Documentation on the Destruction of Hungarian Jewry and the Rescue Attempts," *Yalkut Moreshet* 3 (Winter 2005): 140–1.
29. See Gur-Arie, "History, Law, Narrative," 262ff, for an insightful discussion (on which this paragraph is based).
30. Agranat verdict, 2075 (translation from Gur-Arie).
31. Kasztner Appeal: Cheshin verdict, s. 16.
32. Gur-Arie, "History, Law, Narrative," 267.
33. Agranat verdict, 2096.
34. Kasztner, *Bericht*, 30.
35. Ibid., 31.
36. Agranat verdict, 2095.
37. Kasztner, *Bericht*, 30.
38. Agranat verdict, 2097.
39. Kasztner Trial testimony, March 2, 1954.
40. Agranat verdict, 2117.
41. Kasztner Trial testimony, February 18, 1954.
42. Agranat verdict, 2177.
43. Agranat verdict, 2178.
44. Kasztner Trial testimony, February 19, 1954. Bilsky mistranslates this clause as a result of relying on a misprint in the Halevi verdict instead of on the trial transcript: *Transformative Justice*, 275n56.

45. Agranat verdict, 2179.
46. Kasztner Trial testimony, February 18, 1954.
47. Lahav, however, describes the opinion as "Agranat's finest hour as a judge." See Pnina Lahav, *Judgment in Jerusalem: Chief Justice Simon Agranat and the Zionist Century* (Berkeley: University of California Press, 1997), 133.
48. Agranat verdict, 2178.
49. Olshan verdict, s. 2.
50. Cheshin verdict, s. 12.
51. Silberg verdict, ss. 18, 21. Emphases added.

Conclusion

During the Holocaust in Hungary, the acting head of the country's Jewish rescue operation betrayed his duty to rescue the victims and placed himself at the service of the murderers. The case that Kasztner collaborated with the Nazis can be summarized as follows:

a. The Nazis were determined to avoid panic among their victims leading to large-scale flight from Hungary, as well as outside publicity leading to international pressure on the Hungarian government. The mass murder plan depended on carrying out the deportations at lightning speed behind a wall of secrecy and deception.

b. Kasztner was personally informed of the desiderata of the Nazi plan by Eichmann, Krumey, and Wisliceny; and he learned that bogus official rescue negotiations were part and parcel of the policy of secrecy and deception.

c. Instead of following the dangerous route of going underground and communicating the truth to the victims and the outside world, Kasztner accepted the protection of the Nazis; sanitized their hostage-taking and forced labor schemes as rescue achievements; acted to paralyze the *bona fide* rescue operations of the Zionist underground; helped to deceive scores of thousands of Hungarian Jews into boarding the death trains; and lied to the outside world about Auschwitz.

Since the analysis in this book has been complex, it may be useful to give a brief summary of the facts that led to these conclusions. When the Nazis occupied Hungary, Kasztner and Brand quickly began negotiations and learned that any deal with the Nazis would take the form of "emigration disguised as deportation"—meaning that the Jewish rescue committee would have to assist the Nazis by encouraging the Jews to board the deportation trains. The significance of this condition may have escaped Brand (who displayed almost childlike naïveté), but it could not have been lost on someone as intelligent as Kasztner. The Nazis took advantage of the initial period of negotiations to isolate the Jews from Hungarian society and to drive them into ghettos as a prelude to the deportation to Auschwitz.

When it became clear that the Nazis were not serious about ransom negotiations ("Money for Blood"), Eichmann introduced a new barter proposal ("Goods for Blood"). The essence of this proposal—as Kasztner understood it and described it during and after the war—was that in order to be "rescued," the Jews would be deported to Auschwitz. To the extent that he wanted to pursue this proposal, Kasztner therefore had to facilitate mass deportations to Auschwitz in the name of "rescue." Kasztner, of course, was not fooled by this pretense and understood full well that the offer was a Nazi ruse.

In parallel with the bogus mass rescue negotiations, the Nazis offered an equally bogus scheme to permit the emigration of several hundred Jews, also in the guise of a Nazi deportation. The circumstances of this scheme—the fact that the promised exit date was a lie, the "emigrants" were to be deported by the Nazis on a false pretext, and they had nowhere to go as their entry papers to Palestine had been withdrawn—left little doubt that the "beneficiaries" would be taken hostage by the Nazis in order to guarantee the compliance of the Jewish leadership. Kasztner nevertheless agreed to participate in this hostage-taking plan in order to cement his position as the chief Jewish negotiator and make himself indispensable to the Nazis. To that end, he transformed the Jewish rescue committee from an underground organization working against the law into a client institution of the SS, which depended on the approval of the SS. He also acted to sabotage genuine rescue efforts, such as the missions of the Zionist youth to the provincial ghettos and the resistance plans of the Zionist paratroopers from Palestine, two of whom Kasztner betrayed to the Gestapo.

For as long as Kasztner wished to "negotiate" and enjoy Nazi patronage, he had to obey the will of the Nazis. He had to agree to the *Eichmann-Kommando*'s terms, which included treating the "rescue" deal as a "Reich secret" and therefore preventing panic in Kolozsvár and other ghettos. Multiple eye-witness accounts, plus Kasztner's own admission in his *Bericht*, indicate that Kasztner caused the dissemination of false rumors in order to deceive the Jewish population of the Kolozsvár Ghetto before their deportation to Auschwitz. Likewise, Kasztner grasped the opportunity of the Nazi deportations to Strasshof to claim unearned credit for himself as "rescuer" while facilitating the deportation of tens of thousands of Jews from other ghettos. He even supervised the distribution of the fake "Waldsee" postcards by the *Judenrat* in Budapest in order to reassure the Jews in the capital city before their intended murder.

Just as he misled the Jews inside Hungary, so Kasztner systematically attempted to mislead the Jewish and Zionist organizations abroad that were trying to rescue them. In his messages and letters to the outside world, Kasztner painted a fraudulent picture of his "negotiations" and pretended that the deported Hungarian Jews were alive and well in the fictitious location of "Waldsee," when he knew that they were being gassed in Auschwitz at a staggering rate. He did this at the behest of the Nazis in what was plainly a concerted disinformation effort.

When the imminence of Germany's defeat became clear, SS leaders began to construct their alibis. They recognized Kasztner as an ideal defense witness. They introduced him to premier mass murderers who stood to benefit from his testimony, such as Himmler, Jüttner, and Höss. They invited Kasztner to the heart of the Third Reich and gave him unheard-of privileges for a Jew, including SS passport and SS residence. After the war, despite initial hesitations, Kasztner ultimately did what was expected of him: he acted to help several high-ranking war criminals.

This close bond between the perpetrators of the genocide and the man who was meant to be obstructing them calls for a fuller explanation. At the end of his first meeting with Kasztner, in which Brand—not Kasztner—acted as the Jewish spokesman, Eichmann's right-hand man Krumey saw fit to confer unique privileges upon Kasztner. It was Kasztner who was granted not only exemption from the Yellow Star and the right to use a car and telephone, but also the freedom to travel to the provinces to visit his home town. Why did Krumey dispense this reward to Kasztner? Why did Eichmann choose to negotiate with Kasztner, and not with any of the leaders of the *Judenrat*? The fact of the extraordinary status accorded to Kasztner by the SS from the very first encounters with him demands an explanation: SS officers were determined from the outset to recruit him as a collaborator, and they succeeded in doing so.

If it is wrong to deny Kasztner's crimes, it would be equally wrong to exaggerate them. Kasztner was an accessory to murder, but he was not one of the murderers: it was the Nazis and the local antisemites who perpetrated the degradation, torture, and massacre of Hungary's Jews. Kasztner did not desire the deaths of the victims; surely he would have saved them if the killers had allowed him to do so. The tragedy is that upon realizing that Eichmann's SS unit would *not* tolerate any genuine rescue effort and that the "rescue negotiations" were a mere distraction from the extermination plan, he chose to sacrifice his conscience to his ambition. He agreed to become a puppet "rescue leader" who would sabotage authentic rescue opportunities in return for the unearned status that only his SS masters could provide.

Just as it would be wrong to exaggerate Kasztner's crimes, so it would be wrong to exploit them for partisan ideological purposes. The Kasztner affair became the object of party political hostilities (Herut vs. Mapai) in Israel, and of crude, often antisemitic polemics (Marxist vs. Zionist) abroad. A particularly virulent strain of Soviet Cold War propaganda identified Kasztner as the avatar of a Zionist–Nazi conspiracy to murder the Jews of Europe in order to justify creating the "fascist" State of Israel.[1] Such ideas, if they can be dignified as such, have no contact with reality. The evidence is overwhelming that Kasztner betrayed both the Zionists within Hungary—many of whom risked torture and death to warn the victims and save lives—and the Zionists abroad, who struggled to halt a bloodbath they were powerless to prevent.

It is not very pleasant to conclude that the head of the Jewish rescue committee in Hungary was a collaborator in the genocide of his own people. There is, inevitably, a temptation to avert one's eyes. An emotional argument against telling the whole truth about these events was advanced by Ben-Gurion in a private letter to a journalist in 1955:

> The affair of the *Judenrat* (and perhaps also of the Kasztner case) should, in my view, be left to the tribunal of history in the generation to come. The Jews who were safe and secure during the Hitler era ought not to presume to judge their brethren who were burned and slaughtered, nor the few who survived. . . . This is an abysmal tragedy, and those of our generation who did not experience this hell would do best (in my view) to remain silent in humility and grief. My niece, her husband and her two children were burned alive. Can one speak about that?[2]

Ben-Gurion did not, however, suggest that even *Holocaust survivors* had a duty to remain silent. Did they, at least, have a right to evaluate Kasztner's record? And if so, did others have no right to support them? Furthermore, if it was wrong for anyone who had not experienced the Holocaust to sit in judgment of Kasztner, why was it legitimate for Ben-Gurion's political party to celebrate his role, to select him as a parliamentary candidate, and to appoint him to a senior government post? Ben-Gurion's argument was in fact thoroughly manipulative: he warned his fellow Jews not to judge Kasztner *negatively*, but displayed no qualms at all when the judgment was *positive*.

When Kasztner's defenders failed to silence the critics altogether, they sometimes resorted to unworthy tactics to make their case. Among these was attributing to Kasztner vast rescue achievements that had no foundation in the evidence. The Strasshof operation was repeatedly cited as one of the successes of his talks with Eichmann, even though this idea had been discredited at the Nuremberg Trials, the Kasztner Trial, and the Eichmann Trial.[3] It was also suggested (based on pure "conjecture") that Kasztner had played his part in preventing the deportation of hundreds of thousands of Jews from Budapest.[4] The most extravagant claims were found in the partisan literature published in Israel, where one could learn that "with his own hands, Kasztner had rescued more Jews than any other Jew before or after him."[5] Randolph Braham, the world authority on the Holocaust in Hungary, has corrected the tales of these mythmakers.[6]

The story of Kasztner's collaboration has no happy ending. The Jews of Hungary were largely destroyed. The passengers of the Kasztner Train were taken hostage, held for months in a concentration camp under conditions amounting to psychological torture, and released only because the Nazis were about to lose the war. The Holocaust survivors from Kolozsvár and other ghettos were ignored and forgotten. Kasztner himself was assassinated before he could be brought to justice. The entire episode was subsequently shrouded in a dense fog of misperception. There are no easy answers to such tragedies, but investigations such as this one may contribute to exposing their full horrors to the light of day.

If, as Ben-Gurion maintained in 1955, the issue of Kasztner should have been left to a generation yet to come, that generation has now arrived. It is time to pronounce judgment upon Kasztner's crime.

Notes

1. See, for example, Institute of Jewish Affairs, *Soviet Antisemitic Propaganda: Evidence from Books, Press, and Radio* (London: Institute of Jewish Affairs, 1978), 73–4; Theodore Freedman, ed., *Anti-Semitism in the Soviet Union: Its Roots and Consequences* (New York: Anti-Defamation League, 1984), 28, 335, 573. For the Western Trotskyist version, see Lenni Brenner, *Zionism in the Age of the Dictators* (Chicago: Lawrence Hill Books, 1983), 252–64; Jim Allen, *Perdition* (London: Ithaca Press, 1987).
2. Weitz, *The Man Who Was Murdered Twice*, 230.

3. For example, Bauer, *American Jewry and the Holocaust*, 433; idem, *Rethinking the Holocaust*, 239.
4. Bauer, *Rethinking the Holocaust*, 239; his letter to *Yad Vashem Studies*, 33 (2005), 480–1.
5. Weitz, *The Man Who Was Murdered Twice*, 12.
6. See Randolph L. Braham, "Rescue Operations in Hungary: Myths and Realities," *Yad Vashem Studies* 32 (2004): 21–57.

Source Abbreviations

Bericht: Rezső Kasztner, *Der Bericht des jüdischen Rettungskomitees aus Budapest 1942–1945* (Basel: Vaadat ezrah ve'hatsalah be'Budapest, 1946). English translation: Rezső Kasztner, *The Kasztner Report: The Report of the Budapest Jewish Rescue Committee, 1942–1945*, eds. László Karsai and Judit Molnár (Jerusalem: Yad Vashem, 2013). All citations in the text of this book are from the German original.

Brand-JAE1: Haganah Archive, 80/p187/31, *Note of Conversation Between M.S. [Moshe Shertok (Sharett)] and J.B. [Joel Brand], Aleppo, June 11th, 1944.*

Brand-JAE2: TNA, FO 371/42759, British minutes of Joel Brand's meeting with Moshe Shertok (Sharett) of the Jewish Agency Executive (Aleppo: June 12, 1944).

Brand-SIME1: TNA, KV 2/132, *SIME Report No. 1: Brand, Joel Jeno* (Cairo: July 2, 1944).

Brand-SIME2: TNA, KV 2/132, *SIME Report No. 2: Brand, Joel Jeno* (Cairo: July 21, 1944).

Brand-SIME4: TNA, KV 2/132, *SIME Report No. 4: Interrogation of Brand* (Cairo: July 21, 1944).

Brand-WRB: TNA, FO 371/42807, Interrogation of Joel Brand by Ira Hirschmann of the US War Refugee Board (Cairo: June 22, 1944).

Brand Report: CZA, S26/1248, Joel Brand, *Memorandum über die jetzige Lage der Juden Ungarns sowie der Balkanländer, deren Entwicklung und Vorschläge zur Hazala-Arbeit* (Tel Aviv: January 23, 1945).

CZA: Central Zionist Archives, Jerusalem.

Danzig Archive: Hillel Danzig's personal papers at the Labor Party Archives, Beit Berl College, Kfar Sava, Israel.

DEGOB: National Committee for Attending Deportees, Budapest: http://www.degob.hu

Dinur Archive: Dov Dinur's private archive, now at Yad Vashem Archives, P 54. (Documents courtesy of Eli Reichenthal.)

Eichmann Trial: District Court of Jerusalem, Criminal Case 40/61, *Attorney-General v. Eichmann* (1961).

Freudiger Report: *Report on the Happenings in Hungary From March 19th to August 10th 1944* (Bucharest: October 1, 1944), Kasztner Trial defense exhibit 153.

Grosz-SIME1: TNA, KV 2/130, *SIME Report No. 1: Andor Gross* (Cairo: June 24, 1944).

Grosz-SIME2: TNA, FO 371/42810, *SIME Report No. 2: Andor Gross* (Cairo: June 23, 1944).

Grosz-SIME3: TNA, KV 2/130, *SIME Report No. 3: Andor Gross* (Cairo: July 4, 1944).

IMT: *Trial of the Major War Criminals Before the International Military Tribunal* (Nuremberg: International Military Tribunal, 1948).

Interrogation 1581a: NARA, RG 238, Microfilm Publication M-1019, roll 33: interrogation no. 1581a, Dr. Rudolf Kasztner (July 18, 1947).

Kasztner Appeal: Supreme Court of Israel, Criminal Appeal 232/55, *Attorney-General v. Grünwald* (1958).

Kasztner Archive: the Kasztner family's private archive, now at Yad Vashem Archives, P 54. (Documents courtesy of Eli Reichenthal.)

Kasztner Trial: District Court of Jerusalem, Criminal Case 124/53, *Attorney-General v. Grünwald* (1954–5).

Komoly Diary: the diary of Ottó Komoly, Yad Vashem Archives, P 31/44.

London Affidavit: Rezső Kasztner, Affidavit (London: September 13, 1945) in *Trial of the Major War Criminals Before the International Military Tribunal* (Nuremberg: IMT, 1948), Vol. XXXI, Document 2605-PS, 1–15.

NARA: National Archives and Records Administration, College Park, Maryland.

NCA: *Nazi Conspiracy and Aggression* (Washington, DC: US Government Printing Office, 1946).

NMT: *Trials of War Criminals Before the Nuernberg Military Tribunals Under Control Council Law No. 10* (Washington, DC: US Government Printing Office, 1952).

Palgi Report 1: E. Nussbacher (Yoel Palgi), draft mission report (Budapest: April 15, 1945), Kasztner Trial prosecution exhibit 40.

Palgi Report 2: TNA, WO 208/3405, *Report on Sgt. Noah Nussbecher (Micky) of "A" Force Intelligence Section (MI9)* (undated).

Shertok Report: CZA, Z4/31283, preliminary report by Moshe Shertok (Sharett) to the Zionist leadership in Britain (London: June 27, 1944).

Springmann-SIME1: TNA, KV 2/129, *SIME Report No. 1: Samuel Springmann* (Cairo: May 15, 1944).

Springmann-SIME2: TNA, KV 2/129, *SIME Report No. 2: Samuel Springmann* (Cairo: May 21, 1944).

Springmann-SIME3: TNA, KV 2/129, *SIME Report No. 3: Samuel Springmann* (Cairo: June 1, 1944).

Tamir Archive: Shmuel Tamir's private archive in Israel.

TNA: The National Archives, Kew, London.

YVA: Yad Vashem Archives, Jerusalem.

Important Names

Nazis

Becher, Kurt: Heinrich Himmler's economic representative in Hungary.
Clages, Gerhard: Gestapo/SD officer in Budapest who dealt with the Jewish rescue
   committee.
Eichmann, Adolf: SS officer in charge of organizing the Final Solution.
Himmler, Heinrich: overall commander of the SS.
Höss, Rudolf: camp commandant of Auschwitz.
Hunsche, Otto: a member of Adolf Eichmann's SS unit.
Jüttner, Hans: commander of the Waffen-SS.
Kaltenbrunner, Ernst: head of the SS-RSHA and initiator of the Strasshof operation.
Krumey, Hermann: Adolf Eichmann's SS deputy; negotiated with the Jewish rescue
   committee in Hungary.
Schellenberg, Walter: head of foreign intelligence for the SS.
Veesenmayer, Edmund: Adolf Hitler's representative in Hungary.
Wisliceny, Dieter: a member of Adolf Eichmann's SS unit; negotiated with the
   Jewish rescue committee in Hungary.

Secret Agents

Grosz, Bandi: courier for the Germans, the Hungarians, the Jewish rescue com-
   mittee, and various intelligence agencies; chosen by the SS to accompany Joel
   Brand on his mission to Istanbul.
Klausnitzer, Erich: Gestapo/SD officer in Budapest. His superior was Gerhard
   Clages.
Laufer, Fritz: Gestapo/SD agent involved in the Goods for Blood talks. His superior
   was Erich Klausnitzer.
Schmidt, Johann: head of the Abwehr cell in Budapest.
Winninger, Joseph: a member of Johann Schmidt's Abwehr cell in Budapest; a
   courier for the Jewish rescue committee.

Hungarians

Baky, László: fanatical antisemite in Hungary's Interior Ministry and close ally of
   Adolf Eichmann.
Endre, László: fanatical antisemite in Hungary's Interior Ministry and close ally
   of Adolf Eichmann.
Ferenczy, László: commander of the Hungarian gendarmes who rounded up,
   tortured, and deported the Jews.
Garzoly, József: head of Hungarian counter-espionage.

Horthy, Miklós: Hungary's head of state, retained as figurehead during the Nazi occupation.

Szálasi, Ferenc: head of the fascist Arrow Cross.

Sztójay, Döme: pro-Nazi Prime Minister of Hungary.

Jews

Avriel, Ehud: Zionist rescue activist in Turkey.

Bader, Menachem: Zionist rescue activist in Turkey.

Balázs, Endre: head of the Kolozsvár Ghetto; cousin of József Fischer.

Barlas, Chaim: Zionist rescue activist in Turkey.

Biss, Andre: friend of Rezső Kasztner; cousin and enemy of Joel Brand; replaced Kasztner on the Jewish rescue committee in Hungary.

Brand, Joel: member of the Jewish rescue committee in Hungary, who received Adolf Eichmann's Goods for Blood offer and was sent on a mission to Istanbul accompanied by Bandi Grosz.

Brand, Hansi: Joel Brand's wife; member of the Jewish rescue committee in Hungary; had an affair with Rezső Kasztner.

Danzig, Hillel: friend of Rezső Kasztner and prominent Zionist in Kolozsvár.

Fischer, József: father-in-law of Rezső Kasztner; head of the Jewish community in Kolozsvár and later of the *Judenrat* in the Kolozsvár Ghetto.

Freudiger, Fülöp: head of the Orthodox community in Budapest and member of the *Judenrat* in Budapest.

Goldstein, Peretz: Zionist paratrooper from Palestine sent to Budapest on a British military mission; died in a Nazi concentration camp.

Hermann, Dezső: friend of Rezső Kasztner and prominent Zionist in Kolozsvár.

Kasztner, Rezső: acting head of the Jewish rescue committee in Hungary; assassinated in Israel after being branded a Nazi collaborator in the Kasztner Trial.

Komoly, Ottó: chairman of the Jewish rescue committee in Hungary, who in practice deferred to Rezső Kasztner; murdered before the end of the war.

Krausz, Moshe: head of the Jewish Agency's Palestine Office in Budapest; enemy of Rezső Kasztner; responsible for large-scale rescue operations in Hungary.

Marton, Ernő: friend of Rezső Kasztner and prominent Zionist in Kolozsvár.

Mayer, Saly: Swiss representative of the American Jewish Joint Distribution Committee (JDC).

Palgi, Yoel: Zionist paratrooper from Palestine sent to Budapest on a British military mission; escaped from Nazi captivity and survived the war.

Pomerantz, Venia: Zionist rescue activist in Turkey.

Schwalb, Nathan: Zionist rescue activist in Switzerland.

Schwartz, Joseph: head of the American Jewish JDC in Europe.

Schweiger, Moshe: member of the Jewish rescue committee in Hungary; arrested by the Nazis soon after the occupation; eventually released from Mauthausen concentration camp by Kurt Becher for alibi purposes.

Springmann, Sámuel: member of the Jewish rescue committee in Hungary; left the country shortly before the Nazi occupation.

Stern, Samu: head of the modernist Neolog community in Budapest; first leader of the *Judenrat* in Budapest.

Szenes, Hannah: Zionist paratrooper from Palestine sent to Budapest on a British military mission; executed by the Hungarians.

Szilágyi, Ernő: friend of Rezső Kasztner and member of the Jewish rescue committee in Hungary.

Vrba, Rudolf: Slovak Jewish escapee from Auschwitz; coauthor of the *Auschwitz Protocols*.

Weissmandel, Rabbi Michael: head of the Working Group, the Jewish rescue committee in Slovakia.

Wetzler, Alfred: Slovak Jewish escapee from Auschwitz; coauthor of the *Auschwitz Protocols*.

Israelis

Agranat, Shimon: Supreme Court judge hearing the appeal from the Kasztner Trial.

Ben-Gurion, David: head of the Jewish Agency and leader of the Jewish community in Palestine; first prime minister of Israel.

Cheshin, Shneur Zalman: Supreme Court judge hearing the appeal from the Kasztner Trial.

Cohen, Chaim: Attorney-General of Israel and prosecutor during the Kasztner Trial.

Dobkin, Eliahu: Jewish Agency official in Palestine.

Goitein, David: Supreme Court judge hearing the appeal from the Kasztner Trial.

Grünbaum, Yitzhak: head of the Jewish Agency's rescue committee in Palestine.

Grünwald, Malkiel: pamphleteer and defendant in the Kasztner Trial.

Halevi, Benjamin: District Court judge in the Kasztner Trial.

Olshan, Yitzhak: Supreme Court judge hearing the appeal from the Kasztner Trial.

Shertok, Moshe: head of the Jewish Agency's political department in Palestine; later (as Moshe Sharett) prime minister of Israel during the Kasztner Trial.

Silberg, Moshe: Supreme Court judge hearing the appeal from the Kasztner Trial.

Tamir, Shmuel: Malkiel Grünwald's defense lawyer in the Kasztner Trial.

Tel, Amnon: prosecutor during the Kasztner Trial.

Glossary

Abwehr: German military intelligence agency, led by Wilhelm Canaris until February 1944, thereafter absorbed by SD foreign intelligence under Walter Schellenberg.

Aliya: Jewish immigration to Palestine/Israel.

Arrow Cross: Hungarian fascist party, led by Ferenc Szálasi, which took power on October 15, 1944, and perpetrated atrocities against Jews.

Auschwitz Protocols: eye-witness account of the mass murder process at Auschwitz, compiled from the testimonies of Rudolf Vrba and Alfred Wetzler, young Slovak Jews who escaped in April 1944.

Bericht: Rezső Kasztner's book-length report to the 22nd Zionist Congress in 1946, *Der Bericht des jüdischen Rettungskomitees aus Budapest 1942–1945* ("The Report of the Jewish Rescue Committee of Budapest, 1942–1945").

Brand Mission: Joel Brand's journey from Budapest to Istanbul in May 1944 to convey Eichmann's Goods for Blood offer to the Jewish Agency and the West.

Columbus Camp: SS-guarded "preferred camp" on Columbus Street, Budapest, for the Jewish candidates for the Kasztner Train.

Eichmann-Kommando: Adolf Eichmann's special SS unit, the *Sondereinsatzkommando-Eichmann* or *Judenkommando*, representing Department IVB4 of the SS-RSHA, responsible for organizing the Final Solution.

Europa Plan: ransom proposal by the Working Group in Slovakia to the SS, promising a $2 million payment for the lives of Europe's Jews.

Final Solution: Nazi euphemism for the policy of killing all Jews.

Gestapo (*Geheime Staatspolizei*): the Nazi secret police.

Goods for Blood plan: SS barter proposal in 1944, promising the emigration of up to a million Jews from Nazi-occupied Europe in return for ten thousand trucks and other goods allegedly needed by Germany.

Halutz ("Pioneer"): a member of the Zionist youth movements.

Hashomer Hatzair: an extreme leftist Zionist youth faction.

Herut: right-wing political party in Israel, the successor to the Irgun, and the main component of today's Likud Party.

Horthy Veto: Hungarian Regent Miklós Horthy's decision to stop the mass deportations of Jews to Auschwitz, announced to his ministers on June 26, 1944, but not enforced until July 7–9, 1944. The decision came too late to save the provincial Jews but postponed the imminent destruction of the Jews in Budapest.

Ihud Olami: pre-state international association of Labor Zionists.

Irgun: pre-state right-wing Jewish underground organization established by Revisionist Zionists.

Jewish Agency: the representative Jewish body in Palestine under the British Mandate.

Joint Distribution Committee (American Jewish Joint Distribution Committee, Joint or JDC): worldwide Jewish relief organization based in the United States.

Judenkommando: see *Eichmann-Kommando.*

Judenrat: Jewish Council established by the Nazis to administer Jewish communities in occupied Europe.

Kasztner Train: special transport of 1,684 Hungarian Jews negotiated by Rezső Kasztner with the SS during the mass deportations to Auschwitz. The passengers were supposed to go to a neutral country but were instead held hostage in the Bergen-Belsen concentration camp and released in two convoys during August and December 1944.

Kasztner Trial: Israeli criminal trial of Malkiel Grünwald for libelling Rezső Kasztner as a Nazi collaborator and Holocaust profiteer. The Jerusalem District Court largely exonerated Grünwald in 1955, concluding that Kasztner had "sold his soul to the Devil." After Kasztner's assassination the Israeli Supreme Court reversed key parts of the verdict in 1958.

Kenyérmező ("field of bread"): fictitious agricultural work site in Hungary used to camouflage the deportation to Auschwitz.

Knesset: Israel's parliament.

Mapai: Israel's Labor Party, which led all governing coalitions until 1977.

Mizrachi: Orthodox religious Zionist faction.

Mordowicz–Rosin report: eye-witness report of the mass murder of Hungarian Jews in Auschwitz, compiled from the testimonies of Arnost Rosin and Czesław Mordowicz, Jews who escaped from the camp at the end of May 1944.

Musy Train: special transport of one thousand two hundred Jews from Theresienstadt to Switzerland, negotiated by the Swiss politician Jean-Marie Musy with Heinrich Himmler in 1945.

Neolog: the modernist or reformist Jewish religious stream in Hungary.

Palestine Office: Zionist department in the Jewish Agency facilitating immigration to Palestine. In Budapest in 1944, headed by Moshe Krausz.

People's Tribunal of Cluj: postwar investigation of Hungarian war criminals in North Transylvania, ceded from Hungary to Romania in 1945.

Reichsführer-SS: Reich leader of the SS, that is, Heinrich Himmler.

RSHA (*Reichssicherheitshauptamt*): Reich Security Main Office, the SS institution responsible for security and intelligence work against domestic and foreign enemies of Nazi Germany. Founded by Reinhard Heydrich, later under the command of Ernst Kaltenbrunner.

Revisionists: right-wing Zionist faction established by Vladimir (Ze'ev) Jabotinsky; its members formed the Irgun and later the Herut and Likud parties.

SD (*Sicherheitsdienst*): SS security service, with domestic and foreign intelligence functions.

SF: Swiss francs.

Tiyul ("trip"): Hebrew code word for cross-border smuggling of Jews.

Vrba–Wetzler Report: see *Auschwitz Protocols.*

Waldsee: fictitious work site in Germany used to camouflage the fate of Jews deported to Auschwitz.

War Refugee Board (WRB): US government agency, established by President Roosevelt in January 1944, for the rescue of persecuted civilians in Nazi Europe.

Working Group: Slovak Jewish rescue committee led by Rabbi Michael Weiss-mandel and his secular Zionist cousin Gisi Fleischmann. Initiated the Europa Plan negotiations with the SS and later disseminated the Auschwitz Protocols.

Yellow-Star House: building in Nazi-occupied Budapest, marked by the Yellow Star, in which Jews were concentrated.

Yishuv: Jewish community in Palestine during the British Mandate.

Bibliography

Aronson, Shlomo. "Israel Kasztner: Rescuer in Nazi-Occupied Europe, Prosecutor at Nuremberg and Accused at Home." In *The Holocaust: The Unique and the Universal: Essays Presented in Honor of Yehuda Bauer*, edited by Shmuel Almog, David Bankier, Daniel Blatman, and Dalia Ofer, 1–47. Jerusalem: Yad Vashem, 2001.

———. *Hitler, the Allies and the Jews.* Cambridge: Cambridge University Press, 2004.

———. "New Documentation on the Destruction of Hungarian Jewry and the Rescue Attempts." *Yalkut Moreshet* 3 (2005): 137–46.

———. "Keitzad nitzal geto Budapest? [How Was the Budapest Ghetto Saved?]." *Dapim Journal: Studies on the Shoah* 21 (2007): 55–73.

Avriel, Ehud. *Open the Gates!* New York: Atheneum, 1975.

Bader, Menachem. *Sad Missions.* Tel Aviv: Sifriat Poalim, 1979.

Barri (Ishoni), Shoshana. "The Question of Kastner's Testimonies on Behalf of Nazi War Criminals." *The Journal of Israeli History* 18, no. 2–3 (1997): 139–65.

Bauer, Yehuda. "The Negotiations Between Saly Mayer and the Representatives of the SS in 1944–1945." In *Rescue Attempts During the Holocaust: Proceedings of the Second Yad Vashem International Historical Conference*, edited by Yisrael Gutman and Efraim Zuroff, 5–45. Jerusalem: Yad Vashem, 1977.

———. "The Mission of Joel Brand." In *The Holocaust in Historical Perspective*, 94–155. Seattle: University of Washington Press, 1978.

———. *American Jewry and the Holocaust: The American Jewish Joint Distribution Committee, 1939–1945.* Detroit: Wayne State University Press, 1981.

———. *Jewish Reactions to the Holocaust.* Tel Aviv: MOD Books, 1989.

———. *Jews for Sale? Nazi-Jewish Negotiations, 1933–1945.* New Haven, CT: Yale University Press, 1994.

———. *Rethinking the Holocaust.* New Haven, CT: Yale University Press, 2001.

———. "The 'Protocol of Auschwitz.'" *Yalkut Moreshet* 3 (Winter 2005): 125–36.

———. "Letters." *Yad Vashem Studies* 33 (2005): 479–89.

Beit-Zvi, S. B. *Post-Ugandan Zionism on Trial: A Study of the Factors That Caused the Mistakes by the Zionist Movement During the Holocaust.* Tel Aviv: privately printed, 1991, 2 vols.

Benshalom, Rafi. *We Struggled For Life: The Hungarian Zionist Youth Resistance During the Nazi Era.* Jerusalem: Gefen, 2001.

Bilsky, Leora. *Transformative Justice: Israeli Identity on Trial.* Ann Arbor: University of Michigan Press, 2004.

Biss, Andre. *A Million Jews to Save*. London: New English Library, 1975.

Braham, Randolph L. *The Destruction of Hungarian Jewry: A Documentary Account*. New York: World Federation of Hungarian Jews, 1963, 2 vols.

———. "The Role of the Jewish Council in Hungary: A Tentative Assessment." *Yad Vashem Studies* 10 (1974): 69–109.

———. "The Official Jewish Leadership of Wartime Hungary." In *Patterns of Jewish Leadership in Nazi Europe, 1933–1945*, edited by Yisrael Gutman and Cynthia Haft, 267–85. Jerusalem: Yad Vashem, 1979.

———, ed. *The Tragedy of Hungarian Jewry: Essays, Documents, Depositions*. Boulder, CO: East European Monographs in association with Columbia University Press, 1986.

———. "The Rescue of the Jews of Hungary in Historical Perspective." In *The Historiography of the Holocaust Period*, edited by Yisrael Gutman and Gideon Greif, 447–66. Jerusalem: Yad Vashem, 1988.

———. *The Politics of Genocide: The Holocaust in Hungary*. Boulder, CO: Social Science Monographs in association with Columbia University Press, 1994, 2 vols.

———. "What Did They Know and When?" In *Studies on the Holocaust: Selected Writings, Vol. 1*, 21–49. Boulder, CO: Social Science Monographs in association with Columbia University Press, 2000.

———. "Rescue Operations in Hungary: Myths and Realities." *Yad Vashem Studies* 32 (2004): 21–57.

———, ed. *The Geographical Encyclopedia of the Holocaust in Hungary*. Evanston, IL: Northwestern University Press in association with the United States Holocaust Memorial Museum and Rosenthal Institute for Holocaust Studies, 2013, 3 vols.

Braham, Randolph L., and Scott Miller, eds. *The Nazis' Last Victims: The Holocaust in Hungary*. Detroit: Wayne State University Press in association with the United States Holocaust Memorial Museum, 2002.

Braham, Randolph L., and William J. Vanden Heuvel, eds. *The Auschwitz Reports and the Holocaust in Hungary*. Boulder, CO: Social Science Monographs in association with Columbia University Press, 2011.

Brand, Joel and Hansi Brand. *Ha'Satan veha'nefesh* [*The Devil and the Soul*]. Tel Aviv: Ladori, 1960.

Breitman, Richard. "Nazi Jewish Policy in 1944." In *Genocide and Rescue: The Holocaust in Hungary 1944*, edited by David Cesarani, 77–92. Oxford: Berg, 1997.

———. "Himmler and Bergen-Belsen." In *Belsen in History and Memory*, edited by Jo Reilly, David Cesarani, Tony Kushner, and Colin Richmond, 72–84. London: Frank Cass, 1997.

———. "Other Responses to the Holocaust." In *US Intelligence and the Nazis*, edited by Richard Breitman, Norman J. W. Goda, Timothy Naftali, and Robert Wolfe, 45–72. Cambridge: Cambridge University Press, 2005.

Breitman, Richard, and Shlomo Aronson. "The End of the 'Final Solution'? Nazi Plans to Ransom Jews in 1944." *Central European History* 25, no. 2 (1993): 177–203.

Cesarani, David, ed. *Genocide and Rescue: The Holocaust in Hungary 1944.* Oxford: Berg, 1997.

Cohen, Asher. "He-Halutz Underground in Hungary: March–August 1944." *Yad Vashem Studies* 14 (1981): 247–68.

———. *The Halutz Resistance in Hungary 1942–1944.* Boulder, CO: Social Science Monographs in association with Columbia University Press, 1986.

Conway, John S. "The First Report about Auschwitz." *The Simon Wiesenthal Center Annual* 1 (1984): 133–51.

———. "The Holocaust in Hungary: Recent Controversies and Reconsiderations." In *The Tragedy of Hungarian Jewry: Essays, Documents, Depositions*, edited by Randolph L. Braham, 1–48. Boulder, CO: East European Monographs in association with Columbia University Press, 1986.

———. "The Significance of the Vrba-Wetzler Report on Auschwitz-Birkenau." In *I Escaped From Auschwitz*, Appendix I, 289–324. London: Robson Books, 2006.

Dean, Gideon. "The Kastner Affair." *The Reconstructionist*, January 27, 1956, 9–15.

———. "The Kastner Affair II." *The Reconstructionist*, February 10, 1956, 13–19.

Dinur, Dov. *Kastner: giluyim hadashim al ha'ish u'fo'olo [Kasztner: New Lights on the Man and His Deeds].* Haifa: Gestelit, 1987.

Erez, Zvi. "Hungary—Six Days in July 1944." *Holocaust and Genocide Studies* 3, no. 1 (1988): 37–53.

———. "Why Were the Jews of Budapest Not Expelled in August 1944?" *Yalkut Moreshet* 2 (2004): 9–40.

Florence, Ronald. *Emissary of the Doomed: Bargaining for Lives in the Holocaust.* New York: Viking, 2010.

Freudiger, Fülöp. "Five Months." In *The Tragedy of Hungarian Jewry: Essays, Documents, Depositions*, edited by Randolph L. Braham, 237–96. Boulder, CO: East European Monographs in association with Columbia University Press, 1986.

Friling, Tuvia. "The Zionist Movement's March of Folly and Tom Segev's *The Seventh Million*." *Journal of Israeli History* 16, no. 2 (1995): 133–58.

———. "Nazi-Jewish Negotiations in Istanbul in Mid-1944." *Holocaust and Genocide Studies* 13, no. 3 (Winter 1999): 405–36.

———. *Arrows in the Dark: David Ben-Gurion, the Yishuv Leadership and Rescue Attempts During the Holocaust*, 2 vols. Madison: University of Wisconsin Press, 2005.

———. "Istanbul 1942–1945: The Kollek-Avriel and Berman-Ofner Networks." In *Secret Intelligence and the Holocaust*, edited by David Bankier, 105–56. New York: Enigma Books, 2006.

Fuchs, Abraham. *The Unheeded Cry.* Brooklyn, NY: Mesorah Publications, 1984.

Gelber, Yoav. "Zionist Policy and the Fate of European Jewry, 1943–1944." *Studies in Zionism* 4, no. 1 (Spring 1983): 133–67.

Gilbert, Martin. *Auschwitz and the Allies.* London: Mandarin, 1991.

Gur, David. "Missions of the Zionist Youth Movements in Hungary to the Provincial Cities in 1944." *Yalkut Moreshet* 2 (Winter 2004): 77–85.

————. *Brothers for Resistance and Rescue: The Underground Zionist Youth Movement in Hungary During World War II*. Ramat-Gan: The Society For the Research of the History of the Zionist Youth Movement in Hungary, 2006.

Gur-Arie, Hemda. "History, Law, Narrative: The 'Kastner Affair'—Fifty Years Later." *Dapim Journal: Studies on the Shoah* 24 (2010): 223–68.

Hecht, Ben. *Perfidy*. Jerusalem: Gefen, 1999.

Kádár, Gábor, and Zoltán Vági. *Self-Financing Genocide: The Gold Train, the Becher Case and the Wealth of Hungarian Jews*. Budapest: Central European University Press, 2004.

Kádár, Gábor, Schmidt van der Zanden, Christine, and Vági, Zoltán. "Defying Genocide: Jewish Resistance and Self-Rescue in Hungary," in *Jewish Resistance Against the Nazis*, edited by Patrick Henry, 519–46. Washington, DC: Catholic University of America Press, 2014.

Kasztner, Rezső. *The Kasztner Report: The Report of the Budapest Jewish Rescue Committee, 1942–1945*, edited by László Karsai and Judit Molnár, 53–330. Jerusalem: Yad Vashem, 2013.

Kranzler, David. *The Man Who Stopped the Trains to Auschwitz: George Mantello, El Salvador, and Switzerland's Finest Hour*. Syracuse, NY: Syracuse University Press, 2000.

Lahav, Pnina. "Blaming the Victims—The Kasztner Trial." In *Judgment in Jerusalem: Chief Justice Simon Agranat and the Zionist Century*, 121–44. Berkeley: University of California Press, 1997.

Laqueur, Walter. "The Kastner Case: Aftermath of the Catastrophe." *Commentary*, December 1955, 500–11.

Linn, Ruth. "Genocide and the Politics of Remembering." *Journal of Genocide Research* 5, no. 4 (2003): 565–86.

————. *Escaping Auschwitz: A Culture of Forgetting*. Ithaca, NY: Cornell University Press, 2004.

————. "Rudolf Vrba and the Auschwitz Reports: Conflicting Historical Interpretations." In *The Auschwitz Reports and the Holocaust in Hungary*, edited by Randolph L. Braham and William J. Vanden Heuvel, 153–209. Boulder, CO: Social Science Monographs in association with Columbia University Press, 2011.

Löb, Ladislaus. *Dealing with Satan: Rezső Kasztner's Daring Rescue Mission*. London: Jonathan Cape, 2008.

Lustig, Oliver. *Blood-Bespotted Diary*. Bucharest: Editura Ştiinţifică si Enciclopedică, 1988.

Major, Robert. "The Holocaust in Hungary: About the 'Rescue' of Hungarian Jewry in World War II." *Jewish Currents*, December 1965, 6–13.

Maoz, Asher. "Historical Adjudication: Courts of Law, Commissions of Inquiry and Historical Truth." *Law and History Review* 18, no. 3 (Fall 1990): 577–606.

Mayer, Egon. "Jewish Holocaust Rescuer Murdered in Tel Aviv: A Personal Memoir." *Moment Magazine*, August 31, 1995.

Mendelsohn, John, ed. *The Holocaust: Selected Documents, Vol. 15, Relief in Hungary and the Failure of the Joel Brand Mission*. New York: Garland Publishing, 1982.

Mnookin, Robert H. "Rudolf Kasztner: Bargaining With the Nazis." In *Bargaining with the Devil: When to Negotiate, When to Fight*, 53–82. New York: Simon & Schuster, 2010.

Molnár, Judit. "The Foundation and Activities of the Hungarian Jewish Council, March 20–July 7, 1944." *Yad Vashem Studies* 30 (2002): 93–123.

Nedivi, Ayala. *ha-Misrad ha-Erets Yisre'eli be-Budapesht: pe'ulotav bi-tehum ha-hatsalah ba-shanim 1943–1945 ve-ofen 'itsuvan ba-zikaron ha-kolektivi* [*The Palestine Office in Budapest: Its Actions in Saving Jews from 1943–1945 and Their Formulation in the Collective Memory*]. PhD Dissertation, Haifa: Haifa University, 2009.

———. *Ben Kra'us le-Kastner: ha-ma'avak le-hatsalat Yehude Hungrayah* [*Between Krausz and Kasztner: The Struggle for the Rescue of the Hungarian Jews*]. Jerusalem: Karmel, 2014.

Orr, Akiva. "The Kastner Case, Jerusalem, 1955." In *Israel: Politics, Myths and Identity Crises*, 81–116. London: Pluto Press, 1994.

Palgi, Yoel. *Ruach gedolah ba'ah* [*A Great Wind Came*]. Tel Aviv: Ha'Kibbutz Ha'Meuchad, 1946.

———. *Into the Inferno: The Memoir of a Jewish Paratrooper Behind Nazi Lines*. New Brunswick, NJ: Rutgers University Press, 2003.

Pasternak-Slater, Ann. "Kasztner's Ark." *Areté* 15 (Autumn 2004): 5–40.

Porat, Dina. *The Blue and the Yellow Stars of David: The Zionist Leadership in Palestine and the Holocaust, 1939–1945*. Cambridge, MA: Harvard University Press, 1990.

———. "The Protocol of the Meeting Between Representatives of the Yishuv and Joel Brand in Aleppo, Syria, June 1944." *Yalkut Moreshet* 3 (Winter 2005): 147–60.

Porter, Anna. *Kasztner's Train: The True Story of an Unknown Hero of the Holocaust*. New York: Walker Publishing Company, 2007.

Reichenthal, Eli. *Ha'omnam nirzach paamayim? Parashat Kastner breija mechudeshet* [*A Man Who Was Murdered Twice? A Re-examination of the Kasztner Affair*]. Jerusalem: Bialik Publishing, 2010.

Reuveni, Sari. "Horthy and the Jews." *Yalkut Moreshet* 1 (Winter 2003): 158–99.

Ronen, Avihu. *Ha'kerav al ha'hayim: Ha'shomer ha'tzair be'Hungaryah, 1944* [*The Battle for Life: Hashomer Hatzair in Hungary, 1944*]. Givat Haviva: Yad Ya'ari, 1994.

Rose, Paul Lawrence. "Joel Brand's 'Interim Agreement' and the Course of Nazi-Jewish Negotiations, 1944–1945." *The Historical Journal* 34, no. 4 (1991): 909–29.

Rosenfeld, Shalom. *Tik Plili 124: Mishpat Grunwald-Kastner* [*Criminal Case 124: The Grünwald-Kasztner Trial*]. Tel Aviv: Karni, 1955.

Rothkirchen, Livia. "The 'Europa Plan': A Reassessment." In *American Jewry During the Holocaust*, edited by Seymour Maxwell Finger, Appendix 4:7, 1–26. New York: American Jewish Commission on the Holocaust, 1984.

Rozett, Robert. "Child Rescue in Budapest, 1944–5." *Holocaust and Genocide Studies* 2, no. 1 (1987): 49–59.

———. "Jewish and Hungarian Armed Resistance in Hungary." *Yad Vashem Studies* 19 (1988): 269–88.

——. "From Poland to Hungary: Rescue Attempts, 1943–1944." *Yad Vashem Studies* 24 (1994): 177–93.

Segev, Tom. *The Seventh Million: The Israelis and the Holocaust*. New York: Owl Books, 2000.

Shaked, Michal. "Historyah be'veit ha'mishpat u'veit ha'mishpat ba'historyah [History in the Court and the Court in History]." *Alpayim* 20 (2000): 36–80.

Stern, Samu. "'A Race With Time': A Statement." In *Hungarian Jewish Studies*, edited by Randolph L. Braham, Vol. 3, 1–47. New York: World Federation of Hungarian Jews, 1973.

Świebocki, Henryk, ed. *London Has Been Informed: Reports by Auschwitz Escapees*. Oświęcim: Auschwitz-Birkenau State Museum, 1997.

Szamosi, Annie. *Rudolf Kasztner in History, in Testimony and in Memory*. MA Thesis, Toronto: York University, 2006.

Szita, Szabolcs. *Trading in Lives? Operations of the Jewish Relief and Rescue Committee in Budapest, 1944–1945*. Budapest: Central European University Press, 2005.

Tamir, Shmuel. *Ben ha'aretz hazot [Son of This Land]*. Tel Aviv: Zemorah-Bitan, 2002, 2 vols.

Tibori Szabó, Zoltán. "The Auschwitz Reports: Who Got Them and When?" in *The Auschwitz Reports and the Holocaust in Hungary*, edited by Randolph L. Braham and William J. Vanden Heuvel, 85–120. Boulder, CO: Social Science Monographs in association with Columbia University Press, 2011.

Vági, Zoltán, László Csősz, and Gábor Kádár. *The Holocaust in Hungary: Evolution of a Genocide*. Lanham: AltaMira Press in association with the United States Holocaust Memorial Museum, 2013.

Vago, Béla. "Budapest Jewry in the Summer of 1944: Ottó Komoly's Diaries." *Yad Vashem Studies* 8 (1970): 81–105.

——. "The Intelligence Aspects of the Joel Brand Mission." *Yad Vashem Studies* 10 (1974): 111–28.

Vrba, Rudolf. "Footnote to Auschwitz Report." *Jewish Currents*, March 1966, 22–28.

——. "The Preparations for the Holocaust in Hungary: An Eye-Witness Account." In *The Nazis' Last Victims: The Holocaust in Hungary*, edited by Randolph L. Braham and Scott Miller, 55–101. Detroit: Wayne State University Press in association with the United States Holocaust Memorial Museum, 2002.

——. *I Escaped From Auschwitz*. London: Robson Books, 2006.

Weissberg, Alex. *Desperate Mission: Joel Brand's Story*. New York: Criterion Books, 1958.

Weissmandel, Michael Dov. *Min ha'meitzar [From the Abyss]*. New York: Emunah, 1960.

Weitz, Yechiam. "Changing Conceptions of the Holocaust: The Kasztner Case." In *Studies in Contemporary Jewry, Vol. X: Reshaping the Past: Jewish History and the Historians*, edited by Jonathan Frankel, 211–30. Oxford: Oxford University Press, 1994.

——. "The Herut Movement and the Kasztner Trial." *Holocaust and Genocide Studies* 8, no. 3 (Winter 1994): 349–71.

———. "Mapai and the 'Kastner Trial.'" In *Israel: The First Decade of Independence*, edited by S. Ilan Troen and Noah Lucas, 195–210. Albany: State University of New York Press, 1995.

———. *The Man Who Was Murdered Twice: The Life, Trial and Death of Israel Kasztner*. Jerusalem: Yad Vashem, 2011.

Index